Psychological Analysis of Economic Behavior

George Katona

McGraw-Hill Book Company, Inc.
New York   Toronto   London

PSYCHOLOGICAL ANALYSIS OF ECONOMIC BEHAVIOR

III

First McGraw-Hill Paperback Edition, 1963

PREFACE

This book is based on the thesis that economic processes stem directly from human behavior and that this simple but important fact has not received its due in modern economic analysis. The author has set for himself the task of describing a psychological approach to economic analysis and the current research in the field of economic behavior.

The book is not written for the scholar alone. It is addressed to everyone who is interested in what is going on in present-day American economic life and who believes that studying the behavior of consumers and businessmen is a worth-while undertaking. The book is also intended to be used by students at our colleges. Several years of experience in offering psychological-economic courses to both undergraduate and graduate students have convinced the author that there is a great need for courses which integrate two or more disciplines. He hopes that the availability of an interdisciplinary textbook will promote the establishment of courses of this kind.

As the first chapter attempts to show, resources both of economics and of psychology need to be used to arrive at a realistic analysis of economic behavior. The book therefore includes psychology, that is, the presentation of methods, findings, and principles which traditionally belong to that discipline. It includes economics, that is, the discussion of data and theories contained in books and periodicals under the name of that discipline. Yet, to follow the argument, it is not necessary to be familiar with both psychology and economics. The author has aspired to present psychological principles so as to be understandable to readers whose background is primarily economic, and economic principles so as to be understandable to those whose background is psychological.

Because the book is meant for the general public as well as the expert, each chapter is divided into text and "Notes." Reading of the text, unencumbered by numerous footnotes, suffices for the understanding of the argument. The notes contain additional data, report the sources of the data, and refer to confirmatory or contradictory evidence found in literature.

The author is, of course, alone responsible for the selection and presentation of the findings and principles. He is, however, greatly indebted to several persons and organizations without whose aid the book could not have been written. For the past ten years he has been engaged in large-scale empirical studies which, by their very nature, represent group activities. First

iii

of all, he has drawn heavily on findings of the Surveys of Consumer Finances conducted by the Survey Research Center—a division of the Institute for Social Research of the University of Michigan—for the Board of Governors of the Federal Reserve System.

Although the author has been in direct charge of these surveys since their inception, he is only one of several research workers whose joint endeavor is represented by the surveys. Rensis Likert, Director of the Institute for Social Research; Angus Campbell, Director of the Survey Research Center; and, at earlier times, Dorwin Cartwright, now Director of the Research Center for Group Dynamics, are primarily responsible for the development of the methods used in the surveys and their application to economic questions. Among members of the Survey Research Center staff, the author's indebtedness is greatest to Eleanor E. Maccoby, Janet A. Fisher, John B. Lansing, James K. Dent, and Kent E. Winter for the analysis of data; to Charles F. Cannell for interviewing; and to Roe Goodman and Leslie Kish for sampling. Among members of the Division of Research and Statistics of the Federal Reserve Board, substantial contributions to the surveys were made by Ralph A. Young and Woodlief Thomas, the present and the previous Director of the Division, and by Emanuel T. Weiler, Henry H. Villard, Duncan McC. Holthausen, Homer Jones, Clarke L. Fauver, and Irving Schweiger. Thanks are due the Board of Governors of the Federal Reserve System for their forward-looking attitude in providing financial support to the surveys. Grants of the Rockefeller Foundation to the University of Michigan and funds of the Survey Research Center were also utilized in the analysis of survey data.

For several years in the past the author worked as a psychologist. As will be obvious to psychologists reading this book, he has been most strongly influenced by the late Max Wertheimer, the founder of Gestalt psychology. It was in the psychology of thinking as developed by Wertheimer that the author found the key for the analysis of economic behavior. For some years the author worked as an economist. In this field he is especially grateful for the many suggestions of Jacob Marschak, who in 1942 as Director of the Cowles Commission for Research in Economics at the University of Chicago invited him to direct field studies among businessmen. Results of these studies and of experience gained in conducting them have been utilized in this book. Financial contributions of the Cowles Commission, the National Bureau of Economic Research, and the Rockefeller Foundation made those studies possible.

This book has been in the making for almost ten years. During that time the author had a grant-in-aid for research from the Carnegie Corporation, worked as a Fellow of the John Simon Guggenheim Foundation, and directed research at the Cowles Commission, at the Division of Program

Surveys of the U. S. Department of Agriculture, and at the Survey Research Center. In these years he has learned much from his students in New York, Washington, and Ann Arbor. As professor of economics and of psychology at the University of Michigan, he is glad to acknowledge his indebtedness to the chairmen of the two departments, I. L. Sharfman and Donald G. Marquis, who have both recognized the importance of the interdisciplinary approach.

Inevitably the author has discussed his ideas with many of his colleagues and friends, and some of them were good enough to read parts of preliminary drafts of the manuscript. Although he may not have made sufficient use of their valuable suggestions, the author is greatly indebted to Fritz Machlup of the Johns Hopkins University, A. D. H. Kaplan of Brookings Institution, Kenneth E. Boulding of the University of Michigan, and Lawrence R. Klein and James N. Morgan of the Survey Research Center for their aid in the clarification of economic problems. He also gratefully acknowledges similar assistance in the field of psychology by Angus Campbell, Rensis Likert, Theodore M. Newcomb, and Edward L. Walker of the University of Michigan.

In manner of presentation and style, the book profited from the invaluable and painstaking editorial work of Sylvia Eberhart. In addition, Sylvia M. Kafka aided substantially in an attempt to simplify the presentation. To his wife, Marian Katona, the author owes his deepest gratitude for constant help and encouragement.

GEORGE KATONA

ANN ARBOR, MICH.
February, 1951

CONTENTS

CHAPTER 1

THE NEED FOR PSYCHOLOGY IN ECONOMICS

In this book we shall cut through the time-honored boundaries of two scientific disciplines, economics and psychology. We shall look at economic processes as manifestations of human behavior and analyze them from the point of view of modern psychology. We shall find that the investigation of spending, saving, investing, or determining prices or the size of output has much in common with the study of such other human activities as learning, thinking, voting, or getting along with one's employees or one's wife. All forms of behavior are elicited by the environment. But human beings do not react to stimuli as automatons. It is necessary, but not enough, to know about the objective circumstances in which people behave differently. People's attitudes, motives, and frames of reference shape their perception of the environment as well as their behavior. In order to understand economic processes, as well as other manifestations of behavior, subjective variables must also be studied.

Two critical reactions are often aroused when such a program of study is formulated. Some people shrug their shoulders and assert that there is nothing new in the program. Economists, they feel, have always considered human behavior. To be sure, pure economic theory—the logical analysis of interrelationships among different processes in an ideal or imaginary economic system—may have made use of unrealistic psychological assumptions. Such pure theory, however, in the eyes of these critics, has paved the way for the study of economic processes as they actually occur.

Nothing, others argue, can be gained by linking economics to psychology. Economics is the most advanced of all social sciences, they maintain, just because at any early stage of its development it gave up the confused and muddled thinking that results from considering the immense variety of human behavior. It proceeded by using the scientific method of abstraction. It made progress by separating the basic variables and studying the relationship between them—for example, between income and consumption, or between money supply and price movements—instead of losing its bearings among the innumerable deviations and aberrations that occur because of human frailty.

In opposition to such arguments, this book purports to show that it

3

makes a difference in our understanding of economic processes if we focus our attention on the human actors and on the psychological analysis of decision formation and action. For economic processes are the result of people's behavior and are influenced by different patterns of behavior. More specifically, it will be shown in the book that studying the motives, attitudes, and expectations of consumers and businessmen contributes to the understanding of spending, saving, and investing. Modern psychology provides conceptual as well as methodological tools for the investigation of economic behavior. The results of psychological-economic studies will supplement the traditional analysis of supply, demand, income, and consumption.

The past and present relationship between psychology and economics requires further discussion. The assertion that economics has commonly disregarded psychology has to be explained and clarified. It has to be shown what parts of economics are covered by the psychological analysis of economic behavior and how such analysis is related to psychology.

ECONOMICS WITHOUT PSYCHOLOGY

The usual definitions of economics serve to distinguish economics from physical sciences and technology, and not from social sciences and psychology. They indicate that the analysis of material resources as such and of the technological aspects of producing wealth is not the subject matter of economics. Its starting point is the fact that material resources do not abound in unlimited quantities. They are scarce in comparison with human needs and wants. Therefore, people must decide and choose what and how they will produce, distribute, and consume. In brief, economics studies human behavior in allocating and disposing of scarce means; it analyzes human behavior toward wealth and scarcity.

From these and similar definitions of the subject matter of economics, it follows that the dividing line between economics and psychology is hard to draw. Nineteenth-century scholars were fully aware of this fact, and their studies fell into the common domain of political economy, moral philosophy, and psychology. The concept of the rational man—driven by his self-interest and the principle of seeking pleasure and avoiding pain, and endowed with "perfect" knowledge and foresight—was the property of all these disciplines.

How, then, did the separation of economics from psychology come about? What we are interested in is not simply the development of separate disciplines but what the economist Wesley C. Mitchell described, and deplored, as "nonintercourse with psychology."[1] We shall list a few considerations

[1] Wesley C. Mitchell, "Human Behavior and Economics," *Quarterly Journal of Economics*, Vol. 29, 1914, p. 1.

that contributed to changing the attitudes of scholars as well as the procedures they used. First, there was a widespread and well-justified reaction against nineteenth-century psychology. It was realized that human behavior was more complex than, and perhaps different from, what rationalistic-hedonistic calculations implied it to be. Second, the young discipline of psychology separated itself from the social sciences. In experimental laboratories, it concerned itself with physiological processes or what may be called simple behavior. The gap between the studies of such phenomena as reaction time, the association between nonsense syllables, and conditioned responses, on the one hand, and fluctuation of prices or investments, on the other, was unbridgeable. In addition to laboratory experiments with a few human subjects or rats, psychologists and psychiatrists turned to the study of abnormal behavior. Evidence unearthed about the role of unconscious motives, of caprice and prejudice, could hardly be used to understand the recurrent movements in spending and saving.

There may have been a third important consideration that contributed to the exclusion, from economic studies, of the human subjects who produce, distribute, and consume wealth. Long before the preponderance of behaviorism and psychoanalysis among the schools of psychology made intercourse between psychology and economics difficult, it was widely believed by social scientists that psychological factors were indeterminate and not measurable. Psychology thus seemed irreconcilable with the goal of economists to establish an exact science that would yield laws of general validity. This aim could be achieved by developing a logical system in which economic laws and principles were deduced from assumed premises. As a second step, then, attempts were made to replace the unrealistic assumptions of speculative theory with others conforming more closely to observed facts.

Strictly speaking, the conditions of the validity of ideal economic laws include, first of all, the concept of the economic man. This ideal, admittedly nonexistent "person" seeks one goal, namely, the maximization of his own satisfactions or profits; and, having complete knowledge of the means available to attain that end and knowing exactly what everyone else involved will do, he is able to weigh the various possibilities against one another rationally. Furthermore, it is assumed in traditional pure theory that society consists of unorganized individuals who have free access to the production and consumption of goods that are interchangeable. These assumptions having been made, it was possible to study the functioning of an automatic, self-regulatory market and to answer the question: How *should* human beings behave to maximize their satisfactions and profits?

Few economists, however, have been satisfied that economics should be merely a normative discipline. Therefore, the premises restricting the scope of inquiry have been gradually revised. For example, theories of various monopolistic and quasi-monopolistic practices have been added to the theory of pure competition. Similarly, static principles describing a stationary state of economic processes have been replaced by principles dealing with changes in time. Attempts have been made to substitute principles having to do with uncertainty, risk, and speculation for the assumption of complete knowledge. Finally, in some cases, economic motives other than profit maximization have been postulated.

Economic analysis, even at this stage, however, reveals but faint traces of the science of psychology, which in the meantime has developed far more complex insights into behavior. Psychological variables have been either disregarded or oversimplified in economic studies designed to establish enduring regularities. Deviations from these regularities, often observed in individual instances, have been thought to cancel out, on the average or in the long run, or to represent topics for later studies of applied science that might follow the phase of "exact," idealized analysis.

Although economic analysis in the main continues to disregard empirical psychological studies, it is not devoid of psychological assumptions. Most commonly it proceeds on the premise that human beings behave mechanistically. If it were true that human beings could be counted on to show invariably the same reactions to the same developments in the economic environment, the human factor could rightfully be excluded from economic studies. If human beings were automatons, so that if the same stimuli prevailed the response would necessarily be the same, psychology could, indeed, be thrown overboard. It is this "mechanistic psychology"—the assumption that under given external conditions, human reactions are entirely determined by those conditions—which has led economic analysis to what may be called the reification of economic data. Supply, demand, income, and capital are then viewed as the things themselves with which economics is concerned. The "behavior of money" and the "behavior of prices" are studied as if money and prices themselves were the actors influencing developments, and not the human beings who have the money or set the prices.

Let us consider briefly a few examples of economic analysis which are based on the assumption that human behavior is mechanistic. The statements to which we shall refer here will be studied in detail in later chapters. As our first example, we may cite the statement that "consumer expenditures are a function of income." This is usually understood to mean that, given the income (or the disposable income, and perhaps its distribution as well as the income in preceding periods), the amount of consumer expenditures can be determined and predicted from past performance. For under the same income conditions, human beings will spend the same proportion of their income. Therefore it is not necessary to analyze the behavior of the people involved. Seeking the motives or attitudes underlying their action becomes superfluous.

"The rate of business investment is a function of profits" is a further illustration of the same assumption. There is no need to study how businessmen perceive their profits or their economic situation, what they want to achieve, or what they hope or fear; the rate of investment is related to one single factor: the rate of past profits, that can be measured easily. To make the analysis more realistic, the concept of profit expectations is, however, sometimes introduced as the factor determining the rate of investment. It is then often assumed that profit expectations are based on, and determined by, past profits—and again the human actors can be shoved off the stage.

The principle "the lower the price, the higher the demand" may serve as another example of the reification of economic concepts. That human beings create the supply of goods, form the demand for goods, and determine their prices becomes unimportant if a one-to-one correspondence prevails between the stimuli (price reductions) and the responses (increased demand).

Finally, we may quote the most common explanation of inflation. We learn that "inflation is the result of an increase in money supply" or, in a more precise form, that "inflation is the result of purchasing power exceeding the available supplies." The meaning here is that general and considerable price increases are the necessary consequences of the stated external conditions. It is assumed that the behavior of the human beings who charge and pay the increased prices is determined by those conditions. The statement, oft-repeated during the war, that "more money competes for fewer goods" is then not just an innocent metaphor or a shorthand expression. It becomes a scientific statement explaining the sequence of events and making it unnecessary to raise the questions of why, when, and under what conditions human beings use their increased supply of money to compete for the available quantity of goods.

"Economics with mechanistic psychology" might then be a more accurate phrase than "economics without psychology." But the latter is equally appropriate if by "psychology" is meant the scientific discipline as we know it today and not a priori psychological assumptions. Psychology is an empirical discipline. It acknowledges one source of evidence only, namely, controlled observation. It aims at the establishment of relationships between specific conditions and specific forms of behavior, rather than general laws of human nature. Because of the pliability and modifiability of behavior, psychology is skeptical about broad generalizations that posit invariable interrelationships. Human beings are capable of utilizing past experience and have great latitude within the limitations set by external forces.

A few economists have, in recent years, attempted to do justice to these solidly established tenets of modern psychology. There have come into being the beginnings of an "economics with psychology," which tries to find out what actually takes place when people—as consumers, businessmen, or policy makers—make economic decisions and act with respect to material goods. The prevailing complex conditions of economic life are taken as the starting point of the analysis. The method of first setting up ideal conditions and then approaching realistic conditions step by step is abandoned. Study is shifted from the atomistic consideration of individual economic choices to the relation of individuals to groups and to group action. The main questions posed are: What kinds of behavior occur and what kinds of decisions are made under different conditions by different groups of people? Decisions about producing, buying, selling, price setting, investing, and saving are then analyzed.

The conditions of decision formation encompass both external events and psychological states or, more correctly, the psychological field of the persons or groups making the decision. The psychological field includes people's perception of events—those events of which they are aware—as well as their motives, attitudes, and expectations.

The psychological study of economic processes is possible because human decisions, and human behavior in general, are governed by laws, that is, are not arbitrary, unpredictable, indeterminate. While human beings are not marionettes pushed around by external forces, the latitude of their choice itself is subject to scientific analysis. Differences in perceptions, motives, and attitudes are measurable and can be related to causal factors.

PSYCHOLOGY WITHOUT ECONOMICS

Psychology is usually defined as the science of behavior. It is not just the study of mental behavior—of perceiving, learning, thinking. Nor is it merely the study of motives or of emotions, or of the development of behavior from childhood to old age or from "normal" to "abnormal" states of mind, or of individual differences in behavior. Psychology encompasses all these and many other aspects of behavior. It studies the factors that bring forth and determine the different forms of behavior.

Does it follow, then, that economics—and all social sciences—are parts of psychology? If it were true that the general principles of behavior, once established, would exactly determine human actions under all specific circumstances, it might be so argued. But human behavior is so rich and has so many different manifestations that it must always be studied under specific conditions. There is a wide gap between the laws and conditions, for example, of learning, thinking, or goal seeking, and the conditions determining behavior toward the production, distribution, and consumption of goods. To bridge that gap, it is important to establish general principles of human behavior, but it is not enough. Nor is it enough to know the economic facts. What is necessary is to study specifically behavior of producing, distributing, and consuming.

Is economic psychology therefore applied psychology? If the term "applied psychology" has any meaning, it is that psychology is first developed and the finished product is then taken and transferred to another specific field. Few people would say that child psychology, for example, is applied psychology in this sense. On the contrary, child psychology is developed by studying children's behavior. Just so, economic psychology can only be developed by studying economic behavior. To be sure, principles established by analyzing child behavior or economic behavior cannot contradict principles derived from the analysis of other forms of behavior, but they can and do supplement and enrich those principles. Economic psychology then both borrows from and contributes to the study of other forms of behavior.

Such economic psychology is, however, a very young discipline. While many economists have at least recognized the problem, and some have included psychological principles in their studies of economic behavior, there have until very recently been but few psychological investigations into such common forms of everyday behavior as buying, selling, investing, going into business, increasing production, and the like. Still more unfortunately for the development of the young discipline, psychological investigations of motivation, habit formation, incentives and aspirations, or group belonging, which have used diverse fields of human activity to test hypotheses, have usually disregarded economic behavior. Businessmen's and consumers' motives in acquiring assets, their adopting or abandoning habits of spending or saving, or their forming and acting upon expectations—to mention only a few of the major problems of economic psychology—require specific studies that have been neglected by psychologists.

The psychological analysis of economic behavior can, nevertheless, make use of conceptual as well as methodological principles of modern psychology. It must not consist merely of broadening economic analysis by adding to the traditional variables a few new variables, such as habits or attitudes. Psychology aims to do more than to describe what people do under certain conditions. It attempts to discover why they act as they do under those conditions. It is "dynamic" insofar as it studies the motives and forces that bring about and explain behavior. Psychology must serve to make economic analysis, likewise, truly dynamic by shedding light on the question of why as well as what.[2] Indeed, the basic need for psychology in economic research

[2] Differences in the meaning of the term "dynamic" in economics and in psychology will be discussed in the next chapter.

consists in the need to discover and analyze the forces behind economic processes, the forces responsible for economic actions, decisions, and choices.

"Economics without psychology" has not succeeded in explaining important economic processes and "psychology without economics" has no chance of explaining some of the most common aspects of human behavior. And yet very little work has been done that has made use of the facilities of both disciplines. Is this the case because interdisciplinary research is inherently more difficult than any other research?

To be sure, students of economic psychology must have knowledge of both economics and psychology. Yet it might be argued that both economics and psychology are at present such vast and complex disciplines that mastery of either one alone would constitute a lifetime task. How could anyone be an expert in both? The answer is that it is hardly possible to master all forms and branches of economics or all forms and branches of psychology. Some knowledge may be acquired by one person of the psychology of learning, the psychology of perception, abnormal and clinical psychology, social and child psychology, testing, etc., but no one person can be a productive research worker or teacher in all those fields. The same is true of mastering economic theory, economic research methods, money and banking, labor, institutional and international economics, and so forth. The usual boundaries of the various traditional disciplines are, however, quite arbitrary. Why should not some aspects of economics and some aspects of psychology be studied together, rather than different aspects of either field alone? It is clearly possible for one person to be both an "economist" and a "psychologist" in the sense of having a background of knowledge in both disciplines, and it is also possible to specialize in "economic psychology." Such specialization involves not only some information in both economics and psychology but, above all, a specific point of view, namely, an empirical attitude: concern with actual developments and belief in the possibility of finding out what has happened and why.

In this book we shall begin by referring, briefly, to certain general principles of both economics and psychology, for the purpose of bringing about an understanding of the tasks ahead. For the most part, however, the book will discuss neither psychology nor economics as such (in the traditional sense). As has been said, the psychology of economic processes cannot be developed without regard for the inherent features of these processses. Therefore, economic problems will be raised and studied from the psychological point of view. The order of the book is determined by the significance of the economic processes to be analyzed.

PSYCHOLOGICAL ECONOMICS

While it is true that economic processes always result from people's behavior toward scarce resources, economics is much broader than the study of this behavior. What phases of that discipline remain outside the special domain of psychological economics?

The first obvious answer to this question has already been given. Empirical research, directed toward finding out under what circumstances and why consumers and businessmen make their decisions, is not all that should be done in studying economic processes. Economic theory, the ivory-tower discipline of setting up assumptions and deducing consequences from them, is necessary and useful. Simplified models that consider, for instance, the interaction between two countries or two firms which produce and trade only two kinds of goods have their function and merit. They not only serve to show the types of action that are possible under certain conditions but also pave the way for empirical research by presenting it with hypotheses. Empirical research can hardly ever accomplish its task if it consists merely of a haphazard registration of events. The analysis of economic behavior needs guides and standards which can best be obtained from theory—not necessarily from economic theory alone but from psychological theory as well. Moreover, such empirical analysis not only tests and verifies theory but may also initiate and clarify it.

While the dividing lines between economic psychology and economic theory are not too clear-cut, the psychological analysis of economic behavior obviously does not include all empirical studies or all knowledge acquired by empirical methods concerning economic processes. Much of what is called institutional economics—the analysis of institutions, both as to structure and functions—is not directly dependent on psychology, because institutions must also be studied without regard to the persons who created them, who operate them, or who are influenced by them. Similarly, historical economics, or economic history, is usually not based on psychological analysis. What has happened in the past is not susceptible of present-day direct observation. Finally, and most importantly, even with respect to current economic events and processes there exists a statistical, econometric approach which is not necessarily psychological. Economic data, such as amounts of production and profit, of income and expenditures—though they are the results of how human beings have acted—must also be studied without regard to the actors, their motives and attitudes. Therefore, the point to be set forth in this book is not that economic psychology supplants or makes superfluous the other more usual way of studying those data, but that the study of the interrelationship of data is not sufficient of itself and must be supplemented by psychological analysis. Econometric studies and the psychological analysis of economic behavior have, however, much in common. Both approaches aim at the establishment of general, empirically tested propositions or, more specifically, at the discernment and measurement of quantitative relations between relevant variables.

Our psychological analysis will be directed toward an understanding of the major decisions and choices of consumers (Part Two) and businessmen (Part Three), and of those decisions of consumers, businessmen, and policy makers which contribute to economic fluctuations (Part Four). In thus restricting our investigation we are cognizant of neglecting other economic problems equally susceptible of psychological analysis. Prominent among them are those in the fields of labor economics and of international economic relations. Labor economics is, of course, one of the few economic fields in which psychologists have worked in the past and in which economists have made use of psychological and sociological concepts and methods.[3] Relatively little is, however, known about the psychological processes that enter into international economic relations, that is, about the human behavior responsible for fluctuations in foreign exchange, international trade, or balances of payments.

The main shortcomings of this book do not consist, however, in the exclusion of certain fields of economic behavior but rather in the incompleteness of the treatment of consumer and business behavior. Empirical research is a slow process of formulating, testing, and revising hypotheses. All too often, we shall not be able to do more than bring together some materials and formulate hypotheses, rather than present empirical findings that would support or contradict them.

Under these circumstances, is the publication of this book premature? Should research workers first devote all their energies to empirical investigation and postpone any systematic treatment until a complete presentation and definite solution of all major problems become possible? It is ultimately for the reader to answer these questions. The author agrees that what is called for, right now, in the next few years, and in the next decades, are empirical studies of economic behavior. But such studies require a frame of reference. A systematic presentation of a new point of view fulfills an important function at an early stage of research. Future research is bound to be stimulated if the outlines of the structure are clearly perceived, missing links pointed out, and the integration of new pieces of evidence made possible.

---

[3] In analyzing wage negotiations and the respective roles and behavior of management, workers, and trade unions, as well as employee productivity and its relation to work satisfaction and morale, psychological problems abound and many of them have already been successfully tackled.

NOTES TO CHAPTER 1

Concerning definitions of economics and the relation of pure theory to economic analysis, see Lionel Robbins, *An Essay on the Nature and Significance of Economic Science,* London, 1932, and T. W. Hutchison, *The Significance and Basic Postulates of Economic Theory,* London, 1938.

For a brief and succinct presentation of the materials developed by economists, reference may be made to the paper by Sumner H. Slichter, "The State of Economics" (in *Items,* Social Science Research Council, Vol. 3, pp. 25*ff.*, September, 1949). Slichter emphasizes that in addition to tools and concepts, case studies, historical studies, hypotheses, and simplified economic models, the economist must develop "propositions which have some generality and which have been found to be consistent with more or less comprehensive bodies of evidence." This last, most important objective has, however, been greatly neglected. Slichter cites reasons "for the failure of economists to break out of the realm of speculation and to develop tested propositions." He expresses the opinion that the next few decades will bring more rapid progress in collecting propositions about economic behavior that have been tested by means of empirical studies.

Demands for closer relations to psychology have been repeatedly voiced by economists during the past fifty years. As examples, essays by W. C. Mitchell (for instance, "Human Behavior and Economics," *Quarterly Journal of Economics,* Vol. 29, 1914, pp. 1*ff.*) and J. M. Clark may be cited. Clark wrote in 1918:

"The economist may attempt to ignore psychology, but it is sheer impossibility for him to ignore human nature. . . . If the economist borrows his conception of man from the psychologist, his constructive work may have some chance of remaining purely economic in character. But if he does not, he will not thereby avoid psychology. Rather, he will force himself to make his own, and it will be bad psychology" ("Economics and Modern Psychology," *Journal of Political Economy,* Vol. 26, p. 4).

That psychologists carry the major responsibility for separating psychology from economics appears to be the opinion of F. H. Knight, who has rightly said that there has been "in modern psychology . . . an increasing emphasis on unconscious motivation, and on the 'prejudice' and caprice in the conscious motives of men" (*The Ethics of Competition,* New York, 1935, p. 241).

As late as 1947, E. G. Nourse blamed both psychologists and economists, each for neglecting the discipline of the other:

"As to the real nature and force of human motivations and the pregnability of behavior patterns, our knowledge is woefully inadequate. Does this not reflect failure of economists to bring the resources of psychology to bear as fully as they might on the problems with which we economists must deal and the failure of the psychologists to exploit adequately the field of economic behavior as an area for fruitful psychological study?" ("The Employment Act of 1946 and a System of National Bookkeeping," *American Economic Review,* Vol. 37, Supplement, 1947, p. 27.)

No references will be made to various sociological or socio-psychological approaches to economics that have been developed in the past both in the United States and in Europe. We are concerned with the procedures commonly adopted in current economic analysis, and not with the history of economics. One common practice has been for economists to formulate their own psychological laws without seeking recourse in psychology. The most conspicuous example is the "fundamental psychological law" of J. M. Keynes (discussed in Chapter 7). Without borrowing from any work of psychology, Keynes refers to a "psychological characteristic of human nature" to explain the relation between changes in consumption and changes in income (see *The General Theory of Employment, Interest, and Money,* New York, 1936).

Another frequently used device has been described by A. G. Hart as "the widespread bias toward treating 'psychological' factors in fluctuations solely in terms of 'errors.'" To remedy the bias, Hart demands that economic models give explicit recognition to plans and expectations. But "there has long been a tendency to shy off from plans and estimates on the ground that they are 'not observable'. . . . In fact [they are] observable if we adopt correct procedures" ("Liquidity and Uncertainty," *American Economic Review,* Vol. 39, Supplement, 1949, p. 180).

A widely held opinion is reported by Gottfried Haberler when he says that certain "reactions are conventionally called psychological because of their (in a sense) indeterminate character" (*Prosperity and Depression,* Geneva, 1937, p. 134). Haberler argues that "psychological factors come into consideration in economic theory in connection with anticipations and expectations" (*op. cit.*) but believes that it is almost impossible to find out anything about expectations (*op. cit.,* 1941, 3d ed., p. 252). The assumption that psychological factors need to be studied in economics only in connection with expectations will be shown to be far too narrow. Moreover, the most usual treatment of expectations as well as of uncertainty has, as we shall see later, made as little use of modern psychology as the more traditional studies of supply and demand.

Traditional economic analysis has been attacked by Elton Mayo on the grounds that it is atomistic. He demands that economists take into consideration such strong motivational forces as the desire to be associated in work with others (*The Social Problems of Industrial Civilization,* Cambridge, 1945).

CHAPTER 2

WHAT KIND OF ECONOMICS?

Two questions must be clarified before we can embark on our task, the psychological analysis of economic behavior. First, we shall describe, in a brief and preliminary form, the kind of economics with which we are here concerned. Then, in the next chapter, we shall discuss the kind of psychology that enters into economic analysis.

EMPIRICAL MICROECONOMICS

The clarification of the concept economics will proceed in four steps, which, however, are closely interrelated. In each of the four areas of study we shall indicate the kind of economic analysis we shall take up, contrasting it to the one which does not constitute the subject matter of our investigation.

1. We shall study economic processes as they occur under particular conditions. This means, first, in a negative sense, that we are not concerned with ideal or dogmatic economics. Geometry is the prime example of a science which is developed from a few general propositions (axioms). Physics and chemistry likewise concern themselves with fundamental laws that are generally valid. There is a great temptation to establish general laws of economics which govern economic processes at all times and under all conditions. Modern biological and social sciences, however, in dealing with human nature, set up more modest objectives. Instead of attempting dogmatically to establish the laws of human behavior, they seek to find out what particular conditions occasion each of the many diverse forms of behavior that human beings display. Similarly, we shall ask under what conditions economic behavior of a certain type, and under what conditions economic behavior of another type, is more likely to occur.

Empirical findings based on observation of economic behavior will take the place of dogmatic statements or of pure reasoning. From hypotheses tested and revised through controlled observation, generalizations can be derived about the probable connection between specific conditions and specific results.

Ideal principles of economics, meant to be universally valid and applicable to all conditions, are usually established by making certain assumptions

15

which restrict the scope of economic studies. Unlike pure theorists, we shall not assume at the outset that rational behavior exists or that rational behavior constitutes the topic of economic analysis. We shall study economic behavior as we find it. In describing and classifying different reactions, as well as the circumstances that elicit them, we shall raise the question whether and in what sense certain reactions may be called "rational." After having answered that question and thus defined our terms, we shall study the fundamental problem: Under what conditions do more and under what conditions do less rational forms of behavior occur? In this manner we shall avoid the necessity of distinguishing between relevant and irrelevant forms of economic behavior, or between "economic" variables, on the one hand, and psychological or noneconomic variables, on the other hand.

Another distinction, which is customary in economic analysis but cannot be used in our studies, is the one between economic statics and economic dynamics. All too frequently, economic processes are first studied under conditions in which all magnitudes relate to the same period of time. This static theory is then transformed into dynamic theory by introducing variables relating to different periods of time. In modern econometrics, dynamic analysis differs from static analysis by nothing but the fact that in dynamic analysis every quantity is dated. Variables that are measured at different dates appear in the same equation so that their time lag is considered. We shall not only be concerned solely with dynamic analysis, which we shall not attempt to derive from a preliminary static analysis, but shall also use the term dynamic in a somewhat different sense from the one just described.

In psychology, the term dynamic is introduced when the question is raised how and why a person does what he does. Concern with motives of behavior or, more generally, with the forces that bring about and explain behavior and its changes characterizes dynamic psychological analysis. This concern goes beyond the consideration of time lags or correlations between dated magnitudes. Analysis of economic behavior cannot rest satisfied with establishing correlations, for example, between dwelling occupancy rates in one year and building rates in the next year, or asset holdings in one period and rates of spending and saving in the subsequent period. We must ask under what conditions and why the antecedent situation influences the later behavior; in other words, we must inquire about the forces that elicit behavior.

2. We shall study economic processes in the United States in the twentieth century. Since direct observation of the economic processes of, say, ancient Rome or Egypt is not possible today, we have already excluded economic history from the scope of our endeavor. There is no logical reason to exclude economic behavior in present-day Russia, or the South Sea Islands. Economic psychology in any country, even a communistic or

primitive one, is theoretically possible. For practical reasons, however, the analysis in this book is directed toward and applied only to the present American economy.

The first of these reasons can be stated simply in terms of the author's scope of information. He is most familiar with studies of current economic behavior in his own country. But such an explanation might raise the question of why he has thus limited the area of his studies. The answer is that empirical research—in contrast to dogmatic theorizing—is modest and slow. It consists of a gradual exploration of different conditions and of behavior under those conditions. It does not present final solutions but at best represents a step forward to be implemented by further research. Instead of raising questions about differences or similarities between different cultures, traditions, or frames of reference, it seemed best to concentrate on one culture. Even with respect to present-day American economic behavior, the task is much too large to be accomplished and only some, all too few, conditions and reactions will be studied.

3. We shall study economic processes as affected by human decisions. Because human beings have some power in determining what happens in our economy, the so-called self-regulatory market economy cannot constitute the starting point of our analysis. Instead of assuming that prices, size of production, amount of purchases, etc., are set for us by impersonal factors, we shall seek to ascertain the forms, conditions, and limits of the human decisions that affect them. The self-regulatory market economy will be considered as a "limiting case" in which human decisions are least spontaneous. What economists have called "administered prices" and "monopolistic competition" will be acknowledged as the major problems in present-day American economy.

E. G. Nourse distinguishes between automatic prices, which emerge spontaneously in free markets consisting of unorganized producers and buyers, and authoritarian prices, which are fixed by the order of an authority.[1] Besides these, there are other situations in which the seller has some power to set the prices of his products. Such prices are called by Nourse "administered prices." Except during wartime (under price control), they are the common prices in the United States, even though the "power" of manufacturers, wholesalers, and retailers may be severely limited or may even exist only in their imagination. But invariable connections between situations and prices are rare; self-regulatory markets exist only under ideal assumptions; and the conditions and limits for sellers' setting their own prices need to be investigated.

There is only one retail store at the corner of Main and First Streets which sells a certain piece of furniture. Only the Chevrolet Motor Company

---

[1] E. G. Nourse, *Price Making in a Democracy,* Washington, D.C., 1944.

sells Chevrolet automobiles. In this sense, both sellers have a monopolistic position. But, of course, they do compete with other sellers. The same or similar pieces of furniture, and automobiles of similar performance, are sold at other accessible places. And all sellers of furniture and automobiles compete with sellers of other kinds of goods for the people's favor and money. Product differentiation (*e.g.,* between Chevrolet and Ford), in contrast to the standardized goods of the traditional market economy, and the presence of some degree of freedom in setting prices, coupled with restraints emerging from the competitors' actions, are essential features of what is described as "monopolistic competition." This situation represents the realistic starting point for the analysis of current American economic behavior.

4. We shall study economic processes in their relation to individual consumers and firms. Aggregative economics is not enough. It does not suffice to operate with aggregate data that refer to the entire economy as a unit, or to certain large parts of it as units. Yet such aggregate data as national income, the expenditures and savings of all consumers, or estimates of aggregate production, sales, profits of all or certain types of business firms represent the major topics of present-day economic-statistical analysis.

It is widely acknowledged that aggregate data need to be supplemented by what are called microeconomic data, that is, information in which individual families or firms each represent a unit. One reason this need has been felt is that aggregative, or macroeconomic, data give not only an incomplete but often a misleading account of an economic process or situation. Aggregative statistics may tell us, for example, that the national income—the income of all the people in the United States—rose from 200 to 220 billion dollars in a certain year. This is an increase of 10 per cent of total income, or a 10 per cent increase of average family income. It is possible—but very improbable—that in this case the income of every family rose by 10 per cent. It is also possible that the income of half of the families rose by 20 per cent and that of the other half remained unchanged. Or that the income of a small number of families increased greatly while that of most families declined. Aggregates do not tell the whole story. They do not indicate what changes have taken place or what the current situation is. We need to know whether relatively few families received most of the 220 billion dollars, or whether the aggregate income was quite evenly distributed among all families. Information about the distribution of aggregates and of the changes in aggregates can serve to correct misleading impressions and to avoid false conclusions.

This is, however, only part of the argument. Microeconomic data— information on how aggregate income, savings, profits, etc., are distributed among individual families or firms—have still another function. They provide the link with psychological variables and the basis for a dynamic analysis of what happened and why it happened.

Our aim is to analyze behavior—decisions and actions of consumers and businessmen—and the motives, attitudes, and other factors underlying and determining behavior. Does the national economy behave? Can we study the motives and attitudes of all businessmen or all steel producers as a unit? In the next chapter we shall discuss the central problem of social psychology, the question of group decisions and group motivation. Suffice it to say at present that as the result of analysis we may discover that, in certain instances, such concepts are justified. It is possible that in certain instances "psychological groups" exist, the members of which are all subjectively in the same situation and therefore react uniformly. But this is not known at the outset; the psychological analysis must therefore always be directed toward the individual unit. The decision formation of individual persons must be studied in order to determine the differences as well as the similarities, the individual as well as the group factors. Psychological data referring to individual units must be compared with economic and financial data—income, savings, sales, profits, etc.—referring to those same units, not to aggregates.

Two quotations may illustrate this point further. In his analysis of the history of the 1920's, Joseph A. Schumpeter said at the 1945 meeting of the American Economic Association: "If, in a given year, one industry makes 100 millions and another loses 100 millions, these two figures do not add up to zero or, to put it less paradoxically, the course of subsequent events generated by this situation is not the same as that which would follow if both had made zero profits. This is one of the reasons why theories that work with aggregates only are so misleading." [2] And Arthur F. Burns wrote in his 1946 annual report as director of the National Bureau of Economic Research as follows: "Although broad index numbers or aggregates give useful summaries, they tell nothing of the processes by which they are fashioned." [3]

The processes by which aggregate data are "fashioned" include the processes by which consumers and businessmen arrive at economic decisions, the end products of which add up to statistical aggregates. The analysis of the formation of these decisions—for example, why do people reduce their rate of savings or firms increase their capital expenditures—can be conducted only at the level of individual families and firms. The

[2] Joseph A. Schumpeter, "The Decade of the Twenties," *American Economic Review*, Vol. 36, Supplement, 1946, p. 5.

[3] Arthur F. Burns, *Economic Research and the Keynesian Thinking of Our Times*, New York, 1946, p. 22.

situation that generates subsequent events—to use Schumpeter's words—is represented by microeconomic data, not by aggregates.

How microeconomic financial data supplement aggregate data, and how they tie up with psychological data, will be shown in this book. A brief reference to a concrete example may, however, be in order here. Suppose that, as happened during the Second World War, there has been a rapid accumulation of liquid assets among consumers, and it becomes necessary to predict whether they contribute seriously to a threat of inflation. We cannot attempt a prediction solely on the basis of the aggregate amount of liquid assets. If a large part of these assets is in the hands of people of moderate income, there is much more danger of a sharp inflationary increase in the demand for consumer goods than if the greater part is held by the much smaller proportion of people who have large incomes and who, because they are not numerous, cannot affect the market for consumer goods so strongly. We must therefore know first of all how the new accumulation of liquid reserves is divided among the population. Then we must know how the holders regard them—whether, for example, these people are eager to buy cars, refrigerators, radios, and to spend their liquid assets for these purposes, or whether they are sensitive to the dangers of depression and wish to hold on to their savings. By means of microeconomic data we are able, first, to learn whether the liquid assets are spread thinly among all income groups, or concentrated among particular income groups; second, to tie individual holdings of liquid assets to the attitudes and motives of their individual owners. Only after we have such information can we interpret the significance of the aggregate accumulation of assets.

THE LAW OF LARGE NUMBERS

Our discussion must be interrupted by a counterargument. Certain objections to our line of thought are important, not only because they are widely held, but also because they have a sound core and serve to clarify the meaning and use of microeconomic data.

You just can't mean what you say, some people may tell us. In studying economic behavior, it is just not possible to be concerned with individual families or individual firms as such. Suppose you analyze carefully the spending and saving of John Smith. You find out everything about his past and present, his income, his occupation, his family relationships, his health, his tastes, etc.; you make an inventory of everything he has—money, home, automobile, and so forth—and you get a full explanation of why he spent so much and saved so much. Suppose you even do this time-consuming job with many individuals, what do you have then? When economists say that they are interested in the principles of economic behavior, they do not mean the individual circumstances that make every single case different from every other. They are interested in the regularities persisting in very many or all cases and are therefore primarily concerned with aggregates or averages.

From this premise the argument becomes more general. Granted that individual families and individual firms do not behave in an automatic, mechanistic manner. Still, so the argument runs, this does not matter for the economy as a whole. There is an "inertia of large numbers." Individual differences cancel out. Differences in motives and attitudes, and even the freedom of every single person or firm to act differently, are then of no interest and can be disregarded. The actions of very large groups of people or of all the people as a whole can be predicted from the given circumstances. The regularities of large numbers, which are the only ones that interest the economist, are susceptible to analysis without regard to the psychological differences and uncertainties prevailing in individual cases.

From this thesis follow specific statements on prediction. We are told: What an individual will do is uncertain, what thousands of individuals will do is not equally uncertain. Reliable predictions can be made on the probable actions of thousands of individuals but not on the probable actions of a few individuals. For, with respect to thousands of people, or the entire economy, past relationships will repeat themselves. It is not possible to predict how each single person will use his money. But without knowing which individuals will buy cars or will save money, it is possible to predict how many cars will be bought and how much money will be saved jointly by all the American people. The law of large numbers is the basis of economic analysis and economic predictions. And aggregative economics alone is important and possible; why should we lose our way in innumerable unimportant details?

Let us set down the true core of that argument. Consider first the simple case of tossing a coin. If I toss a coin once, I cannot tell whether it will fall heads or tails. The chances are equal; I may be right or wrong when I predict. But if I am going to toss the coin 1,000 times, I can make a number of well-justified predictions. I may predict, for instance, that I will not get 1,000 heads; the chances that my prediction will be wrong are very, very slight. I may further predict that of the 1,000 tosses there will be between 490 and 510 heads, and I can calculate the probability of that prediction.

These principles form the basis of actuarial tables. Life insurance companies cannot predict how long any individual will live and are not interested in such a prediction. They can, however, predict, on the average, how long a very large group of people, of equal age at present, will live and can therefore calculate the life expectancy of an individual for their purposes.

We may apply these principles to a further economic example. If an investor puts all his money into one single bond issue, he cannot predict with certainty that this bond issue will not default. Suppose, however, he diversifies his investment and purchases a bond of each of 100 different issues. Does this give him greater assurance? Can he say that total loss of his money—the default of all 100 bond issues—is less probable? Yes, under one condition. Insofar as the different bond issues are acted on by independent causes, the total loss of money invested in 100 issues is much less probable than the loss of money invested in one issue. If, however, the same cause—say, war or inflation—affects all bond issues, the large number will not help. The same is true of tossing the coin. Or, to change the simile, if the dice are loaded, my prediction that I will not shoot number 6 one hundred times in a row may not come true. Actuarial tables apply only if each person's life span is determined independently of every other person's, and the same cause—say, an atomic bomb—does not wipe out all the people.

More generally, the law of large numbers applies to economic stiuations if only random factors prevail so that individual differences cancel out. If the decisions of thousands of families or firms are due to independent causes, it is true that what thousands will do is more certain than what one will do. But if the same factors influence very many people at the same time in the same direction, the deviations add up instead of canceling out. We shall later study, and contradict, the assertion that individual consumer expectations may be disregarded because they cancel out when large numbers of consumers are considered. At this point, it suffices to say that we do not know in advance which factor, and especially which psychological factor, varies in a random manner among a multitude of people and which operates in the same direction with all. We can and, as we shall see, we must apply the law of large numbers, but only after studying individual cases and putting them together into homogeneous groups.

That the decisions and actions of thousands of persons may be due to the same causes is only one of the objections to the indiscriminate application of the law of large numbers. Let us consider again the argument that we can predict what thousands will do, but not what one person or a few persons will do. To what extent is the second part of that statement correct? Suppose the one person in question is myself, the writer, or you, the reader. It so happens that I can predict with great assurance whether I will buy a car during the next year. You may be able to predict whether you will marry next year, whether you will have an increase or decrease in income, whether you will buy a house. To be sure, in one or the other instance you may be uncertain, and one or the other of your predictions (expectations) may not come true. But it is not correct to say that there is no basis whatsoever for predicting what individuals will do. Individuals know or believe they know many things that will happen to them. And we—the psychologists or economists—can ask them. Furthermore, people are often not only able but also willing to give honest answers. Predictions about the future behavior of a few individuals are by no means certain, but it is questionable whether they are always more uncertain than predictions about the future behavior of many individuals. Only if nothing were known and nothing could be found out about the factors influencing the decisions and actions of a few individuals would the thesis be true that the law of large numbers is the only key to predictions.

What, then, is our purpose in investigating the behavior of individual families and firms? It is true that what we are interested in are regularities, that is, correspondences prevailing under similar conditions. But it is only by studying individual families and firms that we can learn whether or not regularities prevail, and under what conditions and in what groups of people they prevail. The aim of such an analysis is not the description and understanding of individual cases. An analysis of the financial position and the decision formation of individuals makes it possible to place the individual cases into homogeneous groups so that the law of large numbers can be applied. When large numbers of individual instances are found to be similar—when the same reactions are found under the same circumstances—we no longer run the risk of adding indiscriminately apples, pears, and oranges.

Since the objective of microeconomic analysis is not the description of individual cases, microeconomic data will be presented as "distributions." Data about aggregate national income must be supplemented by facts concerning distribution of income, that is, by information on the proportion of those who receive high, medium, and low incomes. Data on change in income must also be expressed in terms of the frequency of those who had income increases and decreases (within the high-, medium-, and low-income groups). We could—and will in later chapters—go further and break down each of those groups, for instance, according to their savings rates (high, medium, and low savers) and also according to many other relevant characteristics. Each of these groups must consist of many individual cases. The more we have, the better. The law of large numbers does apply and a "cell" (a homogeneous subgroup of individuals) consisting of many persons is greatly preferable to one consisting of only a few persons. We may make mistakes because of insufficient analysis of individual cases and include in what we consider homogeneous groups nonrandom factors which do not cancel out. But the chances of avoiding such errors are far greater if data are obtained on the micro- than on the macroeconomic level.

Analysis of economic behavior, then, will be undertaken here from a specific point of view. First, negatively, this study will exclude certain forms of economic analysis. It will not seek to arrive at dogmatic statements or general principles that are valid under ideal circumstances. Further, it will not be restricted to an analysis of the self-regulatory market economy and will not be satisfied to stay on the aggregative level. In contradistinction, this empirical study will be directed toward economic behavior *here and now,* that is, toward the present-day decisions and actions of American consumers and businessmen. Its aim will be to determine the probable types of behavior under different conditions. For that purpose, it will analyze the distributions of the economic position and the behavior of individual consumer units and firms.

NOTES TO CHAPTER 2

The discussion of the relation of aggregate, or macroeconomic, data to microeconomic and attitudinal data draws heavily on the author's paper, "Contribution of Psychological Data to Economic Analysis," *Journal of the American Statistical Association,* Vol. 42, 1947, pp. 449*ff.*

Concerning the accepted terminology in economics, we may quote J. R. Hicks, who defines economic *statics* as "those parts of economic theory where we do not trouble about dating," in contrast to economic *dynamics* "where every quantity must be dated" (*Value and Capital,* Oxford, 1939, p. 115). Similar definitions are used by econometricians. "A theory [is] called 'dynamic' when variables relating to different moments appear in one equation" (J. Tinbergen, "Suggestions on Quantitative Business-Cycle Theory," *Econometrica,* Vol. 3, 1935, p. 241).

References concerning the use of the term dynamic in psychology will be given in the Notes to Chapter 3. It suffices to mention here that the term is used in connection with the study of motives, forces, and answers to the question why, both in gestalt psychology and in psychoanalysis. While in dynamic analysis actually presented by economists only few traces can be found of the psychological meaning of the term, some broader definitions of dynamics may also be quoted from the economic literature. For instance, Jacob Marschak says that economic dynamics studies "the causation of changes of data" (*Econometrica,* Vol. 6, 1938, p. 325). Or, T. Haavelmo refers to "dynamic relations showing the *forces* directed towards an eventual equilibrium" (*Review of Economic Studies,* Vol. 16, No. 40, 1950, p. 80; italics in original).

The "inertia of large numbers" was discussed long ago by the famous nineteenth-century economist W. S. Jevons and in more recent times by Z. Clark Dickinson (*Economic Motives,* Cambridge, 1922, pp. 206*ff.*). The statement "What an individual will do is uncertain, what thousands of individuals will do is not equally uncertain" (p. 21, above) was adapted from Fritz Machlup's article "Why Bother with Methodology" where, however, it is expressed in terms of the difference between decisions of a few monopolists and many competitive sellers. Machlup writes: "The decision of the one, two, or three managers of the official Bank Monopoly is uncertain. The tendency of the decisions of thousands and thousands of wheat-growers is far from being equally uncertain" (*Economica*, New Series, Vol. 3, 1936, p. 42).

That conclusions derived from calculating probabilities apply to the distribution of risks and to diversification only "insofar as the different issues are acted on by independent causes" has been clearly shown in a paper by D. H. Leavens ("Diversification of Investments," *Trusts and Estates*, May, 1945).

For a popular presentation of the view that predictions are possible with respect to the prospective behavior of all people but are not possible with respect to the behavior of individuals, we may refer to Henry A. Wallace's pamphlet *Sixty Million Jobs*:

> "No one is wise enough to say ahead of time exactly how each one of our 60 million job-holders and business units, or their families, will use their money. . . . The insurance company, in the actuarial tables, depends on the laws of large numbers. In the same way, without saying which individual will buy what car, or which one will prefer to buy a house, business and government statisticians, pooling their resources, can estimate pretty closely from past experience and current trends how a large group of consumers will react to more income or less income, how much of their income farmers will spend for machinery, and how much business will use for new investment" (p. 60). (Reprinted from *Sixty Million Jobs* by Henry A. Wallace, Simon and Schuster, publishers. Copyright, 1945, by the Wallace Fund.)

Or we may quote a recent statement made by Tibor Scitovszky in his review of Boulding's book, *Economic Analysis*. These formulations likewise do not do justice to the function of microeconomic analysis.

> "The main advantage of aggregate analysis [is]: our ability to say more about the behavior of a large group than about that of an individual. It is the very essence of macro-economics that, because group behavior is more regular than the behavior of any single member of the group, we can establish statistical laws and make specific statements about a nation's reaction to a change in incomes, or prices, or liquid asset holdings, while we can make only very general statements about the individual's reaction to the same changes. This is not brought out at all by Professor Boulding" (*American Economic Review*, Vol. 39, 1949, p. 755).

It is interesting to note that another book review which appeared in the same journal three months later stresses the greater degree of uncertainty attached to macroeconomic results rather than the alleged regularity of group behavior. Fritz Machlup says of Erich Schneider's *Einführung in die Wirtschaftstheorie* (Tübingen, 1947) that "the best passage in the book, in my opinion, is the exposition of the relationship between micro- and macro-economics." He quotes Schneider's statement to the effect that the number of relationships that enter into microeconomic analysis is too large to be really useful. This number can be reduced by aggregating the "acting economic units" and thereby

". . . obtaining a greatly simplified picture of the relationships relevant to the process as a whole. . . . Naturally, such a macro-economic theory leads to results which are less enlightening and more uncertain than the results of a theory designed to explain the relationships between the smallest economic units. The significance of the results of a macro-economic theory and its quantitative reliability will be smaller the larger the size and the smaller the actual homogeneity of the groups with which the analysis operates. . . . Hence it is incumbent upon economic theory to make both types of analysis: a 'detail' analysis of the relationships between individual economic units and a 'bold-strokes-of-the-brush' analysis of the relationships between groups composed of individual economic units" (*American Economic Review*, Vol. 39, 1949, p. 991).

The example presented in the text concerning the distribution of personal liquid-asset holdings accumulated during the war and the owners' attitudes toward their assets is taken from consumer surveys that will be cited extensively in later chapters of this book. It may be permissible to quote here how in 1946 the microeconomic and psychological analysis led to predictions that later proved to be correct.

"In summary: the personal liquid-asset holdings are concentrated among a relatively small proportion of the people. The implications of this fact can be studied from the viewpoint of either the large or the small holders: What effects would action taken by many small holders have, as compared with the effects of action taken by a few large holders?

"It appears that even if 50 percent of all spending units decided to use all their liquid assets, but these were the poorest units (those who have the smallest amounts of liquid assets), only small amounts of money—3 percent of all personal liquid assets—would be involved. The circumstance that might induce many small holders to use their accumulated liquid reserves at the same time is, of course, widespread unemployment or depression. . . . Since unemployment would affect most immediately the people who have the smallest asset holdings, it appears probable that its effect on the use of liquid assets would not be great.

"On the other hand, a simultaneous decision on the part of the small percentage of spending units who hold large amounts of liquid assets to use these resources would be of great importance. Since 10 percent of the units hold 60 percent of the assets, the decisions of the top 1 or 2 percent govern the use of substantial amounts of money. It is improbable that much of this money would be used for consumption purposes. For the most part the huge aggregate amounts held by the top holders can be used only for investment purposes" (*National Survey of Liquid Asset Holdings, Spending, and Saving*, Part One, Division of Program Surveys, U.S. Department of Agriculture, May, 1946, pp. 11*f*.).

The survey report goes on to show that holders of large as well as small liquid assets intended to hold on to their bank deposits and war bonds. Using accumulated liquid assets for the purchase of consumer goods was considered an inappropriate use by the majority of the holders. (These points will be discussed in greater detail in Chapters 5 and 6 of this book.) Therefore, the conclusion was drawn that during the first few postwar years personal liquid-asset holdings would not be used on a large scale for the purchase of consumer goods.

CHAPTER 3

WHAT KIND OF PSYCHOLOGY?

There is one conception of man and of human behavior which, if it were valid, would make economic psychology, and psychology in general, impossible: what a person does, thinks, or feels is uncertain, unpredictable, not lawfully determined. In contrast, psychology is founded on the conviction that it is possible to establish scientific principles of behavior. Behavior is susceptible of analysis and measurement. Furthermore, some principles of behavior have already been established. To be sure, the principles currently known and accepted are not final. Every scientific discipline is at all times in a stage of growth and development. We can confidently expect to achieve greater knowledge and understanding in the future. On the other hand, psychology is no longer by any means an infant discipline.

There are those who may object: The trouble is not that there is no psychology, but that there are many psychologies. Different schools of psychology emphasize different aspects of behavior and propose different, often contradictory, principles. What is correct in this opinion again characterizes any growing discipline. Several paths may lead to the same mountain peak; it is useful to start the exploration of the peak from all sides. Moreover, the differences between psychological schools are greatly overemphasized. Sometimes such overemphasis may be useful for the sake of clarifying the differences. There are, however, among all present-day scientific psychologists fundamental agreements which are of great import to economic psychology.

Certain major principles and concepts of modern psychology will be presented in this chapter. Some, which will be discussed in the first section, are rather universally accepted, although there may be differences in formulation and emphasis among psychologists. Others, such as the principles of organization referring to the relation of parts to their whole and of individuals to groups, represent, however, the viewpoint of a specific school of psychology. In a certain sense, this book constitutes a test of these principles. It would represent additional evidence for the validity of the psychological principles here presented if they proved useful and fruitful in the task of analyzing economic behavior.

What are the main characteristics of modern psychology? And what are

28

the major theorems of psychology that will be used in analyzing economic behavior?

BASIC PRINCIPLES

1. Psychology is an empirical discipline. There is one, and only one, way to establish whether a psychological statement is correct, namely, by means of empirical evidence. Frequently, of course, a decision about what is correct would be premature, because the empirical studies have not been completed. But in principle, such a decision is possible, and all psychologists agree on how the decision must be sought. Statements not susceptible of empirical validation have no place in psychology.

The term "empirical research" has a specific meaning. It involves, first, controlled observation. Armchair considerations and what is believed to be common sense or a matter of common knowledge do not constitute scientific evidence. Likewise, casual observation and observation possible only to one individual are ruled out. Controlled observation, and especially its most developed form, experimentation, produces results that can be checked by other scientists. Controlled observation consists of identifying and singling out factors that prevail in many, apparently different, situations.

Second, empirical research involves the relating of many different controlled observations to one another. It does not consist of a description of a bit of experience here and another bit there, or a planless procedure of observation in a given situation. Empirical research must be guided by hypotheses or theories. It progresses by testing hypotheses through controlled observation, setting up new or changed hypotheses on the basis of that observation, testing them again, improving them further, and so on. Hypotheses must be valid for more than one set of observations. Instead of being constructed to explain one observation, they must be applicable to a variety of diverse facts and enable the research worker to deduce new facts.

2. There are two conceptions of behavior, molar and molecular. Our psychological analysis is directed toward molar behavior. Physiology and physiological psychology are directed primarily toward molecular behavior; that is, toward segmental activities, such as muscle contractions, limb movements, heartbeats, gland secretion, and so on. But such activities as coughing, chewing, swallowing, sweating are not the only possible units of behavior. There are also molar units of behavior, well defined from a starting point to an end point, in which recurrent similarities may be apparent in spite of differences in molecular activities.

Let us take a simple example. I sit at my desk, to the left of the door; the bell rings; I get up to open the door. Or, I stand to the right of the door; the bell rings; and I turn to open the door. On the molecular level, my activities may differ greatly: different muscles and movements may be involved, and in one case I may open the door with my left hand, in the other case with my right hand. But the two molar units of behavior are similar. They would differ if in the one case I was expecting a friend and in the other case fearing an unpleasant visitor, although probably some of the molecular activities would be the same in both cases. A man driving home for dinner, or a politician delivering a speech are further examples of molar units of behavior. This conception of behavior disregards molecular activities, not because they are unimportant, but because it is concerned with a different level of analysis and has different aims and purposes.

3. Behavior is characterized by plasticity within broad limits. Disregarding wear and tear, one can say of machines that they do the same thing over and over again. In this sense, human behavior is not repetitive. Doing the same thing the second time may differ from doing it the first time. There is maturation and there is learning. On the molar level, psychology is not concerned with reflexes that may be established by the neurophysiological structure once and for all. This structure itself is plastic. It is affected by previous actions. Therefore, the central problem of psychology is change in behavior.

Learning, in the broadest sense of the term, is a basic feature of any organism. The human organism acquires forms of behavior, it acquires forms of action, of knowledge, of emotions. What has been done does not necessarily belong only to the past and is not necessarily lost. It may or may not exert influence on present behavior. Under what conditions and in what ways past experience affects later behavior is one of the most important problems of psychology.

To be sure, there are limits to the plasticity of behavior. Certain limits are clearly set by the neurophysiological structure. For instance, human beings cannot learn to run a mile in two minutes. The neurophysiological determinants of certain other limits are not known. Yet the quantity of knowledge we are able to acquire is not infinite, and the speed of learning likewise has definite limits. Within rather broad limits, however, the possible variations are tremendous in number and kind, and these variations and their regularities represent the subject matter of the analysis of behavior.

The influence of the neurophysiological structure on behavior will, like molecular behavior, be disregarded in our analysis. We are concerned here with what has been called "higher mental processes." In studying economic behavior—for instance, the formation of decisions on buying, selling, pricing, producing—the question of what is innate and what is acquired behavior does not concern us. All these forms of behavior are learned behavior in the sense that they develop and change with experience. Not the limits of plasticity and learning, but rather the variations in making use of experience, represent the main issues in the analysis of economic behavior.

4. Psychological analysis makes use of intervening variables. A certain kind of so-called objective research might be conceived of as consisting of a complete recording of the situation and of the response of the human organism to that situation. Both the situation and the response might be recorded by moving pictures, sound recorders, and similar instruments. But empirical categories alone do not suffice for an understanding of behavior. This purpose requires conceptual tools that go beyond the data presented by objective recordings. They would be sufficient only if there were, of necessity, a one-to-one correlation between the stimulus (or situation) and the response. But, because of the plasticity of behavior, it is not to be expected that the same organism always reacts to the same situation in the same way. A stimulus sets the occasion for behavior. The response is the result of more than the stimulus alone. Something goes on in the organism which may be deduced from its response. The term "intervening variable" is used to denote those factors or constructs that are not directly observable by recording situations and responses but are postulated to explain behavior. The basic scheme of psychological analysis is: situation—intervening variables—overt behavior.

Psychological principles and hypotheses must make use of intervening variables. Examples of such variables are the concepts of organization, habit, motive, attitude. Their manifestations—as, for example, verbal behavior, emotional behavior, differences and similarities in behavior—are susceptible to observation. In exceptional instances, mechanistic connections between stimuli and responses might occur and a description of behavior which makes no use of intervening variables might not be incomplete. Even then, however, the absence of the influence of intervening variables could be determined only by making use of that concept. Intervening variables are essential to psychological analysis because without them our description of behavior would remain incomplete, our understanding of behavior limited, and our predictions of future behavior incorrect.

ORGANIZATION WITHIN A FIELD

Behavior is always organized within its field. The principles of organization need to be discussed in some detail. They serve to clarify the basic thesis of the psychological analysis of economic behavior: Instead of relating the environment to economic processes, we must study the relation of the perception of the environment, and of the perception of changes in the environment, to organized behavior. Our discussion of the principles of organization will adhere to the teachings of field and gestalt psychology.

Let us take two human beings who are confronted with the identical situation. We may say that their "geographical environment" is the same. Their responses to the same geographical environment may, however, not be the same. This is not a complete description of what has been going on. It may be that the "behavioral environment" of the two people is not the same. The geographical environment is represented by the external factors present; the behavioral environment by what the two people themselves see, hear, smell, feel. People do not see all that is given, and they do not necessarily see an object as it is given. Their perceptions are organized. What a person perceives—and therefore what affects him—depends on the organization of his perception.

Organization of perceptions, as well as of behavior, results in unified wholes. All items or parts are influenced by the whole to which they belong. The whole is different from the sum of its parts (which does not necessarily mean that the whole is more than the sum of its parts). The change in one item or part may or may not affect the whole or the other items and parts, depending on the role and function of the part within the whole. An organization has structure, often a focus or central feature, which may or may not be a given part, and it has one or many peripheral parts. The whole is segregated from other wholes. In a broad sense, the psychological whole is represented by the field of behavior. Behavior takes place within a field, is influenced by its field, and, in turn, influences the field.

These broad theoretical formulations require clarification. We shall first present simple illustrations of the statement that what we see represents an organized response. Nine points on a blackboard (Fig. 1a) may be seen as

(a)   *(b)*   *(c)*

FIG. 1. Examples of Simple Perceptual Organizations.

three horizontal rows, or three vertical rows, or a square with a central point. Which organization prevails at a given moment depends on such perceptual principles as proximity and similarity, as well as on past experience. Organization may encompass more than is objectively given. Figure 1b is seen as three horizontal rows because of the operation of the principles of proximity and similarity, although points alone constitute the stimuli.

Similarly, Fig. 1c is seen as three horizontal rows, the middle one of which is shorter than the two other rows. The fact that certain points are missing in the middle row influences the organization of what we see.

The three horizontal or vertical rows on the blackboard stand out from their background. They are, in our perception, a figure separated from the ground. The organized whole of the given figure is segregated from the background and from any other parts which may be present in our perception. The powerful influence of perceptual organization, and of the perceived boundaries of the organized figure, may become apparent if we try to solve the following task. Let us try to draw four straight lines crossing each of the nine points of Fig. 1a without lifting the pencil and without retracing. (The reader is urged to try to solve this problem before reading further.) For most people this is a very difficult task, and many fail to solve it. It can be solved easily, however, if we disregard the boundaries of the square and go beyond the limits of the figure (see the solution of the task in the Notes to this chapter). The given perceptual organization makes it, however, difficult for us to do so.

Perception of movement may serve to illustrate further the statement that what we see is always an organized whole, depending on laws of organization. In the drawings of Fig. 2, points represent small lights which are made

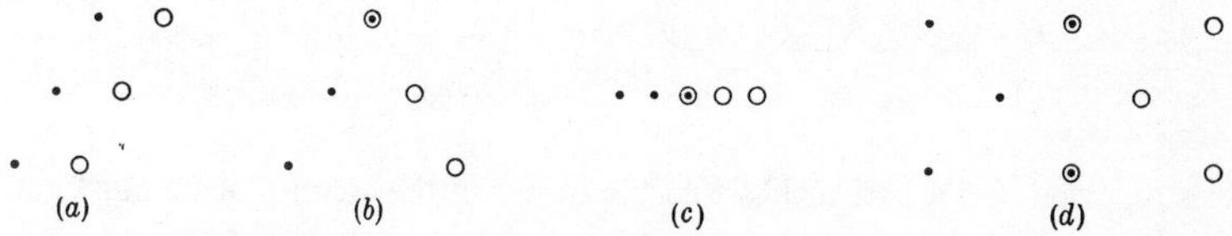

FIG. 2. Schemes of Experiments on the Perception of Movement.

visible first, and circles represent small lights which are made visible right after the lights represented by points have been extinguished. Points within circles remain visible during the entire experiment. In the example, the scheme of which is presented in Fig. 2a, we see first a line (not three simultaneous light flashes) and we then see it move to the right. Movement is perceived (if the interval between the two groups of light flashes is suitably chosen). If our experiment is made according to the scheme of Fig. 2b, a line appears to pivot toward the right; the one point which is objectively lighted during the entire experiment does not move. But in an experiment made according to the scheme of Fig. 2c, a line appears to move from the left to the right; movement is seen at every point of the line, even at the point where, objectively, everything remains unchanged (no light is extinguished and no new light presented). Finally, in an experiment with the scheme of Fig. 2d, we see an X moving to the right; the two points marked with both a point and a circle, though they do not change, are seen as moving to the right.

Specific principles of perceptual organization are of no particular interest for our purposes. Nor are we concerned with the origin of the regularities of perceptions. The main point is that there is no one-to-one correspondence between given stimuli—objective changes in the environment—and the resulting perceptions.

The examples thus far presented were selected to illustrate the thesis that the role and function of each part is determined by the whole situation. This statement may be broadened by saying that the meaning of an event is dependent upon, and derived from, the whole situation. Since this psychological view will be widely used later on—when we shall discuss the meaning of a given income or income change, for instance—further simple illustrations are in order. They will be taken from psychological processes that are somewhat more complex than perception. Thinking and problem solving start out from a perceptual organization (the problem situation as perceived) and proceed by reorganizing or restructuring the situation.

In a parlor game, the question is raised how to make a single chain out of five chains, each of which consists of three interlocking rings (Fig. 3).

FIG. 3. Starting Point of a Problem-solving Experiment.

It is reported that a jeweler has told the owner of the chain that he must cut the third ring of the first part, put it around the first ring of the second part, and solder the cut. This operation he must repeat three times; altogether he must cut and solder four rings. Can the same result be achieved by a smaller number of operations? Many people answer no even after studying the problem for a long time. The solution,[1] which appears to be extremely simple to one who has found it (or been shown it), is psychologically difficult because it involves reorganizing a stable organization. There is a strong tendency to perceive Fig. 3 as consisting of five equal parts, separated by four gaps, in accordance with the working of the principles of proximity and similarity. In order to solve the problem, the first three rings must be seen as gap fillers, instead of as having the same function as the other four parts. Solving the problem, therefore, involves changing the meaning of certain parts. The original meaning, as well as the new one, is determined by the whole situation.

[1] Each of the three rings of the first part is cut and used as a link connecting the other parts.

As a further example, we present the problem of obtaining the sum of the first 10 whole numbers. Suppose the procedure of adding $(1 + 2 = 3, 3 + 3 = 6, 6 + 4 = 10,$ etc.) is ruled out and the person confronted with the task does not know the equation

$$\Sigma = \frac{n(n + 1)}{2}$$

By reorganizing the numbers, some people solve the problem. They see that 1 and 10 "belong" to each other, in the same way as 2 and 9, 3 and 8, and so on, in the framework of the task situation. Each of these pairs has the same sum (11 in our example), and there must be half as many such pairs as there are numbers (5 pairs). Originally, 1 and 2 belonged to each other; solving the problem consisted of changing the grouping and meaning of the individual figures.

1 2 3 4 5 6 7 8 9 10

These examples may serve to illustrate several further field concepts. The whole situation which determined the restructuring of the perception encompassed much more than the visual images of circles or numbers and their pattern. It consisted of a task, and the desire or willingness to solve that task. The psychological field of the person confronted with the task had a direction. The person was motivated in a certain way, and forces in the field pushed him toward one specific organization and not toward another. Motives, attitudes, and also emotions are parts of the field (the whole situation) in the same way as the perceptual parts. In certain rare psychological situations—of which Fig. 1 or 2 may serve as examples—motives and attitudes do not play a substantial role. Usually, however, they contribute to the organization of the field or even determine it. Even simple perceptions of the same environment may differ for a hungry person and for a person who has just finished a good meal. The role that motives and attitudes play is again a function of the field.

Motives are the forces which pull the organism in a certain direction, toward certain ends and goals. They represent the answers to the question why. (Why did I go to a certain meeting? Why did I write this book?) Attitudes represent generalized viewpoints which make us regard certain situations with favor and others with disfavor. The general points of view that influence our perceptions and behavior over extended periods need not have the feature of affecting us pro or con. When that feature is lacking and yet a perceptual or cognitive context is present, we speak of a frame of reference. The terms used and their exact definitions are not very important. Often it does not matter much whether we speak of motives, attitudes, or frames of reference. I hear over the radio a plan to introduce an excess-profits tax on corporation earnings. I view this proposition with favor (or disfavor) because I am motivated by "social" considerations (or by opposition to interference with "the profit motive"), or because my attitudes are procontrol and prolabor (or anticontrol and probusiness), or because my frame of reference consists of the "prevailing large business profits" (or of need for larger business investments).

Motives, attitudes, and frames of reference influence the organization of perceptions of the environment as well as of reactions to the environment. Human action is response within a field and not an automatic, mechanical reaction to stimuli. Because of the influence of intervening variables, two individuals may respond to the same situation in different ways, and one individual may respond to two different situations in the same way.

Instead of motives and attitudes, we may also make use of other terms which, however, do not fit quite as well into our later analysis of the complex psychological processes that constitute economic behavior. Needs, wants, and tensions represent certain forms of powerful motivation. It does not matter whether one says that a certain action was determined by need for food or that the person was motivated by hunger; in both cases one refers to parts of the psychological field and to field forces. Similarly, if one speaks of drives, field forces are meant. Finally, motives of behavior may be described as striving for satisfaction or striving for avoidance of dissatisfaction. This description is justified if these are the intervening variables that provide the most satisfactory explanation of the response.

Thus far we have described the complexity of psychological fields but have not discussed their changes or their origin. Nor have we gone into the question of why motives or attitudes play a great role in certain fields and a small role in other fields. These questions lead back to the problem of learning and the utilization of past experience. For attitudes and motives are acquired or learned. An analysis of learning in terms of field psychology is an essential tool of economic psychology. It will be taken up in the next chapter on the basis of examples from both economic and noneconomic behavior.

THE INDIVIDUAL AND THE GROUP

Up to now our analysis has been conducted in terms of the psychology of individuals. Are the principles of social psychology different? When we speak of groups, instead of individuals, do we have to use a different or a changed psychology?

A modern textbook of social psychology gives the following clear-cut answer to this question: "To understand [social behavior] we must study both individual life and group life, in terms of a single body of coherent concepts and principles." [2] Psychological processes occur only in the individual being, not in the group; only the individual acts, not the group. But the individual does not think and act in the same way irrespective of whether he is or is not a member of a group. Action in groups—social behavior—may differ greatly from individual action, but must and can be explained in terms of the same psychological principles. The cue to the understanding of group behavior is that the group plays the same role that has been assigned to the whole (or the whole situation) in the previous discussion. Just as a stimulus or a motive is part of its whole or field, so is the individual part of his field, usually of his group.

We are then in a position to derive certain important principles of social psychology from our previous discussion. First, we learned that an individual item may be part of several different wholes and may differ according to the whole to which it belongs in the given situation. In terms of social psychology this means that the individual may at certain times of a day be a factory worker or a student, in other words, he may belong to the group of workers or students. At other times, the same individual may be father and husband, his whole situation or group being represented by his family. At still other times, he may be a club member or a member of a political party.

Furthermore, belonging to different groups is not restricted to different times. It may be that at a certain time a student is nothing but a member of the group of his classmates, or a factory worker a member of his work crew (Fig. 4a). It may, however, be that a student belongs not only to the group

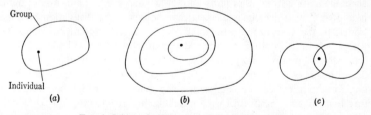

Fig. 4. Schematic Examples of Group Belonging.

of his classmates but also to the group of the entire student body of a university (or the factory worker belongs to the group of all workers at the factory) or to all students (all workers) in the country. Students and factory workers may also belong at the same time to the group of all Americans

[2] T. M. Newcomb, *Social Psychology,* New York, 1950, p. vii.

(Fig. 4*b*). There are further possibilities of divided membership: a worker may be at the same time a member of the factory group (those employed by the XYZ Corporation) and of a union which includes workers from other factories (Fig. 4*c*), or he may even be the only member of a group who is at the same time also a member of another group (for instance, of his family, when he worries at work about his child's illness).

Membership in a group is meant here as belonging in a psychological sense. In this sense, we are not family members, and not Americans, when we are fully engrossed in our work at the factory or classroom.

The individual has a different role and function according to the group (whole) to which he belongs. It is not to be expected that the individual will behave the same way in different group situations.

The same principles apply to individual and to social psychology. Item *x* as part of the whole *A* may, and usually will, differ from the identical item *x* when it is part of the whole *B*. On the other hand, item *x* as part of the whole *A* may be equivalent to, and elicit the same response as, item *y* as part of the whole *B*. The items *x* and *y* may be lights or sounds or individual human beings; the wholes *A* and *B* may be perceptions and psychological fields of an individual, or groups. In both cases, we find that the structural properties of the parts are influenced by the wholes to which they belong, and that the wholes may have structural properties that differ from the properties of the parts.

Among the principles that account for differences in the behavior of an individual according to the group to which he belongs, the most important one concerns the role of the part within the group. A part may be the center or focus of its whole and the major determinant of the whole itself. But a part may also be a peripheral or insignificant one which is subject to influences emanating from other parts and the whole. What comes first to mind in applying these principles to social psychology is the distinction between leader and member, or between an interested, wholehearted member and one who is only accidentally in a group. But what is meant is much more. There are "strong groups," or group situations that are compelling, powerful determinants of individual behavior. Playing football or marching in a military formation may serve as examples of situations in which behaving in a way that does not conform to the requirements of the situation is difficult and is felt as deviant behavior. On the other hand, a student attending a lecture in which he is not interested may serve as an example of belonging to a "weak group" or being in a group situation where the behavior requirements of the situation are not paramount.

The individual behaves, not the group. But the individual may behave as an individual or as part of a "we." Even in a group situation, the action of the individual may be affected only slightly by the group. In other instances, the "ego" may play an unimportant role and the individual may act as a part of the whole. The we may be the family, the college, the factory, the trade union, the football team, or the American nation. We shall come back to this problem when we discuss the motives of a corporation executive. It suffices to say here that individual-centered behavior may differ from we-centered behavior and that conflicts between the two are possible. Also, pursuit of individual interest is not the only form of motivation and not necessarily the basic form of motivation.

In the "we situation" it is meaningful to speak of "group forces" or "group motives" (although groups do not have motives, but group members may share motives). Conscious identification of an individual with his group is one instance of the effectiveness of such forces. Being subject to the same stimuli and the same requirements of the situation is another instance. The soldier marching in a group need not identify himself consciously with the other soldiers in his group and still his behavior will be group-determined. Similarly, buying by consumers or pricing by businessmen may be group-centered without identification with the group and without imitation. Imitation and suggestion are phenomena which may reinforce the group situation and group coherence, but are not necessary conditions of belonging to a group and acting as a we. On the other hand, reciprocal reinforcement of motives of different individuals belonging to the same group—"social facilitation"—will frequently be recognized in economics as in any other interpersonal behavior.

In addition to groups to which one belongs, there are "reference groups" from which an individual may derive standards for his behavior. He may measure his performance with reference to that of a certain group even though he is not a member of that group. Or a group situation as perceived by an individual may determine his attitudes even though he does not belong to that group. A person moving to a wealthy part of the city, inhabited by people to whom he does not belong and by whom he is not accepted, may nevertheless adopt the opinions and behavior of his neighbors. Both group belonging and reference groups will be found to play a role, for example, in consumption expenditures.

Group coherence and group-centered motivational forces are usually most pronounced in groups composed of interacting members who are united in what has been called the face-to-face situation. Somewhat weaker forces result from belonging to a group in a general or imagined sense. The we which becomes the subject of action instead of the ego is most commonly the small group with which one is associated daily—the family, the work crew, the colleagues, or, in the case of an executive or an official, the corporation or agency. The broader groups of all workers, all businessmen, all government officials, or all Americans, or the reference groups—

whether they are real or exist only in one's imagination—are less conducive to group feeling and group action.

The fundamental lesson of field psychology, and of social psychology based on it, is that the psychological study of parts, and of individuals as parts, requires the study of the given whole situation. But is this possible? Is the whole situation not so complex as not to be susceptible of scientific study? The answer is that the whole situation does not encompass everything that happens at a given moment. That it is raining outside, in front of my window, may, but need not, be part of my field. That I am a union member, or a convinced Republican, may or may not enter into my field when I act in a certain way. The whole has "closure." It is organized in such a way that it is unified and delineated from other items that do not belong to it. Similarly, groups are segregated from other groups. It is often easier to take the relevant whole qualities into account than to describe even a few of the given parts or items. Yet even where the study of the determination of the part by its whole, or the analysis of group belonging, is difficult, it must represent the method of psychological analysis.

NOTES TO CHAPTER 3

Empirical research has been characterized in the text as different from mere empiricism. Concerning the relation of observation and experiment to hypothesis and theory in psychology, see "Standards for Appraising Psychological Research" by Dael Wolfle, Rensis Likert, D. G. Marquis, and R. R. Sears, *The American Psychologist*, Vol. 4, 1949, pp. 320*ff*.

On molar and molecular behavior, as well as on intervening variables, see E. C. Tolman, *Purposive Behavior in Animals and Men,* New York, 1932, and Kurt Koffka, *Principles of Gestalt Psychology,* New York, 1935. The concept of molar units of behavior is used for the study of behavior and motivation in K. F. Muenzinger's *Psychology, the Science of Behavior,* New York, 1942.

From the very extensive literature on dynamics in psychology, we shall cite only the work of Wolfgang Koehler, *Gestalt Psychology,* New York, 1929, and *Dynamics in Psychology,* New York, 1940; and of Kurt Lewin, *A Dynamic Theory of Personality,* New York, 1935, and *The Conceptual Representation and the Measurement of Psychological Forces,* Durham, N.C., 1938. These books, and Koffka's volume cited earlier, are also the basic sources for the study of field and gestalt psychology. Field and gestalt psychology have, especially in the past, been sharply contrasted with behaviorism. But the original behaviorism of the Watsonian type has practically disappeared during the last two decades; furthermore, no matter what school they belong to, all psychologists study behavior. Differentiation between field psychology and what may be called "elementarism" is, however, still justified. On the differences between psychological theories, see R. S. Woodworth, *Contemporary Schools of Psychology,* New York, 1948, rev. ed.

The author's research in psychology, and his formulations in the text, have been most strongly influenced by Max Wertheimer, who has been rightly called the father of gestalt psychology. The discussion of the role of organization and the illustrations presented in Figs. 1, 2, and 3, as well as the "Gauss problem" (adding the first ten whole numbers), were borrowed from Wertheimer's work, which has been only partly published in his posthumous book, *Productive Thinking*, New York, 1945. See also Wertheimer's papers on perception of movement (*Zeitschrift für Psychologie*, Vol. 61, 1912), on principles of organization (*Psychologische Forschung*, Vols. 1 and 4, 1921 and 1923), and on items and parts (*Zeitschrift für Psychologie*, Vol. 129, 1933).

The task of drawing four straight lines through nine points without lifting the pencil or retracing, from N. R. F. Maier's article in the *Journal of Comparative Psychology*, Vol. 10, 1930, was used by the author to illustrate the concept of frame of reference in his paper in the *American Journal of Sociology*, Vol. 49, 1944, p. 342. The solution of the task is presented in Fig. 5. On frames of

FIG. 5. End Point of a Problem-solving Experiment.

reference and attitudes, see also Hadley Cantril, *The Psychology of Social Movements*, New York, 1941, and M. Sherif and H. Cantril, *The Psychology of Ego Involvements*, New York, 1947.

Regarding the age-old problem of the distinction between trees and forests, or individuals and groups, the following discussion by Kurt Lewin may be quoted:

"There is no more magic behind the fact that groups have properties of their own, which are different from the properties of their subgroups or their individual members, than behind the fact that molecules have properties, which are different from the properties of the atoms or ions of which they are composed.

"In the social as in the physical field the structural properties of a dynamic whole are different from the structural properties of subparts. Both sets of properties have to be investigated. When one, and when the other, is important, depends upon the question to be answered. But there is no difference of reality between them.

"If this basic statement is accepted, the problem of existence of a group loses its metaphysical flavor. Instead we face a series of empirical problems" ("Frontiers in Group Dynamics," *Human Relations*, Vol. 1, 1947, p. 5).

Two excellent textbooks on social psychology must be referred to with respect to groups and social behavior: David Krech and R. S. Crutchfield, *Theory and Problems of Social Psychology*, New York, 1948, and T. M. Newcomb, *Social Psychology*, New York, 1950. On the concepts of ego and we, which are not used in the psychoanalytic sense, see Chapter XIV of Koffka's book, cited above.

CHAPTER 4

PAST EXPERIENCE AND EXPECTATIONS

We turn to the analysis of change in behavior. We concluded in the last chapter that most human behavior, and especially complex human behavior, is learned behavior. The motives, attitudes, and frames of reference, and also the principles of perceptual organization which influence the behavior of human adults, are dependent on past experiences. They affect decision and action in familiar as well as new situations. How past experience is utilized we have not yet studied.

Two ways through which behavior may change will be excluded from consideration. Maturation and growth, on the one hand, decay and injury, on the other, do affect behavior but—like the molecular aspects of behavior in contrast to the molar aspects—they are of little interest in studying economic behavior. The third, and for us the only important, form of change in behavior is learning. Learning results in doing something in a different way, usually better, than before. It has two forms: we may learn through stamping in (memorizing, drill) and through understanding.

TWO FORMS OF LEARNING

We shall begin the discussion of the general principles of learning through understanding by first presenting an example taken from geometry. The relevant points of these principles can be most easily clarified through mathematical examples. Suppose the reader is asked to find the area of a trapezoid (Fig. 6a). He may have learned the formula in school but have forgotten it by now (as will no doubt be true of most readers). He may, however, remember something about the area of a square or parallelogram or, by thinking about what area means (for instance, the area of his back yard), he may find out how to measure the area of that simple figure. The area of the parallelogram consists of the number of small squares into which the parallelogram is divided, that is, of a times h; we have to measure the sides a and h and the problem is solved (Fig. 6b). At this point some people will give up. They are unable—or are not sufficiently motivated to try seriously—to make the transition from Fig. 6b to 6a and to discover what they have to measure to find the area of the trapezoid. Others, however, will discover the solution, or may be helped to discover it. One of sev-

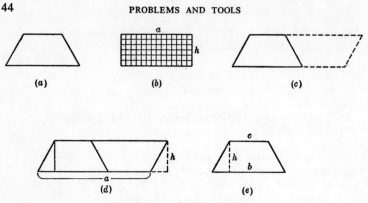

FIG. 6. Steps in Problem Solving.

eral possible ways of discovery is the following. The two ends of the trapezoid are "disturbing"; they are the parts which make the trapezoid different from the parallelogram. How can we get rid of those disturbing areas? Suppose we try to find the area not of Fig. 6a, but of twice that area—by cutting the trapezoid out of paper twice and placing the two figures side by side, the second one upside down, as in Fig. 6c. Then we get a "more regular" figure. We can transform that figure into a parallelogram by cutting off the left corner and placing it at the right (Fig. 6d). The area of the new figure will be a times h. What is the length of a? The line a is equal to the sum of b and c (Fig. 6e); that is how we put the two trapezoids together. Therefore, we have to measure the two sides b and c, add their length, and multiply this by the length of line h; then we obtain the area of two trapezoids; by dividing the result by two, we obtain the area of one trapezoid: $\frac{(b+c)h}{2}$. This formula is, of course, identical with the one stated in textbooks: $\frac{h}{2}(b+c)$.

In psychological terms, however, the two identical solutions are not the same. If we are told that in order to find the area of a trapezoid, we must, first, add the length of the two parallel sides, then draw a perpendicular line (the height), and, finally, multiply half of the height by the sum of the two parallel lines, we will—usually—not understand what we are told to do. Why just one-half the height? If we memorize the formula, the concept "half the height" has—for nonmathematicians—no meaning.[1] It has been shown by experimentation that the results of the two processes of arriving at the

[1] Demonstration of the mathematical proof of the formula, as is done in school, is usually of no more help in bringing about an understanding of it, though, to be sure, some pupils may gain an understanding of the problem even though they have merely

same result—the answer to the question, "What is the area of a trapezoid?" —are different. If we discover the solution ourselves, we remember the result better and for a longer time than if we memorize the formula. And we are able to apply what we learn through solving the problem to many similar and even rather different situations, which we cannot do after just memorizing.

Through solving the problem, we have learned something. Of what did problem solving consist? We reorganized the field. When the problem was presented—What is the area of Fig. 6a?—the psychological field consisted of two parts, the figure and the problem, between which there was a gap. Solving the problem, discovering the solution, consisted of closing the gap. Generally, understanding consists of the reorganization of parts so that the gaps are closed. Through understanding we obtain an integrated field. The parts acquire new meaning, consisting of their role and function within the new integrated whole. Learning, in certain instances, consists, then, of the discovery of new meanings through reorganizing the field.

The process of learning through understanding could have been illustrated by the problem, discussed in the previous chapter, of adding consecutive numbers. We solved that problem and learned through understanding when we reorganized the field and saw that the first and last number, the second and the second from last, and so on, belonged together. That process differed from learning by heart the formula $\Sigma = (n+1)\frac{n}{2}$. To clarify further aspects of understanding, we shall turn to an economic example.

The following question, asked in a nation-wide survey in the fall of 1942, was studied by the author at various later periods: "If personal income taxes are increased next year, will this affect prices in general, or won't it make any difference to the prices?" [2] Some people answered that if income taxes were raised (1) prices would not be affected; others said (2) that prices would go up; still others, (3) that prices would go down. Further questions showed that some people who gave the first answer did not see any connection between the two ideas, tax increase and price movement.

memorized the formula and learned its proof. For mathematicians, of course, the formula, and the concept "half the height," is meaningful and elegant.

[2] The question was asked in connection with a survey initiated by the Office of War Information concerning the people's knowledge of, and their attitudes toward, anti-inflationary measures. Just as the trapezoid example does not describe the process of understanding of a mathematician, this example does not refer to the thought processes of a trained economist. The latter may rightly say that the question provided too little information, and that countless things might happen after income taxes had been raised. The example is meant to illustrate the principles of thinking and understanding and is not intended as an analysis of the conditions under which tax increases have different effects.

Some people who gave the second answer argued that taxes are costs; that when wages, which are also costs of producing, go up, prices are raised; and that the same thing would happen when taxes are increased. Finally, some people considered the question from the point of view of purchasing power in the hands of consumers and concluded that higher income taxes would reduce the amount of money available for spending.

The three different answers to the same question show what is meant by lack of understanding (answer 1), misunderstanding (answer 2), and true understanding (answer 3). Let us analyze, first, lack of understanding as illustrated by the assertion that raising income taxes would not affect prices. According to the classical theory, it is always the new, the unfamiliar, which we do not understand. Suppose someone reads the Latin words *vis major* for the first time. He does not understand them. Then he looks in the dictionary and finds the definition "act of God." By repeating "*vis major*— act of God" several times, by forming an association between the two, he makes sure that the next time he reads those Latin words he will understand them. Understanding, according to that theory, is the result of association. More and more evidence seems to indicate that this theory is, to say the least, one-sided. Understanding in typical and important instances is not obtained by forming a connection between the new and the familiar. And what we do not understand is not necessarily new or unfamiliar. To many of those who said that raising income taxes would not affect prices, the two ideas, tax increase and price movement, were not unfamiliar, and mere repetition of the two ideas would not have brought about an understanding of the problem. Lack of understanding results not merely from the absence of any connection between two experiences but also from the absence of a framework within which an experience finds its place. Understanding may be lacking with respect to familiar matters, such as prices and taxes, just as well as to new discoveries, such as radar and atomic energy.

Lack of understanding is overcome by viewing previously unrelated items as integral parts of the same context. The greater context may, however, not be the appropriate one. In that case, misunderstanding may result. Those respondents who saw only the similarity between wage increases and tax increases had an inappropriate frame of reference to answer the question. They failed to see the dissimilarity—that higher wages would result in increased purchasing power, while higher income taxes would have the opposite effect—which was central to the problem. Misunderstanding is characterized by lack of structural clarity, despite the presence of a seemingly unifying framework; the relation of the parts to one another is not clarified, the parts do not fit, and gaps or unsolved problems remain.

On the other hand, when tax increases and price movements are viewed within the context of available purchasing power, not only are they related but their meaning and mutual relationship are properly established. Within this frame of reference, the concept tax increase is understood to mean diminution of spendable money. Real understanding requires the integration of all data in such a way that the gaps are closed. To be fully understood, a problem or an experience must be fitted into its proper and consistent context, and its role within that context must be clarified.

The above criteria of understanding are valid even in cases in which there are different ways of understanding the same problem. Suppose we raise the question of whether government deficits are good or bad. Those who feel they understand this question view it within some frame of reference. It may be that of a private household. Living beyond one's income, going into debt to meet expenses, is usually considered bad. It is not acceptable except in a great emergency (*e.g.,* an accident or serious illness). Within this framework, the answer to the question may be that deficits are bad and are tolerable only during an emergency or a war. Other people may think of taxes as means of increasing or decreasing people's purchasing power. Within this context, government deficits are acceptable and even required if it is necessary to increase purchasing power (that is, during a depression); they are unsound and to be avoided if it is necessary to reduce purchasing power (that is, during inflationary times). To shift from the first to the second view—irrespective of whether or not the conclusions are correct—requires a reorganization of the field. The field determines the role and function of the parts and reorganization gives new meaning to the parts.

Change in behavior, then—verbal behavior, in our last example—may occur through reorganizing one's field. Such a change may also occur through carrying over previously achieved understanding. If the reader is asked the question about the area of the trapezoid or about the relation of income taxes to price movements a few days after reading this chapter, he may not reply in the same way as he would have yesterday. There will be no need to solve the problem, he may just recall the solution. The repetition of the identical problem or situation represents, however, only one type of occasion for carrying over past experiences. We repeat our behavior in many situations which we deem to be similar to previous ones. The application of knowledge or past experience is a most frequent occurrence, and it may or may not be appropriate. For instance, using the formula $(n+1)\frac{n}{2}$ to solve the problem of the sum of the consecutive numbers 3 to 10 may be inappropriate and lead to an incorrect solution if one merely substitutes the largest number, in this case, 10, for n.[3] Tax increases may have the same

---

[3] Meaningful application of the formula—or of the understanding previously acquired—may also be made if one remembers that the formula means: Add the first and the last number in the series and multiply this total by the number of pairs.

effects for a manufacturer as wage increases, and still a blind carry-over of this experience to the question discussed above is not satisfactory. Or, to take another example, it was the perceptual framework of the 9 points (Chapter 3, Fig. 1a) which, carried over to the problem of drawing 4 straight lines through the points, made the solution of the problem difficult.

In addition to learning through understanding and to the meaningful application or the blind carry-over of understood experience, there is another kind of learning. I may learn to tap the typewriter at a certain place for S and at another place for T. I then form a connection between certain movements and their results. By repeating this connection often, I learn something without understanding it. Similarly, I may learn telephone numbers by heart or may memorize, as is done in certain psychological experiments, pairs of nonsense syllables. Or, I may repeat and learn by heart the formula for the area of the trapezoid. There are certain ununderstandable connections which cannot be learned in any other way (telephone numbers, for instance, if we do not want to rely on the telephone book). There are other connections (the area of the trapezoid, for example) which may be learned either in a meaningful or in a senseless way. What interests us here is that attaching new items or responses to old items or stimuli is a way of learning. It usually requires frequent repetition and is forgotten relatively fast if not practiced (repeated again).

Habits may be formed in two ways. Habitual or routine behavior may be the result of learning through repetition, or it may consist of carrying over principles, well understood in their original context, from one situation to other situations. Not every course of action or trial serves as a reinforcement of a habit. Trials must be successful or rewarded to be effective. A rat placed in a maze, for instance, in well-known psychological experiments, will form the habit of turning to the left at a certain point if it obtains food at the end of the left alley. Occasional runs through the blind right alley will not create the habit of turning to the right. Reward or success represents the necessary motivational condition for stamping in the behavior.

Conversely, habits may be broken because the habitual response is not rewarded (or is punished), because the situation has changed so that there is no occasion to repeat the habitual response and, sometimes, because of the understanding that the habitual behavior is no longer appropriate.

When, under what circumstances, will we act habitually, do what we have done before, and when will we try to reach an understanding and solve the problem that confronts us? The answer to this question will provide a cue to the analysis of economic behavior.

There is one clear condition for problem solving: we must see that there is a problem. A gap, a question, something puzzling or new must confront us. Or we must be, subjectively, in a crossroads situation where several possibilities are open to us. Tensions must exist, representing strong motivational forces that drive us to embark on a different, unusual task. This situation does not occur frequently. Usually, the situation, even if it is objectively new, appears to have at least some familiar, old features. In most situations we recognize possibilities of old, well-known, and well-tested reactions. The easiest way out, which we apply automatically, is to do the same thing we have done before in similar situations. We apply a principle, or carry over a habitual response, without studying whether that response fits completely, whether it does justice to the requirements of the new situation.

GENUINE DECISIONS AND HABITUAL BEHAVIOR

Now we are in a position to introduce new names for the two kinds of behavior which we have described. Genuine decisions are made occasionally. They require the perception of a new situation and the solution of the problem raised by it; they lead to responding to a situation in a new way. In contrast, habitual behavior is rather common. We do what we did before in a similar situation. Whether we use the word "decision" in such circumstances is immaterial. The main point is that the psychological process involved is different from that in genuine decision. Routine behavior, or using rules of thumb, are suitable terms to describe the second form of behavior.

The difference between the two kinds of behavior can also be pointed out by referring to the much-discussed problem of flexibility or rigidity of conduct.[4] Crossing the street at a particular corner on my way home may exemplify rigid behavior. Many forms of price setting by businessmen represent rigid behavior; they are routine acts, repeated over and over again. Flexibility, on the other hand, is best defined as reorganizing the field and acting in the light of the newly gained understanding.

The terms rational and irrational behavior may also be applied here. These terms are often used so as to indicate the difference between purposive and understandable behavior, on the one hand, and emotional, haphazard, nonunderstandable behavior, on the other. The psychologist does not acknowledge the occurrence of behavior that is not eventually understandable. The only meaning he can give to the concept of rational behavior is based on its description as the weighing of different alternative courses of action and of choosing deliberately among them, according to some principle. This description may be taken to coincide with that of genuine decision making—deciding according to the requirements of the

---

[4] Rigidity is, of course, meant in the molar and not the molecular sense, and is to be differentiated from compulsiveness or fixation.

situation. It can then be contrasted with mechanistic, routine, repetitive behavior.

It has been necessary to contrast the two kinds of behavior sharply. It should not be inferred, however, that there are no intermediate kinds of behavior or that all complex actions can be clearly classified one way or the other. Yet, often enough, such classification is possible, as can be shown by presenting economic examples illustrative of the psychological principles involved.

Our first example of routine behavior, or rigidity in decisions—to be mentioned here briefly and studied again in Part Three—is setting prices by means of the markup principle. Many retailers, for instance, add one-third to the purchase price of an article to arrive at its sales price. When new merchandise comes in, they do not necessarily go through the complex process of studying how their competitors price these goods, they do not experiment with prices to find out how much customers are willing to pay or at what price they would sell the largest quantities and make the highest profit. They price the new merchandise according to their established principle of adding their usual markup to the purchase price.

The crucial question is: when, under what conditions, will this behavior take place and when will the behavior be flexible? We shall cite a few examples of following routine behavior and of giving it up. They are taken from field studies on pricing practices that were conducted during the Second World War.

Many years ago, most restaurants, especially the larger ones, adopted the system of pricing meals according to the cost of the food that went into them. The restaurants calculated their total receipts and the total cost of the food they bought and endeavored to keep the ratio between the two constant. From 1940 to 1943, when food prices rose rapidly and restaurant prices were not subject to price control, this system was maintained unchanged by a great many restaurants. In other words, they increased their prices, or cut down on the quantity or quality of their meals, every time the calculated ratio increased. What does that mean? If food prices increased, as they did in those years, keeping the ratio unchanged brought about a greater difference in dollars between receipts and food costs. Suppose a restaurant operated on a 40 per cent ratio. Then, in 1940, food that cost 40 cents went into a meal priced at $1; in 1943, when food prices had risen 50 per cent, the same food cost 60 cents and went into a meal priced at $1.50. Thus, in 1943, there was a difference of 90 cents, as against 60 cents in 1940, to cover other expenses and allow for profits. Among the other expenses, however, some—for example, for linen and china, and especially rent—went up comparatively little. Then, too, the volume of restaurant business generally increased sharply, so that even unchanged dollar margins would have brought about increased operating profits. Despite these facts, interviews conducted in 1943 with the managers and owners of several restaurants revealed that they had not kept the unchanged ratios with the idea of increasing their profits. They said that they had kept the same ratios because they had learned in the past that that was the right way to run a restaurant. The food-cost principle was maintained unchanged because of the tendency to carry over from one situation to another certain principles that were well understood in their original context; there was no realization that the unchanged application of the old principle meant something different under the new conditions.

We find in this example that price flexibility—the frequent price increases by the restaurants—was the result of extremely rigid principles. This was also the case in a second example in which, however, the inflexible principles brought about lower rather than higher profits. In both situations, a large number of different merchants acted in the same way; mutual reinforcement of individuals belonging to the same group and competing with each other may have facilitated the course of action adopted.

Throughout 1942 and as late as January, 1943, most retailers of clothing, shoes, and furniture maintained their policy of conducting seasonal clearance sales. At that time there was hardly any slow-moving merchandise, changes in style had become much less pronounced, and the retailers' main problem was getting goods rather than selling them. Nevertheless, some retailers went so far as to mark down the prices of the same proportion of their stock as usual. Others marked down less merchandise and sold it at a smaller discount than usual but declared that they would not think of changing the established principle of merchandising, that sales must be promoted by markdowns during certain months and stocks must be cleared by the end of the season. Careful analysis showed that in many cases complex "rational" explanations of this behavior were out of place. There has been no weighing of the profits lost by marking down merchandise against the risk to be taken by discontinuing the clearance sales or by alienating certain customers. The retailers simply continued to make use of their old-established policy without realizing that it did not fit the changed conditions.

Yet, a short time later, in the spring and summer of 1943, most retailers discarded markdowns altogether. This action can serve as an example of the second principle of behavior described above: established policies were changed under the impact of new developments which created a subjectively new situation. It was the great buying wave for clothing, occasioned by the introduction of shoe rationing in February, 1943, and by announcements of forthcoming shortages in civilian goods, that shook the traditional orientation of most retailers and led them to change their policies.

These few examples may suffice to illustrate the thesis that in human conduct flexibility is a function of the subjective realization of new conditions, and rigidity a function of the lack of such realization. To understand business life, both habitual or routine acts and their abandonment through making genuine decisions must be studied. Because of the frequent occurrence of habitual behavior, business activity cannot be viewed as a process of continuous adaptation to changing conditions.

TIME PERSPECTIVE AND EXPECTATIONS

For the understanding of genuine decision making, we must consider one further psychological concept, that of expectations.

It is the field as given at the present time that determines the response. The intervening variables consist of motives, attitudes, and frames of reference as present in the field structure of the moment. But, as we have said before, past experiences affect, and often determine, the structure of the field. We have at all times a time perspective. The time perspective extends backward as well as forward. Our "life-space" (to use a term of Kurt Lewin) as of a given moment encompasses some of our past experiences, our perceptions of the present, and our attitudes toward the future. The "current" psychological field, of individuals as well as of groups, includes expectations, aspirations, plans, fears, and many other forward-looking attitudes. Expectations are attitudes which, like other attitudes, may shape behavior.

Only a few words are needed to illustrate the extension of the time perspective into the past. Not all our related past experiences affect us at a given moment, because our memory is selective. Sometimes the organization is such that our time perspective extends far back, while sometimes even similar recent events appear to be wiped out.

Take the example of wages and salaries. In the early thirties, many workers considered their incomes low because they viewed them within the framework of how much they had made in the late twenties. The time perspective extended far back to the years of prosperity. But after the Second World War broke out, wage rates were apparently viewed in a different context (high cost of living, other people's incomes, etc.) which was devoid of historical perspective. Similarly, a steel producer, for instance, may have disregarded prewar prices shortly after the end of the war (in his actions, not when he was asked about past prices). For him, the effective time perspective began with the notion that prices were not in correspondence with costs. Or, for a would-be buyer and seller of a house today, the knowledge that the same house sold at a much lower price a few years ago may or may not be relevant. The depression of the thirties is at present "real" for some people, or "real" in certain contexts, and not for other people or in connection with other issues.

The time perspective extends forward as well. Here again there are great differences. It may happen that we live for the moment and our aspirations and expectations play no effective role. The demands of the immediate situation—including, perhaps, the very near future—make us act, for instance, in an emergency. Or, to mention a similar situation that is more significant for our purposes, in selling a shoddy product to a stranger, I may charge an unjustifiedly high price, without considering the effect of this action on my reputation or on future deals. I may, however, in setting a price or in bargaining, be governed by considerations that extend far into the distant future.

Even in instances in which the time perspective does not extend far into the future, expectations are important. We must know about them so as to understand why they appear to be absent or are disregarded. In other instances, how we take the future into account becomes the most important question. How does what we expect to happen influence our present behavior? And how are expectations formed?

The study of expectations forms a part of the psychology of learning, since expectations are not innate or instinctive forms of behavior but rather the result of experience. Therefore, expectations are explained by the same two principles by which all learning is explained, that is, by repetition or understanding (or both). The theory of expectations based on repetition alone is: I expect those things to happen that have happened before, and the frequency of my past experience (the number of reinforcements) determines the strength of my expectations. In other words, if I have experienced the sequence a-b-c-d several times and a-b occur again, then I shall expect c-d to follow, and the more frequently I have experienced the sequence, the more certain I shall be that c-d will follow. The first few words of a poem or song make me expect the next words because I have heard the poem or song frequently before.

But frequency is the determining factor of expectations under certain conditions only. The strongest and the most influential expectations originate in understanding. We shall illustrate this by describing briefly laboratory and classroom experiments which the author made a few years ago.

The subjects in some of the experiments were undergraduates who had had no previous instruction in physics. These students were given a brief explanation of the principle of inertia and of the parallelogram of forces. Then followed the test, which contained such questions as:

Standing at the open window of a speeding railroad car, you aim your rifle directly at a distant stationary target. Would you expect the bullet to hit the target or to pass ahead of or behind it?

A fast and a slow airplane release their bombs when they are directly above their target. Would you expect the bomb of the fast or the bomb of the slow airplane to fall nearer to the target? [5]

These specific questions had *not* been discussed in the instruction period, but those students who had studied the principles were able to find the correct answers. They rightly concluded that the bullet must be deflected by the momentum of the train and the bombs by the momentum of the planes. Could it possibly happen, the students were asked, that their expectations would not be fulfilled? Most of them said definitely not. It was shown in these and similar experiments that new and strong expectations were derived from systematic and well-understood knowledge. In parallel experiments in which the answers to the test questions were memorized, without an understanding of why the one or the other result must occur, much weaker and much less stable expectations were formed. Thus the strength of the expectations was not a function of the frequency of past connections.

In similar experiments, certain simple principles of wartime inflation were explained to students of physics in the fall of 1941: how and why consumer purchasing power increases and civilian supply decreases during a total war, and how changes in supply and demand affect prices. Students who understood these principles expressed the strong expectation that prices would go up the following year. These expectations could not easily be shaken. A comparable group of students read a number of speeches, attributed to persons of high prestige, in which the prediction of higher prices was made several times without any explanation of why the prices would increase. In later tests it appeared that only in a few instances did such reading bring forth the expectation of price increases. It was quite simple to change even those expectations.

Let us recapitulate the implications of these psychological studies for the analysis of economic behavior. If it is true that a restructuring of the psychological field which yields new understandings is a relatively infrequent occurrence and, furthermore, that the strongest expectations result from such a reorganization, several significant consequences follow. First, new expectations bringing forth new decisions cannot be an everyday occurrence in business life. Since the larger context in which new expectations originate does not change very frequently, it is questionable whether busi-

[5] The experiment was made in 1940 before newspapers and periodicals had familiarized the public with the trajectory of bombs.

ness behavior is correctly described as resulting from, and consisting of, a continuous revision of expectations. Business actions are frequently routine in the sense that expectations or changes in expectations play hardly any role in determining them.

Second, when expectations do change, they usually change radically or substantially. The need for the reorganization of a greater context does not usually arise under the impact of slight changes in the environment, nor would such a reorganization be likely to bring about small adjustments in expectations (*e.g.,* it would hardly cause a businessman to expect his sales to increase by 6 rather than 5 per cent). Therefore, when business decisions are determined by the emergence of new expectations, they are likely to be decisions to make radical changes.

Third, it follows from the psychological findings that when expectations change, they are likely to change at about the same time and in the same direction for many individual businessmen. The subjective feeling of a changed situation and the need for reorientation in one's thinking are usually dependent upon general economic, social, and political events which many businessmen experience at the same time. Uniformity or similarity of new decisions need not, therefore, reflect automatic or imitative responses, but may be the result of many individuals' reacting to the same change in the setting.

We thus conclude from psychological considerations that expectations tend to change infrequently, radically, and simultaneously. Illustrations of these assumptions may be drawn from the study of business behavior under price control, in which it was found (1) that businessmen had definite price, sales, or profit expectations only at certain times, and not at all times; (2) that when new expectations arose (*e.g.,* that price control would break down or that the "line would be held"), they usually represented radical changes in orientation; and (3) that such reorientations frequently occurred among many businessmen at the same time so as to form what is often called the "atmosphere" or "climate" in which business operated.

During certain periods, observed in recent investigations, the price expectations of many businessmen and consumers were of the "it depends" type. In reply to questions about the future course of prices, businessmen enumerated various possible developments that might cause prices to go up and others that might result in stable or declining prices. Under these conditions, it was found that price expectations had little influence on business decisions and policies.

In other periods, different forms of behavior were observed. In 1941, for instance, many businessmen were found to be puzzled by the change from a "buyers' market" to a "sellers' market" and sought an explanation for that change. Some of them grasped the relationship between the wartime increase in national income and the decrease in available civilian supplies. They also saw the connection between these developments and prices. The result of this new understanding was the expectation of higher prices. This definite expectation was arrived at by many people independently at the same time; later, of course, it was taken over in a routine way by thousands of businessmen and consumers.

The expectation of higher prices did not prevail, however, at all times during the war. Radical changes in expectations, which decisively influenced business decisions, occurred at certain periods marked by spectacular events. This was the case, for example, in the summer of 1943 when the "hold-the-line order" and the establishment of dollars-and-cents retail ceilings for food products destroyed the expectation prevailing in the spring of that year that price control would break down. In field studies it was found that, in the spring of 1943 and again in the early fall of that year, most business-men gave definite and uniform answers to a question about the probable future course of the prices of their most important products. In the first period they said that prices would "undoubtedly" go up, in the second that they would remain stable. It was also found that these expectations influenced their actions, especially their endeavors to accumulate or not to accumulate inventories.

We shall have ample opportunity in later chapters to contrast expectations based on the reorganization of one's frame of reference with the absence of definite expectations, or with expecting the same thing to happen as happened before, or with expecting what everybody expects or what one reads or is told will happen (without understanding why it should or must happen). Here we shall only mention how these differences relate to the concept of uncertainty, another psychological term widely used in this context.

Uncertainty has several meanings. It may stand for the absence of definite expectations. "I am uncertain about the future course of prices" may mean simply that I do not see any reason why prices should take any definite move in either direction. But uncertainty may also imply concern with future contingencies, fear of adverse developments, definite unfavorable expectations. In that sense, uncertainty represents "lack of confidence." The two meanings must be kept apart. The study of expectations must start with the first meaning of the concept of uncertainty. Only after the presence of definite expectations is determined can the content of the expectations be fruitfully studied.

Routine behavior, or rigidity of business policies, which occurs in the absence of definite expectations, may be detrimental under certain condi-tions and appropriate under other conditions. It will be detrimental if needed action is forestalled through lack of awareness that such action is necessary. It will be appropriate if the feeling that "the future is uncertain" means simply that we cannot and need not have definite expectations and can go ahead with our habitual way of life and safely rely on it.

NOTES TO CHAPTER 4

Much of the content of this chapter is taken from previous publications by the author. His book *Organizing and Memorizing: Studies in the Psychology of Learning and Teaching,* New York, 1940, discusses learning through repetition and learning through understanding, and contains experimental evidence for the differentiation between the two. The major differences in the results of the two forms of learning are shown to occur in that form of utilization of past experience which is called in educational psychology "transfer of training."

The example of the relation between tax increases and price movements was presented by the author in his paper "The Role of the Frame of Reference in War and Post-war Economy," *American Journal of Sociology,* Vol. 44, 1944, pp. 340*ff.* The analysis of rigid and flexible pricing behavior during the war and of wartime price expectations of businessmen is taken from the author's book *Price Control and Business,* Bloomington, Ind., 1945. These examples were used to present the distinction between making genuine decisions and habitual behavior in the paper "Psychological Analysis of Business Decisions and Expectations," *American Economic Review,* Vol. 36, 1946, pp. 44*ff.*

This paper, as well as the author's book *War without Inflation: The Psycholological Approach to Problems of War Economy,* New York, 1942, contains some of the discussion of the origin of expectations presented in this chapter. The experiments on the origin of expectations are described in his paper "On Different Forms of Learning by Reading," *Journal of Educational Psychology,* Vol. 33, 1942, pp. 335*ff.* The basic principles of problem solving, reasoning, and understanding are developed in Max Wertheimer's *Productive Thinking,* New York, 1945.

Theories fundamentally different from those presented in the text are embodied in the teachings of classical associationism, the most important modern representative of which was E. L. Thorndike, and of Pavlovian conditioning. These theories recognize only one kind of learning, namely, repetition and reward. The theory of C. L. Hull (*Principles of Behavior,* New York, 1943) likewise rests on principles of frequency of reinforcement and habit formation.

The point of view that is not accepted in the text may be illustrated by the assumption that understanding is always the result of association (see p. 46 above). This statement is based on the traditional analysis of learning to read, according to which that process consists of forming an association between three elements—a printed or written word, its sound, and its meaning. "To give meaning to an object one must form associations with it" (H. B. Reed, *Psychology of Elementary School Subjects,* New York, 1927). P. W. Bridgman gives a modern version of the theory in dealing with the process that brings about understanding, namely, explaining: "The essence of an explanation consists in reducing the situation to elements with which we are so familiar that we accept them as a matter of course, so that our curiosity rests" (*The Logic of Modern Physics,* New York, 1938, p. 37). We are not concerned here with the question of whether association brings forth the simplest kind of meaning from which other kinds of meaning are developed.

Some experimental evidence has been reported for the statement that judgments and beliefs are formed by repetition and can be manipulated arbitrarily through suggestion and prestige. These experiments would contradict the position taken in the text of this chapter that strong expectations usually originate in understanding, and that strong beliefs result from grasping the intrinsic merit of their contents. For a critical examination and refutation of the associationist experiments, see S. E. Asch, "The Doctrine of Suggestion, Prestige and Imitation in Social Psychology," *Psychological Review,* Vol. 55, 1948, pp. 250*ff.*

For a critical discussion of the different theories of learning, and also of the distinction between "blind fumbling and intelligent searching," see E. R. Hilgard, *Theories of Learning,* New York, 1948.

Regarding routine behavior by businessmen, reference may be made to the volume *Cost Behavior and Price Policy,* by the Committee on Price Determination, National Bureau of Economic Research (New York, 1943). This book contains the statement that the retailer "in all probability" utilizes a rough rule-of-thumb method when he adds a uniform markup to his buying prices (p. 285).

The study of the concepts of expectation and uncertainty in this chapter is preliminary and introductory. It will be resumed and expanded in later chapters, especially in Chapters 6, 7, and 10.

The discussion in this chapter is open to the counterargument that learning and change in behavior are presented exclusively on the cognitive level. The principles of development and adjustment studied in psychodynamics were intentionally omitted (and the study of motivation is postponed to Chapters 5 and 9). To be sure, the forms of need satisfaction, conflict, and what have been called defense mechanisms or mechanisms of adjustment, are of great importance to the basic personality structure of individuals and groups and for the continuity of motivational patterns that constitutes personality. But such mechanisms (which, of course, do not operate mechanistically) as defenses against anxiety, repressions, and rationalizations, developed primarily in and through psychoanalysis, will not be utilized in our study of economic behavior. The author's point of view is not that they cannot or should not be so utilized. As will be stated specifically in the discussion of unconscious motives (Chapter 5), it is to be hoped that future research of economic behavior will make great use of psychoanalytic concepts. But what is available at present does not, in the author's opinion, warrant its inclusion in this book. The use of psychoanalytic concepts may turn out to be of great importance for the understanding of differences between different cultures and of individual differences—to explain, for instance, why the economies of two periods differ, or why two businessmen in the same situation act differently. Their use may not be of such great importance for the understanding of regularities in behavior that are responsible for relationships between, say, income changes and saving or for cyclical fluctuations in the present American economy.

For a discussion of psychoanalytic concepts in the framework of experimental psychology, see E. R. Hilgard, "Human Motives and the Concept of the Self," *American Psychologist,* Vol. 4, 1949, pp. 374*ff.* For a presentation of psychodynamic principles in conjunction with field-theoretic assumptions, see J. H. Masserman, *Behavior and Neurosis,* Chicago, 1943.

PART TWO
CONSUMER BEHAVIOR

CHAPTER 5

PLANS AND MOTIVES OF CONSUMERS

The conception of the rational, economic man has been mentioned before. Applied in its strictest form to consumer behavior, this conception implies that in all their actions involving making and spending money people are driven toward one definite goal, the attainment of the greatest possible amount of satisfaction. This statement contains several assumptions which have encountered doubts and counterarguments during the past decades. It has been argued that satisfactions are not measurable and that, therefore, the thesis cannot be verified scientifically. It has also been maintained that people often do not strive for satisfaction. People act impulsively instead of rationally, according to momentary whims, or suggestions and emotions. In short, we, as consumers, do not plan. How we spend our money depends on fashion, salesmanship and advertising, social background and standards, considerations of prestige, insecurity, and emotional conflicts—all nonmeasurable factors that change constantly.[1] If such a view were correct, consumer economics as a scientific discipline would not be possible.

Opinions have also been expressed that are less extreme than those just formulated but that lead to the same negative conclusion. One of those opinions is that the poor cannot plan ahead, and the rich need not. The poor are concerned only with subsistence; they live from hand to mouth, spending whatever they have for food and shelter so as to stay alive, without any plan or deliberation. The rich, on the other hand, satisfy their whims, purchase whatever comes to their minds. Or, it has sometimes been said that people are divided into classes, not by their economic resources, but by certain inflexible personality traits. There are some careful people, so this opinion runs, who budget their expenditures; they set aside certain amounts for every type of need: for rent, food, streetcar fare, newspapers, cigarettes, and so on. Other people, with different constitutions, spend on

[1] Cf. the following summary by Jacob Viner of what he believes to be the lesson derived from "modern psychology": "Human behavior . . . is not under the constant and detailed guidance of careful and accurate hedonic calculations, but is the product of an unstable and unrational complex of reflex actions, impulses, instincts, habits, customs, fashions, and mob hysteria" (*Journal of Political Economy*, Vol. 33, 1925, p. 373).

whatever need arises at a given moment as long as their money lasts. Both of these views may open the possibility for certain institutional and anthropological studies, but appear to exclude the establishment of principles of consumer behavior.

Consumer behavior is, however, susceptible of empirical investigation. To be sure, the evidence as yet available to answer the question whether consumers do plan and do act with foresight is tentative and incomplete. Likewise, no definite studies have yet been made about the origin of consumer behavior patterns prevalent in the United States today, or about the differences in consumer behavior in different cultures and at different times. But empirical investigations have begun to collect information relevant to the question: When, under what circurmstances, is one kind of consumer behavior likely to occur, and when, under what circumstances, another kind of behavior?

The chief of these investigations to be referred to in this book are the Surveys of Consumer Finances, which have been carried on annually since the beginning of 1946, and with which the author has been associated since their inception. These surveys, consisting of detailed interviews with representative samples of the households of the nation, are described and discussed in Part Five of this book.[2] At this point it is only necessary to say that the investigation must always be directed toward specific forms of consumer behavior. It would be of little value in economic surveys to ask people such a broad question as "Do you plan the spending of your money?" Instead, we must ask a variety of questions and conduct repeated surveys so as to discover what went on before people made certain specific expenditures. We can also ask a man whether he expects to buy, for example, an automobile within a certain future period and, if the answer is affirmative, check later to learn whether he actually bought it. Or, if he said that he did not expect to buy a car and is found later to have actually bought one, we can seek the reasons for his behavior.

DO CONSUMERS PLAN?

In turning to the study of specific forms of consumer behavior, we shall consider first the behavior involved in buying a house. Suppose we find that John Smith has just bought a one-family house for $10,000. If this transaction is studied, or if hundreds of similar transactions are studied by means of detailed interviews conducted with people who have bought houses, or who plan to buy houses, one thing can be established without doubt: In some cases at least, purchases of houses are deliberately planned, discussed, and studied over long periods of time, with alternatives weighed and

[2] See also the Notes to this chapter.

different courses of action thought through. We may find, for example, that John Smith and his wife looked at many houses and that their deliberations included figuring out that their savings could provide the down payment for a $10,000 house and their income could accommodate the monthly payment necessary on a house of that price. Motives for buying a house and attitudes toward the purchase of a house can be studied, and the psychological factors thereby discovered shed light on people's decisions and actions.

Advance planning also occurs, again not necessarily in all instances but assuredly in some, in the case of automobile purchases. Purchases of refrigerators, washing machines, and furniture are other instances in which it could be established that some people do make plans. Further examples of planned, deliberated decisions are contracting life insurance, borrowing money, and making investments.

All these examples refer to what may be called large expenditures that are made sporadically, once in a lifetime, or once in several years, or once in a year. Suppose we should say: "Large expenditures are often planned expenditures." What does this statement mean? In the Surveys of Consumer Finances, a representative cross section of the nation's families were asked year after year whether they expected to buy houses, automobiles, furniture, refrigerators, washing machines, radio or television sets, or other household appliances during the next twelve months, and if so, how much they expected to spend on those items. Then, a year later, another representative sample of families—and in two instances samples of the previously interviewed families—were asked what kinds of durable goods they had bought during the previous year and for how much. It was then found that more purchases were actually made than had been expected at the beginning of the year.[3] Some people who had said, "We do not expect to buy a car [furniture, etc.] next year," had nevertheless bought those goods during that year.

Does it follow that some purchases of durable goods were "planned" and some "not planned"? It is evident that we used these terms to mean planned (or not planned) at the beginning of the year in which the purchase was made. Possibly, then, the occurrence of unplanned purchases (as defined in the surveys) is due to our having postulated too long a time period. Possibly, we would have found more instances of planning if we had conducted monthly instead of annual surveys. There is some evidence for the correctness of this view. In one study, people were asked, first, in January

[3] One exception to that statement is of interest. In the years 1946 to 1948, fewer people bought new automobiles than had said at the beginning of the year that they planned to do so. Because of insufficient automobile production during those years, many people were unable to carry out their plans.

what kind of purchases, if any, they expected to make during the next 12 months. Then, the next January, the same people were asked what purchases they had made during the preceding 12 months and *when* they made those purchases. It was then found that the number of unplanned, or not anticipated, purchases was greater in the second than in the first half of the year, and the number of planned purchases was somewhat greater in the first than in the second half of the year. Some planned and some unplanned purchases occurred, however, a few weeks as well as many months after the inquiry about expectations.

How do unplanned purchases—we continue to use the survey definition of the term—come about? In some few cases—by no means in all—they could easily be explained. Mr. A. B., for instance, who bought a car in May of a given year, although in January of that year he had said, "We haven't thought of buying a new car; I don't think we will buy one this year," explained later that his old car had broken down; the repair costs would have amounted to so much that he had decided to sell his old car and buy another (used) car. We may also quote the case of Mr. C. D., who bought a house a few months after he had said that he did not expect to buy one. He had, shortly after the first interview, been transferred by his firm to another town.

These and many other examples of unplanned purchases point to limitations in our definitions. The car purchase of Mr. A. B. was planned in a certain sense, although only a short time elapsed between the formation of the plan and its realization. Yet, even through conducting monthly surveys, the problem of finding a strict definition of planning would not be solved. It is possible that, in a family of considerable means, one week's planning of the purchase of a car would represent a substantial degree of forethought, whereas for another family two months' planning of such a purchase would be psychologically tantamount to acting on impulse. In order to clarify the problem, we turn then to further survey findings, again accepting, for the sake of convenience, the definition of the terms as used in the annual surveys.

It was found in the surveys that the proportion of planned to unplanned purchases was not the same for all types of durable goods. In each of the postwar years, more used cars than new cars were bought without the expectation of making such purchases; furniture and radio sets were bought without plan more frequently than refrigerators or washing machines; and houses, the most expensive item about which the question was asked, were purchased least frequently without previous anticipation. In general, it was found that the less expensive the item, the larger was the proportion of unplanned purchases. In comparing the prices of actual purchases of furniture and radio sets, for instance, with the expectations expressed at the beginning of the year, it was found that the higher the price, the more frequent had been the anticipation of the purchase. Relatively few table radio sets in the price range of $15 to $30 were mentioned among the purchase plans for the following year, and many more were actually purchased; among radio-phonograph models costing over $100, the difference between plans and purchases was much smaller. Similar findings were made when plans to buy furniture were compared with actual purchases: the purchase of single chairs or tables was less frequently anticipated than that of complete furniture sets for one, two, or more rooms.

It is probable on a priori grounds that the term "large expenditure" should mean different things for rich (high-income) and poor (low-income) families. Some of the available evidence seems to support this view, but the opposite, namely, that the absolute size of the expenditure is relevant, cannot as yet be ruled out. The findings warrant only the following statements: Among all kinds of purchases, there are some that are planned in advance (as the term is used in the surveys); for purchases of more than $1,000, planning is relatively frequent; for purchases of several hundred dollars, somewhat less frequent; and for purchases of less than $100, quite infrequent.

These findings are in accord with what one might expect in the light of psychological research. We may recall the argument presented in the preceding chapter (Chapter 4). Under certain circumstances, when we face a new problem and are in a crossroads situation, we reorganize our field and make genuine decisions. Otherwise, we continue with our habitual patterns of behavior without thinking of alternative courses of action. This argument appears applicable to consumer behavior and serves to replace the unclear terminology of planned and unplanned actions. It implies that what is often called irrational behavior—emotional, affect driven, or irresponsible actions—does not represent a large proportion of consumer activity. Customary or routine behavior takes its place, namely, acting the same way as we acted before under similar circumstances, following habitual patterns without making new decisions and without considering the advantages and disadvantages of our actions. In addition, however, genuine decision making also occurs under certain circumstances, some of which can be described.

Actions that are performed rarely, such as buying a house or a car, borrowing money, or making an investment, qualify, of course, as nonroutine actions. In order that a genuine decision should be made, the possibility of such an action must be perceived. Since perceptions are selective, it may not be enough to be told about the possibility. Reading advertisements about houses for sale, or being visited by a life insurance agent, may help to arouse the need for owning a home or having life insurance, or the need may be primary and may lead us to read or hear about possibilities. When our neighbor or colleague buys a new car, we may or may not be ready to consider doing the same. Multiple and conflicting motivations are the rule, not the exception—as we shall see in a moment—and usually many different factors contribute to making us aware of a need and leading us to make a decision. One important instance of a situation that demands reorganizing our field is the occurrence of something new, like an increase in our income or a new opportunity to purchase something as, for example, when payroll deductions for buying war bonds were introduced.

A genuine decision, once made, usually leads to routine actions over a long period of time. After having decided to buy a house with a mortgage, or a car on installment, we send a check every month to the mortgage bank or installment company. Prior charges on income are fixed expenditures which are made as a matter of routine for a long time after a genuine decision is made. They often represent a very large part of our expenditures. They may include rent and insurance payments, certain regular contributions and dues, and expenditures for the upkeep and use of things previously bought (for instance, gas for the car). To discontinue, not to continue, such expenditures requires a genuine decision.

There are other types of routine expenditures. Little is known about the dynamics of expenditures on food and clothing, but there is no doubt that in many cases they follow habitual patterns. The situation here may differ somewhat from the expenditures just described. It is possible that no genuine decisions are ever made with respect to certain regular expenditures. The patterns may be set by our parents or friends and be taken over by us without deliberation. Or certain spending and saving patterns may be customary in our culture and our habitual behavior may be group-determined. The smaller the single expenditure—relative to our total expenditures—and the more frequent the expenditure, the more probable is habitual behavior. Whether or not such expenditures are formalized in a family budget is not very important. They go on habitually until something disturbs the flow of behavior and leads us to make a new decision. Habitual action may take the form of buying the same quantities and brands the same day of the week in the same store, and also of following advertisements about clearance sales, or studying the windows of many stores before shopping.

This does not mean that all our expenditures on food or clothing are habitual or routine. Changes in our standard of living may be the result of genuine decisions and may lead us to abandon old-established expenditure patterns. The situation is similar with respect to purchases of durable goods or any other large expenditures. Though we usually make a genuine decision to purchase a house or a car or large pieces of furniture, it is possible that with some people, in some cases, even purchases of what economists call postponable goods are made habitually—following past patterns of behavior. For instance, a person may have the habit of exchanging his car for a new one every year or every second year. Habitual expenditures may be planned expenditures in the sense that they are thought of in advance (and recalled at the occasion of an interview). But often they are not salient in people's thinking because they are not deliberated or weighed (and may therefore not be mentioned in an interview).

It is not implied here that what traditionally is called irrational action never occurs. Some of our expenditures may be found to be nothing but the expressions of whims or the results of emotions. What is implied is that by studying only genuine decisions and habitual patterns, we are considering the relevant aspects of consumer behavior. The term "relevant" should denote behavior that is of significance for economic trends and especially for an increase or decrease in consumption or saving by large groups of people.

A few consequences of this view of consumer behavior may be cited at this point. First, although we shall discuss habitual behavior, our main concern must be with genuine decision making. An analysis of such decisions must go beyond recording the external conditions that make them possible. Since reorganizing one's field depends on motives, frames of reference, attitudes, and expectations, it is improbable that such decisions, and therefore people's expenditures, are a function of nothing but income, assets, age, and similar "objective" factors. It is probable that consumer attitudes represent—at least sometimes, or to some extent—independent forces contributing to the shaping of economic processes. The richer a community, i.e., the larger the number of families who are in a position to make many genuine decisions, the more probable it is that "subjective" factors will influence economic developments.

Second, we may point to a conclusion with respect to the priority of spending or saving. Usually a substantial portion of our money outlay will be absorbed by routine actions—prior charges resulting from old, relatively inflexible decisions, and regular habitual expenditures. Therefore, quite often we save what is left over. Sometimes, however, we may decide to save more or to save less and, of course, we make decisions about large or unusual expenditures, which decisions affect our savings. It follows again that consumer economics is concerned primarily with a few important decisions that change the habitual flow of expenditures.

MULTIPLICITY OF MOTIVES

This chapter began by referring to the major implications of the traditional thesis that economic behavior is rational. Having discussed one implication, namely, that consumer behavior is planned behavior, we turn to the assertion that consumer behavior is governed by one paramount objective, the attainment of maximum satisfaction. The problem of consumer motivation is of special importance in the case of genuine decision making, when patterns of behavior are adopted for the first time or when they are changed.

We must first broaden the problem. In the previous section, we spoke primarily of decisions about using one's income, as if consumer economics were identical with consumption economics. For our purposes, however, the dividing line is not between consumption on the one hand and production and distribution on the other, but between the behavior of the household or family and that of the business enterprise or firm. The analysis of the economic behavior of the family must cover not only the motives underlying the ways it uses its income but also its motives for making money.

Concerning making money, the traditional answer is simple: People strive to have the maximum possible income.[4] When reference is then made to a young man who goes to college instead of making money, or to a person who refuses to accept a risky job with a high salary, or who keeps money in a checking account that brings no interest instead of investing it to obtain a high yield, the answer again is simple: Not the maximum income at the given moment is meant, but the highest possible income earned over an extended period. This answer shows that measurability represents a difficult problem with respect to maximum income just as with respect to maximum satisfaction. Neither of these alleged objectives of human endeavor can be measured objectively by an outside observer. The meaning of these goals seems to be: A person does what he deems best. Statements about "maximizing" are too general to contribute to a real understanding of consumer motivation. The problem is not even raised as to why at one given moment a person thinks one thing is best for him and at another moment that a different thing is best for him.

The same is true of other general statements about consumer motivation as, for example, that people strive to maximize their net worth, or to attain power, or approbation, or security. The trouble with such formulations is not merely that acquisitiveness or 'search for security is not a basic drive but rather a means to an end. Even basic drives, such as the urge to reduce tension, do not help in understanding consumer behavior. The question,

---

[4] Such obvious qualifications of the statement as that most people would not work 18 hours a day to make more money are disregarded.

what is *the* motive of consumers, is meaningless. We can only search for the motives of specific actions and decisions. We must, and by means of empirical studies we can, analyze specific psychological fields and seek out the motives that constitute parts of those fields.

Psychology provides us with information that may help us in that search: it is improbable that there exists just one motive in a given instance. There may be such instances, but they will not be the rule. Multiplicity of motives, some reinforcing one another and some conflicting with one another, is much more common. Therefore, research must be aimed toward discerning the patterns of motives entering into specific decision formations, not toward discovering the one motive of all behavior.

Further, we learn from psychological studies concerning the role of the individual and the group that people's motives need not be ego-centered. If, in a given situation, a person is part of a group, he may be motivated by the interests of his group. His motives may be centered around the welfare of his family, his business associates, or his country, and what would be best for his own welfare may be secondary or may not even enter into consideration.

The given time perspective is also relevant for the study of economic motivation. It is possible that in some situations the time perspective does not extend into the future; when that is true, the analysis of motives is relatively simple. If the time perspective does extend into the future, there may be conflict between the desire to satisfy present needs and the desire to prepare for future needs. Psychologically, this question arises: Which of the forces is stronger, those directed toward satisfying present needs or those directed toward satisfying future needs?

Satisfaction of present needs is usually achieved by what is called spending, and satisfaction of future needs by what is called saving. We concluded earlier that expenditures usually represent the prior charges on income, and savings usually what is left over. This is in accord with what the psychologist knows about the role of the immediacy of forces. Immediate rewards usually loom larger than delayed rewards. If strong needs requiring immediate satisfaction are present, future needs may be entirely neglected: if a family has great difficulty in making both ends meet, it may not save despite a desire to save and an awareness of the importance of putting money aside for the future. The principle of immediacy operates in various ways, and sometimes people intentionally act in a way that makes them subject to immediate forces. Some people feel that they will not save unless they are compelled to do so. It has been found, for example, that many people like the payroll-deduction arrangement for purchasing savings bonds because it makes saving a first charge on income. Also, some people who could pay cash from their bank accounts for automobiles and other goods buy them on the installment plan instead. They believe, and say so, that being compelled to meet the monthly installment bills, they will refrain from some other expenditures; if they took the money for the durable goods out of the bank, they would, however, not put it back and would not save.

It follows, further, from the principle of immediacy that saving has its best chance if either many of the immediate needs are satisfied (as is the case with the "rich") or if future needs acquire some degree of immediacy. This may happen if a person, still employed at a fair wage, fears the loss of his job and feels threatened by unemployment. Or the strength of the motives to save may increase with the approach of the birth of a child, or of a son's reaching college age, or of retirement.

The discussion of empirical studies directed toward finding evidence for or against these hypotheses will be taken up later. At this point, we are concerned with the general problem of how to study economic motivation. The problem of conflict between different motives requires further attention.

In the Survey of Consumer Finances conducted at the beginning of 1946, consumers were asked about their various plans and expectations for the year 1946—the first postwar year—and about the reasons for those plans and expectations. It developed that many people expected to spend more for regular living expenses in 1946 than they had in 1945, because they were aware of a rising price trend and expected it to continue. Further, many people planned to buy durable goods in 1946 which they had not bought in the previous war years. They also expressed themselves strongly in favor of saving. They said that saving was, in their opinion, as important after the war as during the war, and many of them said that they would save more in 1946 than in 1945. At the same time, people in general expressed great reluctance to withdraw money from wartime savings: the savings bonds and bank deposits accumulated during the war were meant for the future, they said; they should be touched only in emergencies, or in order to buy a house or establish a business, but not for regular expenditures. A fair proportion of American consumers also thought, and many with very good reasons, that their income would be higher in 1946 than in 1945. Thus, for some families, all expectations and plans were consistent; it was possible that they would all be carried out. But some other families presented inconsistent plans. They expected to spend more and to save more out of an unchanged income. It was impossible for them to act as they said they would. Moreover, they were not clearly aware of the inconsistency in their plans.[5] This means that our investigation served to

---

[5] Some people, of course, budgeted carefully and presented consistent plans. Sometimes they said that these plans were not what they desired but represented what they would have to do.

give us a picture of people's attitudes toward future expenditures and savings but did not indicate what they would actually do. It disclosed people's motives, or needs, desires, and hopes, which were conflicting. They would have to be resolved when decisions were made, or if habitual expenditure patterns prevailed and nothing was left over for saving, they were resolved by default.

This does not mean that the analysis of motives is useless or that future behavior is unpredictable. It means that future behavior cannot be predicted simply by asking people how they will behave. It means, further, that we have just started with the analysis of motivation. It is not enough to list conflicting motives; we must also find out about the strength and immediacy of the motives. In the case of the specific investigation just discussed, for instance, it was possible to predict at the beginning of 1946 that the amounts saved would be considerably smaller in 1946 than in 1945.[6]

In what sense, then, can consumer motivation be studied? Such studies can be undertaken, first, with respect to the motives that entered into a decision made in the recent past. For instance, when it is ascertained that a person has recently bought a car, or has added to his savings, the question of why he acted as he did may be fruitfully raised. Second, motives can be studied that prevail at a given time because, even if they are conflicting and inconsistent, they may influence future decisions. Attitudes toward buying a car during the following twelve months, or toward adding to or withdrawing from savings, represent examples of subjects of such motivational analysis.

But we frequently hear, and rightly, that motives are elusive. This assertion may mean that people themselves do not know why they do certain things, or that even if they knew they would not tell their true motives to a stranger, such as a survey interviewer. More specifically, according to psychoanalytic theory, many motives are believed to be unconscious: what we think to be the reasons for our behavior are for the most part rationalizations. We construct reasons for our actions, reasons that are acceptable to society and that put us in a good light; we even believe that these are our reasons; but the true reasons are different, they are repressed, covered up, and unknown to us.

No doubt there is much truth in this argument. The chances for obtaining really deep-seated motives during a short interview are none too good.

---

[6] Because the investigation showed that (1) most of those who explained how they would resolve inconsistent plans and desires had made the resolution at the expense of future saving; (2) in spite of people's expressed desire to save, certain reasons for saving and for not using accumulated liquid assets were much weaker early in 1946 than early in 1945; and (3) the desire to purchase and own consumer durable goods was expressed in very strong terms.

Repeated and extended psychiatric or psychological interviews would help in many instances, but they are hardly practicable for purposes of large-scale economic investigations. But all this is not too important for our purposes. We are in a position to give three answers to the argument denying the possibility of an analysis of motives. We shall argue, first, that for purposes of understanding economic behavior the difficult task of discovering the hidden motives may not be necessary; second, that the "superficial" answers people give when they are asked why they have acted in a certain way may be of importance; and third, that there is a fruitful method of discovering motives in addition to asking people about their motives.

Regarding the first point: In some occasional cases it happened accidentally that hidden motives were unearthed by survey interviewers. A family with a steady, fair income had had no unusual expenditures and had made no large purchases during the first two years after the war, and nevertheless had spent more than its income, fast reducing its previously inherited assets. Answers to questions about how husband and wife felt about saving and about various expenditures failed to give any clue to their behavior. Because of the chance arrival of a visitor, however, the interviewer found out that the couple drank heavily; a fair part of their income was spent on liquor. In later chapters, when we shall list the findings on the factors contributing to postwar dissaving (spending more than one's income), we shall not mention the factor "alcohol," for which we have some superficial evidence in this one instance and which, of course, may have played a role in many other instances. We are concerned, as stated in Chapter 2, with factors prevailing in a large number of cases, and not with the explanation of the singular, unique case. In analyzing tendencies prevailing in many instances, or in certain well-defined groups of people, we can and must neglect the factors influencing singular cases. To be sure, unhappy marriages, childhood or professional frustrations, and many other circumstances would have to be listed if we were to search for a complete explanation of every instance. But this is not our goal. Motives that appear to account for the increase of dissaving, say, in 1946 and 1947, will be found outside of these deeper factors entering into individual motivation.[7]

Second, superficial conscious motives, and even rationalizations, may often be relevant for economic analysis. To be sure, there are rationalizations that can be safely disregarded and treated as singular, unique cases. Take, for instance, the case of an elderly well-to-do widow living alone with her maid, who disclosed that she spent considerable amounts of money

[7] This argument should not imply that psychoanalysis is unable to contribute to the understanding of economic behavior. The author believes simply that such contributions are not needed at the beginning of economic analysis.

for pictures, bric-a-brac, and furniture because, as she said, it was the duty of childless people to give employment to craftsmen. With this statement as the only information at hand, the clinical psychologist may speculate about her relation to her heirs, or to the craftsmen she employs—but for our purposes those speculations as well as her explanation itself can safely be disregarded. To put our case most strongly: Both the alleged and the true motives of the widow, as well as the addiction to alcohol by the couple mentioned before, can be ignored as irrelevant to any explanation of changes in economic trends, of prosperity or depression.

A different situation prevailed when it was found that not one person but many people gave such straightforward reasons as the following for their having gone into debt to buy new cars in 1946 or 1947, or television sets in 1948: "At last I could get a car; my old car was no good any more"; or, "The kids wanted a television set"; or simply, "We needed a new car." From such "superficial" statements, repeated over and over again, the analyst may conclude that the forces directed toward immediate satisfaction of these desires were strong. From what he knows about the situation prevailing during those years, he may speculate further about the psychological impact of shiny new automobile models seen on the street, in advertisements, and in the possession of neighbors, about the role of suggestion, salesmanship, and, above all, prestige. But for the first step in his analysis, he need not go far. The motives of which people appear to be conscious, which they repeat over and over again until they themselves believe in them—in this case, that the new car or television set was urgently needed—are relevant. They are facts which influence economic decisions.

We shall discuss in a moment the kinds of motives and purposes of saving of which people were aware during the war and of which they spoke repeatedly, and will conclude likewise that they did influence people's behavior even if they were rationalizations. Before doing so, we must discuss the third, and most important, reply we can make to the assertion that motives are elusive and cannot be discovered.

Asking people why they did or did not act in a certain way, and asking them how they feel about certain expenditures or about saving, is only one of the methods of studying motivation. In addition, and perhaps primarily, the analyst can rely on the results of cross tabulations between forms of behavior and certain characteristics of people. A "discovery" made during the war, in the process of analyzing the war-bond campaigns, will illustrate this statement.

In sample surveys conducted during or shortly after every one of the war-bond drives, people were asked why they had bought bonds, how they felt about bonds, what they planned to do with them, and so forth. In replying to such questions, very few people ever mentioned that they had been asked to buy bonds. But the analyst thought of the possibility that solicitation, especially personal solicitation, may have played a role and he proceeded to test his hypothesis. Questions were inserted in the surveys, inquiring whether anybody had called upon the respondent and asked him to buy bonds, whether this had happened at his home or his place of employment, where and what he had heard about the bond campaigns (over the radio, in movies, etc.), and so forth. That hearing about bonds and a knowledge of bond drives (quotas, results, etc.) were found to be positively correlated with bond purchases may not point to any causal factor. It is possible that people who were interested in bonds and purchased them listened more carefully to information about them. But hearing about bonds from general sources made a much smaller difference in bond purchases than did being asked directly to buy by a personal solicitor in one's home or place of work. Many more people who said they had been personally solicited had bought bonds than people who said they had not been solicited. This finding was made separately for different groups of the population studied, for people with high, medium, and low incomes. It appears, then, that personal solicitation did make a difference, although it was not mentioned in answer to the direct question, "Why did you buy these bonds?" It was not the only factor leading to bond purchases, but one of the many prevailing motivational forces. Motives were disclosed both by cross-tabulating characteristics and events and by questioning people about their goals.

Similarly, in order to study the question of why certain people bought cars in a given year, methods of investigation are available that supplement the direct question asked of the buyers, "Why did you buy that car?" We may compare the economic characteristics of those who bought and those who did not buy cars in a given year. We may then find that the two groups differ in their income, their liquid-asset holdings, their age, and in the age and condition of the cars they owned before the buyers made their purchases. We may further compare the attitudes and expectations of the two groups concerning incomes, prices, and general economic conditions. As we shall see later, such cross tabulations frequently reveal important aspects of motivational patterns of which people do not think and do not speak in answer to a direct inquiry about their motives. What factors we seek out for the analysis of motives is not a matter of trial and error but must be guided by hypotheses—psychological or economic—that are relevant for behavior in general.

To repeat: This section is intended to provide evidence for the statement that it is possible to analyze the motivational patterns influencing specific economic decisions. A final example will be presented here to clarify our point of view. We shall contrast the traditional analysis of economic motives with our method of analyzing them.

J. M. Keynes devotes a chapter in his great book [8] to the discussion of the subjective factors determining saving. In brief, his question is: Why do people save? The answer: "There are, in general, eight main motives or objects of a subjective character which lead individuals to refrain from spending out of their incomes." These are "the motives of Precaution, Foresight, Calculation, Improvement, Dependence, Enterprise, Pride and Avarice." These statements are too general to be of much use. It is hardly possible to prove by means of empirical studies that the list is complete or incomplete; this would be primarily a question of the definition of the terms. Nor is it a promising end of investigation to try to show that Precaution is a stronger or weaker force than, say, Independence or Enterprise. The various objectives may occur together in innumerable combinations. No wonder that Keynes makes no use of his list for the purpose of explaining changes in the rate of saving. He concludes that these motives, the force of which varies according to institutions, habits, customs, and standards of life, change slowly and therefore can be excluded when short-period changes in the rate of saving are considered.

Our question is not: Why do people save? It is, rather, a question about the specific set of circumstances in which people are known to have changed their pattern of saving. We may ask, for example: How did it happen that the American people as a whole saved a much larger part of their income during the Second World War than before the war?

Let us list briefly the relevant financial facts. Even in the best years in the period between the two world wars, the American people saved no more than a few billion dollars or a small percentage of their income. Total net savings of all consumers (exclusive of savings by corporate business) were estimated by the Commerce Department at less than 4 billion dollars during the prosperous year 1929, or at about 5 per cent of disposable income (total personal income minus direct taxes). In 1941, for the first time, consumer saving reached 10 billion dollars, in 1942 it jumped to 25 billion, and in each of the following two years it was over 30 billion. In relation to disposable income, amounts saved constituted 22 and 23 per cent in each of the years 1942, 1943, and 1944.

These aggregate data tell only part of the story. Before the Second World War, year after year a large proportion of American families spent more than their income and another large proportion just managed to break even. Exact data are not available, but it appears that in the thirties there was hardly a year in which more than one-half of American families saved any substantial amounts. During the war years, however, 75 to 80 per cent

---

[8] J. M. Keynes, *The General Theory of Employment, Interest, and Money,* New York, 1936, Chap. 9.

of the families managed to save, and a fair proportion saved as much as 30, 40, or 50 per cent of their income.

Why did this happen? In attempting to answer this question, we can do more (and better) than list expert opinions or ask people why, in their opinion, people saved a lot during the war. In accordance with what we have already said about methods of studying motivation, we shall make use of three approaches to the problem. First, we shall consider the statements of people—of a representative sample of families—about why they acted as they did. Second, we shall examine cross tabulations between saving behavior and various other characteristics. Finally, we shall consider types of explanations which people who saved much did *not* mention and for which no indirect evidence was found.[9]

First, how did people talk about their saving and spending during the war? Many people declared spontaneously that they were happy to have saved. They said that they liked to save, wanted to save, and were glad that they had done so. The most common answer given during the war was that they had put money aside for future contingencies. Saving for "rainy days," for unexpected adverse developments like illness or unemployment, for old age, and for the future needs of children were mentioned in explanation of specific actions. People believed that these were the motives of their behavior and considered it right that they had these motives. The statements were often general in nature, although one specific reference to the near future was also made frequently: bad times or a depression might, or would, come after the war and one had to be prepared.

When people were asked specifically what future plans they had for their savings, only two types of answer were made by large numbers: "We would like to own our own house," and "We want to start a business of our own." Most people, however, did not seem to have specific uses in mind for the money they had saved.

Few people mentioned only one motive for having saved. In addition to speaking of a rainy day, or of future business plans, many spoke of saving for the sake of the country. Patriotic motives, or motives indicating some identification of their own interests with those of the country, were expressed with varying degrees of sophistication. There were many people who appeared to believe literally that they were buying war bonds to provide ammunition for the boys abroad, that planes, tanks, and ships could

---

[9] In actual survey procedure, people are asked first about their income and assets and about what they did and what they did not do. After it has been determined that a person bought, for example, $300 worth of war bonds and repaid a $500 debt in a certain year—and did not put any money in a bank account—questions are asked about why he did as he did, what his opinions were of war bonds and savings accounts, and what he planned to do with his bonds.

not be built if they did not provide the money in bonds. Others, who made similar statements ("We are buying bonds to help the war effort") often meant more generally that in the prevaling emergency the country would somehow benefit from such actions. Comparatively few understood war financing well enough to say that by saving—buying bonds—instead of spending, they were helping to lessen the inflationary pressures characteristic of wartime economy. (Most people expressed themselves strongly in favor of keeping prices stable, but only a few connected this attitude with their own spending and saving behavior.)

The foregoing is a description of people's motives for saving as they themselves explained them. What further light is thrown on these motives by our second method of investigation, the gathering of indirect evidence through cross tabulation? As mentioned before, evidence was obtained in the years 1942 to 1946 that the war bond drives were effective. People knew about the campaigns and about quotas set for their communities or groups, and were frequently solicited by mail or in person to purchase bonds. Cross tabulations revealed that advertising helped to some extent, setting quotas to a larger extent, and that personal solicitation was an outstanding factor in influencing people in every group of the population to buy bonds or to buy large amounts of bonds.

It was also found in surveys that during the war most people knew that other people—their neighbors, friends, and colleagues—were buying war bonds, were saving part of their income, or were abstaining from spending in one or the other respect. There was hardly any such verbal expression as "spending a lot of money is out of place during the war," but it appeared that the accepted pattern of behavior, the one which represented climbing on the band wagon, was represented by buying war bonds or putting money in the bank. This was, for most people, not frugality, as manifested by the fact that the physical quantities of goods consumed—of food and clothing, for instance, not of course of automobiles and gasoline, which were not available—reached record levels.

Third, we must discuss possible motivational factors for which no evidence, or negative evidence, was found in wartime consumer studies. For example, we found little support for the argument that it was the rapid and substantial increase in incomes alone which accounted for the wartime saving. In a local survey conducted at the beginning of 1945, it was found that many people whose incomes had not increased during the war had saved, and that some had saved substantial amounts, in 1944. Possibly, however— and we do not have evidence for or against this statement—those whose incomes increased saved more. It is possible, we again do not know, that expenditure standards which were habitual before the war were frequently maintained during the war in spite of much higher incomes, and that therefore more money was left over, that is, more was saved. We shall come back to this important problem later. Here we note only that people did not intentionally keep their wartime living standards at prewar, low-income levels.

Furthermore, wartime savings have often been attributed to' wartime regulations. Because of regulations which prohibited the production of new automobiles and many other consumer durable goods, and restricted building, consumers could not spend money on these goods even if they wanted to. One possibility, then, would be that many people said to themselves that they ought to put money aside for these purposes so as to be able to buy a new car or refrigerator, or to pay for a new roof, when those goods would become available. This question was investigated in detail and a surprising finding resulted: Very few people said that they were saving for such purposes. Further, when people were asked what they would do after the war with their war bonds or bank deposits, hardly any mentioned the purchase of durable goods. Finally, when people were directly asked whether they would consider it an appropriate use of their bonds or bank deposits to pay for automobiles or other durable goods after the war, with relatively few exceptions they answered in the negative. (The same question put with reference to buying a house or starting a business was answered in the affirmative by many more people.) They argued, overwhelmingly, that the money was not being saved for such purposes; that it would be wasting money meant to represent reserve funds if it were spent for such goods; that automobiles and durable goods ought to be bought out of income, not out of accumulated assets.

Another possible reason, which has sometimes been advanced for wartime savings and for which we found no evidence, is that people were forced to save as a result of the shortage of available goods. It has been argued—rightly—that if all the people had decided to spend all or most of their income there would not have been enough goods to go around (and prices would have gone up greatly). According to available evidence about the motives behind the savings of individual families, the shortage of goods played only an indirect role. There was merchandise in the stores; it would have been possible for every single family to have found enough things on which to spend its entire income. To be sure, the situation would have been different if the stores had been stocked with a greater variety of first-rate goods, and new models of durable goods had exerted a great attraction on the buyers. Thus, important forces inducing people to spend were missing. Nevertheless, people did not feel that they had been forced to save. When asked directly, they denied it strongly and argued that they liked to save.

Finally, we may refer to certain theoretical considerations according to which a high rate of saving is connected with high interest rates. Yet the record wartime saving coincided with the lowest interest rates in American history. In the surveys, hardly anybody said that he had abstained from spending in order to have income later in the form of interest. Many people knew of the 3 per cent interest rate on war bonds. But attempts to gather evidence that this interest rate motived people to buy the bonds were not successful. It is impossible to say whether wartime savings would have been lower if the interest had been set at, say, 1 per cent, or higher if the interest had been set at, say, 5 per cent.[10] All that can be said is that people were not consciously driven to their mode of action by the desire for interest income.

The purpose of this discussion of wartime motives for saving has been to illustrate both the possibility and the complexity of studying economic motivation. Why a certain kind of mass behavior occurs—for instance, why most American families saved much more during than before the war—can be studied by collecting microeconomic financial and psychological data. Such studies may be useful in the sense in which the usefulness of scientific research is most properly measured: they may lead to correct predictions. Although the primary purpose of ascertaining motives and attitudes is diagnostic, and the transition from diagnosis to prediction is not simple, the studies just discussed have enabled the analysts to make a few important predictions. It was concluded in 1945 that (1) liquid assets accumulated during the war by the consumers would not be reduced quickly for purchasing consumer goods after the end of the war and (2) while amounts saved would probably drop after the end of the war—because patriotic motives to save and group approval of low spending might disappear—there would remain numerous incentives to save; first of all, the paramount one, the desire to be prepared for a rainy day. The finding that a variety of factors enter into motivations to spend and to save pointed toward the improbability of the mechanistic assumption that with the end of the war the volume of expenditures and savings would be a function of nothing but the disposable income in the hands of individuals.

NOTES TO CHAPTER 5

Although frequent reference was made in this chapter to wartime surveys, most empirical data presented in this chapter and in Part Two are taken from the Surveys of Consumer Finances, conducted annually since January, 1946, by the Survey Research Center of the University of Michigan (or its predecessor organization, the Division of Program Surveys in the U.S. Department of Agriculture) for the Board of Governors of the Federal Reserve System. Reports of the surveys have been published in the *Federal Reserve Bulletin*. For a dis-

[10] It will be shown in Part Five that questions inquiring how people would behave under certain imaginary conditions ("Suppose that . . .") are of little value.

cussion of objectives and methods of the surveys, see Part Five. In addition to findings previously published, some tabulations as well as qualitative and illustrative material that have not hitherto appeared in print are presented in this book. For all these materials, the author is greatly indebted to his colleagues; the surveys represent a cooperative undertaking in which research workers in the Survey Research Center and in the Division of Research and Statistics of the Federal Reserve Board participate.

The problem of planning by consumers has been discussed before in relation to the methods and findings of the Surveys of Consumer Finances by R. A. Young and D. McC. Holthausen in "Values and Limitations of Consumer Financial Surveys for Economic Research," *Federal Reserve Bulletin,* March, 1947, pp. 249–250. The present discussion has made substantial use of the argumentation in that article.

For data on the relation between the number of "prospective purchasers" (those who said at the beginning of a year that they would buy a certain article) and "actual purchasers" (those who said at the end of the year that they had bought the article), see "1949 Survey of Consumer Finances," *Fèderal Reserve Bulletin,* June, 1949, p. 648. The data presented there are based on interviews with nation-wide samples of consumer units, each of which consisted of different respondents. When the same respondents were interviewed twice, within an interval of one year, the findings showed relationships similar to those with different respondents. There were relatively few families among those who purchased new cars in 1948 who, at the beginning of the year, had said that they did

TABLE 1. PRICE RANGE OF PROSPECTIVE AND ACTUAL PURCHASES

Price of furniture to be bought or bought	Anticipated purchases, 1948,* per cent	Actual purchases, 1948,† per cent
Less than $75	11	17
$ 75–$174	19	24
175– 274	15	12
275– 474	20	19
$475 and over	19	22
Uncertain about price	16	6
Total	100	100

* A nation-wide sample of 3,500 spending units were asked at the beginning of 1948 whether they expected to buy any furniture in 1948; 9 per cent answered in the affirmative. The column shows the distribution of the amounts these people expected to pay for furniture.

† Another nation-wide sample of 3,500 spending units were asked at the beginning of 1949 whether they had bought any furniture in 1948; 15 per cent answered in the affirmative. The column shows the distribution of the amounts these people paid for furniture.

SOURCE: 1948 and 1949 Surveys of Consumer Finances.

not plan to do so. The number of unplanned purchases was somewhat greater in the case of refrigerators, and much greater in the case of used cars and furniture.

Table 1 may serve as an illustration of the statement that there is a difference in the degree of advance planning according to the price of the goods purchased. The underestimation of prospective purchases in comparison to actual purchases is larger in the lower than in the higher price ranges. Similar findings were made in different years regarding several other items.

Only one aspect of the study of consumer plans has been discussed in this chapter. To provide evidence for the statement that "some consumer purchases are planned in advance," it was not necessary to cite another aspect of these studies which, however, will be mentioned here in order to avoid misunderstandings. Some people who expressed the intention of purchasing certain articles during the coming year did not buy those articles. Occasional nonfulfillment of plans is, of course, to be expected because circumstances may deteriorate or people may change their minds for other reasons. Furthermore, difficult methodological problems are involved in ascertaining expectations, intentions, and plans, and the present solution of these problems is far from foolproof. The methods of measuring expectations and the question about the predictive value of expressed expectations will be discussed in later chapters. Table 2 may, however, serve to illustrate the relation found to prevail between expressed intentions to buy and subsequent purchases by the same people.

TABLE 2.   REALIZATION OF EXPRESSED INTENTIONS TO BUY NEW AUTOMOBILES

Actual Behavior (determined early in 1949)	Expected to Buy New Cars in 1948,* per cent (determined early in 1948)
Did buy new cars in 1948	52
Did buy used cars in 1948	10
Did not buy cars in 1948:	
Postponed purchase †	12
Explained change in plan ‡	6
Unaccounted	20
Total	100

* Respondents said either that they definitely expected to buy new cars in 1948 or that they probably would; when only those who expressed definite intentions to buy are tabulated, the rate of realization of intentions is somewhat higher.

† Respondents said in early 1949 that they definitely would buy new cars in 1949; there was still a shortage of automobiles in 1948, which may have accounted both for postponement of purchase plans and for buying used cars instead of new ones.

‡ Referred in early 1949 to income or price developments which made for a change in plans.

SOURCE: Spending units interviewed both early in 1948 and early in 1949. These units represent a random sample of urban spending units included in the 1948 Survey of Consumer Finances who did not move in 1948. The analysis of the reinterviews was made possible by a grant of the Rockefeller Foundation to the University of Michigan.

The information on conflicting expectations (p. 72, above) is taken from the first Survey of Consumer Finances conducted at the beginning of 1946 (see the publication of the Division of Program Surveys, U.S. Department of Agriculture, entitled *National Survey of Liquid Asset Holdings, Spending and Saving,* Part III, August, 1946).

The information on wartime motives for purchasing war bonds and attitudes toward war bonds is taken from a series of surveys conducted by the Division of Program Surveys for the War Finance Division of the U.S. Treasury Department. For later publications by those who were primarily responsible for this research program, see Rensis Likert, "The Sample Interview Survey," in *Current Trends in Psychology,* University of Pittsburgh Press, 1948, and Dorwin Cart-

TABLE 3.   EFFECT OF HEARING ABOUT BONDS AND OF SOLICITATION TO PURCHASE
BONDS ON PURCHASES OF SAVINGS BONDS

Characteristic of group *	Purchased savings bonds, per cent	Did not purchase savings bonds, per cent
All spending units:		
Have heard about bonds recently † ..	14	86
Have not heard about bonds recently †	5	95
Have heard about bonds recently ‡ ..	19	81
Have not heard about bonds recently ‡	10	90
Spending units with incomes of less than $4,000: †		
Were solicited in person	25	75
Were solicited by mail	10	90
Were not solicited	5	95
Spending units with incomes of over $4,000: †		
Were solicited in person	46	54
Were solicited by mail	30	70
Were not solicited	14	86
Spending units with incomes of over $2,000: ‡		
Were solicited in person	55	45
Were not solicited	21	79

* The questions were: "During the last three months or so have you seen or heard anything about savings bonds? What sort of things have you seen or heard? Has anyone asked you personally to buy savings bonds recently? Were you asked to buy at home or work or where? Have you received any mail or leaflets about savings bonds?" Those solicited both in person and by mail are tabulated as solicited in person.

†From a survey conducted in July, 1949. The purchases recorded were those made in the first half of 1949.

‡ From a survey conducted in July, 1948. The purchases recorded were those made in the first half of 1948.

wright, "Some Principles of Mass Persuasion," *Human Relations,* Vol. 2, 1949, pp. 253*ff*. Cartwright presents data on the wartime effects of personal solicitation. With respect to postwar effects of the same factor, information is available from studies made by the Survey Research Center for the U.S. Treasury Department in July, 1948 (after the Security Loan Drive), and in July, 1949 (after the Opportunity Loan Drive). Some of the findings of these surveys are shown in Table 3.

Much of the information on wartime savings motives and on attitudes toward the use of accumulated liquid assets is taken from a survey conducted by the Division of Program Surveys at the beginning of 1945 for the Federal Reserve Board. Some of the results of that survey were published in the September, 1945, issue of the *Federal Reserve Bulletin* under the title "Surveys of Liquid Asset Holdings." The results of that survey and of several other surveys conducted in the same period did not confirm a prediction that was widely held at that time and was formulated, for instance, by A. G. Hart as follows: "It is generally agreed that spending for durable goods . . . will be for many consumers substantially free from current-account budget limitations for two or three years . . . cash or money substitutes being on hand" (*American Economic Review,* Vol. 35, Supplement, 1945, p. 346). Postwar surveys showed that some people did pay part of the cost of durable goods purchased by drawing on accumulated assets, but for most people income and installment credit were the major sources of those expenditures. It is, nevertheless, possible that the possession of substantial liquid reserves may have changed people's attitudes toward spending out of income and borrowing during the postwar years. This important question, possibly implied by Hart, will be studied in Chapter 8.

CHAPTER 6

ATTITUDES TOWARD INCOME, ASSETS, AND EXPENDITURES

In studying the choices and decisions confronting consumers, three major concepts may be distinguished. The first one is the receipt of material values, primarily of money. For practical purposes today in America only one kind of money receipt is important, namely, income. The second concept has to do with the material values owned, that is, the assets of consumers. The third concerns the use or outlay of values, primarily what appear to the consumer as expenditures. The subjective meaning and significance of these concepts must be clarified, and the kinds of decisions consumers can make concerning their income, assets, and expenditures must be described.

THE MEANING OF INCOME RECEIVED

It follows from our discussion of consumer motivation that desire for higher income or for making more money cannot be the only economic goal of all people. There cannot be just one economic motive or goal. Motives and goals change with circumstances, with past experiences, and with group belonging. Income is a means toward an end. Money, in our culture, is necessary for many important purposes of life and helps greatly in achieving them. The same is true of security—to which money contributes but with which high income is not identical—as well as of independence, power, or approbation by others. But whatever relations prevail among the various goals that enter into different motivational patterns, income and desire for higher income exert great influence on economic behavior.

In order to study the influence of income on people's motives and behavior, we have to formulate a working definition of the term "income" that can be used as a research tool. Should we deal with income per capita, per income receiver, per family, or what? The attempt has been made to define a functional unit, which may consist of one or of several persons, and which includes only one income receiver, or two or more income receivers whose incomes are pooled and used as a common fund for the purposes of the unit. In many instances, it is a simple matter to recognize such a unit.

86

Suppose that husband, wife, and two children are the inhabitants of a one-family house, that the only one with an income is the husband, and that the family has no dependents living elsewhere. Then it does not matter whether we take the household or the family as our basic unit. But if there are roomers or boarders (not related to the main family) in the household, or family members who are financially independent (for instance, a daughter and her husband living with her parents), the situation is more complicated. The procedure adopted in the Surveys of Consumer Finances was to study the incomes of, and the income distribution among, *spending units*. A spending unit is defined as all related persons living at the same place who pool their income for purposes of their major expenditures. A spending unit may consist of one or more persons. A family—all related persons living in the same dwelling—may consist of one or more spending units. A dwelling unit may contain one or more families. The concept of spending units fits in many cases and enables the investigator to study assets and decisions of "secondary" units living with the main family, but it also has certain drawbacks. For instance, sometimes persons living in different dwellings may pool their income, or may be dependent on the same income. Furthermore, the income of several family members may be pooled for certain purposes (*e.g.,* rent, automobile) and not for others. Probably there is no perfect solution to the problem of selecting a basic unit, but during the first few years after the Second World War, when the housing shortage and other special factors often caused financially independent members of the same family to live together, family income appeared to be a less useful concept than spending-unit income.

The next preliminary question to be discussed is the kind of income to be taken into account. Income is usually measured in the United States in dollars. But in addition to the dollars received in wages, salaries, dividends, profits, etc., a family (or spending unit) may have what is called "income in kind"—free meals, free lodging, food grown on its own farm, and the like. Also, data on aggregate national income usually contain "imputed income," representing, for instance, the expenses saved by people who own their homes. In surveys collecting income data and determining attitudes toward income, both income in kind and what is called imputed income are usually disregarded. Not only is it difficult to determine the size of such "incomes," but it is also probable that they are viewed by most people in a different way from money income. The influence of income in kind and imputed income on people's saving and spending requires, however, careful studies which have not yet been undertaken.

On the other hand, income measurements on the macro- as well as the mircoeconomic level can make use of the distinction between income in dollars and real income. In periods of price increases, a stable $3,000 income in two successive years may mean that the family's real income, in terms of its purchasing power, has declined; in times of price decreases, on the other hand, real income increases if dollar income remains stable. A further complication arises because the same dollar income may have different purchasing power in different parts of the country. In a small rural place, $3,000 may buy more and mean more than in New York City.

Comparisons between incomes at different periods are usually made on the basis of real income. The price level at different periods is taken into account, and the money income is expressed in terms of its purchasing power. For instance, the proportion of families with incomes of, say, over $5,000 in 1948 is not compared with the proportion of families with incomes over $5,000 in 1938 but with that of families with incomes of over, say, $3,300 in 1938 (assuming that $3,300 had the same purchasing power in 1938 as $5,000 in 1948). Though this procedure is, of course, justified, it should not be assumed that money income is void of any psychological reality. In periods of small price changes, it seems that money income alone counts. Getting a higher pay means higher income. When price changes are large or rapid, and when they are widely publicized, as in the first few postwar years, a different situation may arise. Increases in money income may then be felt to mean nothing but compensation for price increases. But even in such situations money income cannot be entirely disregarded. The pay rate in dollars—$1 per hour or $3,600 a year, for instance—has psychological meaning in the sense that people know those rates and measure their achievement and aspiration levels in terms of those rates. Therefore, wage or income reductions may cause frustration, even if they are accompanied or preceded by price reductions of the same extent.

Recently, attempts were made to study the joint effect of changes in income and changes in the cost of living. In the Surveys of Consumer Finances, representative samples of the population were asked the following question at different times: "Would you say you people are better or worse off financially now than you were a year ago?" From the lengthy answers received to this question and to such additional queries as "Why do you think so?" or "What makes you say this?" it became clear that a multitude of different circumstances may influence people's subjective evaluation of their financial situation and its changes. Some people said that they were worse off because of illness or hospital expenses; others that they were better off because their new jobs appeared more secure or contained promises of advancement; and still others referred to an increase or decrease in the size of their families as making them better or worse off. But on the whole, past changes in income and in prices determined most answers. During the period 1946 to 1948 most people appeared to be aware of the rising cost of living and judged their financial position in the light of both income changes and price increases. The number who said they were better off was, during these years, much smaller than the number whose incomes had increased. One spending unit out of every four with an income increase thought, for instance, at the beginning of 1947 that it was worse off than a year ago. Among those with stable incomes, two out of five, and among those with declining incomes, three out of four expressed the same opinion.

Our next preliminary question concerns the time period for which income is measured. It was found in the surveys that for many people annual income had a definite meaning. They usually knew what their annual income was and, especially at the beginning of a year, they knew what it was during the year just previous. The obligation to prepare income-tax returns no doubt contributed to the awareness of annual incomes, but possibly the calendar year was considered a natural unit of accounting even before income taxes were introduced or extended to most income receivers. There are, of course, people who also think of their incomes in terms of their weekly, biweekly, or monthly salary checks, or their hourly wage rates. But others, for instance, businessmen or farmers with sharply fluctuating receipts, do not attach much importance to their incomes per week or even per month. Awareness of annual income level is, of course, not identical with knowledge of the exact amount of the annual income received; especially on the part of seasonal workers, or persons with many income sources, such knowledge may be lacking.

Finally, it is necessary to distinguish between income before taxes and income after taxes. Three developments of the past ten years, the reduction in the amount of tax-exempt income, the considerable increase in income-tax rates, and the introduction of tax withholding, made a very large proportion of the people conscious of the difference. For many purposes it is more appropriate to relate expenditures and amounts saved to disposable income than to income before taxes. But there is also some justification for the first procedure, not only because the conclusions drawn from the two procedures are similar in most instances, but also because subjectively many people still think of their incomes before taxes when they consider their incomes. In very high income brackets the situation may, however, be different.

If two spending units living in the same town make the same amount of money in a given year, we may, of course, say that they have the same income. Psychologically, however, we know only that with respect to income their environment (the stimulus) is the same. What the income means to them may be very different. The meaning of a given income depends on the field in which it is perceived. The field is not necessarily determined by the stimulus alone. What are the factors that influence the perception of income? Some such factors require little discussion. One is age—the same income may mean something different for a young, a middle-aged, and an old person. Another factor is the size of the family (spending unit), the number of dependents who live on the income. Both these factors are of lesser interest with respect to the analysis of economic fluctuations than certain other factors, closely related to each other, that have been studied recently. We shall take up first the role of past income, then that of income aspirations and of expected income, and finally of incomes of others belonging to the same group.

1. Past Income Changes.   Suppose two spending units, *A* and *B,* have, in a given year, the same income—$3,000. But *A* has had the same income for the past few years and never had a higher income; *B,* on the other hand, had a much higher income during the past few years, which dropped to its current level recently. Then it may well be that the same amounts received have different meanings for the two units, and therefore the behavior of the two units in response to the same stimulus—$3,000 received—will differ.

We recognize here the problem of time perspective. Whether past incomes influence the perception and evaluation of current incomes depends on the time perspective of the persons concerned. No general rule can be set up. For instance, it has been recently postulated [1] that the highest past income level always influences the use of a lower current income. Whether or not this is the case will, however, depend on the perspective, which may or may not extend as far back as the highest previous income. Concerning the probable backward extension of people's time perspective, the following hypotheses may be advanced (they require empirical confirmation which is only partly available at the moment):

a. The time perspective will probably encompass recent substantial changes in income. In other words, in a year in which one's income has increased or decreased sharply, the new income level will probably be considered as an increased or a decreased level and not simply as a, say, $3,000 level. The terms "recent" and "substantial" require clarification. Suppose a spending unit had a $4,000 income in 1945, and $3,000 in both 1946 and 1947; will the income in 1947 be considered a low or decreased income? Or, suppose the decline was one of 10 per cent; will this change affect the evaluation of the current income? We do not know the answers to these questions. The answers may differ in different circumstances; they may depend on further contents of the unitary field, to which we now turn.

b. If the income change is considered unusual, it will probably find a place in one's time perspective. Let us take first an example of an income change which is not unusual. A young persons starts working at a relatively low rate, which then increases year after year. It is then probable that his behavior is not greatly affected by memories of his previous low income.

[1] See the references to Duesenberry's and Modigliani's articles in the Notes to Chapter 8.

The same may hold true of regular promotions or of increases due solely to passage of time. Income changes due to change in occupation, however, and, to revert to the previous point, "substantial" income changes may more frequently be considered unusual.

c. The meaning of past income changes and their effect on current behavior depend on expected income changes as well. In addition to the past and the present, the future may also belong to one's time perspective. Therefore it is unjustified to discuss past changes without reference to future changes. We shall take up this problem in a moment.

d. Whether or not an income change is considered unusual may depend on the income trend of other people, especially of those belonging to one's own group. An income increase in which all of one's "colleagues" share may have a different meaning from one which occurs at a time when other people in one's group or even in the entire country have stable or declining incomes (or are thought to have such incomes). This is again a point to which we must come back later.

2. Levels of Aspiration. Psychological findings that are relevant for the understanding of the role of income expectations have been gathered by studying what is called the level of aspiration. In experimental investigations of a wide variety of goal-striving behavior, it has been possible to distinguish different levels of performance. People were often found to be aware of these levels, and they influenced their behavior. Take, for instance, target shooting. There is, first, an ideal level—the perfect score—which is known to be the best possible performance. Then there is the level of achievement, represented by the last actual score or by the average of recent scores. Finally, there is the level of aspiration—the level which the person desires or expects to achieve in his next performance or next performances.

In many kinds of goal-striving behavior it is not possible to say what the ideal is. Such a level has, then, no psychological reality. But the other two levels can be distinguished in almost all instances.

The level of aspiration is usually much lower than the ideal level—if the latter is recognized—but somewhat higher than the achievement level. The factors that influence the level of aspiration have been determined by experimental variation, for instance, by informing subjects engaged in different activities of their scores, sometimes correctly, and sometimes incorrectly by telling them too high or too low scores. It has been found that if a person has scored higher—or thinks he has scored higher—on a second test than on a first, he will aspire to score even higher on a third test. In other words, success raises his level of aspiration. This process goes on until the possibilities of still further improvement begin to disappear. On the other hand, failure, disappointment, frustration tend to lower the level of aspiration. But whether a person feels that he has failed or has been successful depends not on his actual performance, but on its relation to his level of aspiration. That is, if he expected to make a poor score but is told that he has made a fair score, he may aspire to do still better; whereas if he is told that he has done much worse than he expected to, he is likely to have no ambition to improve. In addition, group standards, or scores achieved by others (reference scores), influence the level of aspiration. Knowing that other people with whom one compares oneself have achieved something may supply additional motivation or create added frustration in case of failure.

A golf player, for instance, who takes his game seriously may, at the beginning of his career in the sport, endeavor to achieve a score of 100 or 90. When, after due time, he achieves this score, he may regard himself as no longer in the duffer class and may raise his level of aspiration.

Such findings, made in diverse fields of goal-striving behavior, are directly applicable to economic activities. They appear to contradict the opinion sometimes held that wealthy people are motivated to a lesser extent to add to their wealth than poor people are motivated to acquire some reserves for a rainy day. Similarly, the aspirations of people with relatively high incomes to increase their incomes may be as strong as those of people with low incomes. This deduction from psychological experiments performed with noneconomic activities has been confirmed by interviewing studies concerning attitudes toward income. The results of one such study were summarized as follows: "The more money a person has, the more money he wants." [2] This finding requires confirmation through further investigations. Probably it is not generally valid. Group standards and climates of opinion will have to be taken into account and it will have to be considered that disappointment in attempts to achieve higher income usually reduces the level of aspiration.

More generally: ambition and resignation are not inflexible personality traits with one or the other of which a person is endowed. Past experience shapes people to aspire higher or makes them resigned to their estate and hesitant to strive toward new goals. Limits to what one wants, or levels of aspiration beyond which nothing good can be obtained, are not objectively given. They cannot be defined as, for instance, a $10,000 income or $20,000 in the bank. Limits are real and decisive for our behavior but are constantly changed by us, raised with success and lowered with failure. Not only our own but also our group's success and failure may count. If a person grows up in a small mining town in which his father, brothers, friends also grew up, and if they are all miners, he will be strongly influenced to accept being a miner as his lot, and not aspire further. Thus his

[2] Richard Centers and Hadley Cantril, "Income Satisfaction and Income Aspiration," *Journal of Abnormal and Social Psychology*, Vol. 41, 1946, pp. 64ff. See the Notes to this chapter for details of these studies.

expectations and aspirations will be limited, not by any failure on his part, but by the limits of his group. To be sure, there are exceptions, because psychological limits are not insurmountable, but crossing psychological boundaries requires strong motivational forces.

Goals of behavior are frequently imposed upon us from the outside: for example, in our job we are told to do so and so. Imposed tasks become goals in the psychological sense when we adopt them. The adoption may be an almost automatic process. Psychological experiments regarding unfinished tasks are relevant here. It has been found that even rather uninteresting imposed tasks exert a tendency on us to be finished. When, for instance, people are asked to carry out certain simple manual tasks or solve arithmetic problems and are interrupted before completing those tasks, they later frequently spontaneously return to them. There exists a tendency toward completion or closure. Thus, even a task that was started reluctantly because of external pressure—be it a worker's or a clerk's job, or a business venture—may provide incentives toward its completion. It has been found, furthermore, that satisfactions need not consist of tangible rewards or praise but may be inherent in finishing a job or completing a task. Accomplishing what one wanted to do, reaching one's level of aspiration or coming closer to it, brings forth satisfaction. On the other hand, apparent lack of motivation or absence of striving toward a goal is usually the result of frustration. Failure and disappointment may cause a person to be convinced that his income or his advancement is entirely dependent on others, or on luck, and not on his own work or abilities. Then it may come about that economic activities are apparently not goal-striving activities.

3. Income Expectations. We turn to the discussion of short-range income expectations. If people are asked—as has been done in the Surveys of Consumer Finances—whether "a year from now" they expect to make more money or less money, or if they are asked what amount of income they expect to have during the next calendar year, on what considerations can they base their answers? In the light of the discussion just concluded, we may advance the following hypothesis: Income expectations are based on levels of aspiration or, more specifically, they are based on the same considerations that determine the levels of aspiration. Past performance will then be a major consideration. If a person's income has been going up according to his aspirations, he will expect it to go up further; if, however, he has been unsuccessful in increasing his income, or if contrary to his aspirations his income has declined, he will not expect a higher income.

Recent studies indicate that there is some truth in these assumptions. In some cases, people's income expectations were found to be determined by their past performance and its relation to their aspirations. But in other cases, the assumptions have not been confirmed. The analysis of income expectations had disclosed that only certain past achievements and failures, and not all achievements and failures, influence expectations.

The investigation of income expectations in the Surveys of Consumer Finances, to which we now turn, has a drawback in that it has been applied only to changes in income during one past year and to expected changes during one future year. Further studies that consider longer periods of time are needed. But even from studying the relation between short-range past changes and short-range expectations, we may derive certain conclusions.[3]

a. Among those whose incomes had increased during the past year, many more expressed the expectation that their incomes would go up during the following year than among those whose incomes had declined. Conversely, the frequency of expected income declines was found to be much larger among those who had experienced an income decline than among those with an income increase.

b. Some past income increases and decreases were considered to be "temporary"—subjectively not important, not affecting income expectations. In some cases it was found that people did *not* expect the continuation of past income trends in the future because those were attributed to temporary causes such as illness or unusual, one-time profits and losses. More importantly, it appears that the frequency of "reversals" in income expectations—expecting income declines (increases) after income increases (declines)—differed at different times according to people's "general economic outlook."

Opinions about the general economic situation were found to shape some people's, and sometimes even many people's, income expectations. Most people seem to have an opinion about the probable course of business in general; they either expect good times to come or to continue, or fear that bad times will develop or stay on for some time. The surveys have shown a correlation between optimistic income expectations and optimistic general economic outlook, as well as between pessimistic income expectations and pessimistic general economic outlook. The correlations are, however, far from perfect, reflecting the fact that income expectations depend on other factors, too.

Survey findings obtained during the year 1949–1950 indicate that changes in the relation of past income trends to income expectations are dependent on people's general economic outlook. (The findings are presented in Table 11 at the end of this chapter.) During the first half of the year 1949, people were aware of a slowing down in industrial activity and of a slight deterioration in the general economic outlook. In July, the proportion of

[3] Tables presenting survey findings on income expectations are included in the Notes to this chapter.

both those whose incomes had increased and who nevertheless expected income declines, and the proportion of those whose incomes had declined and who expected further income reductions, was found to be higher than six months earlier. During the second half of the year 1949, industrial activity picked up again and many people thought this sufficient reason to view the future with optimism. At the beginning of 1950, the proportion of those whose incomes had declined and who nevertheless expected income increases was found to have increased sharply. The income expectations expressed at that time were as optimistic as a year earlier, although in 1949 the proportion of people who suffered an income decline was greater, and the proportion who enjoyed an income increase smaller, than in 1948. The often unexpected adverse developments in 1949 had a slight effect on people's attitudes. Early in 1950 the income expectations were primarily influenced by people's general economic outlook rather than by their past income trends.

These findings are in accordance with the theory of the formation of expectations. We learned in Chapter 4 that sometimes we base our expectations on what has happened to us before, while sometimes, when we have reason to reorganize our psychological field, we expect new developments that differ greatly from past trends. Possibly it is hardly ever correct to speak of past trends as determining expected trends. It is our understanding of what happened to us in the past that matters. Sometimes past income increases will be viewed as a steady advance toward higher levels and will raise our level of aspiration and make us expect further income increases; sometimes, however, a past income increase may appear as nothing but a temporary interruption of a downward trend. Similarly, income declines may result in frustration and in lowering our sights. But as the recent survey findings indicate, this need not be the case. The adverse development may be viewed as independent of our own performance, and our aspirations and expectations may be the results of considerations other than the past trend.

On the basis of the studies conducted up to now, we cannot foretell in advance when the one and when the other situation is likely to occur. What we know is (1) that at a given time it is possible to determine what proportion of people expects their past income trends to continue and what proportion expects reversals and (2) that people's economic behavior differs according to whether past income changes are subjectively considered to be temporary or permanent and continuous. We shall study the joint effect of past and expected income changes on spending and saving in Chapter 8. At this point it suffices to draw the conclusion that meaning and effect of past income changes are affected by income expectations. People view their incomes in a perspective which extends forward as well as backward and which contains some salient and important as well as some temporary and unimportant parts.

Up to this point we argued as if all people had at all times a clear notion about their future incomes. This is not quite correct. It was found in the surveys that some people had definite and well-founded expectations concerning the amounts of their future income. Many more people said that they could not tell how much money they would probably make, but they did say that they expected their incomes to remain stable, or to rise or decline moderately, or to rise or decline considerably. There were also people who could not express any definite income expectations. They were at a loss to say what would happen to their incomes, or listed circumstances on which their future incomes depended without being able to decide which of the circumstances was most probable. In the first few postwar years, about one-quarter of all income receivers were found to have no definite income expectations in the sense just described.

Expectations may be of great significance even if what we expect does not come true, because they may affect our behavior at the time we hold them. ·Still, the question about the fulfillment of expressed expectations may be fruitfully raised. In one recent study it was possible to compare actual income trends with the trends that were expected to prevail during that year by interviewing an identical sample of respondents twice with a yearly interval. As shown in the Notes to this chapter (Table 10), a substantial number of respondents predicted the direction of their income changes fairly correctly. Only 13 per cent of the sample were grossly inaccurate in that their incomes went down although they had expected them to go up, or went up although they had expected them to go down. It thus appears that in the majority of cases income expectations represented something more than idle speculation.

4. Other People's Income. The role of group membership has already been recognized by discussing the income of families or spending units instead of that of individuals. Belonging to a group may affect a person's appreciation of his income in other ways, too. One may consider one's income low if it is lower than the income of others in the group, for instance, of workers employed on the same job, and high if it is higher. If belonging to a club is more than a mere formality, and a feeling of identification with the club develops, the same may be true of one's income in relation to that of other club members. Reference groups contributing to the evaluation of one's income may also consist of neighbors or of the parents of children who are schoolmates of one's children. Being or not being in step with others is of special importance with respect to evaluation of income changes. It may determine satisfaction or lack of satisfaction with past income increases and represent the driving force behind desires for further income increases and steps taken to achieve them.

In the preceding discussion, the term "others" meant the small groups to which the individual belongs or his reference groups. Yet much broader groups may also play a substantial and important role in determining the subjective meaning of income changes. All inhabitants in one's town or country may qualify as one's group. In periods of depression, when one knows that the income of most people in the town or in the country has declined, and difficulties in making ends meet are common experiences, an income decline may take on an entirely different aspect than in times when one's own income trend is or appears to be different from that of most other people. The surveys during the war and in the first few postwar years revealed that small income increases seldom brought forth a feeling of satisfaction or progress. People considered them as normal by evaluating the increases in their own incomes in comparison to those of their associates, of reference groups, and of the population at large.

According to some recent views, it is not the absolute level of income that affects the behavior of the income recipient, but his position in the income distribution. In comparing the behavior of a family in the 1920's, for instance, with the behavior of a family at the end of the nineteenth century, it would be useless to select two families with identical money income, even if prices had been the same during the two periods. Since incomes generally advanced during the first few decades of the century, a $3,000 income gave a family a lower percentile position at the later date. Therefore, it has been advocated that comparisons of different periods be made on the basis of comparable deciles—for example, that in analyzing changes in consumer behavior between 1910 and 1940, families in, say, the lowest income decile in 1940 should be compared with families in the lowest decile in 1910. These considerations represent real progress, but it is questionable whether in all cases the entire income distribution should be taken as the reference group. Possibly the position of a family within the income distribution of families belonging to the same occupational group, say the physicians or the skilled workers, is of greater immediate importance.

It is possible for making more money to be the group-accepted criterion of success, and there may exist cultures where this is the case, or there may have been such times in the past. If so, then a person, in order to achieve status in his group, must have a certain income, everyone being evaluated by others according to his income. There is some evidence that at present in the United States this is not the case. At higher income levels the evidence is fairly conclusive. Corporation executives, instead of being proud of the wide publicity their salaries received through publication by the Treasury of all salaries exceeding $75,000, fought this publicity and, in

1949, succeeded in changing the law so as to discontinue the publications. Sociological studies have shown that association among people is not determined solely by income, and leadership or highest esteem is not generally attributed to the person in a group who has the highest income.

If high income in itself is not what creates status and is seen by the income receiver and his associates as a means to an end, the use made of high income becomes important. It is only in rather small and rare groups that conspicuous spending, lavish entertainment, or expensive hobbies appear at present to be approved of, or to be required for attaining group status. Restraint in spending and contributions to cultural or social objectives are widely valued and frequently represent approved group standards.

Far too little is known about prevailing group standards and values as well as about how such values change. Similarly, exact investigations are needed concerning the currently prevailing form and the evolution of individual aspirations. No doubt, what may be called noneconomic aspirations —desire for a happy family life, or friendship, or esteem by others—are interwoven with economic motivations, and the motivational patterns are fluid and may change in different situations. The economic motives themselves are complex. Professional pride or desire to do a good job may be called an economic motive even if it is not clearly connected with achieving higher income. In view of the usual rather extensive time perspective, it is improbable that people in general aspire to high income for the immediate future only. Striving for high income over protracted future periods, or for steady income, brings up the problem of security. The discussion of the desire for security, and also of the desire for power, will be taken up later in connection with the analysis of business motivation. At this point, it suffices to say that income aspirations represent only part of the motivational pattern. Concerning them we conclude that the thesis that people strive for the maximum possible income is too vague to be of much use. Even if maximum or ideal income levels were discernible, they hardly ever represent motivational forces. What is considered possible at a given moment depends to a large extent on people's general economic outlook. Among the given possibilities, people strive to achieve their levels of aspiration, which depend primarily on past achievements and frustrations and on the levels of their reference groups.

ATTITUDES TOWARD ASSETS

From the economist's point of view, three types of assets in the possession of families or households may be distinguished: liquid assets, investments, and inventories. The distinction among the three types is not always clear-cut, and especially with respect to life insurance policies held and homes owned the classification is rather arbitrary. Yet it is useful to begin with a description of the economic categories and to raise the question later whether people's attitudes toward their assets conform with the usual classification employed by the economist.

Liquid assets are defined as cash and its substitutes. In addition to currency held, any asset that is cashable at any time at a fixed and known value is considered a liquid asset. Bank deposits, whether in checking or in savings accounts, and government bonds, especially the savings bonds which are redeemable at any time and therefore need not be sold at a market like other securities, qualify in these respects.

The main examples of investments are corporation stocks, bonds other than government bonds, real estate, business investments (ownership or partnership in an unincorporated business), money lent, and mortgages held. Life insurance policies and owner-occupied houses are usually likewise classified under investments, although it is generally recognized that they are not bought for the purpose of investing money.

Automobiles, furniture, and household implements are the most important forms of consumer inventories. In addition to durable goods, clothing and many other semidurables may also belong in this category. With respect to luxury items, such as jewelry or paintings, the classification is more difficult because they may in some instances be acquired as investments.

Many families have not only assets but also debts. The problem of debts may be disregarded in consumer studies if the concept of assets is replaced by that of net assets—that is, the value of assets minus the debts outstanding. Subjectively, consumers may or may not think in terms of net assets. In other words, it may happen that a person regards the value of his house, on which there is a high mortgage, or of his automobile, when he still owes most of its price, as very small. Such attitudes are indicated in some instances when a person replies to the question "Do you own your home?" "No, I have not paid for it yet." In other instances, however, people do not appear to think in terms of net assets or of net worth. When a person has a debt because of hospital expenses, for instance, he usually considers it a charge against his income and not as something reducing the value of his assets.

Exact information on the total wealth of consumers is not available, and information on the distribution of total wealth is fragmentary. It is very difficult to determine the value of some forms of assets, such as business investments, real-estate holdings, jewelry, and diverse forms of personal property. Fortunately, however, during the last ten years the greatest changes in consumer wealth have occurred in types of assets the size and distribution of which can be and have been measured. During the Second World War, additions to nonliquid wealth in homes and investments were moderate, whereas personal liquid-asset holdings increased considerably. Furthermore, consumer debt decreased substantially through repayment of mortgages and installment liabilities.

According to the best available estimates, personal holdings of liquid assets exclusive of business holdings amounted to 45 billion dollars before the war and to 140 billion dollars at the end of the war. During the four years following 1945, there was a further small increase in the aggregate personal liquid assets.

It is highly probable that in 1939 the 45 billion dollar liquid assets were held by a very small portion of American families. Most families, before the war, had only small amounts of currency or bank deposits and no government bonds. Owing to the large-scale saving that occurred during the war, the situation changed completely. At the end of the war, at least three out of four spending units were owners of some liquid assets, not counting currency, and approximately one-half of all American spending units had more than $500 in bank deposits and government bonds. Even among low-income families, and especially among middle-income families, ownership of liquid assets was widespread. To be sure, most of the large amounts of individual holdings, and therefore the bulk of the total holdings, were in the possession of high-income families. But for the first time in American economic history, low-income families had many billion dollars of liquid assets at their disposal.

Why should people hold liquid assets? Holding liquid assets means, it may seem, making no use of one's money, keeping it in reserve without any return (in the case of checking accounts), or being satisfied with a small return (on savings accounts and government bonds). Therefore, it has been assumed that liquid assets are held pending investment opportunities. Then it would follow that liquid assets ought to be large when investment opportunities are scarce or investment appears unattractive, and small when ample and attractive investment opportunities exist. Or liquid assets may be thought to be large when spending is restricted, as during the war, and ought to be reduced quickly when the purchase of much-needed and highly esteemed goods becomes possible.

There is no doubt that such considerations hold true for some people. For instance, the Surveys of Consumer Finances have occasionally revealed people who had large bank deposits after they had sold common stock and thought that prospects for reinvestment were unfavorable. But the great majority of holders of small as well as large amounts of liquid assets were not in that situation. Nor did they hold their liquid assets in order to use the funds later for the purchase of automobiles or other consumer goods, as we have already seen before when we discussed the motives of wartime saving. Surveys conducted between 1944 and 1949 revealed that most holders of liquid assets regarded most of these assets as permanent investments. They wanted to have reserves for "rainy days" and were reluctant to use them even in adverse circumstances because that would have meant being deprived of reserves in the future.

It may be thought that for many people it is an important consideration to have their reserves in a liquid form so that they can be used whenever they are needed. But according to the surveys, most people did not appear to be conscious of liquidity as a reason for having their reserves in bonds or bank deposits. Also, many people held thousands of dollars in such forms. When asked about the disposition of their assets and their preferences among various kinds of assets, people generally stressed the feature of security. Investments in common stock and real-estate holdings were considered risky by the majority; government bonds and bank deposits, on the other hand, were appraised as safe.

There were, of course, many variations in people's opinions and attitudes. Lack of familiarity with securities or real estate, or need for continuous watchful supervision, were frequent arguments against investments and, therefore, for liquid assets. Need for diversification and desire for larger income were the main arguments against liquid assets and for investments, but such arguments were mentioned by many fewer people. Liquidity was also considered an advantage of certain assets by some people (e.g., "You can get the money easily when you need it"), but some others spoke of the liquidity of bank deposits as a disadvantage: they argued that it was too easy to get one's money out of the bank and spend it.

Studies of war-bond holdings revealed that these assets frequently remained untouched for long periods of time. In the summer of 1948, about one-half of all spending units in the nation owned some government bonds of the Series E type. Over one-third of these spending units had never cashed any of their bonds. From a study of the reasons given for cashing bonds, it was found that purchases of homes and investments in one's business accounted for the largest amounts. Emergencies, especially those caused by sickness or hospital expenses, were the most frequent single reason for cashing bonds, but the amounts used for these purposes were usually small. For buying consumer durable goods bonds were used less frequently. General living expenses were given as the reason for cashing bonds in a substantial number of instances, but the frequency of this reason did not increase during the postwar years when prices advanced rapidly. During the war when, because of the patriotic pressure of bond drives and the payroll-deduction campaigns in factories and offices, many people signed up for larger purchases than they could afford, some of the bonds bought were cashed shortly after their purchase. In the postwar years, however, most people who cashed bonds did so with some regret or misgiving.

They expressed dissatisfaction at not being able to hold on to their bonds, except when they used them for the purchase of homes or businesses. From information compiled about attitudes toward war bonds and toward redeeming war bonds, the conclusion emerged as early as in 1945 that there would be no large-scale bond redemptions after the end of the war and that the rate of redemption would not increase in the postwar years. That this prediction came true may serve to illustrate the value of the study of financial attitudes for assessing short-run trends.

Students of recent developments may think of a further argument against holding liquid assets during the war and the first few postwar years. In this period of price increases, the purchasing power of money invested in government bonds and bank deposits declined steadily and considerably. We referred before to the fact that most people were well aware of the rising trend in the cost of living. Nevertheless, they had no misgiving about the value of their liquid assets. Only very few people realized that the amounts they invested in war bonds during the war years had depreciated, and that this loss of capital was not compensated for by the accrued interest. Consideration of the prevailing inflationary trend or fear of its continuation was, in the period of 1946 to 1948, not mentioned frequently as an argument against putting money into liquid assets, or for putting it into other investments, or for spending the money.

References to inflation were even occasionally made in explaining why saving is important and why saving should be done by purchasing savings bonds or adding to bank deposits. Some well-educated people, especially, were aware of the fact, during the war as well as in the first postwar years, that excessive spending contributes to inflationary price increases. The argument that "by buying war bonds we keep prices down" was more frequent than the other that "in periods of price increases one should not keep money in liquid assets."

Altogether, more than 70 per cent of the nation's spending units had some liquid assets (aside from currency) at the beginning of 1949. How does that compare with the ownership of other assets? There is one type of asset, though frequently small in value, which appeared to be still more widely distributed. Life insurance policies were held by almost four out of every five spending units. Ownership of automobiles comes next on the list: more than one-half of all American spending units had cars at that time. From the point of view of the size of wealth, the most important form of asset is the one which comes next in the order of frequency. It was found that early in 1949 about 45 per cent of all spending units lived in homes they owned—although frequently they had a mortgage debt on their houses.

What are traditionally called investments, in contrast to liquid assets, are restricted at present to a relatively small proportion of American families. Ownership of bonds other than United States government bonds—state, municipal, corporate, or foreign bonds—is very rare among private individuals. There is no doubt that most of these bonds are held by financial institutions, life insurance companies, and trust funds. Approximately 10 per cent of American families owned corporation stock in 1947 to 1949. Such assets were rare among low- and even among middle-income families. The proportion of owners of corporation stock increases sharply among consumer units with over $5,000 income. About 1 out of every 2 units with over $10,000 income was found to be an owner of common stock. Furthermore, holding common stock was concentrated among certain occupational groups. Skilled and unskilled workers and clerical and sales employees rarely held such investments; but close to 20 per cent of professional people, of the self-employed, and of business managers did own them. Finally, it was found in the postwar years that common-stock ownership is less frequent among young people (under 35 years of age), even if they have a relatively high income, than among middle-aged or old people. It appears probable that putting some of one's money into common stock is to some extent group-motivated. If one's colleagues and associates, neighbors, and friends do so, then probably sooner or later one will aspire to have a chance of capital appreciation or high yields through ownership of common stock. Some people expressed this tendency clearly by answering to a question about what they think of putting some money into common stock: "None of my friends does so." [4]

Ownership of real estate other than one's own home appears to be somewhat more widespread than ownership of common stock and is more common among people living in small towns and rural areas than in large cities. Here again, people within groups may act in similar ways and acquire familiarity with the same investments. In addition, some people acquire vacant lots in the hope of building homes sometime in the future.

The main motive for business investments of which those who have such investments are aware, and which they emphasize, is desire for independence. Most of the people with business investments have invested in their own businesses which they manage. They have done so in order to start businesses or to enlarge them or to buy out partners, and much of

---

[4] It is possible that individual as well as group attitudes toward common stock, and therefore also the frequency of ownership of common stock, were different in the years before 1929 from what they were found to be after the Second World War. That fewer young people with high incomes were found to own common stock than older people with similar incomes, and that many of the former held strong adverse opinions about such investments, seems to indicate that a generation reached the age of economic independence and acquired some wealth after 1929 in which common stock is not an accepted form of keeping savings.

their investment has accrued out of profits which were left in their businesses, rather frequently for the purpose of repaying debts. Only a small proportion of people were found to be silent partners in a business or to be looking for investment in other people's businesses. Many of these people were either business owners themselves or lent money to, or participated in, the businesses of relatives or neighbors.

The study of the attitudes toward the three major forms of investment—corporation stock, real estate, and unincorporated businesses—in comparison to the attitudes toward liquid assets, may shed some light on the much-discussed problem of scarcity of venture capital. Lack of familiarity looms as a major factor that makes many people, and even people with substantial income and wealth, unfavorably disposed toward investments. By lack of familiarity we do not mean simply that people have never heard of common stock—although many have not—but primarily that they are not acquainted with its relevant features. Such opinions were found frequently as: "Stock market prices are regulated by a small group of insiders," "Brokers only recommend stock they want to unload," or "You always pay a lot when you buy a stock, but if you want to sell it there is no market for it." It appears that the mechanism of the stock market and its ethical standards are not widely known. Even such misapprehensions as the belief that corporation statements are not trustworthy ("They show high profits when they want to sell their stock") were revealed sometimes.

That liquid assets are preferred primarily because they are considered safe and secure has been stated before. In contrast, investment in corporation securities is usually said to be risky. But risk does not appear to be something from which people always shy away. To be sure, there may have been periods in which venturesomeness was more characteristic of American savers than the 1940's. Yet, even in that period, many people said that they would favor putting some of their money into risky common stock. "If only the chances of winning would be as good as the chances of losing" —they added. Exaggeration of the risks involved (for instance, "One can easily lose everything, even in the best common stock") and fear of what was called the unknown and undeterminable extent of the risks were found frequently.

Life insurance is undoubtedly the most common form of saving and the most common form of investment—but most people do not consider it as either saving or investment. About 80 per cent of American families held life insurance policies in the postwar years, but half of these paid annual premiums of less than $200. Some relatively few people are convinced that life insurance is the best way to save money. Some others appear to think of life insurance in terms of both protection and saving money. Many more, however, view life insurance premiums as a necessary expenditure. These subjective considerations are reflected by the fact that there appears to be no substantial difference in the proportion of income put into life insurance premiums when one compares low-, middle-, and high-income groups. In the first few postwar years, the average premium payments of most income groups amounted to 3 to 4 per cent of income.

Owning one's home is a generally accepted form of behavior on the part of many people, and the aspiration of many others. Except in large cities and except for very young people, most families who do not own their homes either hope to achieve that aim or regret that they are unable to do so. The higher the income, the larger is the proportion of families who own their homes. But in this respect the differences between low- and high-income families are much smaller than with respect to any other types of asset (except life insurance). Even among low-income families, about two out of every five are home owners.

We noted before that money spent for buying one's home is not considered money used. Most people are also aware of the fact that repayment of mortgages adds to their wealth and that expenditures for repairs and improvements on their homes represent money well spent.

Some of the home purchases during the first postwar years were "forced" purchases. Some people who bought homes said that they were compelled to do so in order to find shelter for their families, and would not have bought houses if rental dwellings had been available. These statements, however, appear to refer mostly to the prices paid, which were frequently considered not justified, and not to the preference for rented as against owned quarters.

Some data are available about the frequency of ownership of such major consumer inventories as automobiles, refrigerators, radios, and television sets, but not much is known about consumers' attitudes toward their inventories. It appears, however, that durable goods owned by consumers are viewed in a different light from machinery owned by business enterprises. Nothing comparable to depreciation reserves exists among consumers. While business firms set money aside to cover the loss in value of their equipment with use and time, individuals do not think in these terms. This does not mean that the owner of an automobile considers the money paid for it as wholly spent, since trade-in values are generally figured in buying new cars and also some other durable goods. But it means that replacement of durable goods is not a function of money set aside during the period of the use of such goods, and does not depend simply on length of ownership.

One might think that consumers ought to be divided into two groups, those who have and those who do not have automobiles, refrigerators, vacuum cleaners, etc. Those who do not have these goods might be sup-

posed to need them, while those who have them would be outside the
market as long as their implements are in good operating condition. Sellers
of automobiles and other durable goods know that this is not the case.
They know that the best prospects for new cars are normally those who
bought cars one, two, or three years ago, and the worst prospects those who
have no cars at all. Need for a new automobile and demand for an automobile—on the part of those who have cars in good operating condition,
that is, on the part of recent buyers—appear to be a function, first of all, of
group standards. Belonging to a certain group may imply that one must
have a late-model automobile. Perception of a need for a new car and the
urgency and strength of the motivational forces inducing a person to satisfy
this need are often group-determined. The subjective feeling of saturation
may likewise be dependent on the group situation. First, there are older
people who say that their needs for durable goods are satisfied. When
saturation is mentioned by middle-aged or younger people, it is often
found that they are better provided for than their neighbors or other people
in similar walks of life. Generally, therefore, saturation with inventories at
hand cannot be measured by determining simply what articles are in the
possession of a family. For most people, even for people with considerable income, it is possible to have more or better or newer automobiles,
furniture, household implements, or clothing.[5]

What has been said about saturation with durable goods seems to hold
good of all assets, of liquid assets as well as investments. The assumption
that there is an absolute limit or an ideal level for accumulating assets must
be contradicted. Our knowledge about developments of levels of aspiration presents a cue to this discussion. Suppose a father tries to save as
much as he can from his income in order to send his son through college.
When his savings reach the limit set and are sufficient for his purpose,
the chances are that new, different goals will take the place of the old one.
He may begin saving toward buying a house or toward retiring. This is also
the usual situation if a person does not have a specific purpose for saving.
Having reserves of a couple of thousand dollars may appear the ultimate
of security to a young man who is just about to open a bank account. But
$2,000 may appear to him entirely insufficient a few years later, when his
savings approach this goal. The assumption that saving is a much more
powerful motive for people who have nothing or very little than for people
who have already substantial assets has not been confirmed in any studies.
The reverse statement cannot be proved either, although some considerations

[5] In spite of these general principles, it is possible that—*within* the same group, that
is, among people having the same income, occupation, assets, attitudes, etc.—expenditures for goods vary inversely with stocks of goods. No reliable data are available
concerning this relationship.

seem to support the assumption that the more one has, the more one wants to have.

Does that mean that there are no subjective limits for the accumulation of wealth? Accumulation is limited, for poor as for rich people, by the ever-prevailing conflict between spending and saving. At the same time that larger reserves for "rainy days" or retirement are needed and desired, many other more immediate needs are pressing toward satisfaction. Because of this ever-present conflict, it is possible that large asset holdings may influence some people to spend a greater proportion of their income. They may save less, not because they do not desire to save, but because, having substantial assets, they find it harder to say no—to their wives, children, or to their own desires. We shall return to this question in Chapter 8 when we shall study the spending and saving behavior of people with large and with small liquid-asset holdings during the postwar years.

CHOICE AMONG EXPENDITURES

In studying the origin of consumer demand, one might try to distinguish between enabling conditions and need. Money in the possession of the consumer, that is, first of all his income and second his liquid assets, appears the major condition that enables him to make expenditures. The term "need" may be meant as something psychologically real, of which the individuals concerned are aware or which influences their behavior. Needs are often classified in a continuum, starting from absolute necessities without which life cannot be maintained (food, shelter, some clothing, etc.) and ending with purchases that represent not much more than the expression of a whim and are postponable indefinitely. Such classification is, however, usually made from the point of view of an outside observer. Whether needs can similarly be classified from the point of view of the would-be purchaser, we do not know. If such classifications were possible, they would probably yield lists of expenditures that vary greatly in their composition for different individuals, groups, and cultures.

The discussion of enabling conditions and needs may be of some usefulness in order to point out that in a poor community expenditures for subsistence will predominate. If the incomes of all or most consumers are so low that they barely cover the amounts needed for subsistence, and if no assets are available to be drawn upon to supplement incomes, then demand for, and the sale of, goods that are not "necessary" will be very small. There is some value in the concept of discretionary purchasing power, although it cannot be measured without certain rather arbitrary assumptions. Suppose we were to calculate for different countries, or for the same country at different periods, the amounts needed for subsistence and deduct them from aggregate income. We might then obtain some indication of the amounts available for the satisfaction of needs beyond mere subsistence. When such calculations were made for the American economy, they showed that the discretionary purchasing power, or the "market" for goods other than necessities, was much larger in postwar than in prewar years. This was found to be true after taking price increases into account, and without considering the increases in consumers' liquid-asset holdings.

It may be possible to refine these calculations by determining separately the discretionary purchasing power of different groups. Differences in the frequency of low-, middle-, and high-income groups, and differences in what are necessities for each of these groups, could then be taken into account. But the value of such calculations would be rather limited because, first, what is "necessity" has no fixed meaning, and second, available purchasing power is not the same as demand.

Neither enabling conditions nor needs are fixed, stable quantities. They both may change rapidly and can be influenced. Also, enabling conditions and needs jointly do not determine demand, which is the result of consumer decisions.

The best-known method of influencing enabling conditions is taxation. If income-tax rates are raised—other things being equal (which of course they never are)—income available for expenditures (the disposable income) is reduced, and if income-tax rates are reduced, disposable income is increased. Tax policies may also be used to change the prices of certain goods or all goods (through sales taxes); thereby the relation between money available in the hands of consumers and the price of goods offered for sale may be altered. Exact effects of changes in tax rates, however, cannot be calculated in advance because, as we shall see later, people may react differently to such changes.

A similar situation prevails with regard to a second possible "interference" with enabling conditions, which concerns borrowing. If goods are sold on credit, consumers can purchase them even if their assets do not suffice. Introduction, facilitation, and popularization of credit sales or installment sales are measures which sellers can take to enlarge demand. But the final decision to borrow money is made by the buyer. His freedom in making such decisions is, of course, limited. The limits are set, first, by the availability of credit; and in this respect the rule as made by the lenders is that those who have much (high income, large assets) have much easier access to credit than those who have little. The consumer's latitude is limited, further, by his notion of his ability to repay the debt, that is, again by his present or prospective income and assets, and the other obligations he may have. But within these limits, there is still a wide latitude for consumer decisions to borrow or not to borrow, that is, to create enabling conditions for expenditures.

Needs change, and can be influenced, to a still greater degree than enabling conditions. What comes to mind first of all is the invention or development of new goods. A few years ago, no need for television sets existed. In 1948 and 1949, however, especially in larger metropolitan centers, many people felt strongly that they needed such sets. Similarly, at different times, needs arose for automobiles, refrigerators, vacuum cleaners, and so forth. Through new technological developments, some needs may be supplanted—for instance, the need to purchase ice after the need for a mechanical refrigerator has been satisfied—but new needs do not always cancel old ones, and it is probable that we need many more articles today than our grandparents needed in the last century.

Technological developments include not only the invention of new articles but also the production of better or changed articles. People who have cars that run well and are capable of taking them wherever they wish to go often feel that they need new cars. Why is it that the appearance of new automobile models, or of television sets, creates needs?

First, of course, people must be acquainted with the existence and availability of these goods. Advertising has a major function in this respect. The information is hammered into our minds by constant repetition over the radio, in newspapers, and on billboards. Automobiles occupy an almost unique position in this as in many other respects; since we see the new models constantly on the streets, every owner becomes an advertiser of the product he has bought.

But perceptions, even oft-repeated perceptions, are not sufficient to arouse forces driving us to act. The arousal of needs for specific goods is no doubt complex, and many of its aspects have not been studied. Yet all investigations confirm that our needs—at least today, in most cases—are group-determined. We feel the need to have the same things that other people in our group have or need. We have discussed before some evidence of such motivation in the case of ownership of homes, common stock, and automobiles. The function of the group within our motivational patterns is especially strong in the case of automobiles, where all our neighbors and associates know what we have and what we haven't, and of household implements, where a husband can hardly deny something to his wife which his colleagues or neighbors have not denied to their wives. But these aspects of group life, imitation and conscious striving for prestige, are only superficial demonstrations of more fundamental factors. Within a closely knit whole—a we group—the same kinds of forces are aroused because similar receptive conditions prevail for the stimuli. Many members of a group become aware of certain needs, not by imitating each other, or as a matter of conscious decision, but because the given conditions of life are similar for all members of a group.

Our past experiences, frames of reference, and attitudes are group-influenced. At the time of his marriage, a young man is receptive to a call by an insurance salesman. He buys life insurance, usually not because of a rational weighing of risks or a desire to save, but because it is the thing to do. Acting in a certain way, which happens to be the same way as others act, is the requirement of the situation.

Being part of a field or a group means being subject to similar motivational forces and being receptive to similar demands of the environment. The field plays a role not only in our use of discretionary purchasing power but also in determining what represents necessities and what luxuries. But, for most individuals at least, the situation is fluid. Group belonging is a powerful force but not one which we cannot evade. We can, and often do, by means of genuine decisions, resist the prevailing group forces and act contrary to them. We also can leave the field and sever our belonging to a group.

Far too little is known about these factors. The motivational patterns of consumer expenditures require extensive further studies. It is probable that such studies will reveal various other forms of consumer motivation. For instance, an expenditure may not be an end in itself, but a means to achieve a further, different goal. Or, in buying product A and not product B, chance, prejudice, or suggestion may play a role. We are not in the position to go deeper into the matter. We proceed, therefore, to the final question: Suppose both enabling conditions and need are present, that is, we desire a good which we can afford to buy, will then the purchase always be made?

The answer to this question is obvious: We are often aware of a need for goods which are within our means and which nevertheless we do not buy. The main reason for not buying them is the conflict between different needs. This is the point where the individual exercises the greatest amount of discretion. As we have seen, he can, to some extent, manipulate even the enabling conditions and his need. But he is, to a much greater extent, master of what he demands—at least when it matters, that is, when he does not act habitually but makes a decision. Routine expenditures, which we have seen to be very frequent, are then those expenditures in which enabling conditions and awareness of need do the job alone. Conflicts between different possibilities of satisfying different needs characterize genuine expenditure decisions. And such conflicts, and the need for and the possibility of choosing, are not infrequent.

Undoubtedly not all consumer expenditures enter into conflict with each other. The choice of consumers is limited in a way which was mentioned in the previous chapter but which has received too little attention up to now. There is need to introduce concepts into consumer economics that have been widely used only in business economics. Consumers have fixed charges or make expenditures which, at the moment when they are made, are predetermined by previous decisions.

The study of fixed or prior charges on household budgets should probably be made without distinguishing between what economists consider expenditures and what they consider savings. Premiums on life insurance policies, repayments of installment or mortgage debt (principal as well as interest), rent and charges for utilities, real-estate and income taxes are usually fixed charges. These and many similar outlays of money are frequently made prior even to subsistence expenditures—except in case of dire need, unemployment, or emergencies, when failure to meet the prior charges may plunge the family into the equivalent of bankruptcy. There are other fixed charges, too, which, though less pressing, remove some money outlays from the choice situation. Earlier decisions, such as signing up for payroll deduction to purchase savings bonds or promising to contribute to a charity or to a club regularly in the future, may predetermine later expenditures. Expenses for tuition of children, for the upkeep of homes, for gas to run the car, and many others may fall into the same category.

What, then, are the major consumer choices with which the analysis of consumer behavior is primarily concerned? The answer to this question will differ according to whether we consider restriction or expansion of money outlays. As said before, under the impact of unfavorable or catastrophic developments, consumers do face the problem of meeting their fixed charges and continuing their habitual expenditures. They may then have the choice of which of them to discontinue or to restrict. In the absence of such unfavorable developments, the primary choice of consumers does not appear to concern the question of which but the question of when. Preliminary investigations appear to show that the major question, most commonly raised, is not whether a car or a refrigerator should be bought or a life insurance policy or savings bonds should be contracted for. It is the timing of money outlays that represents the most usual problem of choice. A family needs a refrigerator; the need is psychologically real and possibilities to buy it are given; should the refrigerator be bought "now" or later? Should the purchase of a house, a car, a fur coat, or a man's suit be made or postponed?

We referred before to the fact that when, in surveys, consumers who had bought cars during the year prior to the interview were asked, "Why did you buy the car?" many gave answers of hardly any explanatory value. "I needed the car," "I wanted the car"—were answers which seemed to imply that there was no real conflict or choice present with respect to buying or not buying the car. When, however, the question had the form "Why did you buy the car at that time?" it evoked much more detailed answers. Many people, in reply to that question, referred to the factors that made their need urgent, or discussed income and price developments and prospects. It appears that the timing of certain large purchases was often carefully considered and even debated within the family or with friends. Making expenditures at a given time or postponing them then appears to represent a real consumer choice. The postponement of certain expenditures may result in saving part of the income, while making them at a given time may lead to saving little or even to drawing upon previous savings.

Economic analysis is mainly concerned with consumer choices that have significance not only for the individual himself, and not only for one or a few producers and sellers, but for the trend in the economy. From the point of view of economic fluctuations, the major choice is the one with which we started our analysis and which we resume in the next two chapters, the choice between satisfying current needs and satisfying future needs, the choice between spending and saving. The timing of spending or of saving is of particular importance because of the effect on the economy of "bunching" expenditures for durable goods or of abstaining from such expenditures. The form of saving, that is, the choice between different kinds of assets, is another important choice where consumers exercise great latitude.

The power of consumers to make decisions that affect the entire economy is, of course, limited by outside circumstances, first of all, by their income. But the assumption that decisions by consumers can be disregarded because the multitude of factors that enter into individual decision formation will cancel out is contrary to the facts of group motivation. Since consumer choices are often group-determined, it is probable that similar considerations will influence a great many consumers at the same time. In other words, many consumers will use the latitude available to them in the same way. Therefore, in proceeding with the analysis of the factors influential in consumer decisions, we shall assume that consumer choices contribute to shaping economic developments, at least in the present-day high-income, high-asset economy of ours. Consumers have that power because they can and do make autonomous decisions, and because, as we shall see later, business decisions are sometimes based on the flow of consumer purchases, that is, on consumers' decisions.

NOTES TO CHAPTER 6

DISTRIBUTION OF INCOME AND OF INCOME CHANGES

Statistical data on the distribution of income, income changes, and income expectations need to be presented to supplement the discussion in the text. The most usual way of analyzing distribution of income is by ascertaining the proportion of consumer units that fall into each of different income brackets. This is done in Table 4, which deals with the first few postwar years.

The tables in this section are taken, unless otherwise indicated, from the Surveys of Consumer Finances conducted by the Survey Research Center of the University of Michigan for the Federal Reserve Board. Survey data are presented in per cent of the population covered. The number of spending units in the nation is estimated at less than 47 million in 1946, about 49 million in 1947, over 50 million in 1948, and about 52 million in 1949. For further data on the distribution of income and assets, see the reports of the surveys in the 1949 and 1950 issues of the *Federal Reserve Bulletin*.

TABLE 4.   DISTRIBUTION OF SPENDING UNITS BY SIZE OF INCOME
(Percentage distribution of all spending units)

Annual money income before taxes	1946	1947	1948	1949
Under $1,000	17	14	12	14
$1,000–$1,999	23	22	18	19
2,000– 2,999	25	23	23	21
3,000– 3,999	17	17	20	19
4,000– 4,999	8	10	12	11
5,000– 7,499	6	9	10	11
$7,500 and over	4	5	5	5
Total	100	100	100	100

NOTE: The total income of the over 50 million spending units in the nation in 1948 is estimated from the survey at 176 billion dollars in 1948. If this figure is contrasted with "personal income" as estimated by the Commerce Department—212 billion dollars for 1948—differences in concepts and coverage must be kept in mind. Personal income as defined by the Commerce Department includes income in kind, imputed income, and some income which does not flow to consumers; the surveys do not cover the institutional and the transient population. It is estimated that more than one-half of the difference between 176 and 212 billion dollars is accounted for by these factors. The remaining understatement of income obtained from surveys as against data of the Commerce Department may be due to sampling and reporting errors in the surveys as well as to overestimates by the Commerce Department.

For estimates of the distribution of spending units by size of income *after* taxes, see "1949 Survey of Consumer Finances," Part III, *Federal Reserve Bulletin*, July, 1949.

Income in Table 4 is measured in dollars the purchasing power of which has varied. Prices advanced during the first three of the four years considered, so that a decline in the proportion of units with less than $1,000 or $2,000 income may have represented income increases that kept pace with price increases. If Table 4 were to be extended to prewar years, the information would be of little value in itself. There were considerably fewer units with over $5,000 income before the war than after the war, but $5,000 meant a great deal more before than after the war. And even if the prices paid by consumers had remained stable, standards of living might have changed. It is questionable whether "having a high income" is best defined as having an income of more than $5,000 or more than $10,000. High income may be more adequately characterized as belonging to the top 5 or top 10 per cent of income receivers, and low income as belonging to the bottom decile or quintile in the distribution.[6] Finally, we should note that Table 4 presents the distribution of spending units by income and not the distribution of incomes among spending units.

It is possible to do some justice to these arguments. The distribution of postwar American incomes is presented in Table 5. First, for each year, the spending units were ranked according to the size of their incomes, and then they were divided into ten groups, each containing one-tenth of the units. The limits of each group were different in every one of the four years; the absolute number of all units was likewise different, since the American population rose; the total amount of income also increased year by year. But the table is prepared in such a way that these differences can be disregarded. It shows the percentage of total income received by each tenth of the spending units in each of the years.

TABLE 5. DISTRIBUTION OF INCOME RECEIVED

Spending units ranked according to size of income	Percentage of money income before taxes received by each tenth			
	1946	1947	1948	1949
Lowest tenth	1	1	1	1
Second tenth	3	3	3	3
Third tenth	5	4	5	5
Fourth tenth	6	6	6	6
Fifth tenth	7	7	7	8
Sixth tenth	9	9	9	9
Seventh tenth	10	10	10	11
Eighth tenth	12	12	12	12
Ninth tenth	15	15	15	15
Highest tenth	32	33	32	30
Total	100	100	100	100

The information presented in Table 5 refers to income before taxes, but the proportions of income received by the various deciles of the population are similar even when income after taxes is considered. We learn from the table that in the

[6] Concerning the role of a person's position in the income distribution, see D. S. Brady and R. D. Friedman, "Savings and the Income Distribution," in *Studies in Income and Wealth*, Vol. 10, National Bureau of Economic Research. 1947.

first four postwar years the top 10 per cent of the spending units received about one-third of the total income, while the lowest 10 per cent got only 1 per cent; all units in the top 20 per cent (the top quintile) received somewhat less than 50 per cent, and in the bottom quintile, 4 per cent of the total income. This means—what was of course well known and did not require any proof—that incomes are not equal in the United States. The degree of inequality has been judged by some as extremely large and bound to have disastrous social consequences. According to others, the prevailing income inequality is advantageous, since it produces much-needed incentives to people to better their situation.

It is not easy to obtain information on long-run changes in income concentration because data for more remote years, say, for any period of the nineteenth century, are not available, and data for prewar years are not strictly comparable. It required complex statistical work and the making of numerous estimates to produce Table 6, which compares the 1947 income distribution with that in two earlier years.

TABLE 6. DISTRIBUTION OF INCOME RECEIVED BEFORE AND AFTER
THE SECOND WORLD WAR

Family units ranked according to size of income	Percentage of money income before taxes		
	1935–1936	1941	1947
Lowest fifth	4.0	3.5	4.0
Second fifth	8.7	9.1	9.8
Third fifth	13.6	15.3	15.4
Fourth fifth	20.5	22.5	22.6
Highest fifth	53.2	49.6	48.2
Total ·........................	100.0	100.0	100.0

NOTE: Taken from the *Economic Report of the President,* transmitted to the Congress, January, 1949, p. 91. The methods of computing these data from three different surveys using different methods are described in this report, as well as in the July, 1948, *Economic Report,* pp. 66ff. Table 6 differs from Table 5 insofar as it refers to family units and not spending units and as it attempts to correct for families omitted from one or the other survey, and also for errors of sampling and reporting. Some family units consist of single persons.

No very great differences in the distribution of income appear in this table when a prewar year with rather substantial unemployment (1935–1936) is compared with a prosperous postwar year (1947). The share of the top 20 per cent of the families in total income shows, however, a slight decline. From 1929 to the postwar years, there was probably a rather substantial decline in the proportion of income received by the top income receivers (according to estimates prepared for 1929 by the Brookings Institution).

By using the methods of computation applied in Tables 5 and 6 comparability is achieved but some real and significant differences between different years are made to disappear. Suppose in two different years a given quintile of the families had the same share of total income; does this mean that they were equally well off? Not necessarily, because in one year a 50 per cent share in total income may represent a small, and in another year a large total amount. In one year, expenditures for subsistence may take up most of the income received, and in another year only a small part of it. These considerations apply very decidedly to a comparison of income shares during prewar and postwar years. Aggregate consumer income, and the total income of each quintile or decile of the families, increased greatly from 1935 to 1947, even when measured by its purchasing power.

Income distribution in two consecutive years may be quite similar in spite of a substantial number of changes in income. It may happen that the number of consumer units who moved up from one bracket to another during a given year is similar to the number who moved down from the higher to the lower bracket. Therefore, the data presented before need to be supplemented by data on the distribution of income changes. Table 7 shows that in each of the postwar years income increases were more frequent than income declines.

TABLE 7.   DISTRIBUTION OF CHANGES IN MONEY INCOME BEFORE TAXES
(Percentage distribution of all spending units)

Income in second year as compared with income in first year	1945– 1946	1946– 1947	1947– 1948	1948– 1949
Much larger	17	18	20	16
Somewhat larger	25	31	31	23
About the same	27	30	27	29
Somewhat smaller	16	11	12	16
Much smaller	12	8	6	10
Not ascertained	3	2	4	6
Total	100	100	100	100

NOTE: Income for the "second year" was determined by asking the heads of the spending units 13 questions about different forms of income received by each member of the unit. After this inquiry, the following question was asked: "We found that your income during the year just ended was $_____. Thinking back to the year before that, was your income about the same, or was it larger or smaller than in the year just ended? (If larger or smaller) Could you say that it was much larger (smaller) or only slightly larger (smaller)?" Some respondents reported the dollar amount of their incomes in the previous year. In such cases, income changes of 4 per cent or less were considered as "about the same," changes of 5 to 24 per cent as "somewhat" larger or smaller, and changes of 25 per cent or more as "much" larger or smaller. Other respondents told whether their incomes had been much or slightly higher (lower) or about the same for the previous year.

Reference was made in the text to an attempt to measure people's subjective evaluation of changes in their financial position in addition to changes in their income. Table 8 presents the results of that inquiry at different periods. By comparing Tables 7 and 8, it appears that in each of the first four postwar years the proportion of units whose incomes increased was larger than the proportion who thought that they were better off than a year before.

TABLE 8.   EVALUATION OF CHANGES IN FINANCIAL POSITION
(Percentage distribution of all spending units)

Opinion about financial situation *	Early 1947	Early 1948	Early 1949	Early 1950
Better off now than a year ago	31	29	33	32
Same	30	28	35	32
Worse off now than a year ago	34	39	30	34
Uncertain	2	2	1	1
Not ascertained	3	2	1	1
Total	100	100	100	100

* The questions were: "Would you say you people are better or worse off financially now than you were a year ago? Why do you say so?"

The results of one form of inquiry into people's income expectations are shown in Table 9. The upper part of the table shows that at various periods at least three-fourths of all units were able to answer a question about their income prospects. Further inquiries about the reasons for income expectations and the certainty attached to them revealed that a substantial proportion of both those who expected income increases and those who expected income decreases thought they had good reasons for their expectations. In addition to past achievements and failures, on the one hand, and the general economic outlook, on the other hand, occasionally other factors were also discussed when people were asked to explain why they expected their incomes to go up or go down. Among these we may mention references to a new job recently obtained or to be obtained in the near future, or to a new business venture recently started or planned. Some other people spoke of their being in ill health to explain expected income declines or of their having recovered from illness to explain expected income increases. Finally, forthcoming changes in the number of family members working influenced some people's income expectations. Special studies are needed to investigate the relation of income expectations to the feeling of security or insecurity. It is possible that such attitudes not only shape some people's income expectations but also affect their spending and saving behavior directly.

Table 9 shows also the results of repeated inquiries into attitudes concerning the country's economic prospects. Most people, irrespective of income, occupation, or education appeared to have opinions both about the prevailing eco-

TABLE 9. DISTRIBUTION OF ATTITUDES TOWARD PERSONAL INCOME PROSPECTS
AND THE GENERAL ECONOMIC OUTLOOK
(Percentage distribution of all spending units)

Expectation	Early 1947	Early 1948	Early 1949	July, 1949	Early 1950
Own income a year from now: *					
Income will be larger.........	23	27	27	23	28
Income will be about the same.	42	38	46	41	32
Income will be smaller........	14	10	17	18	11
Uncertain, it depends.........	19	23	9	17	27
Not ascertained	2	2	1	1	2
Total	100	100	100	100	100
General economic outlook: †					
Good times ahead............	55	47	47	38	40
Partly good, partly bad.......	7	6	14	15	15
Bad times ahead.............	22	26	25	31	18
Uncertain, no change.........	14	13	10	14	19
Not ascertained	2	8	4	2	8
	100	100	100	100	100

* The questions were: "How about a year from now—do you think that you will be making more or less money than you are now, or will you be making about the same? Why will that be?" Farm operators are not included in this table.

† The questions were: "Now considering the country as a whole, do you think we will have good times or bad times or what during the next twelve months or so? Can you tell me a little more about what you see for 1949? Do you consider that we are having good times or bad times now?"

nomic situation and about the expected economic situation. They were able to explain what they meant and to give reasons for their opinions. The opinions remained remarkably stable in the period 1947 to 1949. The stability was observed not only with respect to the distribution of the opinions of all people but also with respect to opinions expressed by the same people at different times. For instance, 41 per cent of a sample interviewed both at the beginning of 1948 and of 1949 gave similar opinions at both dates, 20 per cent slightly changed opinions, and only 18 per cent reversed their opinions (the remaining 21 per cent had no definite opinions at either date). This finding seems to indicate that what the surveys found out were not *ad hoc* opinions formed at the time of the interview in order to give some kind of answer, but opinions of some reliability and endurance.

Those who expected good times to come during the first few postwar years were obviously "right." More important is the question of fulfillment of income expectations. The results of an inquiry into that subject are shown in Table 10.

At the beginning of 1948, 26 per cent of a sample expected their 1948 incomes to be higher than their 1947 incomes, and 13 per cent expected them to be lower. In fact, as ascertained a year later, 54 per cent of the same sample had income increases and 29 per cent income decreases. The absolute magnitudes do not seem to be good indicators of future developments, but their relationship was fairly correct. Furthermore, we find that one-third of the sample predicted the trend of their incomes correctly and an additional one-fourth fairly correctly (the expectation "no change" is always more frequent than the actual development "no change").

TABLE 10.   FULFILLMENT OF INCOME EXPECTATIONS

Income	Expected 1948 income as against 1947 income, per cent (first interview)	Actual 1948 income as against 1947 income, per cent (second interview)
Larger (by 5% or more)...........	26	54
About the same...................	49	14
Smaller (by 5% or more)	13	29
Uncertain, not ascertained..........	12	3
Total	100	100

After an interval of 12 months	Expected income (first interview)	Actual income (second interview)		Per cent
Correspondence	....	....		32
	Larger	Larger	19	
	Same	Same	6	
	Smaller	Smaller	7	
Partial correspondence	....	....		24
	Same	Larger by 5-24%	12	
	Same	Smaller by 5-24%	8	
	Somewhat larger or smaller	Same	4	
Lack of correspondence.......	....	....		29
	Same	Much larger	11	
	Same	Much smaller	5	
	Larger	Smaller	7	
	Smaller	Larger	6	
Uncertain, not ascertained ...	....	....		15
				100

NOTE: The sample consisted of 655 urban spending units who were asked early in 1948 about their income expectations (first interview) and early in 1949 about their actual income developments (second interview).

How about the predictive value of average expectations? Hardly anybody would, of course, use the data in the upper left column of Table 10 to predict at the beginning of 1948 that the 1948 national income would be higher than the 1947 national income (although such a prediction, had it been made, would have proved correct). But suppose we presented data on the distribution of income expectations at half-yearly intervals over several years; then the time trend, for instance, of the difference between the frequency of expected income increases over expected income decreases might serve as an indicator of improvement or deterioration in attitudes. To be sure, further studies must be undertaken for that purpose: changes, if any, in the reasons for income expectations must be taken into account; the time trends must be studied separately for low-, middle-, and high-income people; the rate of expected income changes must be considered; and the relation of income expectations to expenditures and savings must be studied at each date.

The results of the study concerning the relation of income expectations to past income changes that has been discussed in the text are presented in Table 11. It is shown in the bottom row of the table that the frequency of upward and downward income changes varied considerably at different times during 1949–1950. (Data on people who had stable income trends are omitted from the table.) Furthermore, it is shown that those with past income increases were at all times more optimistic, and those with past income decreases at all times more

TABLE 11. RELATION OF INCOME EXPECTATIONS TO PAST INCOME CHANGES
(Current earning rate compared to that a year ago)

Expected rate of earning a year from now	Making more now				Making less now			
	Jan.-Feb., 1949	July, 1949	Oct., 1949	Jan.-Feb., 1950	Jan.-Feb., 1949	July, 1949	Oct., 1949	Jan.-Feb., 1950
Will make more.............	35%	32%	39%	43%	22%	22%	22%	30%
Will make the same..........	38	39	39	29	24	26	26	18
Will make less..............	10	15	11	7	21	29	23	16
Don't know, not ascertained..	17	14	11	21	33	23	29	36
Total....................	100%	100%	100%	100%	100%	100%	100%	100%
Proportion of all spending units in each group.........	42%	24%	22%	30%	21%	36%	29%	27%

NOTE: At each of the four dates, representative samples of consumer units were asked: (1) "Are you making as much money now as you were a year ago, or more or less?" (2) "How about a year from now—do you think that you will be making more money or less money than you are now, or what do you expect?" The relation of the answers received to the two questions is presented in the table. For example, early in 1949, 42 per cent of all units said they were making more than a year ago, and of these units 35 per cent said they were expecting to make more a year later. Farm operators are not included in this table.

pessimistic (and more frequently uncertain) than the other group. But the proportion of people whose expectations had the same direction as their past trends, and who showed a reversal in direction, varied at different times. These variations may be understood through studying the variations in the same people's general economic outlook during the year 1949.

Further studies revealed that in October, 1949, more than one-half of those who reported an income decline called it an unexpected development. Optimistic income expectations were found much more frequently among these people than among those who reported that their income had declined according to expectation.

LEVEL OF ASPIRATION

A concise summary of the studies on the level of aspiration is to be found in Chapter 10 of *Personality and the Behavior Disorders,* edited by J. McV. Hunt, Vol. 1, New York, 1944. The chapter is written by Kurt Lewin, Tamara Dembo, Leon Festinger, and P. S. Sears; the first author was mainly responsible for the development of the concept and its experimental verification. The concept has been applied to economic motivations and their relation to remuneration by N. R. F. Maier in *Psychology in Industry,* Boston, 1946, Chaps. 12 and 13.

Concerning the tendency to resume unfinished tasks, the basic experiments are by two pupils of Lewin, B. Zeigarnik and M. Ovsiankina. They were published in the *Psychologische Forschung,* Vols. 9 and 11, 1927 and 1928.

The studies of Centers and Cantril on income satisfaction and income aspiration that were mentioned in the text are based on a sample survey conducted by the Office of Public Opinion Research in Princeton. A relatively small sample of adults—selected by quota sampling—were asked after their current weekly family income was determined: "About how much more money than that do you think your family would need to have the things that might make your family happier or more comfortable than it is now?" ("Income Satisfaction and Income Aspiration," *Journal of Abnormal and Social Psychology,* Vol. 41, 1946, p. 66). The amounts of additional money "needed" were found to increase with income. For instance, persons with a weekly income of about $25 said, on the average, that they would need $16 more; persons with about $50 income that they would need $30 more; and persons with over $100 income that they would need $100 more. In order to understand fully what people had in mind when they answered the question, many more questions should have been asked. (See Part Five for a discussion of sampling and interviewing methods and, especially, of possible pitfalls of reliance on quota sampling and on one single question.) Yet later more detailed studies of Centers seem to provide evidence for the conclusion which he formulates as follows: "The higher people's occupational status is now, the more likely they are to aspire to even higher positions" ("Motivational Aspects of Occupational Stratification," *Journal of Social Psychology,* Vol. 28, 1948, p. 199).

DISTRIBUTION OF ASSETS

Table 12 presents the best available estimates of aggregate data both before and after the war and indicates the tremendous increase in consumers' liquid assets. Statistical information supplementing this table and the discussion in the text is needed concerning the distribution of liquid asset holdings. In the Surveys of Consumer Finances, which consider only liquid assets other than currency holdings, it was found that the great majority of consumer units had some bank deposits or government savings bonds after the war (Table 13). The proportion of owners declined somewhat during the first postwar years; this decline corresponded to an increase in the number of spending units in the nation, so that the number of units holding liquid assets remained substantially stable.

TABLE 12.   ESTIMATES OF AGGREGATE PERSONAL HOLDINGS OF LIQUID
ASSETS BEFORE AND AFTER THE SECOND WORLD WAR
(In billions of dollars)

Type of holding	End of 1939	End of 1945	End of 1948
Demand deposits	7	25	29
Time deposits	28	51	62
Government securities	6	42	40
Currency	4	21	20
Total	45	139	151

SOURCE: *Federal Reserve Bulletin,* July, 1949, p. 794.

TABLE 13.   DISTRIBUTION OF SPENDING UNITS BY SIZE OF LIQUID ASSET HOLDINGS
(Percentage distribution of all spending units)

Liquid-asset holdings *	Early 1947	Early 1948	Early 1949	Early 1950
None	24	27	29	31
$1–$499	26	28	29	27
500–1,999	28	24	22	20
2,000–4,999	14	12	12	13
$5,000 and over............	8	9	8	9
Total	100	100	100	100

* United States government bonds and various kinds of bank deposits; currency is not included.

If liquid assets are ranked according to their size, it is found that a relatively small percentage of all holders own most of the liquid assets (reference to this finding was made in the Notes to Chapter 2). If, however, liquid-asset holdings are set in relation to the incomes of the holders, as is done in Table 14, low-income people are found to hold a relatively small but nevertheless substantial share.

TABLE 14. DISTRIBUTION OF LIQUID-ASSET HOLDINGS BY EACH TENTH OF THE NATION'S SPENDING UNITS, RANKED BY SIZE OF INCOME *

Spending units ranked according to their income	Percentage of liquid assets held		
	Early 1947	Early 1948	Early 1949
Lowest tenth	3	5	3
Second tenth	4	4	4
Third tenth	4	4	3
Fourth tenth	5	4	6
Fifth tenth	7	6	6
Sixth tenth	7	5	6
Seventh tenth	7	7	8
Eighth tenth	9	8	9
Ninth tenth	15	14	11
Highest tenth	39	43	44
Total	100	100	100

* Distribution of liquid assets at the beginning of 1947 was determined by ranking spending units according to their 1946 incomes, at the beginning of 1948 and 1949 by ranking the units according to their 1947 and 1948 incomes, respectively. Liquid-asset holdings include United States government bonds and bank deposits.

The distribution of the frequency of various types of consumer assets and indebtedness among consumers is shown in Table 15. This table does not take the value of the assets into consideration; the owner of a very small life insurance policy or an old jalopy or a small, heavily mortgaged shack is given the same standing as the person who has several thousand dollars in each of his investments. Still, the table shows that there are certain kinds of assets that are relatively widely distributed and others that are held by comparatively few people. The higher the income, the more frequent is the ownership of every type of asset.

When the value of different kinds of assets is considered, the differences between the holdings of low- and high-income groups appear much larger. Low-income groups not only hold assets less frequently than high-income groups but also hold assets of smaller value. Curves drawn for each type of asset rise with income. Yet the various types of assets seem to fall into three groups. There are assets with respect to which the increase of the curves with income is gradual, and even low-income groups hold substantial amounts. Owner-occupied homes, life insurance, and automobiles fall into this category. Liquid assets constitute a second group of greater dependency on income. Investments in real

TABLE 15. FREQUENCY OF SPENDING UNITS HAVING VARIOUS TYPES OF ASSETS AND DEBTS, EARLY 1949

(Percentage of all spending units and of units in specified income groups)

1948 annual money income before taxes	Life insurance	Liquid assets	Auto-mobile	Home or farm*	Other real estate†	Busi-ness‡	Corporate stock§	Mortgage, installment, and consumer debt
Under $1,000	50	44	23	46	10	3	3	28
$1,000 – $1,999	64	59	31	30	12	5	3	38
$2,000 – 2,999	78	65	43	36	11	5	5	51
$3,000 – 3,999	85	78	59	46	14	6	6	60
$4,000 – 4,999	87	87	69	54	17	9	9	65
$5,000 – 7,499	92	94	77	59	28	23	15	64
$7,500 and over	92	99	87	70	44	43	36	60
All units	77	71	51	45	16	9	8	51

* Owner-occupied home or farm.

† Real estate other than home or farm on which owner is living. Includes lots, one- or two-family houses, apartment houses, summer or weekend homes, commercial or rental property, farms owned by nonfarmers, and additional farms owned by farmers.

‡ Full or part interest in a nonfarm, unincorporated business or privately held corporation.

§ Common and preferred stock of corporations open to investment by the general public.

estate, businesses, and securities fall into a third group; substantial amounts of these assets are held almost exclusively by high-income people.

One of the methods used in the Surveys of Consumer Finances to determine consumers' attitudes toward various assets consisted in presenting to the respondents alternative possibilities for investments. No mention was made in that inquiry of life insurance, home ownership, or automobiles because it was thought that, with few exceptions, American families were favorably disposed toward these assets. The question asked what the respondent thought would be the wisest thing for a man to do with money he does not need for his expenses;

TABLE 16. REASONS FOR AND AGAINST HOLDING VARIOUS TYPES OF ASSETS, EARLY 1949 *

(Percentage distribution of spending units with incomes of $3,000 and over)

Reason given †	Type of asset				
	Savings account	Checking account	Savings bonds	Real estate	Common stock
For holding...................	41	18	92	14	8
Safe........................	14	1	48	5	2
High rate of return............	6	‡	34	8	5
Liquid......................	16	4	3	0	0
Familiar with................	‡	‡	1	0	0
Help country.................	0	0	5	0	0
Convenient...................	4	12	0	0	0
Not liquid, favorable..........	1	0	2	0	0
Hedge against inflation........	0	0	0	1	‡
Capital gain expected.........	0	0	0	1	‡
Against holding................	39	19	12	63	69
Not safe.....................	4	1	1	17	28
Low rate of return............	30	9	6	2	1
Not liquid....................	2	0	5	1	1
Not familiar with.............	1	1	‡	6	34
Takes lots of money to buy.....	0	0	0	7	3
Too liquid, unfavorable........	2	9	‡	0	0
No protection against inflation..	‡	‡	‡	0	0
Capital loss expected.........	0	0	0	30	3
No reason given §..............	34	67	24	31	31

* The questions were: "Suppose a man has some money over and above what he needs for his expenses. What do you think would be the wisest thing for him to do with his money nowadays—put it in a savings account or in a checking account, buy government savings bonds with it, invest in real estate, or buy common stock with it? Why do you make that choice? You didn't discuss . . . What do you think of . . . ?"

† When a respondent gave more than one reason for or against holding a specific type of asset, each reason was tabulated. Consequently, the totals exceed 100.

‡ Less than one-half of 1 per cent.

§ Some respondents did not discuss each one of the five types of assets.

whether he should put such money in a savings or checking account, in savings bonds, in real estate, or in common stock. The main purpose of this question was to introduce a further question, namely, why the respondent made the choice he did, and more specifically what he thought of each of the five types of assets mentioned.

Not all respondents had opinions on each of the five types of assets. But among those who expressed opinions, only savings bonds met with overwhelmingly favorable comment. With regard to real estate and common stock, the attitudes were predominantly unfavorable (Table 16).

Annual publications of the Institute of Life Insurance, entitled "Life Insurance Ownership among U.S. Families" and prepared by the Survey Research Center from data collected in the Surveys of Consumer Finances, present detailed information on the distribution of premium payments on life insurance policies.

Regarding the frequency with which owners of durable goods replace these goods by newer models, only sporadic information is available. In 1948, about 80 per cent of the purchasers of new cars did trade in or sell cars when they made the purchases. With respect to purchasers of used cars, the proportion was much lower. It is known that before the war the proportions were somewhat higher but may have been inflated owing to advantageous trade-in terms. In 1948, however, the proportions may have been relatively low because of demand deferred from wartime and satisfied during that year.

As an example of the measurement of "discretionary purchasing power," see the paper "Consumer Purchasing Power—1949," by Arno H. Johnson (J. Walter Thompson Company, New York, 1949; also by the same author, "Market Potentials, 1948," *Harvard Business Review,* Vol. 26, 1948, pp. 11*ff*.). The method used is to deduct from income after taxes in postwar years the "basic living costs necessary to maintain the 1940 standard of living for food, clothing and shelter." The result is called "surplus income for discretionary spending or saving." This surplus income rose from 26½ billion dollars in 1940 to over 100 billion in 1949, according to the calculations presented. The increase between these two amounts is, of course, much larger than the increase in prices from 1940 to 1949.

As to the classification of consumer assets, the discussion in the text is in full accord with the following recent statement by A. G. Hart: "From the standpoint of the motivational problem, no classification of assets and liabilities is perfect" (*Studies in Income and Wealth,* Vol. 12, p. 86, National Bureau of Economic Research, 1950).

CHAPTER 7

SPENDING AND SAVING: THEORETICAL ANALYSIS

The study of the factors that influence consumers in their spending and saving is primarily a problem for empirical research. But long before this research had made progress, an extensive body of economic theory about consumer behavior had been worked out. This is of great advantage for empirical studies because they need not proceed in a haphazard manner but can be directed toward confirming, disproving, or modifying theories. It therefore behooves us to begin the discussion of the problem by recapitulating the theoretical analysis of spending and saving. First, the most developed part of the theory will be discussed, namely, the one applicable to the spending and saving of the entire economy. Afterward, parts of the theory applicable to the spending and saving of individual consumers will be taken up.

MACROECONOMIC MODELS

Our first task is to bring the economic significance of consumer choices into clear focus. An economic model which has recently been widely used may serve to illustrate the role and function of the consumer in our economy. In this model the flow of money in the economy is traced in a simple, schematic fashion. We consider first the payments made and received by the XYZ Telephone Company, which provides telephone service in one of our large cities. The company disburses money for wages and salaries. It purchases equipment and materials. It pays taxes on real property, on telephone billings, and on profits. Finally, it pays interest on its debt and dividends on its common stock. As Fig. 7 shows, wages and salaries go to consumers, payments for materials to business firm, taxes to government (local and national), and interest and dividends either to consumers or to business firms (according to whether the bonds and stocks are held by private individuals or firms). Where does the XYZ Company get the money it pays out? It bills all those who have telephone service, that is, individual consumers, business firms, and government. Those who receive payments from the XYZ Company are not identical with those who make payments to it, and the total amounts paid out to, say, consumers need not

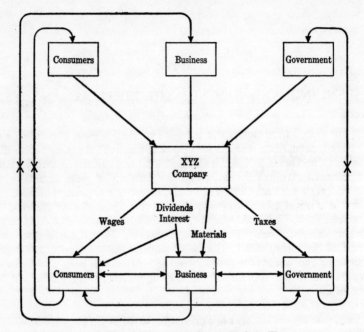

FIG. 7. Money Flow to and from a Business Firm.

be the same as the total amounts received from consumers. Nor must all payments made by the company in a given period of time be identical with all its receipts for that period. The company may operate at a deficit and use previously accumulated reserves or borrow money to cover excess payments; or it may disburse less than it takes in and thus create reserves.

What do the business firms do with the money they receive from the XYZ Company for materials sold to it? They use it to make payments to consumers, business firms, and government. Suppose, then, we change our schematic presentation of money flow and substitute all business firms in the country for the XYZ Company. Now payments made by one business firm to another disappear from the scheme; such payments would occur within the central square of the new figure. All payments made by Business go to Consumers or Government, and all payments received by Business come from Consumers or Government. Let us assume further that Government budgets are in balance; Government disburses exactly and promptly what it takes in. In that case, the money circulation will go on without interruption if Consumers and Business pay out, without any time lag, all that they receive and no more than they receive. If this happens in Period 1, consumer income, the money received by all consumers, will be the same in the subsequent Period 2 as it was in Period 1.

Our schematic presentation has the merit that it focuses attention on interruptions of the money flow which lead to diminution of aggregate income in the next period, and on injections into the money flow which lead to enlargement of aggregate income. How can interruptions of the flow occur? Through saving by Consumers, Business, or Government. Consumers may not pay out all money received in the period in which they receive it; that is, they may save part of it. Similarly, there may be business savings and there may be government surpluses. On the other hand, injections of new money may occur through dissaving. In a given period, consumers, for instance, may disburse more money than they receive by drawing on previously accumulated money or by borrowing. Similarly, there may be dissaving by business and government deficits. The signs X in Fig. 7 indicate the possible points of disturbance.

But what happens to money withheld from circulation? If we had no banks and a cash economy in which all payments received and made by consumers were in currency, there would be only one way to interrupt the money flow: locking currency in one's drawer, hiding it under the mattress—that is, hoarding. In our economy, however, this is a rather unimportant way of saving. Money saved by consumers may be entrusted to business firms (for instance, to banks in which the money is deposited) or to the government (by buying savings bonds). It follows that our schematic presentation is incomplete. There is a connection between the points of disturbance. Consumers may not necessarily interrupt the money flow by saving part of their income. Whether saving by consumers will have adverse effects on the economy depends upon what happens to the money saved. If it goes to banks which pay it out in the form of new loans to business firms, or to government to be paid out for wages and materials, the total money flow will not be reduced. If, however, the banks or government do not put consumer savings to use promptly, the effect of these savings will be to interrupt the flow of income. Similar considerations apply to money saved by business and government and to injections of new money by either source. Government deficits need not increase the money flow, because they may be compensated for by saving on the part of business and consumers.

While the savings of any one sector may be used for expenditures by another sector, aggregate net savings of the entire economy can be used only, if they are used at all, for investments. It is then the crucial question whether aggregate net savings exceed aggregate net investments or whether the latter exceed the former. The size of the income flow during the next period depends on that relation. Interruptions of the money circulation or injections into the circulation may originate with any of the three sectors of the economy. But there is an interaction among all the sectors, and it is the net result of this interaction that counts.

The "nation's economic budget," an economic model of a similar type, summarizes "in a few broad figures the flow of goods and purchasing power through the main sectors of the economy: consumer households, business, government activities, and the international area." [1] It differs from the previous schematic model of money flow insofar as it contains estimates of the dollar amounts of all relevant variables (and also in that it takes into account the net effect of money inflow from, and outflow to, foreign countries). The budget for the American economy for a prewar and a postwar year is reproduced in the Notes to this chapter. The budget presents, first, data on the receipts of all consumers, that is, their income after taxes. Second, it contains data on the expenditures of all consumers, that is, what they have spent on goods and services in the same period. The two amounts were not identical in either of the years considered. Income exceeded expenditures, which means that there was a net saving. Similarly, the economic budget helps us to trace receipts and expenditures of the other sectors of the economy and thus to determine which sector provided funds to another sector and which made use of such funds.

Computed for several years, the nation's economic budget is a useful tool of economic analysis. When, for instance, in January of each year, the President's Council of Economic Advisers prepares a preliminary form of the budget for the preceding year—as it has done since 1947—the student is given information about the relative sizes of the economic sectors and their changes during the year. Further, he is given a picture of the amounts saved or dissaved in each sector and the changes in these amounts. But the economic budget does not present a full account of what has been going on in the economy.[2] We must understand the two major shortcomings of the model: it is aggregative, and it is "ex post."

In view of what was said before, the first shortcoming of the economic budget may be discussed briefly. To the unsuspecting student of the budget it may appear as if all that any consumer saves is used by the other sectors of the economy. This is true of the "net savings" of all consumers taken as a unit. But what some consumers save may be used by other consumers. For instance, consumers may lend money to each other, buy real estate or

---

[1] *The Economic Report of the President,* January, 1948, Washington, D.C., p. 31.

[2] This fact is, of course, well known to the Council of Economic Advisers, the agency primarily responsible for the budget at present. The reports of the Council lay great stress on additional information, some of which will be discussed later.

securities from each other, or may invest some of their savings themselves by building homes. Furthermore, some consumers may save while others may dissave and only the net savings of all consumers appear in the budget. Similarly, much of business saving and business investment is carried out within the business sector, for instance, by what is called internal financing. Corporations usually do not distribute their entire income to their stockholders but retain some earnings and use these funds for new investments. How many consumers and business firms, and what kind of consumers and business firms, save and how much they save, and how many consumers and firms dissave and how much—these questions find no answer in the economic budget. The budget is concerned only with the net aggregate transactions between sectors of the economy. It must therefore be supplemented by microeconomic data.

In the economic budget, the interruptions of and injections into the money flow cancel out. The sum of the amounts saved by all sectors is equal to the sum of the amounts invested by all sectors. To understand this equality, we have to introduce two basic equations that are found nowadays in practically all economic textbooks. The first one represents the definition of saving: Saving is what is left over from income after consumption. If S is written for saving, C for consumption, and Y for income,

$$S = Y - C \qquad \text{or} \qquad Y = C + S \qquad (1)$$

This equation holds good for each individual family, each individual business firm, all consumers, all business firms, and the entire economy. The definition of saving as used is meaningful on the macro- as well as the microeconomic level. We must only be aware that S in the formula may be a positive number (when consumption is less than income); it may be zero (when consumption exactly equals income); or it may be negative (when consumption is greater than income and must be paid for in part by dissaving—that is, by borrowing or by using up previously accumulated assets). Income may be zero or negative in some instances, but consumption always has a positive value.

We now turn to the second basic equation, which defines income as the value of output. Total output consists of output either of consumption goods or of investment goods; it is the sum total of all consumption and investment. Therefore, if we write I for investment,

$$Y = C + I \qquad (2)$$

It follows from the two equations that saving is equal to investment.

$$S = I \qquad (3)$$

The second equation, and therefore also the third one, holds good only on the macroeconomic level. They express aggregate relations which cannot be deduced from relations prevailing among individual households or firms. Furthermore, these equations apply only to realized income and investment and not to intended or planned investments. The aggregate data that enter into the economic budget are data summarizing what has happened in a past period. They show how differences between intended savings and investments were resolved. All amounts saved in the past are accounted for in the budget. It is the necessary consequence of the bookkeeping scheme that an excess of receipts of a sector turns up as an expenditure of another sector, and an excess of expenditures as a receipt of another sector. One person's expenditures are another person's receipts. What people have intended to save and to invest may have been very different. But in attempting to carry out their intentions they influence the income flow. If they start out to save more than is used for investment, the income flow is restricted; if intended investments exceed savings and are financed, for instance, through borrowing, the income flow is expanded. Yet what is said about the equality of past savings and past investments, and the effect of differences between intended savings and investments, applies to the entire economy only and not to individual consumers and firms.[3]

The kind of analysis embodied in the nation's economic budget represents accounting "ex post." This concept and its opposite, accounting "ex ante," have been developed by Swedish economists. Data in retrospect, arrived at by looking backward, represent the material of ex post analysis. Ex ante phenomena, on the other hand, consist of anticipations and plans. Analysis of a forward-looking type, shedding light on the factors determining economic action, is ex ante analysis. The results of ex ante analysis may differ from those of ex post analysis, because by carrying out our plans we may influence and change the given conditions.

We discussed in Chapter 5 the inconsistent spending and saving plans of consumers as they were expressed toward the end of the war. This was ex ante analysis; to find out, after the event, how the inconsistencies were resolved is ex post analysis. In our first graphical economic model, we argued that interruptions of, or injections into, the money flow are possible and will affect future income. This was ex ante analysis because, as we learn from the economic budget, ex post, for the economy as a whole, we do not

---

[3] "This is the vital difference between the theory of the economic behavior of the aggregate and the theory of the behavior of the individual unit," says J. M. Keynes about this point. "The changes in the individual's own demand do not affect his income" and "the amount of his own saving is unlikely to have any significant influence on his own income." (*The General Theory of Employment, Interest, and Money,* New York, 1936, pp. 84 and 85.)

find excess savings or excess investments; what we find is that income in the second period was smaller or larger than in the first.

It may be useful to illustrate the problem with a more specific example. Let us take the ownership of government bonds. Every individual consumer who holds such bonds appears to be his own master. He may decide to own fewer bonds or no bonds at all. Can he carry out his decision? Only if there are buyers of bonds. Suppose the government wants to keep the amounts of bonds outstanding unchanged; it neither buys nor sells bonds. Then it is still possible for individuals to sell their bonds, provided other individuals or business firms are willing to buy them. The bonds offered for sale will exert pressure on the price of the bonds. The lower price may induce some individuals or firms to buy them. If it does not, the sellers must abstain from selling. Ex ante, perhaps, there were at a given moment only sellers, that is, people who intended to sell; ex post, sellers and buyers were equal (not in number but in the amounts they sold and bought). From the aggregate ex post data, we only find that at the end of Period 2 the same amount of bonds was outstanding as at the end of Period 1. From the price trend of the bonds, from information about size and frequency of bond transactions, and from data about the distribution of bonds among individual holders and business firms, we may find out more, even ex post. Ex ante information, that is, information on intentions, plans, and attitudes, will supplement the ex post data. Both kinds of information are needed to gain full understanding of what has happened and why it happened.

THE PROPENSITY TO CONSUME AND TO SAVE

We found in the previous section that interruptions of the income flow, and injections into the income flow, may originate in any of the three sectors of the economy. Whether the behavior of any one sector is more important than that of any other we have not yet studied. From certain propositions of economic theory, it follows, however, that consumers do not play an active or autonomous role.

The functional relation between the disposable income of the community and the expenditures on consumption out of that income is called the propensity to consume. The relation between income and amounts saved out of that income is called the propensity to save. These are, thus defined, aggregative relations and, although it would be possible to speak of the propensity of individual units to consume or to save, we shall reserve these terms for relationships prevailing in the entire economy. John Maynard Keynes, in introducing these concepts, defines the propensity to consume in terms of wage units instead of in money, thus eliminating from the discussion fluctuations of the purchasing power of money income. He then presents his fundamental proposition that "the propensity to consume is a fairly stable function so that, as a rule, the amount of aggregate consumption mainly depends on the amount of aggregate income" (*op. cit.,* p. 96).

What is the basis of that statement? Obviously, so Keynes argues, the amount a community spends on consumption may depend not only on its income but also on other objective circumstances and on the subjective needs and habits of its members. Among the objective circumstances, fluctuations of prices and changes of tax rates are recognized as effective. They are, however, eliminated from consideration by defining income level in terms of disposable income in wage units. Other objective circumstances, for instance, the prevailing interest rate, are found to be of secondary importance. The subjective and social incentives, on the other hand, are believed to change slowly. As we have seen before (Chapter 5), motives to save and to consume are thought to depend on institutions, conventions, and education and, therefore, to differ in different cultures, but are not believed to account for short-period changes in consumption. It is therefore argued that in the short run consumption must depend mainly on the rate at which income is earned.

The rate at which income is earned, however, does change. The central issue which determines the shape of the *consumption function* is: How do consumers react to changes in their income? Keynes answers this question by his discovery of a fundamental psychological law. He says:

"The fundamental psychological law, upon which we are entitled to depend with great confidence both a priori from our knowledge of human nature and from the detailed facts of experience, is that men are disposed, as a rule and on the average, to increase their consumption as their income increases, but not by as much as the increase in their income" (*op. cit.,* p. 96).

Similarly, according to Keynes, people will decrease the amounts they spend as their income decreases, but not by as much as the decrease in their income. Let us repeat the thesis again by dividing it into three separate statements. When, under what conditions, is a community willing to widen or to narrow the gap between its income and its consumption?—this is the first question. The answer is: Only when its income increases or decreases. Except for this circumstance, the propensity to consume will remain stable. If there is a change in the income-consumption relation, what will be the direction of that change?—this is the second question. When income increases, the gap between income and consumption will be widened; when income decreases, it will be narrowed. People will spend a smaller part (and save a larger part) of their income when income increases, and spend a larger part (and save a smaller part) when income decreases. What will be the extent of the change in the income-consumption relation?—this is the third question. The change will be smaller than the change in income. The marginal rate of increase (decrease) in consumption will not be as large as the marginal rate of increase (decrease) in income.

The first statement is a reiteration of the thesis about the stability of the propensity to consume. The second statement is, as Keynes says, "obvious" and "beyond dispute." "When our income is increased, it is extremely unlikely that this will have the effect of making us either spend less or save less than before." [4] That we will spend the same after our income is increased is also unlikely, since we will have more money at our disposal. Will we, therefore, spend all that we gained in income, or will we increase the amount we spend so that the proportion of income spent will be the same at the new level as it was before, or will we spend a smaller proportion of the higher income than of the previous lower income? In due time, we will reach the spending rate which is characteristic of the new, higher income level. But the adjustment to that new income level, so Keynes asserts, is slow.

> "For a man's habitual standard of life usually has the first claim on his income, and he is apt to save the difference which discovers itself between his actual income and the expense of his habitual standard; or, if he does adjust his expenditure to changes in his income, he will over short periods do so imperfectly. Thus a rising income will often be accompanied by increased saving, and a falling income by decreased saving, on a greater scale at first than subsequently" (*op. cit.* p. 97).

The last argument is presented in terms of individual families. It is a psychological statement which cannot be true of the aggregate economy unless it is true, as a rule, of individuals. Here, then, we find a psychological principle of behavior of which psychologists were not aware until it was propounded by an economist.

It follows from the considerations just presented that economic analysis need not be concerned with disturbances in the income flow originating in consumer behavior. For, increases or decreases in consumer saving can be derived from changes in other economic magnitudes. Consumers save either the same proportion of their income as before or, if they change their rate of saving, they do so in response to changes in their income in a way that is regular and predictable. It is in business investments alone, and in government surpluses or deficits, that changes in the income flow originate.

[4] J. M. Keynes, "The General Theory of Employment," *Quarterly Journal of Economics*, Vol. 51, 1937, p. 220.

"In Keynes' scheme investment is a free variable, while consumption is rigidly and passively tied to income." [5]

Only a few words need be said about the stability or instability of the aggregate propensity to consume. If the relation of consumer expenditures to disposable income in the United States is calculated for several decades, prior to the 1930's, it will be found to vary little from year to year. But it has been pointed out repeatedly that a high correlation between annual disposable incomes and annual consumer expenditures is obtained by necessity. Since consumer expenditures amount to about 90 per cent of disposable income, we find simply that the whole is correlated with its greatest part. By using relatively rough measures, fluctuations in the propensity to consume, if they occurred, would be obscured. It is therefore of greater interest to study the correlation between the income series and the series of annual saving. Then the correlation appears to be much smaller. Since available data are rough estimates—both real income and amounts saved are magnitudes that are very difficult to determine for the present time and even more difficult for the distant past—they do not represent proof of either the stability or instability of the propensity to save. After 1930, however, there is evidence of erratic fluctuations in the saving rate. In the years 1932 to 1934, according to the estimates of the Commerce Department, consumer expenditures exceeded income, that is, the economy as a whole dissaved; after 1941, as described before, rates of saving were unprecedentedly high (over 20 per cent in 1942 to 1944); and after 1945, there was a sharp drop which, however, probably did not lower the rate of saving to its 1929 level.

Whether the fluctuations in the rate of saving can be explained in terms of changes in income is again a somewhat disputed question. In years of high national income, the community's rate of saving was, on the whole, higher than in years of low national income. Furthermore, in some years in which national income increased, the rate of saving also increased and, conversely, it decreased in some years in which income declined. The record also indicates some years, however, with different trends. In the first two postwar years, for example, national income increased—probably even if measured by its purchasing power—while amounts saved declined sharply. Also, the extent of the year-to-year changes in saving frequently shows substantial variations instead of a rigid dependence on changes in income. But can we rest satisfied even if, as some students of the problem believe, most of the fluctuations in aggregate savings of the American economy can be explained through the consideration of the two variables, income level and income change? In order to understand how and why the community's propensity

[5] A. F. Burns, "Keynesian Economics Once Again," *Review of Economic Statistics*, Vol. 29, 1947, p. 261.

to save changes, we cannot rely on time series of aggregate data alone. We must also study the developments in terms of the behavior of the units which constitute the economy, that is, we must proceed with studies on the microeconomic level.

Students of economic theory may perhaps point out that our procedure has no relevance for the validity of the Keynesian thesis, which was not meant to apply to microeconomic dynamic processes. To be sure, our objective is to analyze economic behavior and not to confirm or disprove specific formulations of economic theory. But the Keynesian theory provides an analytical tool that has stimulated and guided empirical investigations of spending and saving behavior. Furthermore, our method is in accordance with frequent statements in current economic literature and cán be understood in the light of the following quotations: "From the savings and investment relationship in the Keynesian system, we learn how households and business firms make their decisions about the disposition of their current income." [6] Here the problem is posed as it appears to us who attempt to analyze economic decisions. What can we learn about consumers' disposition of their income? "One of the simplest theories of consumer behavior is: individuals decide on the basis of their income how much they will spend and how much they will save (not spend)." [7] There may be factors other than income that are relevant, but they are secondary. In the words of Schumpeter: The consumption function "posits the existence of a unique relation between consumption and income *alone* (both measured in wage units)." [8] This author goes on to say that the aggregative approach achieves a "drastic reduction in the number of variables." Here we find a specific problem for the analysis of consumer behavior: What is the role of the variable "income" in consumer decisions; can other variables be disregarded, or do we gain valuable additional understanding by taking other variables into account?

Statements that consumers are not merely passive agents, and that it is possible to change the propensity to consume even if income has not changed, have been made recently by several economists. We shall refer to some of them later; at the present stage of our discussion, when we are searching for a program of research, the following statement is of the greatest interest to us. According to A. F. Burns, the main issue is "not that the Keynesians regard the consumption function as fixed, but that they attach

[6] L. R. Klein, *The Keynesian Revolution*, p. 69. Copyright, 1947. Used by permission of The Macmillan Company.

[7] L. R. Klein, "A Post-mortem on Transition Predictions of National Product," *Journal of Political Economy*, Vol. 54, 1946, p. 298.

[8] J. A. Schumpeter, "Keynes and Statistics," *Review of Economic Statistics*, Vol. 28, 1946, p. 195.

slight importance to its wanderings" (*op. cit.,* p. 261). We shall study these "wanderings" and the factors possibly contributing to the fluctuations in individual families' rate of spending and saving.

PRINCIPLES OF SAVING AND SPENDING BEHAVIOR

In the light of the theoretical analysis, two broad hypotheses may be formulated concerning the allocation of income between spending and saving. If the hypotheses prove to be valid, a rather simple and consistent picture of the major consumer choices will emerge. And even if, as is probable, the hypotheses prove to be in need of refinement or revision, they will be of great usefulness. They will not only pave the way for empirical research to be reported later, but may also serve to facilitate for the reader of this book the understanding of the complex factors underlying consumer decisions.

Both hypotheses will be presented first as they apply to decisions of individual consumers, that is, on the microeconomic level. But, as we shall see, each hypothesis has a corollary that expresses relationships among aggregate magnitudes. The first hypothesis is embodied in the following statements: The higher the income of a family, the more will it save; the lower its income, the less will it save. Not only the absolute amounts saved but also the proportions of income saved will be correlated with the income level. Among high-income families we shall find those who save a large proportion of their income, and among low-income families those who save nothing or who dissave (that is, whose expenditures exceed their income). The largest savers will be the people who, having a high income, had money left over after they satisfied most of their needs, and the dissavers the people who, because of their low income, were unable to make ends meet and were compelled to dip into their assets or mortgage their future through borrowing.

Since aggregate income will be relatively high in years in which there are many high-income people (and therefore many large savers) and relatively low in years in which there are few such people, we may formulate a parallel hypothesis on the aggregate level: The higher the national income, the larger will be the aggregate amount saved and the larger will be the proportion of total income saved by the entire community. Aggregate savings will be larger in prosperous years than in years of depression, and the savings of a rich country will be larger than the savings of a poor country.

The second hypothesis concerns income change and is derived from Keynes's discussion of the effects of people's habitual standard of life on their expenditures and savings. A family which has had an income increase will save a larger portion of its new, higher income than it did of its previous, lower income because the adjustment of expenditures to the new income level will not be instantaneous. Conversely, after having experienced an income decline, the proportion of income saved will be reduced. The same relationship may also be expressed in the following way: We consider three groups of families, *A, B,* and *C,* which, in a given period, all have the same income; in the preceding period, however, the income of families *A* was lower, of *B* the same, and of *C* higher. Then we will find that the rate of saving of the three groups of families will not be the same; those whose income increased (*A*) will save the most, those whose income decreased (*C*) the least, and the amount saved by those with stable income (*B*) will occupy the middle position.

On the aggregate level, the second hypothesis says: If national income increases, aggregate amounts saved will likewise increase, and if national income decreases, aggregate amounts saved will decrease.

In order to test these hypotheses, we shall have to raise a number of factual questions. In the next chapter we shall present findings about the relation of the income level of individual families, and of the direction of change in their incomes, to their rate of saving. We shall find that on the whole it is true that the higher the income the larger the rate of saving. But, in the last few years at least, there were also low-income families who saved a high proportion of their income, and there were many high-income families who dissaved. Regarding the relation of income changes to saving, the findings will likewise be complex: some findings will appear to be in accord with the second hypothesis and others will contradict it.

Before discussing the empirical investigations of the factors influencing spending and saving, we must raise certain objections to the two hypotheses on the basis of theoretical considerations. There are more fundamental shortcomings involved in the hypotheses than occasional data which do not appear to fit. The consideration of two variables alone, of income level and income change, instead of the entire psychological field which influences consumers, contradicts basic principles of psychological analysis. The term "income change" is being understood in a piecemeal, atomistic way, as if any income increase of $1,000, or 10 per cent, were necessarily equal to any other income increase of $1,000, or 10 per cent, irrespective of expectations and irrespective of income changes experienced by other people (of the group). Further, the terms "spending" and "saving" are used and related to habits without discriminating between different kinds of expenditures and savings. It appears to be necessary to confront the two hypotheses with what we already know about the psychological principles of consumer decisions in order to derive more complex, but at the same time more satisfactory, statements concerning consumers' spending and saving decisions.

1. Consumer Expectations. Since past income changes constitute a part of people's time perspective, it is psychologically unjustified to study their effects without regard to prevailing income expectations. As argued in the preceding chapter, an increase in this year's income over last year's may have different meanings according to the income development expected for the next year (and also according to income changes that occurred previous to last year). The same is true of income declines. Even if we consider only a two-year period, at least six cases need to be distinguished, which can be presented schematically as follows: (1) ++, (2) +=, (3) +−, (4) −−, (5) −=, (6) −+ (the first sign denotes the direction of the *past* income change, and the second the direction of the *expected* income change. The first and the fourth cases represent continuous trends toward higher or lower incomes, the second and fifth cases income changes to higher or lower levels, and the third and sixth cases changes that are considered subjectively to be temporary. It cannot be assumed a priori that the effects of income increases on saving and spending behavior will be the same in the first three cases and of income decreases the same in the second three cases.

Joint treatment of past and expected income changes appears to be preferable to analyzing each change separately. But the major problem confronting the analysis of the propensity to consume is the omission of the study of expectations. Keynes, who assigns great importance to the expectations of businessmen in shaping their policies, does not take expectations into account when he analyzes the factors influencing consumer behavior. He does list consumer expectations among the "objective factors" which influence the propensity to consume but asserts:

> "*Changes in expectations of the relation between the present and the future level of income.*—We must catalogue this factor for the sake of formal completeness. But, whilst it may affect considerably a particular individual's propensity to consume, it is likely to average out for the community as a whole. Moreover, it is a matter about which there is, as a rule, too much uncertainty for it to exert much influence" (*op. cit.,* p. 95).

Keynes does not present any evidence for his arguments. We shall have to question each of his points. First, is it probable that for the community as a whole different income expectations average out? Second, is it true that as a rule there is much uncertainty about income expectations? Finally, is it to be assumed that uncertain expectations do not exert much influence?

In analyzing the origin of expectations, we found that in some cases people expect that to happen which happened before. If, then, income expectations are based on past income changes, it is unlikely that they will average out: if the past year was a good one, most people will have had favorable income trends and will have favorable income expectations, and the reverse will be the case during a downward trend in the economy. When expectations originate in a reorganized field, the averaging out of expectations is still more unlikely. New events may become generally known, new viewpoints may sweep the country or the business community and lead to the emergence of similar expectations among many people at the same time.

The question concerning the uncertainty of income expectations is a question of fact. As has already been mentioned, during the first few postwar years approximately one-fourth of the consumer units expressed uncertainty in the sense that they could not even make a statement about the probable direction of their future income change. But for approximately three-fourths of the consumer units definite income expectations could be ascertained, and these units could be grouped according to the six cases enumerated earlier. Whether uncertain income expectations exert any influence is a further question about which little is known. Possibly it may become necessary, especially when absence of definite expectations is frequent, to study these instances separately from the six cases.

The arguments used by Keynes are not the only ones which enable the economist to rule out the role of income expectations. The same conclusion was recently reached by different trends of thought. J. W. Angell, for instance, after first assigning a great role to expectations, argues that "The general level of anticipations . . . is equivalent to, and can be replaced by, some summary expression for the recent history of incomes." [9] And L. R. Klein puts it still more strongly when he says: "The expected national income depends upon most recently observed levels of national income (how else can expectations be formed?)." [10] According to this argument, expectations can be disregarded because they are necessarily the same as past trends. In other words, it is asserted that instances which we schematically denoted as plus-minus or minus-plus (past income increase and expected income decline, or past income decline and expected income increase) cannot occur.

We have already refuted the underlying argument. It is not true that we *always* do the same as we have done before in similar circumstances, and that we *always* expect the same as has happened to us under similar circumstances. The same item may become part of a different whole, and such reorganization may fundamentally alter the meaning of the part. More specifically with regard to income expectations, several variables have already been discussed which may cause a reorganization of the field and

[9] J. W. Angell, *Investment and Busines Cycles*, p. 85. Copyright, 1941. Courtesy of McGraw-Hill Book Company, Inc.

[10] L. R. Klein, *The Keynesian Revolution*, p. 63. Copyright, 1947. Used by permission of The Macmillan Company.

may lead people to expect future income increases or decreases irrespective of their past income trends.

We tried to show before that people's general economic outlook—what they believe to be the prevailing trend in the economy—may influence their income expectations. It is also possible that an expectation about the direction in which the economy is moving will influence people's spending and saving behavior directly. What will be the effects of optimism or of pessimism on consumer behavior? Certain conclusions emerge from previous discussions which help us to formulate probable answers to this question. The answers must, of course, be tested through empirical research.

If people believe that depression will come and their incomes will decline, their need to accumulate reserves for the future will gain in immediacy. Pessimistic expectations may then retard spending and may especially impede borrowing for the sake of such large purchases as houses or durable goods. Optimistic expectations, on the other hand, especially if they are held both with respect to the general economic trend and to one's own income, may accelerate spending. They may induce people to satisfy immediate desires and to give lesser weight to their needs for accumulating reserves.

Among further economic expectations that may influence spending and saving behavior, expectations concerning the future course of prices must be taken into account. Suppose a person is convinced that in the near future there will be an increase in the price level, or an increase in the prices of things he desires to purchase. Then he may have good reason to do more buying or to buy certain goods before their prices rise. Conversely, expected price declines may induce people to delay their purchases, to wait until prices have declined, in other words, to save their money until prices go down. Under what conditions such behavior will take place is again a question for empirical studies. At this point, price expectations should merely be listed among the factors that possibly influence consumers' spending and saving decisions.

2. Habitual Behavior. Further psychological considerations need to be taken into account when we consider the plausibility of the hypothesis formulated earlier concerning the relation of changes in income to spending and saving. The assumption that the "habitual standard of life" is changed slowly was applied by Keynes to both income increases and decreases. But in the light of psychological findings, it is hardly justifiable to believe that the effects of improvement and of deterioration of conditions on behavior will be just the reverse of each other. "Reward" and "punishment"—to use customary psychological terms—are not simply opposite poles, but have been found to have qualitatively different effects. Discarding an established habit may be relatively easy if conditions become more favorable, while there may be a stronger tendency to maintain habits if conditions become less favorable.

It is possible that habitual standards of expenditure represent a powerful force in shaping our behavior when we experience an income decline but not when we experience an income increase. In case of an income decline, when adjustments in our expenditures hurt us, we will tend to make no adjustments, or to make insufficient adjustments, or to make the adjustments slowly. Therefore, the proportion of income spent shortly after the income decline may increase. In case of an income increase, however, a different situation may prevail. We know that people as consumers have many unsatisfied needs at all times. They need and desire automobiles, household appliances, clothing, medical care, entertainment, and so on, beyond the quantities with which they provide themselves. When their incomes increase, they may become aware of the possibility of satisfying some of these needs. Thus it is possible that an increase in income may become the occasion for large, long-delayed expenditures.

We have emphasized before that there are no definite limits to economic needs and to consumer demand. If it were true that people in general are saturated with goods, increased income would, of course, lead to increased saving. If, however, needs for consumption goods and services usually surpass actual satisfactions with goods and services, and if, moreover, satisfaction with certain goods gives rise to need and demand for further goods, a different conclusion may emerge.

Improvement in enabling conditions—increased income, for instance— permits the satisfaction of desires that could not be satisfied before. If our most powerful desire, the nonfulfillment of which caused us the greatest frustration, was that we were not able to save, increase in income would lead to increased saving. But increase in income may equally well lead to increased expenditures. And the forces directed toward satisfaction with certain goods may be such that when the barrier is broken by an income increase, we may go all the way and buy so many goods that we will save even less than at our previous lower income level.

Thus we have to conclude that breaking with past expenditure habits may be difficult when it is necessary to give up habitual satisfactions but easy when the possibility opens up to satisfy further desires. Yet, even in the first instance a question arises concerning the meaning of the expression "habitual standards of expenditure." Let us assume, first, that the well-ingrained habits of a family relate to what is considered saving. That family would, for example, habitually put $50 in a bank account every month. Then, of course, the hypothesis about slow changes in habits would lead to conclusions other than previously envisaged. An income decline might then result in maintenance of habitual activities, namely, of putting money in the bank, and therefore in a sharp reduction of the family's expenditures.

This illustration is not entirely unrealistic. Although spending and not saving represents usually the first charge on consumers' incomes, there are exceptions. Certain forms of saving—life insurance premiums or repayment of debts—represent prior charges, and attempts will usually be made to maintain them even in case of a decline in income. Some other forms of saving may be the results of past decisions and carried on in a routine way, and will likewise not be given up easily.

Still, the term "habitual standards" requires clarification primarily with respect to expenditures and not savings. What kind of expenditures are habitual? These are, usually, the expenditures for "necessities" but hardly those that are sporadic and unusual. Among the latter are the expenditures for luxuries, for services, for vacation trips, and for durable goods, such as the purchase of automobiles, household implements, or furniture. During the last few decades, the expenditures on durable goods have become increasingly important in the American economy.

An income decline may have similar effects on behavior with respect to expenditures on durable goods as it has with respect to saving. In response to a reduction in income, a family may cut its expenditures on durable goods drastically. If, prior to the income decline, the expenditures on durable goods have been substantial, it may happen that cutting those expenditures alone will balance the budget after the income decline, and all other expenditures and the amounts saved may remain unchanged. It may also happen in such cases that the amounts saved will increase even though all or most expenditures on nondurables are maintained at their previous level.[11]

It follows that the hypothesis about people's maintenance of their habitual standards of expenditure leads to different consequences as regards spending and saving according to whether a family has spent, prior to the income change, small or large amounts on durable goods (and on other nonhabitual purchases and services). The assumption about slow changes in expenditure habits does not suffice to predict what will happen to the amounts saved by people with changes in income.

All these considerations call for empirical studies. We have raised them in order to show that people's saving and spending behavior is probably subject to manifold influences which were not considered when the two simple hypotheses were formulated at the beginning of this section. Empirical studies must determine whether the various factors discussed in this section need to be taken into consideration. The law of parsimony alone

[11] Schematic calculations illustrating these considerations are presented in the Notes to this chapter.

is not sufficient to exclude those factors. It does not compel us to build a theoretical system comprising few variables, because correctly formulated it says: "Entia non sunt multiplicanda praeter necessitatem." The last two words are of importance. We must find out whether or not the introduction of new variables is necessary.

NOTES TO CHAPTER 7

The Economic Reports of the President, transmitted to Congress as prepared by the Council of Economic Advisers, and published by the U.S. Government Printing Office in January and July of each year since 1947, contain the presentation and analysis of the nation's economic budget. The basic data are taken

TABLE 17. THE NATION'S ECONOMIC BUDGET

(In billions of dollars *)

Economic sector	1939			1947		
	Receipts	Expen-di-tures	Dif-fer-ence	Receipts	Expen-di-tures	Dif-fer-ence
Consumers:						
Disposable income..........	70.2	....	....	173.6		
Expenditures...............	....	67.5			164.8	
Saving.....................	....	....	+2.7	....	....	+8.8
Business:						
Receipts not paid out........	8.6	....	....	19.4		
Investment.................	....	9.0	....		30.0	
Excess.....................	....	....	—0.4	....	....	—10.7
International:						
Government transfers abroad	....	....	....	5.4		
Net foreign investment......		0.9	....	....	8.9	
Excess.....................	....	....	—0.9	....	....	—3.5
Government:						
Cash receipts..:............	15.0	....	....	57.3		
Cash payments.............	....	17.6	....	....	50.7	
Excess.....................	....	....	—2.6	....	....	+6.7
Adjustments..................	—3.3	—4.5	+1.2	—1.4	....	—1.4
Gross national product........	90.4	90.4	0	231.6	231.6	0

* Details may not add to totals because of rounding. Also, for 1947, transfer payments are excluded from totals.

SOURCE: The Economic Report of the President, January, 1948, and January, 1949, U.S. Government Printing Office.

from estimates made by the Commerce Department. As an illustration, the budgets for a prewar and a postwar year are reproduced in Table 17.

In the discussion in the first section of this chapter, certain complex factors were disregarded so as to focus the attention on a few essential points. Practically any modern introductory textbook of economics may serve to supplement the discussion. For a more complex analysis of the relation between saving and investment, Chapters 6 and 7 of J. M. Keynes's book, *The General Theory of Employment, Interest, and Money,* which is frequently quoted in the text, may be referred to. Keynes's "fundamental psychological law" is presented in Chapters 8 and 9 of his book.

It is hardly necessary to say that the objective in discussing certain aspects of Keynes's theory in the text is not to criticize it. Students of the theory may point out, for example, that Keynes's entire system is formulated at the static level. The concept "income change" is said to relate, in Keynes's theory, to a static functional relationship, while in our discussion it has been used in a "dynamic" sense (change from one income level in Period 1 to another level in Period 2). Whether our discussion applies strictly to Keynes's formulations is, however, irrelevant for our purposes. References to Keynes's book are in order because fruitful dynamic hypotheses can be derived, and have been derived, from Keynesian thinking. It is a great achievement of Keynesian theory that it has stimulated further research, although not always exactly along the lines envisaged by the creator of the theory. Even if later research goes beyond the original theory, and even if it contradicts certain specific formulations of that theory, that research is greatly indebted to the original theory. Students of consumer decisions concerning the allocation of income may therefore subscribe to A. H. Hansen's tribute to Keynes, written shortly after the death of the master:

"It has been my conviction for many years that the great contribution of Keynes's General Theory was the clear and specific formulation of the consumption function. This is an epoch-making contribution to the tools of economic analysis." ("Keynes and the General Theory," *Review of Economic Statistics,* Vol. 28, 1946, p. 183.)

For the distinction between ex ante and ex post analysis, see Bertil Ohlin, "Some Notes on the Stockholm Theory of Savings and Investment," *Economic Journal,* Vol. 47, 1937, and Gunnar Myrdal, *Monetary Equilibrium,* London, 1939.

Theoretical analysis has been separated in this chapter from empirical studies. Actually, of course, the two are closely interconnected. Both theoretical arguments concerning the influence of changes in income on behavior and empirical studies based on these arguments have been presented by the author in his article "Effect of Income Changes on the Rate of Saving," *Review of Economics and Statistics,* Vol. 31, 1949, pp. 95*ff.*

The hypotheses that expecting bad times to come and expecting prices to go down may lead to saving more, and expecting good times to come and expecting prices to go up may lead to spending more, were used to guide empirical studies on business behavior in which the author participated during the war (see George Katona, *Price Control and Business,* 1945). The two hypotheses were also discussed in the author's paper "Psychological Analysis of Business Decisions and Expectations," *American Economic Review,* Vol. 36, 1946, p. 58.

As we shall see in the next chapter, the evidence for the hypotheses is far from conclusive. Some recent authors appear, however, to assume that the hypotheses are generally valid and need not be refined. For instance, K. E. Boulding writes: "The expectation of rising prices leads to larger expenditures" (*The Economics of Peace,* New York, 1945, p. 137). S. H. Slichter states: "Optimistic expectations (belief that one's income will rise or that tax rates will fall) encourage spending. Pessimistic expectations (belief that one's income over the long run will fall, that tax burdens will rise, or any other fears for the future) encourage saving" (*Financing American Prosperity,* Twentieth Century Fund, 1945, p. 284n). In the same volume, Slichter as well as J. H. Williams, J. M. Clark, and Fritz Machlup argue that the propensity to consume and to save may be subject to influences emanating from consumer expectations and other factors.

Contradiction of the notion that consumers may be saturated with goods and services constitutes the leitmotiv of H. G. Moulton's book on the *Controlling Factors in Economic Development* (Brookings Institution, Washington, D.C., 1949), and is expressed by him, for instance, in the following title of a section: "The Expansibility of Consumption" (p. 123).

The history of the treatment of expectations in the economic literature is characterized by repeated shifts in emphasis. A period in which expectations were almost entirely neglected was followed by a period in which it was assumed or implied that ever-present and constantly changing definite expectations about income, business trends, and prices shape the economic processes. After having thus been assigned a great role, the concept of expectations was, however, frequently thrown overboard. This feat was accomplished by substituting past trends (of income, sales, production, prices, etc.) for the expected trends. If income expectations, for instance, were always the function of current and past income, only these data, which can be determined easily, would need to enter into the economists' equations. Measurement of expectations could then be avoided.

Sometimes more complicated and yet essentially similar assumptions were made about the origin of expectations. Instead of the past trend, changes in that trend were assumed to determine the expectations. Suppose, for instance, that prices advanced during the past few months but the rate of increase slowed down (that is, the price increases were larger three months than two months ago and larger two months ago than last month). Then a further slowing down of the price increases or even stable or declining prices would be anticipated. This case is somewhat more complicated but nevertheless is closely related to the case of expecting to happen what has happened in the past.

Consideration of various theoretical possibilities emerging from the recognition of past trends has led to a discussion of expectations which is divorced from psychological considerations and is carried out without recourse to empirical research. The major example of this treatment is J. R. Hicks's book *Value and Capital* (Oxford, 1939). Another example, of a somewhat different nature—it contains psychological speculations—is G. L. S. Shackle's book *Expectation in Economics* (Cambridge, England, 1949). Such discussions of theoretical possibilities may be of great usefulness—we shall have opportunity to make use of Hicks's concept of elasticity of expectations in later chapters—but should not replace empirical studies directed toward finding out what people expect in different circumstances and why they expect what they do.

It remains to be said that recognition of the fact that the study of expectations is a psychological-empirical problem is not lacking in the economic literature. For instance, Shackle himself wrote that because "it is, after all, the decisions of individuals which determine what will happen" there is a "need to study the psychology of expectations as a process of the individual mind" ("The Expectational Dynamics of the Individual," *Economica*, Vol. 10, 1943, p. 99). J. A. Schumpeter argued that we must "discontinue the practice of treating expectations as if they were ultimate data and treat them as what they are—variables which it is our task to explain"; and "unless we know why people expect what they expect, any argument is completely valueless which appeals to expectations as *causae efficientes*." [6]

Hypothetical calculations may serve to illustrate the possible consequences

TABLE 18. HYPOTHETICAL CALCULATIONS CONCERNING THE EFFECTS OF INCOME INCREASES AND DECREASES

Year	Income after taxes	Expenditures		Saving
		"Habitual"	Durable goods	
A. Income increase				
Year 1.......	$4,200	$3,800	$200	$200
Year 2.......	5,000	4,000	800	200
or Year 2.......	5,000	4,000	900	100
or Year 2.......	5,000	4,000	700	300
B. Income decrease				
Year 1.......	$5,000	$4,000	$700	$300
Year 2.......	4,200	3,800	100	300
or Year 2.......	4,200	3,800	0	400
or Year 2.......	4,200	3,800	200	200

[6] J. A. Schumpeter, *Business Cycles*, Vol. 1, pp. 55 and 140. Copyright, 1939. Courtesy of McGraw-Hill Book Company, Inc.

of the assumptions that (1) there are habitual expenditures which change slowly in the case of income changes, but they do not encompass all expenditures; (2) nonhabitual expenditures—especially those on durable goods—that were large before an income decline or small before an income increase are greatly restricted or expanded after a change in income; (3) saving is for consumers a residual item, it represents what is left over after spending out of income. The calculations (Table 18) show that under such circumstances amounts saved may remain unchanged, or may increase, or may decrease after an income change.

The only purpose of these calculations is to show that the thesis about habitual expenditures does not suffice to predict saving behavior. It is not implied that consumers will actually behave as presented in the table.

CHAPTER 8

SPENDING AND SAVING: EMPIRICAL STUDIES

We turn now to the study of empirical data indicating the relation of spending and saving behavior to various factors that may influence it. The data cited are taken from the Surveys of Consumer Finances and refer to the first few postwar years. Empirical data concerning one given period cannot serve as conclusive proof of the validity of hypotheses. But they can be usefully applied to refute hasty generalizations, or to revise hypotheses so as to clarify the problems involved and pave the way for further research. Practically every period is unusual or exceptional in one or another respect. In considering observations referring to the first few postwar years, it should be kept in mind that this was a relatively prosperous period of high employment and income which followed war years during which demand for a variety of consumer goods could not be satisfied.

Our empirical material has other shortcomings, too. It is taken from sample surveys consisting of interviews with approximately 3,500 spending units. Sample surveys may yield, if properly conducted, reliable information on the order of magnitude of certain data. The number of cases in the Surveys of Consumer Finances is large enough to clarify the relations that exist between two variables among all the spending units in the nation. But the number of cases available in a "cell" is much smaller and represents a serious handicap to research if there is need to investigate the interrelation of more than two variables (for instance, of past income changes, expected income changes, and amounts saved), or if the relation of two variables is to be studied separately within various groups (income groups or occupational groups, for example). Because of the effect of sampling and reporting errors, information based on small cells is often inconclusive. Some differences between small subgroups in the sample may show up, but they may not be statistically significant and cannot be used, therefore, either to confirm or to refute hypotheses. Investigations using more complex statistical methods are under way and are directed toward overcoming, at least partly, these difficulties. But for the time being, the discussion based on such data as are available must be restricted to the clarification of interrelations between two or, at the most, three variables.

The annual Surveys of Consumer Finances do not contain questions, and therefore do not provide information, about every form of people's spending and saving behavior. For the sake of restricting the length of each interview and avoiding inquiries into recurrent small expenditures which people could not recall for a period of an entire year, no questions are asked about expenditures on food, clothing, amusements, and the like. The two types of data the measurement of which represents the major objective of the surveys, and which will be used in this chapter, are expenditures on durable goods and amounts saved. Even these measurements represent, however, a very complex task. Almost a hundred questions are asked of the survey respondents to obtain information from which, then, in the course of the process of analyzing the interviews, it is determined how much a spending unit has spent on durable goods and how much it has saved. By deducting these amounts from the unit's income (after taxes) a rough measure of all other expenditures is obtained.

How the information collected in the interviews—on the price paid for an automobile bought, on savings bonds purchased or cashed, on mortgage debt repaid, etc., etc.—is put together depends on the definition of the terms "expenditure on durable goods" and "amounts saved." In defining savings, not much use can be made of the concept as it exists in the minds of the people concerned. What people regard as savings differs greatly from individual to individual and often excludes important items that represent provisions for the future (*e.g.,* life insurance premium payments). Nor can such concepts as the difference in wealth (net worth) between the end and the beginning of a year be used to define savings as determined in surveys. Even if depreciation on the family's automobile or additions to its furniture and clothing could be determined, a definition of saving would emerge that would not be sufficiently distinct from that of spending and would differ from most traditional statistical compilations of amounts saved. Moreover, changes in the prices of securities, real estate, and other assets influence a person's net worth; they represent, however, gains or losses that are independent of his income.

The definition of saving used in the Surveys of Consumer Finances represents a compromise solution, which is in accord with the equation, savings plus expenditures equal income. The net sum of those relatively infrequent outlays which are not used for the satisfaction of immediate needs is considered saving. Thus a definition is obtained that is similar to (but not identical with) the definition used by the Commerce Department in determining aggregate savings. Both definitions consider money spent for the purchase of durable goods as expenditures. Thereby differences between money irrevocably spent for food and the wealth acquired by spending money for the purchase of an automobile or a refrigerator are disregarded. On the other hand, money spent for the purchase of a house or for improvements on one's house (not for repairs) is considered money saved.

One final shortcoming of all measurements of amounts saved must be mentioned. It is not possible to differentiate completely between consumer activities and entrepreneurial activities. Insofar as business is conducted by corporations, the separation is feasible. But consumer and business activities of owners of unincorporated businesses can often not be distinguished from each other. All transactions of farmers are included in the surveys, although farmers are entrepreneurs as well as consumers. With respect to owners of unincorporated businesses other than farms, a separation of business expenditures and savings from consumer expenditures and savings has been attempted in the surveys (but new funds invested and profits left in one's business are treated as consumer savings).

BEHAVIOR OF PEOPLE WITH HIGH AND LOW INCOMES

Our first task is to present factual information concerning such questions as the following: What kind of people save? In what form do people save? Is saving uniformly distributed among all consumers, or are there any substantial and regular differences among them? In accordance with the basic hypothesis developed in the last chapter, we have to study first of all the relation of amounts saved to the income of the savers.

During every year there are some people who save, that is, spend less than their incomes, and some people who dissave, that is, spend more than their incomes by supplementing them through drawing on previously accumulated assets or borrowing. The aggregate savings figures represent the difference between the amounts saved by those who saved and the amounts dissaved by those who spent more than their incomes. From the Surveys of Consumer Finances, it appears that in the first four postwar years 60 to 65 per cent of the spending units saved, and 27 to 34 per cent dissaved, while the remaining small proportion of units spent just what they earned.[1] In each of these years, the amounts saved by the savers were larger than the amounts dissaved by the dissavers. The difference decreased from 1945 to 1948, the aggregate "positive savings" in the latter year being only twice as large as the aggregate "negative savings."

How do people who save differ from people who dissave? There are some differences between these groups according to the type of community in which they live, the number of persons in the spending unit, the age, educa-

[1] Table 24 in the Notes to this chapter shows how saving was distributed during the first four postwar years. Most tables that present statistical information supplementing the text are included in the Notes.

tion, and especially the occupation of the head. Yet most of these differences are either small or are related to differences in the income of the different groups. What is the relation of saving and dissaving to level of income? Table 25 (in the Notes) shows the proportion of units at five different income levels who saved, broke even, or dissaved in 1947 and 1948. It indicates that the proportion of savers increases with income and, further, that the "zero savers"—units who neither save nor dissave—are most frequent among low-income people and almost nonexistent among high-income people. With respect to negative savers, no uniform finding presents itself: they are almost equally frequent at most income levels (although somewhat less frequent at very high income levels).

In these calculations, only the frequency of saving and dissaving is considered, without regard to the amounts saved or dissaved. It is, however, possible to consider the amounts as well and calculate distributions of amounts saved by the savers, of amounts dissaved by the dissavers, and amounts of net savings of the various income classes. As shown in Table 26 (in the Notes), "positive savings" (the amounts saved by the savers) are correlated with income: the higher the income, the larger are the amounts saved. The top income receivers saved substantial proportions of the aggregate positive savings. In the distribution of the amounts of negative savings, however, there appears to be no clear-cut relation to level of income. Dissaving, during the first few postwar years at least, was not a form of behavior characteristic of low-income people alone. The share of the top-income groups in total dissavings was as large as the share of the bottom-income groups.

If, within each income group, positive savers and dissavers are considered jointly, that is, if the net savings of each income group are determined and related to the net savings of the entire community, very pronounced relations to income level become apparent. In the years 1947 and 1948, for instance, 30 or 40 per cent of the lowest income receivers dissaved as a group (the amounts dissaved by the dissavers in these groups exceeded the amounts saved by the savers in the groups). The top-income group, that is, those 10 per cent of the spending units who had the largest incomes, were responsible for most of the net savings of the economy.

Comparison of the distribution of amounts saved in postwar years with that of prewar years is subject to substantial errors because of differences in the survey methods used to determine the amounts saved. But it appears probable that a larger proportion of units saved during the postwar years than in 1935–1936. During that one prewar year for which estimates are available, only the top 40 per cent of income receivers (as a group) saved, and the 60 per cent below them on the income scale dissaved. Moreover, during 1935–1936, the concentration of net savings among top income receivers appears to have been more pronounced than during the postwar years.

Top income receivers are responsible for a much larger share of the total amounts saved than would correspond to their number. But people with high income not only do most of the saving, they also do most of the spending, especially for goods which do not belong in the category of necessities. More of the people with high incomes buy automobiles and other durable goods than people with low incomes. Furthermore, high-income people buy higher priced goods than do low-income people. Of the entire expenditure on durable goods made by all consumers in 1947 and 1948, the top 20 per cent of the income receivers were responsible for approximately 45 per cent (Table 27). With respect to expenditures for clothing, food, and rent, the concentration among top income receivers is less pronounced. Still, high-income people represent the best market for practically all commodities.

On the average, high-income people, although they buy more goods and higher priced goods, save higher proportions of their income than do people with smaller incomes. In other words, they allocate their incomes differently. As Table 28 shows, they save a much higher proportion, spend only about the same proportion for durable goods, and spend a much smaller proportion for food and rent.

The finding that dissaving is not a form of behavior characteristic of the low-income groups alone makes it necessary to raise a question concerning the saving behavior of the "poor." The question may be asked in the following way: Suppose we divide all consumer units into those who save much, save a little, save nothing, and finally, who dissave; do lower income people characteristically fall into any one of these groups? For the first postwar years, the question can be answered unequivocally: Those we have called the zero savers, people whose expenditures equal their income, are the poorest of the groups. In 1948, for instance, of all zero savers, more than one-half had incomes of less than $1,000 and about 80 per cent less than $2,000. Furthermore, it was found that zero savers differed from all other groups in that they contained by far the lowest proportion of those who owned liquid assets or had purchased durable goods.

While it is true that most zero savers have low incomes, it is not true that most low-income people are zero savers. This discrepancy is caused partly by the fact that there are low-income people who cannot be called poor. This is true of people with negative income, who are usually business-men with net losses in a given year, and of some retired people with considerable means. Second, even among poor low-income people there are many who save, though usually small amounts. Life insurance and re-payment of mortgages or other debts are common forms of saving among some low-income people. Other forms of saving are, however, relatively rare among those with low incomes.

This last observation indicates that our procedure of considering the total saving of each spending unit irrespective of its form may not have been the most appropriate one. As reported earlier, some saving is not due to decisions made during the year when the amounts have been saved. Payments of life insurance premiums, payments into retirement funds, and repayments of mortgage principal represent such "contractual saving." It appears that contractual saving is much less dependent on income than is saving in other forms. Almost all spending units with incomes of over $3,000 were found to have saved some money in these ways, and even among units with lower income the majority made contractual payments that are classified as saving. When the amounts saved in these forms are expressed in proportions of income, we find that in 1948 there were only small differences among low-, middle-, and high-income people. Therefore, the much higher proportions of income saved by high-income people must go mainly into other forms of saving.

The forms of saving by the upper-income groups appear to vary greatly. Some families with substantial income save primarily through adding to their liquid assets, others through buying houses or investing in securities or businesses. Likewise, considerable variations are observed in the forms of saving if the performance of identical upper-income families is studied over two consecutive years.

Because of their very great share in the total savings of the economy, the behavior of the top income receivers is of particular interest. Data available from the small sample surveys conducted up to now yield, however, little information about the 1 or 2 per cent of families who are at the top of the income scale. Concerning their income development, tax reports provide valuable data, but their spending and saving behavior requires studies of special samples which have not yet been undertaken.

EFFECT OF PAST AND EXPECTED INCOME CHANGES

We shall take up next the question raised in the previous chapter about the effect of past income changes on saving behavior. Suppose we divide all consumer units in the nation into five groups, those who in a given year had much larger incomes than in the previous year, those who had somewhat larger incomes, those who had the same incomes, those who had somewhat smaller incomes, and finally, those who had much smaller incomes than in the previous year. Table 19 shows that there were differences in the saving performance of these five groups. They can best be summarized by concentrating our attention on the frequency of the dissavers (who spent more than their incomes) and the "high savers" (who saved more than 20 per cent of their incomes).

As has been expected, on the basis of theoretical considerations, dissavers appear to be most frequent among units with substantial reductions in income. But, contrary to expectations, the proportion of dissavers does not decrease gradually as one proceeds to the other groups and is not the smallest in the group with substantial income increases. On the contrary, the latter group, spending units whose incomes increased greatly, contains a slightly greater proportion of dissavers than some of the other groups. At the same time, the group with substantial income gains contains the largest proportion, and the group with substantial income declines the smallest proportion, of high savers.

Since the general level of prices advanced during the years considered, those who, in the table, are marked as having had stable money incomes had a decline in real income. Only the group with "much larger" money

TABLE 19. RELATION BETWEEN PAST CHANGES IN INCOME AND PROPORTIONS OF INCOME SAVED

(Percentage distribution of spending units in each group)

Rate of saving in 1947	Much larger*	Somewhat larger†	Same‡	Somewhat smaller†	Much smaller*
	1947 money income before taxes compared with 1946 income				
Negative...................	30	25	25	29	44
Zero......................	5	5	13	7	9
Positive:					
1 – 19% of income........	40	49	44	44	33
20% or more of income....	25	21	18	20	14
Total.................	100	100	100	100	100
Rate of saving in 1948	1948 money income before taxes compared with 1947 income				
Negative...................	32	28	27	35	46
Zero......................	6	5	9	4	6
Positive:					
1–19% of income..........	37	48	46	39	32
20% or more of income....	25	19	18	22	16
Total.................	100	100	100	100	100

* Increase or decrease by 25 per cent or more or, in some cases, assertion "much larger" or "much smaller."

† Increase or decrease by 5 to 24 per cent or, in some cases, assertion "somewhat larger" or "somewhat smaller."

‡ Change between plus 4 and minus 4 per cent or assertion "same."

incomes qualifies clearly as having had an increase in real income. It appears, therefore, that in the years under study a substantial proportion of people who had increases in real income are characterized by two forms of distinctive behavior: some of them saved more and some of them spent more (in proportion to their incomes) than people with stable or slightly declining real income. The one distinctive form of behavior of people with large income declines, on the other hand, is a relatively high frequency of spending more than the income received. These findings, shown in Table 19 to prevail among all consumer units, are confirmed when units at various income levels are studied separately. There is evidence that the direction of income change, irrespective of differences in income level, is responsible for some differences in saving rates.

Before discussing the implications of these findings, we turn to the presentation of data on the relation between income expectations and rates of saving. Table 20 shows that the differences in the saving behavior of groups with different income expectations are small but consistent. The proportion of savers is larger among those who expect their incomes to decline than among those who expect their incomes to increase. Conversely, there are more dissavers among people who expect income increases than among those who expect income declines.

TABLE 20. RELATION BETWEEN EXPECTED CHANGES IN INCOME AND PROPORTIONS OF INCOME SAVED

(Percentage distribution of nonfarm spending units in each group)

Rate of saving	Next year's rate of income expected to be—		
	Higher	About the same	Lower
1947			
Negative	36	24	31
Zero	5	9	4
Positive:			
1–19% of income............	39	49	40
20% or more of income.......	20	18	25
Total	100	100	100
1948			
Negative	36	28	26
Zero	3	8	4
Positive:			
1–19% of income............	41	47	47
20% or more of income.......	20	17	23
Total	100	100	100

Next, following the requirements set for the investigation in the previous chapter, we turn to the analysis of the joint effects of past and expected income changes. The findings (see Table 29 in the Notes to this chapter) confirm what might be expected on the basis of the preceding two tables. Although they are based on relatively few cases, the following tentative conclusions appear to be warranted:

1. Income expectations have an effect on the saving performance. If those with past income declines are divided into groups according to whether they expect their incomes to increase, decrease, or remain stable, differences are found in the saving data; similarly, if those with past income stability or past income increases are divided into three groups, the saving .rates of the groups are found to differ. As to the direction of the differences, it can be stated that (in both years studied) there were more dissavers among those who expected income increases than among those who expected income decreases, and (in 1947) more high savers among those who expected income decreases than among those who expected income increases.

2. The largest proportion of dissavers is found (in both years) among those with past income decreases and expected income increases. In other words, an income decline that was believed to be temporary was frequently associated with spending more than one's income.

3. The smallest proportion of dissavers is found (in both years) among those whose incomes had not changed and were not expected to change. Income stability was not associated frequently with spending more than one's income.

Presentation of findings concerning the relation between income changes and the purchase of durable goods is next in order. In considering first the effect of past income changes, substantial differences are observed. The proportion of people who made such purchases and especially the proportion who spent large amounts on durable goods is by far the largest among those whose incomes have advanced considerably. Durable-goods expenditures are least frequent and involve the smallest amounts among units whose incomes declined substantially or remained stable (Table 21). It appears that improvement in income position encourages, and deterioration in that position discourages, the satisfying of needs and desires for durable goods.

Definite relations are also apparent between income expectations and durable-goods purchases. Expectation of higher incomes is associated with more frequent and larger purchases of durable goods than expectation of lower incomes.

The data provide clear-cut indications, however, that the direction of past and expected income changes cannot be the only factors determining

TABLE 21. RELATION BETWEEN PAST CHANGES IN INCOME AND PURCHASES OF DURABLE GOODS

(Percentage distribution of spending units in each group)

Expenditures for durable goods* in 1947	Much larger	Somewhat larger	Same	Somewhat smaller	Much smaller
	1947 money income before taxes compared with 1946 income				
None.....................	50	54	65	58	60
$1 – $199.................	14	15	13	14	14
200 – 999................	23	21	16	18	19
$1,000 or over.............	12	9	6	9	6
Not ascertained............	1	1	†	1	1
Total...................	100	100	100	100	100

Expenditures for durable goods* in 1948	1948 money income before taxes compared with 1947 income				
None.....................	43	48	62	51	65
$1 – $199.................	15	16	11	15	10
200 – 999................	26	27	17	24	17
$1,000 or over.............	16	9	9	10	7
Not ascertained............	†	†	1	†	1
Total...................	100	100	100	100	100

* Include amounts paid for automobiles, furniture, refrigerators and other household appliances bought minus trade-in values. See also footnotes to Table 19.

† Less than ½ per cent.

purchases of durable goods. Even among units whose incomes had declined and were expected to decline further, there were a considerable number who spent substantial amounts on durable goods.

The findings about the relations of past and expected income changes to rates of saving and to rates of durable-goods expenditures have been presented separately, but in fact they are not independent of each other. To be sure—as will be shown in a moment—buying durable goods is not the only "reason" for low rates of saving or for dissaving. But people who, in a given year, spend substantial amounts on durable goods usually save less than people with similar incomes who do not purchase such goods. Conversely, among dissavers, expenditures on durables, and especially large expenditures on durables, are much more frequent than among savers. Thus one factor responsible for the relatively high proportion of dissavers among people with substantial income increases may well be their inclination to purchase durable goods.

Although the available empirical data are far from sufficient to prove the point, they present ample indications for the relevance of the theoretical considerations developed in the previous chapter. First, it appears that expectations—not only income expectations, but also the general economic outlook, which factor has not been shown separately—influence people's perception of their income developments and their spending and saving behavior. Second, it seems clear that adjustment of spending and saving to a changed income level is not smooth and not instantaneous. But a principle relating to maintenance of habitual standards of expenditures after increased or decreased income is not sufficient to account for all the observations. Under certain circumstances, such a principle appears to be effective. When their incomes decline but are expected to increase again, people tend not to cut their habitual expenditures, and therefore many of these people will save little or will even dissave. When declines in income are expected to be permanent, the lag in adjusting expenditures and its effect on saving behavior appears to be less pronounced.

When income increases, there is evidence of a kind of behavior contrary to the one deduced from the assumption of maintaining expenditure standards. Some people take income increases which they consider permanent, or as leading to even further income gains, as an incentive for large expenditures on durable goods and for "overspending" (spending more than one's income) in general.

These considerations help in the urgently needed task of placing the discussion of saving behavior within the framework of cyclical fluctuations. Since business upswing is characterized by a great frequency of income increases and of optimistic expectations, we find that an upward business trend may generate certain attitudes and behavior that contribute to its continuation. But income increases alone need not produce optimistic expectations, and the expectations are important for behavior. When income increases are coupled with pessimistic expectations, they are associated less frequently with purchases of durable goods and with dissaving. Such attitudes may therefore promote saving and contribute to the downturn itself.

Very little is known about the factors influencing saving behavior during a depression. Regarding economic "stagnation," it may, however, be pointed out that during the first few postwar years income stability (unchanged income during the past year and expected stable income during the next year) was associated with a relatively low frequency of durable-goods purchases and of dissaving. It appears that certain expenditures are not made unless there is some strong impetus present.

DIFFERENT KINDS OF DISSAVING

The factors contributing to high rates of *spending* deserve special attention. We shall proceed with an analysis of dissaving—spending more than one's income—which is a somewhat narrower concept than high rates of spending. In the light of findings already presented, dissaving appears to be a rather complicated phenomenon. On the one hand (1), a relation was found between dissaving and decline in income. On the other hand (2), dissaving is related to expenditures for durable goods, which in turn are more frequent if incomes increase. Furthermore, dissaving is not clearly associated with any one income level although, undoubtedly, (3) the need to supplement one's income is greater at lower than at higher income levels. On the other hand (4), people cannot dissave unless they have some financial strength. They must have assets to sell, previous savings to draw on, or credit that enables them to borrow money, and these circumstances are usually more frequent at upper income levels. It follows that dissaving can hardly be a unitary phenomenon that originates in one kind of circumstance only.

Analysis of the characteristics and behavior of spending units who dissaved during the postwar years revealed that there are at least three—there may be more—different kinds of dissaving. Dissaving may occur (1) because of inability to meet necessary expenditures out of income, (2) because of unwillingness to keep usual expenditures at the level of income, and (3) because of willingness to make unusual expenditures.

One major circumstance in which the first kind of dissaving occurs is illness or other emergencies. If large emergency expenditures become necessary, for instance, for hospital expenses, a family may draw upon previously accumulated assets (if it has any) or borrow money (if it has credit) to cover its expenses and to maintain, nevertheless, its habitual standard of life.

The most typical instance of the second kind of dissaving is what we have called "temporary income decline." If, because of unemployment, change of job, or reverses in business profits, the income in a given period is smaller than it used to be but is expected to rise again, a family may be more than willing to keep its habitual expenses even if doing so involves drawing on accumulated assets or borrowing.

Separation of the first two kinds of dissaving is, of course, not possible in every instance. Whether unemployment, for example, is classified under the first or the second category will depend upon the circumstances. Likewise, income decline due to retirement may represent an instance of either the first or the second kind of dissaving. We do not know enough about the varied motivational patterns that may lead to dissaving to proceed further with that analysis.

But it is important to differentiate the third kind of dissaving from the first two. Unusual expenditures may consist of purchases of automobiles or other durable goods, or of various types of semidurable goods, or of vacation trips, moving expenses, and also of certain luxury expenditures. When dissaving is due to such expenditures, it is found to have features that differ greatly from other kinds of dissaving. First of all, dissaving due to purchases of durable goods appears to be positively correlated with income: the higher the income level, the more frequent is that type of dissaving. On the other hand, dissaving due to income declines or to emergency expenditures (without purchase of durable goods) appears to be inversely correlated with income level: the lower the income, the more frequent are those kinds of dissaving. Second, dissaving due to purchases of durable goods, unlike other kinds of dissaving, appears to occur more frequently when incomes increase than when incomes decline.

Statistical data on the relative frequency of different kinds of dissaving are summarized in the Notes to this chapter. They yield only rough approximations, because not infrequently several different circumstances contributed to dissaving on the part of the same family. It must also be kept in mind that the available data clarify the circumstances in which dissaving occurs under prosperous economic conditions only. It is probable that dissaving due to purchases of durable goods will be relatively frequent in prosperous times or during the upward phase of the business cycle when optimistic income expectations prevail. On the other hand, decline in income is, of course, more frequent during the downward than the upward phase of the cycle. But without further investigation the statement cannot be made that dissaving due to income declines is characteristic of depression. What was called temporary income decline may be an income decline during prosperous times because that is the period when optimistic expectations will be prevalent. It is also possible that decline in income will lead to dissaving in good times only, because in these times one's income trend is felt to differ from the income trend of other members of one's group and maintaining habitual standards of expenditure will appear more desirable than in periods of general income decline or depression.

Is it to be expected that dissaving will be more frequent in periods of depression than in periods of prosperity? Regarding dissaving due to the willingness to undertake 'unusual expenditures, the reverse conclusion emerges. When dissaving is due to illness or emergencies, cyclical factors may not play a major role. Declines in income, as we have just argued, likewise need not induce more people to dissave during a depression than during prosperous times. Of course, there may be kinds of dissaving during a depression that we have omitted from our study, which was based on data obtained during years of relatively full employment. Thus we are not in the position to give a definite answer to the question raised.

We next turn to the problem of repetitiousness as against reversal in spending and saving behavior. The analysis of dissaving yields certain definite conclusions in this respect. Probably, for most families, a year of dissaving will be one preceded and followed by years of saving. It will not happen often that a family dissaves in every one of several successive years. Retired people may do so, or certain wealthy people who suffer emergencies or reverses during several years in succession. But sizable durable-goods purchases that cause dissaving are commonly bunched in certain years—for instance, the year of marriage or the year of purchase of a house—and the year following the one in which unusual purchases were made will often be a year used for repayment of installment or other debts incurred previously and therefore a year of saving. Similarly, decline of income which extends year after year will hardly be considered a temporary decline and will therefore not usually lead to dissaving.

Investigations covering a period of only two years confirm the conclusion just reached. In each of the years 1947 and 1948, about 30 per cent of all spending units dissaved. Therefore, the maximum possible proportion of those who dissaved in either year would be 60 per cent (assuming that none of the units dissaved in both 1947 and 1948); the minimum possible proportion would be 30 per cent (assuming that all the dissavers dissaved in both years). A study covering the financial behavior of identical urban respondents revealed that among those who dissaved during the first year, 1947, only about 40 per cent dissaved during the second year, 1948 (namely, 12 out of 31, see Part A of Table 22). Similarly, among those who dissaved in 1948 only 40 per cent had dissaved also in 1947. Reversal of behavior, such as dissaving in the first year and saving a high proportion of one's income in the second year, or saving much the first year and dissaving the second year, occurred more frequently. Altogether, almost one-half of all spending units (48 per cent) were found to have dissaved in one or the other year, namely, 12 per cent who dissaved both years, plus 19 per cent who dissaved only in the first year, and 17 per cent who dissaved only in the second.

That dissaving is not repeated often during consecutive years is not surprising. Since bequeathing money to one's heirs is not the only and not the strongest motive for saving, it is to be expected that there will be years during most people's life history in which the amounts previously saved are used. Occasional dissaving may be called one major purpose of saving. Such behavior is facilitated by a feature of the American economy which enables consumers to make large expenditures before saving money to pay for the

TABLE 22. REPETITION OR REVERSAL OF SAVING BEHAVIOR AND OF
PURCHASES OF DURABLE GOODS IN TWO CONSECUTIVE YEARS

A. Saving behavior   Per cent

Saved in both 1947 and 1948.....................................	49
Dissaved in both 1947 and 1948.................................	12
Saved in 1947,* dissaved in 1948...............................	17
Dissaved in 1947, saved in 1948 *..............................	19
Broke even in one year, saved the other year.......................	1
Broke even in both 1947 and 1948................................	2
Total	100

B. Purchases of durable goods †

Bought durable goods in both 1947 and 1948.......................		25
Spent similar amounts each year...............................	12	
Spent greatly different amounts each year........................	13	
Bought durable goods in one of the two years only..................		38
In 1947 but not in 1948.......................................	18	
In 1948 but not in 1947.......................................	20	
Bought no durable goods in either 1947 or 1948....................		37
Total		100

* A few spending units who broke even in 1947 (zero savers) and dissaved in 1948
or who dissaved in 1947 and broke even in 1948 are included.

† Automobiles, furniture, refrigerators, and other household appliances.

SOURCE: 655 urban spending units interviewed early in 1948 about their saving and
spending in 1947 and early in 1949 about their saving and spending in 1948.

goods purchased. Borrowing on installment means dissaving in a given
period and must ordinarily be followed by periods of repayment of debt,
which is a form of saving.

The data presented also show that dissaving cannot be thought of as
an unusual form of behavior. Nor is it necessarily undertaken reluctantly
or with misgivings, when every other avenue of balancing one's budget
fails. It is not an index of hardship. With some families it represents hardship. With others, however, it is a sign of willingness to spend; it is then
both an indication of prosperous economic conditions and a factor contributing to them.

Table 22 contains information not only about the frequency of reversals
in saving behavior—transition from saving to dissaving, or from dissaving
to saving, in two consecutive years—but also about the frequency of repetitiousness in saving behavior. About one-half of all spending units in the
sample saved in both of the two years studied. The majority of these units
saved similar proportions of their incomes in the two years. Similar behavior
in two consecutive years was especially frequent among units who saved
small proportions of their income (less than 10 per cent). One major factor

contributing to this repetitiousness in behavior is to be found in what has been called "contractual saving." The amounts saved in form of life insurance premiums, payments into retirement funds, and repayments of mortgages were, of course, similar in two consecutive years with most spending units.

Expenditures for durable goods show greater variability from one year to the next than amounts saved. The extent of repetitiousness in the purchases of identical urban spending units during 1947 and 1948 is shown in Part *B* of Table 22. We see that the proportion of people who bought durable goods in only one of two consecutive years is much larger (38 per cent) than the proportion who bought any such goods in both years (25 per cent).

It appears probable that large nonhabitual expenditures—not only for the purchase of durable goods but probably for various other purchases as well—represent the most variable form of consumer behavior. It may, of course, happen that in two consecutive years aggregate consumer expenditures for durable goods will remain the same although different people did most of the buying in the two years. But this need not happen; the inherent instability in the same people's durable-goods expenditures may, and often does, produce great variations from one year to the next in the amounts of aggregate expenditures.

THE ROLE OF PRICE EXPECTATIONS

In discussing, in the preceding chapter, the possible influence of expectations on people's spending and saving behavior, price expectations were also mentioned. The assumption that price expectations affect the purchase of durable goods and the amounts saved was not confirmed in the first few postwar years. Possibly the assumption was not tested in a satisfactory way. What would have been necessary would have been to determine the price expectations prevailing before or during the period for which spending and saving behavior was investigated. What was actually done was to inquire about price expectations at the end of that period and to relate them to previous purchases and to purchases planned or anticipated during the following year.

Groups of people who, at a given time, expected the price level to go up, and groups who expected it to go down, were found to be practically equal both with respect to their past purchases of durable goods and past saving rates. Some people who expected prices to decline reported that they had postponed some purchases they had planned in view of what they considered to be the prevailing price trends. But, nevertheless, the group holding such expectations spent money on durable goods at rates similar to those people who anticipated different price trends.

When the relation of price expectations to buying intentions was studied, some differences were found. In 1949, for instance, somewhat more of those people who expected prices to go down said they intended to buy automobiles and other durable goods than of those who expected prices to remain stable or go up.

Further inquiry about price expectations yielded information which may contribute to an understanding of the findings. First, especially in 1948 and at the beginning of 1949, the expectation of price declines was strongly associated with the expectation of good times to come. A substantial proportion of people believed that what was needed for a continuation of prosperous times was a decline in prices. Inflation was considered the danger leading to an economic collapse and price declines the good thing that would enable people to buy more and thus guarantee high employment.

Second, it was found that at no time during the first few postwar years did people expect quick or substantial price changes. With very few exceptions, the American people envisaged in these years price increases or decreases of about 5 or, at the most, 10 per cent during the 12-month period to follow. Thus it is not permissible to generalize from the postwar findings about the probable effects of anticipating large or rapid price changes.

Third, it was found that price expectations fluctuated during the first few postwar years to a much larger extent than some other expectations. At the beginning of 1946, for instance, the majority of people thought that prices would be going up; at the beginning of 1947, that prices would be going down; in July, 1947, people were about evenly divided; in January, 1948, the majority again thought that prices would increase; and a month later most people expressed the opinion that prices would go down. In contrast, people's general economic outlook remained fairly stable during these years; the majority of people thought at all these times that conditions would remain good or even improve further.

Finally, we may refer to a finding about the origin of price expectations during the first few postwar years, which finding may be related to the instability of these expectations. In the surveys just discussed, people were asked why they expected prices to go up or down and why they thought that times would remain good or bad, or their own incomes would increase or decrease. Explanations of price expectations consisted in large part of references to recent events and recent past trends of prices. Logically, it hardly can be considered an explanation to say that prices will be going up or down because they have been going up or down recently, but such opinions were more widely held than opinions about underlying factors producing inflationary or deflationary pressures. Explanations such as "Prices always go up after a war" or, after the increases of 1946 and 1947, "What goes up must come down" likewise appear to testify to the impersonal and somewhat superficial nature of prevailing price expectations. At the same time, many of those who expected good times to come explained quite clearly what they had in mind, namely, why in their opinion large demand, satisfactory wages, or high employment would prevail. People frequently referred to their own experiences in the employment market and business, or to their inability to purchase certain goods during the first few postwar years. During 1949, equally detailed explanations were given by those relatively few people who expected a depression to come, and these explanations again seemed to convey an impression of personal concern with business trends. Many of the explanations of income expectations were even more convincing: references to wage increases to be won by the unions, to impending promotions, or to an anticipated upturn or downturn in the respondents' own businesses were frequent. It is therefore possible that differences in the "intensity" of expectations account for differences in the influence of expectations on behavior.

Under these circumstances it is not permissible to conclude from the available survey data about the influence of price expectations on consumer behavior that price expectations are always of little influence. This may be the case under certain conditions that require further study, but need not be the case under other conditions. We shall come back to this point again when we discuss the role of psychological factors in promoting or retarding inflationary movements.

LIQUID ASSETS AND SAVING

We must consider the effect of one further variable on the rate of spending and saving. As said before, dissaving is not possible unless one has credit or assets to expend. Therefore, the frequent occurrence of dissaving during the first few postwar years may have been related to the high asset holdings of consumers. More generally, people's asset position may be an important factor in spending. In the words of Gottfried Haberler, "We must assume . . . that consumption is not only a function of income but also of wealth (and liquid wealth in particular)." [2] The Notes to this chapter contain several formulations of this hypothesis, which all agree on the assumed direction of the effect: the larger their assets, or the larger their liquid assets, the more will consumers spend out of their income. The explanations of why people should behave that way vary. Sometimes it is

[2] Gottfried Haberler, "The Place of the General Theory of Employment, Interest, and Money in the History of Economic Thought," *Review of Economic Statistics*, Vol. 28, 1946, pp. 191*f.*

stated simply that people with great or with substantial wealth would spend more freely; sometimes it is explicitly assumed that there is a saturation in the process of accumulating wealth so that the more a person has, the smaller his incentive to save. With respect to liquid assets in particular, it is occasionally assumed that they are acquired in order to have funds for investment or for spending; if the latter purpose is carried out, great liquid assets induce spending. The last hypothesis was especially popular toward the end of the war when, as we saw before, it was frequently thought that the wartime accumulation of government savings bonds and bank deposits was due to inability to spend and would therefore lead, during the postwar years, to increased spending on the part of those who had accumulated liquid reserves.

Usually the hypothesis is formulated on the aggregate level as referring to wealthy as against poor communities. The transition from the aggregate to the microeconomic level may, as is occasionally acknowledged, require posing a second question: Who holds the liquid assets? The argument is advanced that if the liquid assets are largely in the possession of people with high incomes, the assets can exert only a small influence on increasing the consumption of the entire country, since high-income people do not need to draw on their assets to satisfy their desires for goods.

It is, however, possible to see the relation of asset holdings to spending and saving in an entirely different light. One may argue that large liquid-asset holdings result from large amounts saved in the recent past, and that people who have been able and willing to save much in the past may be the very ones who will most likely save much in the future. Within each income group there are some people with large assets and some with small assets. In some cases these differences are due to inheritance; in some they are due to previous differences in income of people who are now in the same income group. But in many cases the differences in wealth of people with similar incomes are due to the fact that some people habitually save greater proportions of their income than do others—that they are more thrifty or have smaller obligations. Some of these people, it seems probable, would continue their habit of saving relatively large portions of their income.

Empirical studies directed toward investigating the influence of asset holdings on the rate of saving and spending have not progressed far up to now. No data are available with respect to the influence of total assets. Some information has, however, been obtained from the Surveys of Consumer Finances about the influence of liquid-asset holdings (United States government savings bonds and various kinds of bank deposits). Unfortunately, it has not yet been possible in these studies to isolate the effect of liquid-asset holdings from the effects of other factors that influence saving, notably changes in income and income expectations. The available information consists simply of the relation of size of liquid-asset holdings to rate of saving. This relation, as found among consumer units as a whole in 1948, is shown in Table 23; data for 1946 and 1947 show similar relations. (The same computations have been made separately for different income groups and are presented in the Notes.)

TABLE 23. RELATION BETWEEN LIQUID-ASSET HOLDINGS AND PROPORTIONS OF INCOME SAVED

(Percentage distribution of spending units in each group)

Rate of saving in 1948	Liquid-asset holdings at beginning of 1948			
	None	$1 – $499	$500 – $1,999	$2,000 and over
A. Data obtained from a sample of 3,500 cases, representative of all spending units				
Negative..............	21	30	40	34
Zero.................	18	3	2	1
Positive..............	61	67	58	65
1 – 9%............	38	32	22	20
10 – 29%...........	17	27	24	25
30% or more........	6	8	12	20
Total.............	100	100	100	100
B. Data obtained from a sample of 655 urban spending units interviewed twice				
Negative..............	23	27	31	31
Zero.................	16	1	1	1
Positive..............	61	72	68	68
1 – 9%............	39	35	32	22
10 – 29%...........	19	30	26	28
30% or more........	3	8	10	18
Total.............	100	100	100	100

NOTE: The data presented under A are taken from one survey. Respondents were asked at the beginning of 1949 about their liquid-asset holdings at the beginning of 1948 and about the amounts they saved in 1948. Some memory errors, involved in that procedure, are eliminated from the tabulations presented under B, where liquid-asset holdings were determined at the beginning of 1948 and 1948 savings at the beginning of 1949.

Those who have no liquid assets at all probably have to be considered as a special case and not simply as the group at the low end of the scale of liquid-asset holders. They cannot, of course, dissave by reducing liquid assets. They can dissave in other ways—by selling nonliquid assets or by borrowing. But as they are predominantly from the lower income groups, as their total wealth will probably be small and their credit standing not as good as other people's, these ways of dissaving are also less accessible to them. Hence we should expect to find—and we do find, in Table 23—that they include the smallest proportion of dissavers. But the proportion of dissavers and zero savers, taken together, is as large in this group as it is in the other groups. Those who have no liquid assets differ from the other groups in two respects: they contain the largest proportion of zero savers and the largest proportion of small savers.

How does the rate of saving of owners of small liquid assets differ from that of owners of large liquid assets? The data indicate two differences. First, in most income groups, the proportion of dissavers appears to be somewhat larger among those with large than among those with small liquid assets. Second, the proportion of high savers, spending units who saved more than 30 per cent of their incomes, is larger among those with large than among those with small liquid assets. In other words, there is some evidence that two kinds of motivational forces are connected with large liquid-asset holdings. Some holders of large liquid assets, in each income group, appear to be motivated to save much, and some holders to dissave. Although, to emphasize again, the results are not conclusive and require confirmation through separating the influences of different factors, it seems that there is a grain of truth in both hypotheses with which we started our discussion.

We do not know under which circumstances one or the other of the two contradictory influences will be more powerful. We are not in the position to make a statement about the probable behavior of a community with high assets as against a community with small assets. Furthermore, generalizations from the data obtained during the first postwar years may not be warranted. It is possible that the role and function of asset holdings among the motivational forces to spend and to save varies according to the prevailing business trend.

The requirements emerging from these investigations for further studies are obvious. It is necessary to make statistical studies that will reflect the joint effect of several variables. It may also be necessary to obtain more information about people's attitudes toward liquid assets. In the discussion in this section, holders of liquid assets were differentiated simply according to the size of their holdings. Possibly if holders of liquid assets are separated according to their attitudes toward the assets or their motives for saving, some aspects of our preliminary findings might be clarified. Like changes in income, liquid-asset holdings should not be treated as isolated variables but as factors that play a role in shaping people's motivational patterns to spend or to save. Finally, better understanding of the influence of asset holdings, as well as of some other variables, on saving behavior might be obtained if it were possible to study performance and attitudes of the same families over several years by making repeated interviews.

PROGRAMMATIC REMARKS

The function of the scientist is, as we may well repeat at this point, to formulate propositions of some generality in the light of available evidence. The propositions should serve the purposes of understanding past developments, promoting the collection of new evidence, and predicting future trends. This work necessarily involves a process of simplification. The multitude of diverse findings must be sifted and relationships between certain variables singled out. In concentrating our attention on the final process, we may distinguish several different methods through which we may arrive at predictions.

One method of predicting is that of analogy. Suppose we had asked ourselves in 1945 about production or employment trends during the first few years after the Second World War; using the method of analogy, we would have begun by studying the economic trends following the First World War. Similarly, in order to foresee developments that are expected to occur after an inflationary period, we would study what happened following previous inflationary movements.

The main problem involved in using this method concerns the question of what is analogous. Sometimes this question is easily answered, for example, if only one single similar instance is known. Usually, however, we must choose which of several past occurrences to consider. Furthermore, we must decide whether and how known changes between the situation studied and the so-called analogous situation should be taken into account. There exists hardly any scientific method which gives a clear-cut answer to these questions, and thus predicting by analogy is often more a matter of guesswork than of science.

Another method of predicting is projection. In the simplest case, we may plot the trend of one given variable during a number of past years up to the present and extend the line into the future through freehand extrapolation. There are, however, many more complex methods of projection, too. For instance, it is possible to omit certain past data in making the extrapolation because of their "unusual" nature; or acceleration and deceleration of the past trend may be taken into account.

The method of projection becomes much more complicated and useful when the projection is based on several variables and their interrelation. This task may involve a complex work of analysis. For instance, in trying to predict future population trends we may decide that we should not simply project the past trends. We may find that the future trend of population depends upon three factors, namely, mortality, fertility, and immigration or emigration. Then, in turn, each of these three factors may be studied and projections made concerning certain aspects of the three factors.

This method of projection leads to correlation analysis and regression equations. It is easy to understand their great role. Suppose we want to predict future birth rates (fertility). Birth rates are no doubt the function of several variables, among which some are difficult to predict (*e.g.,* the spread of birth-control practices) but others relatively easy. One of the most important variables, namely, the proportion of women in the child-bearing age groups, is easy to predict, since obviously (neglecting immigration) the maximum number of women in a given age group—say 20 to 25—10 years from now will be the number of women living now aged 10 to 15. Since mortality can likewise be predicted within reasonable margins of error, there is some use in postulating that—other things being equal—future birth rate is a function of the proportion of women in various age groups at present.[3]

This formulation leads us to our immediate problem, namely, the widespread use of such equations at $C = fY$ or $S = fY$, where C stands for consumption, S for saving, f for function, and Y for income before or after taxes. The formulation "consumption is a function of income" is useful for prediction only if future income can be determined more easily than future consumption. (Just as the statement "the birth rate is a function of the proportion of women in various age groups" is useful for prediction because the future sizes of these age groups can be more easily predicted than the birth rate itself.) Although future income is as difficult to predict as future consumption, economists have found a way out of the dilemma. During and shortly after the last war, frequent calculations were made in which the amount of future national income was postulated under certain important conditions. The question raised was: How large must national income be in order to guarantee full employment? It was possible to derive answers to this question by defining, first, what is meant under full employment and by assuming constant prices. The procedure was to estimate the number of people in civilian employment in a given future year, the hours worked per week, the productivity (or changes in productivity) of the workers, and finally the taxes to be paid (in order to derive income after taxes). After future national income was thus determined, consumption expenditures and amounts saved were estimated by projecting the past relation of those variables to national income or gross national product.

These calculations were frequently criticized and attacked, especially when, during the first few postwar years, predictions based on them were far off the mark. In this respect, there was an analogy to the prediction of birth rates, which likewise proved incorrect in the same period. That actual

---

[3] In addition, of course, fertility rates of women in each age group are taken as known or are projected. This variable is omitted from the discussion for the sake of the analogy to be developed presently.

developments in a given period differ from the predicted relationships need not disprove the validity of the method. In this case, however, the failure of postwar employment predictions pointed toward basic weaknesses of the method. One of these was the concentration of attention on one factor—income—in determining the rate of consumption and saving, and the disregard of other factors. Second, the assumption is implicit in the projection of the relation between consumption and income that this relation does not vary cyclically or secularly. Finally, and more generally, regression formulas assume that people will continue to act as they have, or that what happened in the past yields the best clue to what will happen in the future.

As we have repeatedly stated, repetitiveness of behavior does occur, and it may be true that projecting past relationships will give a correct picture of future relationships. But whether or not that will be the case cannot be known in advance. Some scientific information, not contained in the commonly used regression formulas, is needed in order to know whether at any given moment it is permissible and useful to apply those formulas. This information must be of a kind which sheds light on causal relations. For it is possible that a high correlation observed during a given period between such aggregative time series as data on income and retail sales is purely accidental and does not reveal regularities in people's behavior.

In this connection, a further point, of somewhat different import, may also be raised in listing the fundamental weaknesses of regression formulas. To insist that such formulas derived from past data state the relationships that will exist between economic magnitudes in the future may discourage work on other approaches to the problem. It is probable that in the past the preponderant use of the time-series approach, both in theory and in statistical analysis, has done disservice to economic research by impeding the study of the "wanderings" of the consumption function.

It is hardly necessary to state that these considerations do not imply that the aggregative time-series approach is useless or should be abandoned. What is meant here is that that approach needs to be supplemented by other approaches. Time series derived from microeconomic data represent one kind of additional information that needs to be used. In addition to relations that prevail between aggregates, time series of relations between frequency distributions, indicating differences in consumption and saving patterns of different groups, need to be used.

Furthermore, attitudinal and motivational data must supplement the time-series approach. The ultimate aim of the research worker in this respect is obvious. Information on prevailing attitudes may present a clue to the probability of repetitive or nonrepetitive behavior, that is, the continuation of past trends or the inauguration of new developments. Data on motives and expectations provide a clue for dynamic analysis. They are to be used to determine the causal factors that make people behave in one or another way under given circumstances.

These considerations lead us back to the problem of methods of scientific prediction. Is it possible that, in enumerating at the beginning of this section the various methods of predicting, we omitted one, namely, the use of attitudinal data and, especially, the use of expressed expectations?

One possible way to argue would be to assume that data on expectations give us measures of what will happen. In other words, by ascertaining consumer plans for the purchase of durable goods (through surveys of representative samples of consumers), we would obtain data concerning the future demand for durable goods; or, as has been more commonly argued, by determining the expected rate of manufacturers' capital expenditures (through surveys of representative samples of manufacturers), we would obtain advance data about their future investments.

It is questionable whether this is the proper use of data on business or consumer expectations. The immediate purpose of psychological studies and of economic surveys as well is diagnostic: we want to obtain as complete an account as possible of the psychological field as it prevails at a given moment. This field encompasses people's views of the past, their perceptions of the present, and their attitudes toward the future. Expectations are attitudes in which we are interested because they, like any other attitudes, may shape behavior. But complete diagnosis, if obtained, may serve as a basis for predictions, though the transition from diagnosis to prediction is a complex and as yet unsolved process.

We have discussed already the proper use of data on income expectations. A finding that the majority of families expect their incomes to go up has hardly any predictive value about the future national income. But, as we argued in the Notes to Chapter 6, from a time trend of the differences between expected income increases and expected income declines, we may conclude that expectations have taken an optimistic or a pessimistic turn; this finding, then, in conjunction with data about the usual influence of expectations on spending and saving, may be of some predictive value.

Similarly, answers to the question, "Do you expect to buy a new car between now and a year from now?" do not enable us to predict the size of automobile sales during the next year. But by studying the time trend of the answers, we may, under certain circumstances, draw the conclusion that the market for new cars is in better, the same, or in worse shape than it was six or twelve months earlier. To draw such conclusions, we have to check upon the trend of intentions on the part of people in different income and asset groups and also on the trend of expectations to buy cars in different price ranges. We have to find out about the age and condition of the cars owned at the given time, and we have to study the relation of buying intentions to these and other variables. Our purpose is to ascertain people's motivational patterns. We have to know not only how many people desire to buy cars during the next year but also why they so desire and how motivational patterns vary with circumstances and relate to behavior.

These considerations regarding the significance of measuring people's expectations apply likewise to the functional relationships discussed in this chapter. Why do we study the relation of past and expected income changes to saving? In order to establish general principles of behavior that will help us to understand what has happened. If and when, however, we are in the possession of information regarding principles of behavior under different circumstances, we also arrive at clues to what will probably happen.

What we have actually done with respect to isolating and measuring the influence of various factors on spending and saving falls far short of that objective. Much work remains to be undertaken in refining aggregative time series, obtaining microeconomic time series, and measuring attitudinal and motivational factors. And even if there is progress in all these respects, there remains the big task of integrating the various approaches. There is need to build a theory of transition from microeconomic to aggregative data and for checking hypotheses suggested by any one of the approaches through the others. It is not possible to assert confidently that our ability to predict future trends will become satisfactory when all the approaches have been developed and are used jointly. But there can be hardly any doubt that scientific progress lies in that direction.

NOTES TO CHAPTER 8

The amounts saved by each spending unit are determined in the Surveys of Consumer Finances by requesting information about changes in the various asset and liability items that make up the balance sheet of the unit. For example, each survey respondent is asked whether he has any United States government bonds; if so, how much he has in such bonds, and how much he had a year ago in such bonds. From this information, the unit's "additions to saving" or its "withdrawals from saving" through this one source are determined. The same procedure is repeated for all other forms of saving for each calendar year.

The definition of saving as used in the surveys consists therefore of "additions" and "withdrawals" that are taken into account. The additions are: increases in holdings of government bonds and various kinds of bank deposits; purchases of securities and real estate; repayments of debts; payments of life insurance premiums and into retirement funds; cost of building, of structural additions, and of major improvements on buildings owned; amounts lent; new investment in business, and profits left in business owned; purchase price of farm machinery. The withdrawals are: decreases in holdings of government bonds and various kinds of bank deposits; sales of securities and real estate;

amounts borrowed; lump-sum receipts from life insurance policies; repayments of debts received; amounts, other than profits, taken out of businesses owned; inheritances and large gifts of money and bonds received.

Most consumers have both additions to and withdrawals from saving. If the former exceed the latter, the unit is a positive saver, and in the opposite case it is a dissaver.

Some items of information requested are relatively easy to obtain and are subject, as various tests indicate, to relatively small reporting errors. Some other items, however—for example, the excess of amounts spent for the purchase of common stock over the amounts received from the sale of stock—are subject to sizable errors. The findings presented, therefore, do not show exact values but only their probable order of magnitude.

Attention must be called here to further shortcomings of the available data and the definitions used. Some relevant information cannot be obtained from individual consumers. For example, most consumers do not know (and cannot know) what proportion of the life insurance premiums they pay represents "savings" (therefore, in the survey definition of savings, the entire amount of premiums is so considered). Similarly, home owners cannot tell about the annual "depreciation" on their houses, and the surveys adopt a definition of savings that does not make allowance for any depreciation.

The most important differences between the survey definition of saving and that used by the Commerce Department in estimating aggregate personal saving are that the surveys do not include in the savings schedule changes in inventories and depreciation on farms and homes, and that the surveys include all insurance premium payments (not only additions to insurance reserves) and additions and improvements to houses owned. The differences between the definitions used by the two agencies, and also by the Securities and Exchange Commission, have been discussed in the paper of J. N. Morgan in the June, 1950, issue of the

TABLE 24. DISTRIBUTION OF SPENDING UNITS ACCORDING TO PROPORTION OF INCOME SAVED

(Percentage distribution of all spending units)

Rate of saving	1946		1947		1948		1949	
Negative....................		27		28		31		34
Minus 25% or more.........	11		9		11		12	
Minus 10 – 24%.............	7		8		8		9	
Minus 1 – 9%...............	9		11		12		13	
Zero........................		8		8		6		6
Positive....................		65		64		63		60
Plus 1 – 9%.................	24		30		28		26	
Plus 10 – 19%..............	16		14		14		14	
Plus 20 – 29%..............	10		8		9		9	
Plus 30 – 49%..............	9		7		8		8	
Plus 50% or more...........	6		5		4		3	
Total....................		100		100		100		100

American Economic Review. This paper also presents information about the aggregate amounts of savings obtained by the three agencies.

For a more detailed account of the methods used in obtaining saving data and for the distribution of saving in the postwar years, the reader is referred to the articles on the Survey of Consumer Finances in the August, 1948, and January, 1950, issues of the *Federal Reserve Bulletin*. Table 24, presenting the distribution of proportions of income saved, is taken from that publication.

Statistical data on the relation of positive and negative saving to level of income are presented in Tables 25 and 26. For more detailed data and discussion of the problem see the author's article, "Analysis of Dissaving," *American Economic Review,* Vol. 39, 1949, pp. 673*ff*.

TABLE 25. FREQUENCY OF POSITIVE AND NEGATIVE SAVING AT
DIFFERENT INCOME LEVELS
(Percentage distribution of spending units in each income quintile)

	Spending units ranked according to money income before taxes*				
	Lowest fifth	Second fifth	Third fifth	Fourth fifth	Highest fifth
1947					
Negative savers.............	29	30	29	31	23
Zero savers................	24	9	3	2	†
Positive savers.............	47	61	68	67	77
Total....................	100	100	100	100	100
1948					
Negative savers.............	36	32	31	30	26
Zero savers................	20	7	3	1	†
Positive savers.............	44	61	66	69	74
Total....................	100	100	100	100	100

* Units were ranked according to 1947 or 1948 incomes in order to determine the frequency of savers and dissavers in 1947 and in 1948, respectively.
† Less than 0.5 per cent.

Tables 27 and 28 indicate the differences in the allocation of income among high-, middle-, and low-income units. The estimates, and especially those for "other consumer expenditures" that were not measured directly but calculated as a residual item, are subject to sizable errors.

Data on the relation of past and expected income changes to saving and to expenditures on durable goods are presented by the author in his paper "Effect of Income Changes on the Rate of Saving," *Review of Economics and Statistics,* Vol. 31, 1949, pp. 95*ff*., and in the forthcoming paper by the author and J. A. Fisher in Volume 13 of *Studies in Income and Wealth* ("Postwar Income

TABLE 26. DISTRIBUTION OF AMOUNTS SAVED BY EACH TENTH OF THE NATION'S SPENDING UNITS, RANKED BY SIZE OF INCOME *

(In per cent)

Spending units ranked according to their income	Positive saving		Negative saving		Net saving	
	1947	1948	1947	1948	1947	1948
Lowest tenth..........	1	1	15	17	—11	—17
Second tenth..........	1	2	6	10	—2	—7
Third tenth............	2	2	7	7	—1	—3
Fourth tenth...........	4	4	5	8	2	—1
Fifth tenth.............	5	5	6	9	4	2
Sixth tenth............	6	7	11	7	3	6
Seventh tenth..........	7	8	10	9	6	6
Eighth tenth...........	8	11	10	9	6	15
Ninth tenth............	14	15	11	11	16	19
Highest tenth..........	52	45	19	13	77	80
All units.............	100	100	100	100	100	100

* The amounts saved by all positive savers (who spend less than their income) are called positive savings; the amounts dissaved by all dissavers (who spend more than their income) are called negative savings; and the difference between the two amounts is called net saving. The three amounts, determined separately for 1947 and 1948, are taken as 100, and the table shows the share of each income decile in those amounts. Ranking by income was done separately for 1947 and 1948.

TABLE 27. DISTRIBUTION OF TAXES, NET SAVINGS, EXPENDITURES ON DURABLE GOODS, AND OTHER CONSUMER EXPENDITURES, BY INCOME LEVELS, 1948

(In per cent *)

Spending units ranked according to their income	Type of expenditure or saving			
	Federal income taxes	Net saving	Automobiles and other durable goods†	Other consumer expenditures‡
Lowest fifth...........	1	—22	4	8
Second fifth...........	5	—3	10	13
Third fifth............	9	8	17	18
Fourth fifth...........	16	21	25	22
Highest fifth..........	70	97	44	39
All units............	100	100	100	100

* Details may not add to totals because of rounding.
† Amounts spent minus trade-in values.
‡ Include mainly expenditures on nondurable goods and services.

TABLE 28. PROPORTION OF MONEY INCOME ALLOCATED TO TAXES, NET SAVINGS, EXPENDITURES ON DURABLE GOODS, AND OTHER CONSUMER EXPENDITURES, BY SPENDING UNITS WITHIN EACH INCOME FIFTH, 1948

Type of expenditure or saving	Per cent of total income within each income group				
	Lowest fifth	Second fifth	Third fifth	Fourth fifth	Highest fifth
Federal income taxes........	1	4	5	6	13
Net saving.................	—31	—2	3	6	14
Automobiles and other durable goods*..........	8	8	9	10	8
Other consumer expenditures†	121	90	83	78	65
Total...................	100	100	100	100	100

* Amounts spent minus trade-in values.

† Include mainly expenditures on nondurable goods and services.

Changes of Identical Consumer Units," National Bureau of Economic Research, 1951). These articles also contain data on the relations of income changes to saving and to purchases of durable goods within different income groups. It is shown that similar relations prevail in most income groups. A possible exception is to be noted inasmuch as past and expected income changes seem to have the smallest effect on the rate of saving of families with high income.

Regarding the combined effect of income changes that actually occurred and that were anticipated, a table from the author's above-mentioned paper in the *Review of Economics and Statistics* is reproduced here (Table 29). The conclusions drawn have been called tentative because they are derived from a joint consideration of all spending units in the middle-income ranges and are nevertheless based on a relatively small number of cases. In addition, difficult survey problems arise with respect to the timing of income expectations. The surveys were conducted and the income expectations determined shortly after the end of the calendar year for which the amounts saved were ascertained. The investigation therefore rests on the assumption that in general there were no substantial changes in income expectations during the months prior to their measurement. Studies carried out by interviewing the same respondents twice tend to confirm that this was probably the case with many families during the years studied.

Income expectations have been determined in the surveys in two ways. At the beginning of 1949, for instance, respondents were asked what their 1948 incomes were, and then whether they expected their incomes for 1949 to be larger, smaller, or the same. This type of inquiry is the basis of Table 29. It does not represent a determination of expectations alone, since it also takes some past income changes into account. Suppose that the salary rate of an employee was raised in, say, October, 1948, from $3,000 to $3,600 per annum. Assume further that the employee does not expect any changes in his pay rate during the following year. Then, in an interview conducted in January, 1949, he would have

TABLE 29. RELATION OF PAST AND EXPECTED INCOME CHANGES TO PROPORTION OF INCOME SAVED

(Percentage distribution of spending units with $1,000 to $3,999 income in each group)

Rate of saving in 1947	1947 income smaller than 1946 income; 1948 income expected to be—			1947 income same as 1946 income; 1948 income expected to be—			1947 income larger than 1946 income; 1948 income expected to be—		
	Smaller*	Same	Larger	Smaller*	Same	Larger*	Smaller*	Same	Larger
Negative	33	32	44	32	23	36	30	28	32
Zero	7	3	6	7	17	7	3	2	6
Positive:									
1–19% of income	39	44	37	40	50	46	43	53	45
20% or more of income	21	21	13	21	10	11	24	17	17
Total	100	100	100	100	100	100	100	100	100

Rate of saving in 1946	1946 income smaller than 1945 income; 1947 income expected to be—			1946 income same as 1945 income; 1947 income expected to be—			1946 income larger than 1945 income; 1947 income expected to be—		
	Smaller*	Same	Larger	Smaller	Same	Larger*	Smaller*	Same	Larger
Negative	32	26	44	**	18	32	28	26	31
Zero	4	2	2		9	6	4	4	2
Positive:									
1–19% of income	44	51	35		47	37	42	45	43
20% or more of income	20	21	19		26	25	26	25	24
Total	100	100	100		100	100	100	100	100

NOTE: The subgroups presented in the 17 columns of the table consist of 80 to 450 spending units. Six groups consisting of only 80 to 150 cases are marked with an asterisk to indicate that those data are less reliable than the data in the other columns. Two asterisks indicate a group which consisted of so few cases that reliable saving data could not be computed for it.

"Same" refers to less than 5 per cent change in income, "larger" and "smaller" to increases and decreases of 5 per cent or more.

180

to say that he expected his income for 1949 to be somewhat higher than his income for 1948 (namely, $3,600 against $3,150).

Another approach to studying income expectations, which refers exclusively to future changes, has also been used. Respondents were asked, at the beginning of a calendar year, whether a year from "now" they expected their incomes to be higher, lower, or the same. This form of the question was used in Table 20 in the text (and in Table 9 of Chapter 6). The two types of inquiry into expectations yielded similar results regarding their relation to saving and spending.

Detailed data on the different kinds of dissaving were presented in the author's paper in the 1949 *American Economic Review*. The discussion in that paper was heavily drawn upon in the text. Table 30, adapted from that article, shows that large purchases of durable goods and temporary income declines have a much stronger association with dissaving than with saving. Two other variables likewise show different frequencies among savers and dissavers, but the differences are smaller. The data in the table contain "duplications"; some dissavers, for instance, reported both "illness" and large purchases of durable goods. When all duplications are eliminated from the table, it appears that the four

TABLE 30. RELATION OF FOUR SELECTED VARIABLES TO SAVING AND DISSAVING

Variables	Percentage of spending units having each variable among those who—							
	Saved				Dissaved			
	Any amount		Over $500		Any amount		Over $500	
	1947	1948	1947	1948	1947	1948	1947	1948
Illness, emergency............	25	24	22	25	32	37	33	32
Temporary income decline....	4	3	4	4	10	8	10	8
Other income decline.........	13	10	11	11	13	15	19	18
Large purchase of durable goods...................	12	14	19	22	27	30	41	49

DEFINITIONS: *Illness, emergency.* The heads of each spending unit were asked the following question: "Did anything unusual happen in _____ to influence your savings? For instance, were there any large expenses for such things as illness, moving, or contributions for the support of others; or were your expenses unusually low for some reason?" All those who in answering this question referred to medical expenses, hospital expenses, childbirth, and death were put in this group.

Temporary income decline. All spending units who had lower incomes in the year studied than in the previous year and who expressed the opinion that in the following year their incomes would be higher. Lower and higher were defined as a difference of at least 5 per cent.

Other income decline. Spending units whose income declined from 1946 (1947) to 1947 (1948) by at least 5 per cent and who are not included in the previous group.

Large purchase of durable goods. Spending units who purchased automobiles or other selected consumer durable goods for at least $500. The trade-in value of old cars was not included in the purchase price.

factors jointly "explain" a very substantial proportion of the incidence of dis-saving (two-thirds to three-fourths) but a much smaller proportion of positive saving. Still, it must be kept in mind that there are dissavers who neither spent large amounts on durable goods nor had income declines and illnesses; further-more, even dissavers who fell into these categories may have been induced to dissave for other reasons.

The author's paper in the *American Economic Review* also shows that spend-ing units who made large purchases of durable goods *and* dissaved are more frequent in high- than in low-income brackets. Spending units who had income declines or illness and emergencies *and* dissaved are more frequent in low- than in high-income brackets.

The relation between saving behavior and expenditures on durable goods is also shown in Table 31. The frequency of large expenditures on durable goods is much higher among the negative savers than among the positive savers. Zero savers—who spent all they made, not more, not less—are characterized by infre-quent purchases of durable goods.

TABLE 31. EXPENDITURES FOR AUTOMOBILES AND OTHER DURABLE GOODS
WITHIN SAVINGS GROUPS

(In per cent)

Expenditures on durable goods	Positive savers		Zero savers		Negative savers	
	1947	1948	1947	1948	1947	1948
None..................	61	57	85	81	44	41
$1 – $499..............	27	29	14	17	29	29
$500 and over..........	12	14	1	2	27	30
Total................	100	100	100	100	100	100

The analysis of the relation between income expectations and intentions to purchase durable goods presents a corollary to the findings reported on the relation between income changes and past purchases of durable goods. Data obtained in three consecutive annual surveys concerning the relation between three types of expectations and intentions to purchase automobiles and other durable goods are presented in Table 32. Although the differences are not large, and sometimes statistically not significant, they are consistent at different periods of time and with respect to different kinds of goods: more people who expected good times to come, or their incomes to increase, planned to buy automobiles and other durable goods than people who expected bad times to come, or their incomes to decline. The differences between groups with various price expecta-tions are less pronounced. Only one of the six investigations revealed a signifi-cant difference: in 1949 more people who expected prices to fall than who expected prices to rise planned to buy durable goods other than automobiles. The table has, of course, grave shortcomings since it singles out the expectations

TABLE 32. RELATION BETWEEN INTENTIONS TO BUY AUTOMOBILES OR
OTHER DURABLE GOODS AND VARIOUS ATTITUDES

(Data from surveys conducted early in 1949, 1948, and 1947)

Will and probably will buy—	Proportion of prospective buyers in each group, per cent								
	General economic outlook			Income expectation			Price expectation		
	Good	Uncertain	Bad	Higher	Same	Lower	Higher	Same	Lower
Automobiles:									
In 1949	13	7	9	16	9	13	10	9	12
In 1948	14	7	9	16	10	10	10	11	13
In 1947	14	8	10	15	11	13	11	11	13
Other durable goods:									
In 1949	27	21	20	29	22	18	19	21	26
In 1948	25	18	20	30	21	19	23	20	24
In 1947	24	15	19	25	21	22	20	22	22

without regard to past income changes and other variables. The table shows that among spending units who at the beginning of 1949 thought that the general economic outlook for 1949 was good, 13 per cent said that they would or probably would buy automobiles in 1949 (and, therefore, 87 per cent said that they would not buy or were undecided), etc.

TABLE 33.   RELATION BETWEEN ACTUAL OR PROSPECTIVE AUTOMOBILE PURCHASES
AND VARIOUS FINANCIAL TRENDS AND ATTITUDES, JULY, 1949

	Percentage of all spending units in each group who—	
	Bought cars Jan.-July, 1949	Plan to buy cars in 12 months following July, 1949 *
Current income:		
Larger than a year ago.	14	16
About the same	11	9
Smaller than a year ago.	10	9
Evaluation of personal financial situation:		
Better off than a year ago.	16	19
About the same.	11	10
Worse off than a year ago.	10	7
Evaluation of current economic situation or of economic prospects: †		
Times are (will be) good.	13	14
Times are (will be) bad.	6	8

* Includes only those who said "will buy."
† Past purchases are related to the evaluation of the current economic situation, prospective purchases to that of the expected economic situation.

With the downturn in production and increase in unemployment during the first half of 1949, the proportion of people who felt they were worse off than they had been a year before and who expected bad times to come increased somewhat. Thus a survey conducted in July, 1949, constituted a good opportunity to test the relation of various attitudes to past and expected purchases. Findings made in this survey are presented in Table 33. They show, on the whole, larger differences between the buying behavior of different groups than observed in previous surveys. Possibly, although there is no assurance in this respect, pessimistic attitudes and expectations were held with greater conviction in July, 1949, than earlier.

Information on the distribution of price expectations at different times during the years 1946 to 1949 is presented in Table 34. Substantial changes in the expected trend of prices are revealed, in sharp contrast to the relative stability

TABLE 34. CONSUMER PRICE EXPECTATIONS FOR THE YEAR AHEAD
(As reported at intervals from 1946 to 1949)

Prices*	Per cent of all spending units							
	Early 1946	Early 1947	July, 1947	Jan., 1948	Feb. 14-Mar. 5, 1948	July, 1948	Early 1949	July, 1949
Will go up...............	53	13	32	50	15	42	8	7
Will remain the same.......	21	22	29	22	29	25	20	34
Will go down.............	8	46	29	16	39	15	55	48
Conditional answers.......	13	17	9	10	15	16	15	10
Not ascertained...........	5	2	1	2	2	2	2	1
All cases...............	100	100	100	100	100	100	100	100

* The question was: "What do you think will happen to the prices of the things you buy during the next 12 months—do you think they will go up, or down, or stay about where they are now?"

of income expectations and of the general economic outlook observed in the same period (see Table 9 in Chapter 6). Regarding the relation of price expectations to saving, we shall report only one of several inconclusive findings: Both among spending units who in January, 1949, expected prices to go up and among those who expected prices to go down, the same proportion, namely, 29 per cent, dissaved in 1948.

J. S. Duesenberry ("Income-Consumption Relations and Their Implications" in *Income, Employment and Public Policy: Essays in Honor of Alvin H. Hansen,* New York, 1948) appears to relate dissaving in 1935–1936 to unemployment and to incomes that were low in comparison to previous incomes. This relation is possible, but as he himself states, cannot be proved on the basis of data available from the Study of Consumer Purchases. Duesenberry's major thesis that "cyclically, the aggregate propensity to consume depends on the ratio of current income to the highest income previously achieved" (pp. 79*ff.*) disregards the possibility of a systematic relationship between income increases and the propensity to consume. Also, Duesenberry's statement is probably too broad; the highest income previously achieved may not affect the propensity to consume under all circumstances and in all future years. It should also be noted that recent studies revealed substantial errors in people's recollection of the income they had received 12 to 24 months earlier. Recall appears to be "falsified" by developments that have occurred between an event and its recall. Only people's recollection of their previous income may affect their current spending and saving behavior, and not their true previous income.

Franco Modigliani likewise argues that the proportion of income saved is a function of the highest income realized in any year prior to the one studied (in Volume 11 of *Studies in Income and Wealth,* National Bureau of Economic Research, New York, 1948, pp. 369*ff.*).

We are, however, in substantial agreement with the major thesis of another recent paper. George Garvy ("The Role of Dissaving in Economic Analysis," *Journal of Political Economy*, Vol. 56, 1948, pp. 416*ff.*) writes: "There is no logical reason for relating the motivations of two distinct groups of consumers—positive and negative savers—to the same set of causal factors" (p. 416). But during 1946 to 1948, we found no confirmation for the following statement made by Garvy: "The presence in the population of relatively large groups of families who have suffered a loss of income accounts probably for the bulk of dissaving" (p. 423).

Among empirical studies of the "lag" of consumption behind changes in income, Mordecai Ezekiel's investigations ("Statistical Investigations of Saving, Consumption, and Investment," *American Economic Review*, Vol. 32, 1942) and L. A. Metzler's brief paper ("Three Lags in the Circular Flow of Income," *Income, Employment and Public Policy: Essays in Honor of Alvin H. Hansen*, New York, 1948) may be mentioned. Both papers study the relation of aggregate consumption to aggregate changes in income and both suffer from the incompleteness of the basic data used. Ruth P. Mack, in her excellent paper on "The Direction of Change in Income and the Consumption Function" (*Review of Economic Statistics*, Vol. 30, 1948), presents microeconomic data from various surveys and points to a number of problems connected with this as well as with time-series analysis. She argues that the expenditures for some commodities will probably be affected differently from the expenditures for other commodities under the impact of income increases and decreases. This argument points toward the need for empirical studies of different types of consumer expenditures, which are not available at present.

Further important factors associated with the role of income changes may be the recency, extent, and group-psychological meaning of such changes. Jacob Marschak called attention to these factors by raising the question about the spending behavior of the *"nouveaux riches"* (in his Foreword to H. Mendershausen's *Changes in Income Distributions during the Great Depression*, National Bureau of Economic Research, New York, 1946).

The following quotations may serve to illustrate the statement in the text that many economists seem to assume at present that large asset holdings induce people to spend at a relatively high rate. Some of these statements, as well as others made for instance by Pigou and A. G. Hart, refer to changes in the "real value of assets." Insofar as the value of asset holdings is increased or decreased solely by price deflation or inflation, a new problem is raised with which we are not concerned.

"The rate of saving is not only an increasing function of the level of real income, but also a diminishing function of the wealth the individual holds" (Gottfried Haberler, *Prosperity and Depression*, 1941, 3d ed., p. 499).

"The most obvious hypothesis would seem to be that the consumption function will shift upward because of the accumulation of liquid reserves" (Gottfried Haberler, *Review of Economic Statistics*, Vol. 28, 1946, p. 191).

"The rise in the real value of assets will lessen the need for additional saving and hence increase the fraction of any given level of real income that the community will wish to consume" (Milton Friedman, *American Economic Review,* Vol. 38, 1948, p. 259).

"A rise in the real value of the community's assets will raise the average propensity to consume. I do not see how either the existence or the direction of the effect can be denied" (Milton Friedman, *American Economic Review,* Vol. 39, 1949, p. 953).

"Generally speaking, the higher and more widespread the liquid asset holdings in relation to income and prices, the lower the expected rate of saving" (Irwin Friend, *Survey of Current Business,* September, 1949, p. 15).

"The availability of liquid assets raises consumption generally by reducing the impulse to save out of current income" (*Survey of Current Business,* May, 1950, p. 10).

It is interesting to note that some of these statements are formulated as if they expressed established facts, although no evidence is available about liquid-asset holdings reducing the impulse to save, and that statement is hardly in accord with findings of psychology. (The reader is referred to the discussion of the "saturation theory" in Chapter 6.)

That the effect of liquid-asset holdings on spending and saving depends on the distribution of the assets has been stated by Alvin Hansen: "With respect to the effect of increased liquid assets . . . on the consumption function, that all depends upon who it is that holds the liquid assets. If the liquid assets are largely in the possession of the rich, the consumption function can rise very little" (*Review of Economic Statistics,* Vol. 28, 1946, p. 185).

The table presented in the text concerning the relationship of liquid-asset holdings of different size to saving behavior needs to be supplemented by data which eliminate the possible income effect. Does the relationship found among all spending units in the nation hold good if the behavior of low-income or middle-income or high-income spending units is considered separately?

Table 35 presents an attempt to answer this question. It appears that there are some differences in the behavior of different income groups and there is more variability within income groups than among all spending units (which may be due to the smaller samples involved). Yet the conclusion that the proportion of high savers increases as liquid assets increase is confirmed in every one except the lowest income group. The conclusion that the proportion of dissavers increases as liquid assets increase is likewise confirmed in the different income groups, except that the available data for the middle-income group are inconclusive.

One of the first detailed applications of the method of economic forecasting that consists of the projection of past relationships is contained in the pamphlet *Markets after the War* by S. Morris Livingston, published first by the Bureau of Foreign and Domestic Commerce of the Department of Commerce (U.S. Government Printing Office, Washington, D.C., 1943), and reprinted by the Committee on Economic Development. The most important table in this publication, entitled "A Hypothetical Projection of Expenditures by Commodity Groups Based on Past Relationships to the Gross National Product," carries a note

(Percentage distribution of spending units in each income fifth)

Income group and rate of saving in 1948	Liquid asset holdings at beginning of 1948			
	None	$1–$499	$500–$1,999	$2,000 and over
Lowest income fifth				
Negative	21	44	52	56
Zero	32	9	9	5
Positive	47	47	39	39
1–9%	28	22	15	25
10–29%	13	19	15	7
30% or more	6	6	9	7
Total	100	100	100	100
Second income fifth				
Negative	23	27	49	36
Zero	14	4	—	6
Positive	63	69	51	58
1–9%	42	40	27	25
10–29%	16	24	17	18
30% or more	5	5	7	15
Total	100	100	100	100
Third income fifth				
Negative	16	38	36	36
Zero	7	1	2	—
Positive	77	61	62	64
1–9%	49	30	22	22
10–29%	22	26	29	27
30% or more	6	5	11	15
Total	100	100	100	100
Fourth income fifth				
Negative	25	20	43	34
Zero	8	—	—	—
Positive	67	80	57	66
1–9%	39	34	24	15
10–29%	19	34	24	31
30% or more	9	12	9	20
Total	100*	100	100	100
Highest income fifth				
Negative	.....	19	25	28
Zero	.....	—	1	—
Positive	.....	81	74	72
1–9%	.....	34	21	18
10–29%	.....	33	30	27
30% or more	.....	14	23	27
Total	†	100	100	100

* Small cell; data subject to larger sampling errors.

† Not presented because of the very small number of cases.

saying, "this is not a forecast." But the author says later: "While they are in no sense forecasts, many of the items are probably sufficiently accurate to serve as a preliminary basis for planning as well as a starting point for market analysis."

Three important papers entitled "Forecasting Postwar Demand," by Arthur Smithies, S. Morris Livingston, and Jacob L. Mosak, were presented at a meeting of the Econometric Society in September, 1944, and published in *Econometrica*, Vol. 13, 1945. In these papers, gross national product is estimated under full-employment conditions, and postwar consumer expenditures, government expenditures, and business investment are calculated in the light of past relationships. The authors are well aware of the problems involved in using this method. For instance, Mosak says: "The analysis is based on certain income and expenditure relationships which prevailed in the period 1929–40. The projection of these relationships implies that the war and the reconversion period to follow will have no significant long-run effect on the producer and consumer habits with which we are concerned" (p. 25). Or: "It is assumed that the volume of consumer expenditures in the postwar period will bear a stable relationship to the aggregate volume of disposable income. This assumption also represents an extreme oversimplification" (p. 33).

The same method was used in a great variety of postwar forecasts. For a discussion of the methods used, see L. R. Klein, "A Post-mortem on Transition Predictions of National Product," *Journal of Political Economy*, Vol. 54, 1946, pp. 289*ff*.

The method of regression formulas derived from two or three aggregative time series was severely criticized with respect to its principle and to details by W. S. Woytinsky, in his article "Relationship between Consumers' Expenditures, Savings, and Disposable Income" in the *Review of Economic Statistics*, Vol. 28, 1946, pp. 1*ff*. Use has been made in the text of some of the arguments advanced by Woytinsky. This article was further discussed in five papers which appeared later in the same volume of the same periodical ("Five Views on the Consumption Function," *op. cit.*, pp. 197*ff*.). In addition to L. H. Bean, Irwin Friend, Dorothy S. Brady, and E. G. Bennion, G. Katona and R. Likert pointed to the variety of different factors that need to be considered in addition to the income-consumption relationship.

One of the broadest applications of regression formulas to future developments is contained in the volume *America's Needs and Resources* by J. Frederic Dewhurst and Associates (Twentieth Century Fund, 1947). Projections are made in this book not only on the basis of past regression lines but also on the basis of one-time relationships obtained in a single survey. For instance: "An approximate picture of the probable distribution of the cash income of consumers in 1950 can be obtained by 'projecting' the results of a field survey of cash income distribution in 1941 made jointly by the Bureau of Labor Statistics and the Bureau of Agricultural Economics" (p. 65). The basic assumption involved is clearly stated in the Foreword: ". . . we project this curve (obtained from past measurements) into the future, assuming that we can continue to act as we have in the past . . ." (p. vii). The final words of the extensive volume point, however, to some unsolved problems and thereby cast doubt on the validity of the methods used. "Whether we increase output per man hour during the next decade . . . will not be determined by 'projecting past trends.' It will be determined . . . by a multitude of actions and decisions on the part of individuals. . . . It would be folly to overlook the human element in what is generally conceived to be progress in industrial America. . . . In the last analysis it is people who make 'progress' " (p. 687).

After completion of the manuscript, an extensive discussion of the predictive value of expressed intentions and plans appeared in print. In Volume IV of the *Studies in Social Psychology in World War II* (by Samuel A. Stouffer and Associates), entitled *Measurement and Prediction* (Princeton University Press, Princeton, N. J., 1950), John A. Clausen discusses the wartime questionnaire surveys in which members of the armed forces were interrogated about their postwar plans (of employment, going into business, further schooling, etc.). There is fundamental agreement between some of the general conclusions drawn by the author and the text of this chapter. In the opinion of Clausen, expressed intentions "may be regarded as representing an organization of attitudes toward a particular goal" (p. 580); they are of great assistance in making predictions, but "even if a complete and accurate knowledge of the individual's plans and intentions could be secured by questionnaire, the predictive value of such plans and intentions would remain in question" (p. 689).

During the past few years, econometricians have turned to the study of the simultaneous interdependence of several variables. When consumption expenditures or amounts saved are related to such variables as income changes, income expectations, or asset holdings, in addition to level of income, "behavioral equations" may be derived which summarize the factors responsible for past performance. As said before (Chapter 1), modern econometrics and psychological economics may go hand in hand. Specifically, it is hoped that many of the shortcomings of the analysis carried out in this chapter will ultimately be overcome by the use of the method of simultaneous functional equations.

PART THREE

BUSINESS BEHAVIOR

CHAPTER 9

BUSINESS MOTIVATION

Before turning to the analysis of major decisions made by business firms (Chapters 10 and 11), we must first consider the objectives which firms seek to attain through their decisions and actions. Regarding both business motivations and decisions, we can rely on a variety of observations and case studies, and can also make use of psychological concepts and findings. But empirical investigations that would provide quantitative information about the frequency of various kinds of motives, or of various kinds of decisions, under different conditions, are almost entirely lacking. The discussion in this as well as the following chapters will therefore deal primarily with principles on a hypothetical level rather than present tested generalizations.

It may be argued that there is no need for a discussion of the objectives and goals of business firms: what was established about the motivational patterns of households and consumers must apply to business motives as well. A person is not fundamentally changed when he leaves his home in the morning and enters his business office. Irrespective of whether at a given moment his role is that of consumer or business owner or business executive, the same multiplicity of pecuniary and nonpecuniary motives must be effective. Individual circumstances determine the structure and focus of the motivational patterns; it is therefore futile to search for one paramount business motive.

On the other hand, it may be maintained that in functioning as a businessman—owner, manager, or executive—the psychological field is fundamentally different and is always structured in a specific way. Being engaged in business may mean a more "rational" or more calculating attitude. This argument may imply that business decisions are thought through more carefully than consumer decisions. Business decisions are considered and deliberated, with alternatives weighed and resolved according to some principle or criterion, whereas consumer decisions are frequently either habitual and conventional or emotional and whimsical.

We shall find that there is some truth in both points of view. The second view is embodied in traditional economic theory, according to which the objective of businessmen is the maximization of profits. People are in business in order to make profits. Businessmen want to make profits and want to make the maximum possible profits. This point of view has not, however, gone uncontradicted. It has been argued that it is one-sided; that sociological, anthropological, and psychological studies have revealed that businessmen do not strive for profits alone; that striving for security, power, and prestige plays an important role, in conjunction with, or even in opposition to, the profit motive. These arguments seem to imply that the first point of view is the more correct one, and that motives are not what make business behavior different from consumer behavior.

Evidence to be presented later about the wide prevalence of habitual behavior in business life points in the same direction. It is not at all certain that genuine decisions play a larger role in business than in consumer behavior. Nevertheless, there can be no doubt that in present-day American business thinking the function and role of profits is substantial. We shall try, therefore, to understand the psychological meaning of profits, of striving for profits, and of striving for maximum profits, before we proceed to the discussion of more complex motivational patterns of businessmen.

PROFIT MOTIVE AND PROFIT MAXIMIZATION

1. What Are Profits?   The concept "profit" must be clarified first. Profits are not objectively given data. After they have been determined for a given period and especially after they have been reported and published, they may assume the role of facts in the minds of people outside the business firm and even of those who determined them. But determining how much profit was made in a given period is not an operation of simple fact finding or arithmetic. It involves subjective considerations and is influenced by the attitudes and motives of the business owners or managers.

The simple definition of profits as the difference between what a commodity costs the seller and what he sells it for does not cover all that enters into the determination of profits, except in certain simple situations that are not typical in business life. Let's say John Jones, a bookkeeper, collects stamps as a hobby. One Saturday afternoon, while he is making the rounds of the stamp dealers to see what he can buy to add to his collection, a dealer offers him $3 for a stamp he once bought for $2. Because John has seen another stamp he would rather own, he accepts the offer, figuring that it has netted him a $1 profit. For John Jones the determination of costs is simple. He does not consider the value of his own time in effecting the transaction, or overhead, or taxes, or the need for maintaining reserves.

When we apply our definition of profit to business life, however, we meet with some difficulties. The price for which goods are sold is easily enough determined, and it is a relatively objective procedure to determine the total amount of sales for a year. But what is the cost of a commodity? What are the costs of producing a Chevrolet car and what are the total annual expenses of the Chevrolet Company?

In determining their costs, businessmen are guided by accounting practices and conventions which are not rigid and unchangeable and which leave them much latitude. Of course, there are costs that are objectively measured—wages and salaries and the cost of raw materials, for instance. But costs also depend on depreciation rates, on valuation of inventories, on allocation of overhead, advertising, sales, and developmental expenses. Multiproduct firms, dealing in several products, are the rule and not the exception, which means that the cost and profit of a specific product depend on the allocation of joint costs. How to apply the accounting principles, when to deviate from them, whether to transfer some "profits" to special reserve funds or to draw on such funds—all this depends on subjective considerations, on the businessman's frame of reference and expectations.

To be sure, the businessman's latitude is severely limited. Habits are powerful constraining forces. Businessmen habitually determine the excess of their net assets at the end of a year over their net assets at the beginning of the year and make their valuations of their assets in a conventional way. Also, naturally, the facts themselves present upper and lower limits to valuations. And yet, habits can be given up and new decisions can be made. Often, with regard to cost allocation, developmental expenses, and reserves, decisions must be made. In other words, the exact amount of profits shown depends on business decisions.

All this is, of course, well known insofar as the general principles are concerned. With respect to the different considerations that enter into the process of cost and profit determination under different conditions, our knowledge is limited. Empirical studies concerning the dynamics of those processes are needed. But what we have said about the subjective character of profits may suffice as an introduction to the problem with which we are concerned. The analysis of profit motives, to which we now turn, will proceed in stages, although the different aspects of the problem are interrelated. The first question to be taken up refers to the "subject" of the profit motive, the person, group, or institution seeking profits. The second concerns the time period within which profits are considered. The kind of profits considered and the means by which profits are achieved will then be discussed and will lead to a study of pecuniary motives that are not directly or not primarily profit motives.

2. Profits for Whom? If a man is engaged in a business of his own, if he uses exclusively his own funds and has no employees, the problem as to the subject of the profit motive may not arise. It may be said that he strives to make profits for himself and for nobody else. The problem is somewhat more complicated in the case of a large business enterprise in which the owner, the major partner, or the holder of the majority stock is also the principal manager. Still, the two cases are similar. But how about the large corporations, which at present account for the bulk of American production and distribution? As a rule, the "owners," that is, the holders of common stock, are widely scattered, and there is no individual holder or group of holders who control a substantial share of the capital. Business funds are supplied not only by those who purchase common or preferred stock but also by those who invest in bonds, and by banks as well as by suppliers and customers. Neither the stockholders nor the lenders are, as a rule, the managers of the corporation, nor do they have a substantial direct influence on the management's decisions. The ownership interest of the management itself is usually very small. Yet the management is self-perpetuating and frequently supervises itself by controlling the selection of members of the board of directors or by relegating that board to an advisory position. Although there are marked differences in this situation among American corporations, there can be no doubt that complete separation of ownership and management functions is a widespread situation. Therefore, we must ask: For whom do business executives strive to make profits?

The legalistic answer to this question is: The owners hire the manager to make profits for them, the owners. In sharp contrast to this assertion, one may quote recent statements of a number of corporation executives to the effect that they have responsibilities toward their stockholders, employees, and customers, and strive to strike a balance among these three groups of interests. Psychological studies of group membership, of belonging to, and identifying oneself with, groups, lead to a view which appears to be different from both statements.

If all motives were ego-centered, one might argue that the managers strive to maximize their own salaries or remuneration. The objective of getting the highest possible profit for oneself from the corporation's activities, that is, the objective of "milking" the company one directs, may prevail in one or the other exceptional instance, but it is contrary to the institutional patterns prevailing in our economy.

Furthermore, this objective is contrary to psychological principles of group belonging. We are not only part of our family, or of groups consisting of our neighbors or business associates, but the we with which we identify ourselves may also comprise our business enterprise. Although exact investigations are not available, it is probable that as a rule business managers identify themselves with the businesses they manage. Identification with the business in which one is employed may exist even in low-level employees or may occasionally be missing in high-level employees. But usually the corporation or business enterprise has psychological reality for at least the executives. It is perceived by them as acting, as having objectives of its own, and as persisting beyond their association with it. The psychological reality of the firm appears to be especially pronounced in the minds of executives when management responsibilities are divided among several persons, as is frequent with many of the large corporations that are not managed by an autocratic president and his subordinates.

It follows that the corporation manager, as a rule, does not think separately of the interests of the owners, the employees, and the customers. On the contrary, he may think of the interests of *his* corporation without regard to the special interests of owners, employees, or customers. He thinks and acts as if it were his corporation, even if he has no ownership share in it. Improvement in the situation of the business enterprise brings him genuine satisfaction, and deterioration in its situation causes genuine worry, without regard to whether the improvement or deterioration affects his own position.

But we reported earlier that group belonging varies from time to time. At a given moment, during a conference with a customer, for instance, a business executive may identify himself with his firm, and a few minutes later he may think and act as a family member to whom social relations with this customer may be important. Ego-centered motives of business executives may then be in conflict with business motives. But it seems—although no definite statement can be made about this—that usually they are not. Institutional practices may have contributed to this situation. It has been found, for instance, that moderate increases or decreases in corporation profits rarely have a direct effect on the executives' remuneration or on the assurance with which they hold their positions. The personal motivation of the executives—to satisfy their ego, to have power, security, and larger and larger income—may be and often is satisfied through identification with their firms. Rivalry between executives of the same firm exists. But usually it seems to take the form of striving for a larger share for one's own department. The production vice-president wants larger funds for engineering developments, the sales vice-president wants larger advertising budgets, and so on, because they think that this is in the best interest of the firm. Ego-centered motives may be responsible for the executive's thinking but they do not detract from his identification with the firm.

It appears, then, that the current widespread split between ownership and management functions does not provide valid arguments against the role assigned to the profit motive in our economy. As a rule, a salaried executive will strive for profits for his firm. This conclusion may be somewhat restricted through the extension of group belonging beyond the limits of the business enterprise. As we have said before, people are members of several groups at the same time and identify themselves with several groups. Although a business executive may have the strongest identification with his own enterprise, he may at the same time be a member of larger groups.

The entire trade or business he is engaged in—say, steel, automobile, or cigarette manufacturing—may constitute such a group, and the executive of one company may endeavor to establish a satisfactory market for steel, automobiles, or cigarettes, instead of devoting himself exclusively to his company's affairs. Identification with one's country may result in patriotic motivation which, like identification with one's trade, may represent a restrictive influence on the identification with one's business. We shall take up the problems posed by these larger "wholes" when we discuss the question of the kind of profits for which businessmen strive.

3. Profits—When? The profits for which businessmen and business executives strive are, of course, future profits. The conception of maximizing future profits is a difficult one even in pure theory, as exemplified by such a typical formulation as: "The entrepreneur maximizes the present value of his prospective net receipts." In setting up mathematical models, economists have devised several approaches to the question of what businessmen should do. Sometimes, in the models, past profit rates are substituted for expected profits; sometimes future profits are discounted so that a dollar's worth of next year's profits has a higher current value than a dollar's worth of profits to be made two years hence; and sometimes large uncertain future profits are equated with smaller but certain profits. Are any of these procedures justified in the sense that they correspond with what businessmen actually have in mind? This question leads us to the study of businessmen's time perspective and their profit expectations.

Survey findings appear to indicate that businessmen as a rule have some profit expectations. They concern either specific transactions or the total profits of the firm. In contemplating and discussing large deals—be they accepting orders, purchasing goods, or making investments—expected profits are referred to, as revealed by company records as well as interviews with businessmen. Advance budgeting, a common accounting practice, tends to make the profit expectations definite. But often enough the figures written down are considered as illustrations only, or different contingencies are represented by several sets of figures. Similarly, businessmen, if induced to do so for the purpose of presenting their arguments to their bankers, directors, or colleagues, or to answer opinion questionnaires, may estimate that the next year's sales of their firm should be 12 per cent higher, and the next year's profits 8 per cent higher, than the preceding year's. What is meant, in most cases, is the expectation of an upturn, somewhat larger in sales than in profits, of an order of magnitude approximately indicated by the figures.

We showed above that the determination of profits depends upon subjective considerations. It is rather generally agreed that businessmen have even greater latitude in estimating expected profits than in calculating past profits. Definite opinions about future profits—as expressed in such statements as, "The firm will make $50,000 in this transaction" or "Next year's profits will be 8 per cent higher than last year's"—are no doubt held with lesser certainty than opinions as to current profits. But the direction of a change in profits, or whether a future transaction will be profitable or unprofitable, is often thought to be known with great assurance. The general knowledge that the future is uncertain, or the experience that one has been wrong in the past, is frequently disregarded. Businessmen in their business planning, just like consumers in other kinds of decisions, are found to have definite expectations of the type of "I expect an upward (or downward) trend" or "This would work out well (or badly)," which they hold with great confidence.

On the other hand, it cannot be said of businessmen—any more than of people in other walks of life—that they have definite expectations all the time concerning all matters of interest to them. Such expectations arise only when the future matters: when the time perspective extends far enough and when there is need for genuine decisions rather than going on with habitual patterns of business action.

There is ample evidence for contradicting the statement that every business action is based on definite expectations. Take, for instance, a retailer who reorders some merchandise. He may do so following customary practices (rules of thumb). He places an order when his stocks are depleted—and in large firms a relatively low-level employee may do so when a predetermined point of inventory depletion has been reached—without giving any thought to probable future sales or profits. But reordering may also be the result of a genuine decision. It may then be done even though stocks are still plentiful. Because of new developments and anticipations the retailer may decide on a policy of increasing his stock of given merchandise. He may expect sales and profits in some lines of goods to increase, or shortages to develop, and such expectations may shape his decision and action.

We previously raised two questions with respect to expectations; it seems that the answers to both questions are the same for business and for consumer expectations. First, when, under what circumstances, do definite expectations arise? Only when strong motivational forces create a problem situation and call for genuine decisions. Second, what is the origin of expectations? This question is, of course, closely related to the first.

Profit expectations may be based on one's own past business experience. If circumstances are expected to be similar in the future to what they were in the past, future profits may be gauged according to past profits. But profit expectations may also be based on considerations other than one's own business experience. Among the variety of factors that may play a role, the general economic outlook appears to loom largest. In numerous surveys, businessmen have usually been found to have opinions about the trend of business fluctuations, opinions sometimes independent of their own business experiences. They have opinions about whether the economy is prosperous or a depression prevails, and whether the general business trend points upward, downward, or is uncertain in its direction.

Empirical investigations of business attitudes have not progressed far enough, and it is, therefore, not possible to list all the factors that may shape profit expectations and to assign frequency values to them. But it is probable that, in addition to the general economic outlook, new technological developments in one's own firm or in a competitor's firm, as well as assured or alleged knowledge about competitors' plans and intentions, play a role in reorganizing a businessman's frame of reference. In view of the multitude of such influences, it is not permissible for the scholar to identify expected profits with past profits without special studies or to argue that as a rule expected profits are based on past profits.

One further problem must be mentioned because it may be of special importance in business life. Suppose developments occur that call for new considerations and decisions. Psychologically, the stimuli and motivational forces press toward a reorganization of the field. But the reorganization is not achieved. Definite expectations do not emerge. In simple terms: The businessman cannot make up his mind about what will happen and what he should do. Among consumers, under such conditions of uncertainty, we encountered two frequent types of reactions: taking no action or continuing with the habitual pattern of behavior. It is possible that this happens in business life, too. Postponing a decision is the easiest and simplest way out. It is, however, also possible that even under conditions of great subjective uncertainty business decisions must be made. How and in what direction—these are questions for future research. Some recent theoretical considerations suggest answers—such as equating large uncertain profits with small, more certain profits—but no evidence is known to the author supporting this or any other view.

What, then, can we conclude about the profit motive? Since, at least in instances when they matter, future profits have psychological reality, it is possible for businessmen to be motivated by them and to work and act to attain them. But expected profits are rarely exact quantitative data. Businessmen can often distinguish between more or less satisfactory avenues of action, but they can hardly ever know what decision will result in maximum future profits. It would appear, therefore, that studying the amounts of profits businessmen expect is not among the most urgent tasks of research. Empirical studies might better turn toward determining the length of the prevailing time perspective and the certainty or uncertainty of profit expectations under different circumstances. The answer to the question,

"Profits—When?" will vary greatly, and it may be useful to investigate the relation of the answers to such variables as business structure, business cycles, and business attitudes.

4. What Kind of Profits? The term "maximum profits" must be qualified further. The instances in which the term has a clear, unequivocal meaning are rarely typical of business life. Suppose I want to sell my house and have three offers for it. The meaning, then, of maximization is clear: I will accept the highest of the three offers. But complicating factors may enter even into such a simple case. Given certain expectations, I may decide not to accept any of the offers but to close up or rent the house and wait for a higher future offer. In business transactions there is usually even greater question as to the best way of making the most profit. There are usually many more alternatives than in the case of wanting to sell a house, and it is, as a rule, not possible for a businessman to weigh rationally all possible alternatives and to decide which will yield the highest profits.

Does, then, profit maximization mean striving toward the highest *known* profit? Methods to increase profits may be known and may, nevertheless, be shunned. The typical American businessman is not a fly-by-night trader who charges all that the traffic can bear. This statement means, first, that profits are not sought by any and all means. Certain ways of making profits are excluded by law: businessmen in general do not attempt to maximize their profits if doing so involves the risk of going to jail. Other means of maximizing profits are excluded by conventions. There are, in most trades, certain things that are just not done. To offend customers, suppliers, competitors, employees, or public opinion in general is usually considered bad business even if it should lead to higher profits. This means that maximization is restricted by the extension both of the ego and of the time perspective. Insofar as businessmen consider the future of their businesses or as they identify themselves with their markets or their customers, they would not produce or sell shoddy goods in order to achieve higher profits.

That the term "maximization" must include such considerations as maintenance of the firm's good will or the reputation of its brand name is not the only qualification we have to consider. Unusually high profits may, in the opinion of some businessmen, lead to the introduction of new taxes or of government regulation and control. They may lead to wage demands on the part of the employees. Or they may lead to the entry of new firms into the business field. Therefore, it may be that less than what is known to be the maximum possible profit is sought. How do these questions add up? If businessmen strive for profits but not for maximum profits, what is their clear aim? It may be that they seek to attain "satisfactory" profits. Satisfactory profit is a psychological concept. It is meaningful only if there exist habitual standards that make it recognizable to businessmen. Empirical studies currently available are not sufficient to enable us to give a final answer in this respect. But it appears probable that, at least in many cases, striving for satisfactory profits has real meaning and represents a force motivating business.

Standards exist according to which current and expected profits are being evaluated. Within our institutional setup, the preceding year's profits represent the most important standard. Corporations generally publish their profits in comparison with those made the year before. Our newspapers contain daily a large number of reports of the type "The XYZ Corporation in the last quarter (or the last year) made $3.10 per common share, as against $2.78 a year ago." Similarly, in internal balance sheets and in budget calculations, profits are usually compared with those made the year before. It may happen, of course, that the standard is set not by the last year's profits but by the average profits or by the highest profits achieved in several preceding years, or by some rates of return on sales or capital. Whatever is the case, one meaning of the term "satisfactory profit" evolves clearly: It should not be lower than the preceding year's profit, or should not be lower than whatever is considered the standard profit. Striving toward satisfactory profits means, first of all, attempting to avoid a reduction in profits. Not to make less money than last year, or than whatever is considered "normal," appears to be one of the strongest motivational forces of businessmen.

What else do satisfactory profits mean? How much more do businessmen desire to make than they made the year before, or than they think is their normal profit? It is not possible to give a definite answer to this question, but it appears that regular, gradual, small advances in the profit rate are usually preferred to large upward jumps. Because of adverse effects upon public opinion, legislation, customers, and labor, unusually high profits are not generally desired or sought.

The standard which gives meaning to the term satisfactory profit may be found in other firms' profit development instead of in that of one's own business enterprise. Not doing worse than one's competitors may replace the aim of not doing worse than the preceding year. Doing slightly better than one's competitors may take the place of doing somewhat better than the year before. In times of a general business decline, the term satisfactory profits may have a different meaning than in times of a business upswing. During a depression, profit reductions may be expected and considered satisfactory, provided they are smaller than the profit reductions shown by competitors.

Some preliminary investigations seem to show that not only satisfactory over-all profits but also satisfactory profits in different lines of one's business may act as motivational forces. Businessmen appear to be highly conscious of the "margin" (rate of gross profit) on each of their usually numerous products and often look for high-margin items to add to their lines. There is some evidence that manufacturers and wholesalers, as well as retailers, sometimes introduce new articles because their margin appears high. Insofar as this observation can be confirmed, the profit motive appears to be a force contributing to changes in established business practices and to diversification and expansion of business firms.

Thus there are numerous tasks for future empirical studies on the role and function of profit motives. First of all, however, information is needed about the profit standards businessmen have in mind and about any other standards they may use in measuring their success or failure. In this connection, certain preliminary investigations make it probable that pecuniary motives exist that are not directly profit motives. It has been found that interest in business volume often transcends interest in business profits.

When in recent studies top executives of large corporations were asked about their own and their competitors' profits during preceding quarters and years, it was found that they frequently did not have the answers at their fingertips. When, however, they were asked about their own and their competitors' volume of business, and especially about their own and their competitors' share in the total market, exact answers were quickly forthcoming. Such findings are, of course, not conclusive, and it cannot be proved at present that the view to be set forth is correct. But it is possible that some businessmen gauge their success primarily in terms of their relative volume rather than in terms of their profits. Our newspapers and trade journals regularly publish the share of General Motors, Ford, Chrysler, and other automobile manufacturers in the automobile market; of Lucky Strike, Chesterfield, Camel, and other cigarette brands in the cigarette market. Businessmen in general know their own and their leading competitors' share in the trade, know of orders received by their competitors, and direct their business rivalry primarily toward increasing their share in the market.

Striving for volume, attempting to increase one's share in the market, may serve the purpose of securing profits in the long run. In a formal sense —in theoretical methods—of course, the aim "maximum volume" will rarely be exactly the same as the aim "maximum profit." We are, however, concerned only with the direction of the motivational forces, and it appears that the two drives usually reinforce each other rather than conflict with each other. But it may also happen that increase in volume or the growth of one's firm is desired irrespective of its contribution to future profits. This would imply that striving toward larger volume may become an objective in itself. It may then be related to the social desires of businessmen. This is the problem which we shall take up next when we raise the question about the role and place of pecuniary motives within the framework of business motivation.

THE MOTIVATIONAL PATTERNS

We know that the psychological field usually contains diverse forces driving us toward different aims. Some of them may conflict and some may reinforce each other. If it were true that businessmen are single-minded, governed by nothing but the profit motive, then we would have to assume that human beings change when they enter their business offices. That one single motive becomes paramount, and the motivational pattern is ruled by one objective alone, may occasionally happen in family life, in the sphere of scientific research, or in business. But this cannot be assumed to be generally true under all circumstances. The investigation of motivational patterns in business must begin with an enumeration of the variety of factors which have been found to enter into these patterns, and must then proceed to the question of whether under certain conditions some of the motives become prevalent while others fade away.

In listing the factors that may play a role in business motivation, we may refer first to the biological needs that drive men to secure subsistence. Another basic motivational force is relief of anxiety which, in the case of business activities, may lead to striving for security. One possible way of achieving subsistence as well as security, in our institutional setup, is through making money. We engage in business in order to make money, which we desire, need, and plan to use for the sake of other more basic or more immediate satisfactions. In certain circumstances, the means may become ends, and we may strive for profits for the sake of the profits themselves. More generally, however, the desire for security implies striving for continuous, regular income rather than short-period maximum profits. The anxiety-security mechanism may be much stronger in the negative than in the positive sense. Avoidance of bankruptcy, avoidance of business losses, and avoidance of a decline in profits may on this level of motivation be stronger drives than those directed toward increasing profits.

Next we must take social needs into account. The phenomenon of group membership makes the desire to occupy an esteemed, a high, or even an outstanding position in one's group understandable. We strive for approbation by those belonging to our group. We desire prestige among our business associates, neighbors, and fellow citizens; our ambitions are linked with the esteem and opinion of others regarding our position and progress.

The urge for prestige may develop into a desire to influence other members of our group, to control or dominate them—in short, into a striving for power. There are indications that the prevailing institutional setup has greatly enhanced the desire for power among American businessmen. This desire is closely connected with the striving for profits and the striving for regular and secure profits. A business firm which rules and dominates its market is usually more profitable and has less to fear from sudden adverse developments than a firm which is in a weak position vis-à-vis its suppliers, competitors, and customers. The relative size of a firm in its trade, as well as the absolute size of the firm's physical assets and capital funds, is related to the firm's power position. Outstanding and acknowledged quality of the product or the service of a firm, or the popularity of its brand name, is a further means that makes for supremacy of the firm over its competitors and customers. Striving for control of the market may become the motivational factor of the highest visibility, because it is interlocked with several other motivational forces.

With respect to striving for power, ego-centered motivations of business executives often coincide with their business or group motivations. A president of a weak firm may be a dictator in his own office but must assume a subordinate role in negotiating with suppliers and customers. The head or executive of a powerful firm may, however, exercise power all around and thus satisfy personal as well as business drives.

The feeling of achievement is, however, not necessarily accomplished through the reaction of other people. Inherent satisfactions may be derived from a job well done without the approbation or even awareness of others. Professional pride may be derived from business activities even if they do not contribute to prestige or power. There are values and satisfactions in self-realization, and there is dissatisfaction in tasks not completed, in failure, in not getting ahead with a task. Desire for progress or for growth may be the joint result of subsistence needs, of social needs, and of the urge toward self-realization. Because of our identification with the business enterprise which we own or manage, or in which we are employed, these forces again may be centered in the business firm instead of in our own advancement. Self-realization may be achieved through the progress or growth of the business enterprise of which we are a part.

We said before that the going concern is commonly viewed as a living entity of itself. Self-realization of a business concern represents, then, a topic worth further study. A corporation is not conceived by its executives simply as an organization making money, or making automobiles. It has to carry out its functions, complete the tasks taken up, and expand to justify itself. It has been recently pointed out that here may be found one of the most important explanations of the fact that our large corporations are continuously expanding in diverse fields that are often foreign to their original activity. Small investments may be made, for instance, in order to study the use of by-products or waste products. When some progress has been achieved, the task once begun is pushed toward completion. There is a drive, perhaps even a compulsion, to follow through after one has begun. Or materials purchased from other firms are studied, then manufactured experimentally in a pilot plant, and ultimately manufactured on a large scale. Or the technical know-how in the firm's laboratories drives toward self-realization and, ultimately—to give one example—General Motors becomes the leading producer of Diesel locomotives.

The structure that results from the interplay of the diverse motivational forces must be assumed to vary greatly under different conditions. When, under what conditions, will one or the other motive play a leading role? Empirical studies have not progressed far enough to permit a definite answer to this question. Nevertheless, we may contrast two extreme business situations and try to describe the differences in the motivational patterns that would prevail under the two different sets of conditions. We shall take up first the business enterprise that is in a precarious situation; for instance, a new firm with insufficient capital struggling to stay in business, or any business firm under adverse conditions or in the midst of a severe depression. Then, disregarding intermediate situations, we shall discuss the motivational forces that may influence a well-established firm operating under prosperous conditions.

The first major difference between the psychological fields in which business firms operate under the two situations is probably in their time perspective. In the first case, what will happen years from now hardly enters into consideration. Long-range transactions that would bring large profits after many years, investments that would pay only after some time, are ruled out. The immediate problems are pressing. The main aim is survival. The means to this end may be sought and found in quick profits, even though they may be lower than possible future profits. Or, they may be found in transactions that contribute to liquidity and solvency. To reduce debts or to build up liquid funds may become the strongest business motive. Under these conditions, not only will the pecuniary motives be of short range, but they will also prevail in preference to nonpecuniary motives. Satisfaction of social needs, self-realization, or the urge for growth will play minor roles.

In the case of a well-established business firm operating under prosperous conditions, the time perspective will usually extend into the relatively distant future. Transactions that may not bring any profit for a number of years and long-range investments may be contemplated. Whether or not they will be made will depend on the businessman's expectations. The nature of the profit expectations, their degree of certainty, and all the factors shaping those expectations will greatly contribute to decision formation.

Not only the time period considered but also the scope of the motivational forces will be extended under prosperous conditions. The company's volume and its share in the market will become important considerations. The good will of the firm or the reputation of the firm's brand name may be given greater weight than the size of liquid assets and profits. Reputation among customers and among suppliers may be assigned large pecuniary value. Beyond the desire to maintain a strong market for his goods, the businessman's interest may extend to the entire country. Maintenance of full employment and avoidance of depression may become goals that influence specific business decisions.

The so-called nonpecuniary motives may loom large in the case of well-established businesses operating under prosperous conditions. Improving the living and social standards of the firm's employees or even of the town in which the factory is located may be viewed as being in the interest of the firm itself. Employee relations and productivity of the employees may be thought to be improved by such indirect means as building recreational facilities or hospitals, or by slum clearance. Desire for prestige will be interwoven with more specific business motives.

All this adds up to a weakening of the motivational forces directed toward high immediate profits. Furthermore, under these conditions businessmen will be aware of dangers inherent in large profits and will study the vulnerability of a condition which may be viewed by others as representing excessive profits.

We have discussed two extreme situations. Naturally, intermediate conditions prevail very often, that is, conditions which the businessmen consider neither precarious nor highly prosperous. Not much is known about the motivational patterns prevailing under intermediate conditions, but it is probable that both the length of the time perspective and the role played by social needs increase as we go farther from the first and approach the second extreme situation. Furthermore, striving for increased profits may be more prevalent in a situation that is relatively close to precarious conditions, and striving to avoid reduction in profits more prevalent in a situation that is relatively close to prosperous conditions.

Two paradoxical conclusions emerge. It appears, first, that the worse the situation, the more powerful is the urge toward high or maximum immediate profits, and the less powerful the nonpecuniary motives. Second, it appears that the desire to avoid a decrease in profits may be stronger than the desire to increase profits.

Differences in business situations other than those between precarious and prosperous conditions should be studied with regard to their influence on the structure of motivational patterns. It is possible, for instance, that prevalent motivational patterns may differ as between new and old industries or relatively competitive and relatively monopolistic fields of business. It has been argued that businessmen in new industries (for instance, in the airplane industry or electronics) are characterized by a much greater degree of venturesomeness than businessmen in old industries (for instance, in the railroad or coal-mining industry). Or it is possible that in business fields in which there are no established leaders and into which entry is easy (as examples, women's dress manufacture or the laundry or the baking industries may be mentioned) a much greater degree of uncertainty and a shorter time perspective prevail than in such fields as the aluminum or the automobile industry, where the few established firms are believed to occupy a secure position.

These considerations point toward important tasks for future research. First, the facts themselves must be established and, second, careful studies must be undertaken to shed light on the causes of the differences in motivational patterns—provided such differences are found to prevail. The two tasks are closely connected, because it is possible that the age of an industry or its degree of competitiveness as such does not make for differences in business motives. It may be that, without regard to the business structure, there are periods in each industry in which business leaders, so to speak, relax and are interested only in preserving what they have; and other periods in which striving to expand and to gain advantages over competitors are most significant. (In the "old" railroad industry, for instance, the introduction of lightweight, air-conditioned trains and Diesel engines may have constituted expansion.)

Those who assume that the motives of executives in old and new industries differ sometimes explain the differences by the traits of the executives themselves. Men of inherently conservative character are thought to seek employment and advancement in old industries, while men of imagination, endowed with an enterprising spirit, strive to promote new industries. Yet another type of causation, namely, the shaping of personalities by the atmosphere and conditions prevailing in the industry in which one works and with which one identifies oneself, appears possible and even more probable. On the other hand, there may be instances in which a business executive relinquishes his position and enters a different field of business because his own motivational pattern is not in accord with that of the business in which he has worked.

Information is needed, furthermore, about the motives of executives of large as against small business firms. It may be argued, and it has been said, that large firms with large staffs tend to be bureaucratic; not only the day-to-day work but also the decision formation is routinized, that is, follows established rules. Therefore, for large firms, it is difficult, if not impossible, to deviate from habitual business procedures that are directed toward preserving the *status quo* instead of toward gaining new advantages.

Small firms, on the other hand, are described as flexible; they may change their decisions frequently and even embark on adventures.

On the other hand, however, small firms are usually in a more precarious position than large firms. Therefore, possibly only large firms can make the really long-range plans that are needed for new ventures. Furthermore, small firms usually require outside financing for expansion, while large firms often have substantial liquid reserves or can use profits for such purposes. Strings are commonly attached to borrowing money, and the consent of the lenders to any but conservative procedures is rarely obtainable. In these respects, again, the facts themselves are disputed and require study. The question is whether the size of their business is a factor shaping or even determining the outlook, the ambition, and the motives of businessmen.

The prevailing structure of the motivational patterns in the American economy has been changing in the past and will no doubt change in the future. Capitalism as we know it now differs from nineteenth-century capitalism and probably from future capitalism. What has been described, for instance, as the probable differences in the motivations of prosperous and weak business firms may not have existed a few decades ago and may not be true a few decades hence. The frame of reference of a business community may vary greatly from time to time and from country to country. There are some indications, but hardly any reliable data, that in the nineteenth century in the United States the appreciation of, and the striving toward, higher profits was more pronounced than now, and certain motivational forces played a role at that time which we have omitted from consideration. We have not referred, in describing the present situation, to businessmen's pleasure in risk taking or even in gambling. Nor have we given any consideration to the possibility that some people may consider business as an adventure or as a way to get rich quickly, or that some may seek the thrill of playing with other people's money.

The given description of the current situation applies to a period in which many businessmen assume a somewhat apologetic viewpoint. Instead of being proud of profits made, they see a need to justify them and, in some cases and in a certain sense, to excuse them. It is, of course, possible that this represents nothing but tactics, that is, an attempt to influence wage negotiations, tax legislation, or other public policies. It is also possible that it represents a superficial rationalization or is completely insincere. Still, in all probability, the point of view, if repeated over and over again, changes the psychological field both of those who pronounce it and those who hear it. The motives and actions of businessmen who proclaim publicly and proudly their objective of making large profits may differ greatly from those of businessmen who are apologetic about their profits.

Much further empirical research is needed with respect to the characterization of currently prevailing motivational patterns, their relation to business structure, and their origin. Such research is possible because business motives, like other intervening variables, can be analyzed by observing business behavior under different conditions as well as by recording the explanations businessmen themselves give of the reasons for their behavior.

NOTES TO CHAPTER 9

During the past few years there have been a number of studies that have departed from discussions of the theory of profit maximization and turned toward the analysis of business motivation as it is found in modern business. The material of these books and papers is mostly taken from observations by the authors, derived usually from lifelong association with business leaders and, in a few instances, from the interrogation of samples of businessmen. As said before, the study of business motivation is at present in the qualitative, or case-study, phase. Exact quantitative data on the frequency of different motivational patterns in different circumstances are not available.

E. G. Nourse's book *Price Making in a Democracy* (Washington, D.C., 1944) may be mentioned first, because the author raises and analyzes such crucial questions as "How much money?" "Profits by what means?" and "Profits for whom?" Nourse emphasizes the role of the desire to grow—as a matter of pride and achievement—and of the objective to create the kind of market in which the firm, as well as its competitors, can thrive.

C. E. Griffin in *Enterprise in a Free Society* (Chicago, 1949) devotes several chapters to business motivation. Among what he calls "noneconomic motives," he discusses desire for power, prestige, social approval, and independence, as well as businessmen's creative desires, competitive impulses, and ethical standards. Griffin points to the importance of the "urge for volume" and asserts that "increased volume, to a considerable extent, is an end in itself, not merely (as it is often described) a means of increasing profit rates" (p. 158). He argues that "the simple fact that most American business leaders would prefer to sell more goods at substantially the same prices rather than the old volume at higher prices is one of the most important features of our economy" (p. 159).

K. E. Boulding makes the following interesting assumption about the relation between striving for profit and for volume: "At low outputs the businessman would be willing to expand his business even at the cost of a certain diminution in profits, whereas at high outputs an expansion of the business is troublesome and risky, and even if higher profits result from the expansion, it may not be considered worth the trouble." ("The Incidence of a Profits Tax," *American Economic Review*, Vol. 34, 1944, p. 569.)

R. A. Gordon's book, *Business Leadership in the Large Corporation* (Washington, D.C., 1945) studies the incentives of business executives as distinct from motives relating to the business firm. Information about the respective roles of financial and nonfinancial incentives—for instance, about the role of the fact that the salaries and bonuses of presidents are mostly independent of the firm's profits—is well documented. But the conclusion that "the profits of the firm are not a primary incentive to the majority of top executives in our largest corporations" disregards the possibility (or probability) of identification with the firm.

The same author in his paper "Short-period Price Determination in Theory and Practice" (*American Economic Review,* Vol. 38, 1948) introduces the term "satisfactory profits." "I suspect," he says, "that 'satisfactory profits,' as vague as that criterion is, is frequently a more accurate description of the primary objective than 'maximum profits.' This is particularly likely to be true of mature, successful firms" (p. 271). Gordon does not raise the question whether the criterion must of necessity always be vague. (It may be mentioned that Gordon, in the same article, criticizes dynamic theory which "has not progressed much beyond the point of setting up a highly mechanical type of relationship between past experience and present expectations as to the future," *op. cit.,* p. 286.) In the same volume of the *American Economic Review,* L. G. Reynolds writes: "There may be little interest in *maximum* profits so long as actual profits are up to conventional standards" (p. 298).

Another reference to differences in motivation under different conditions is to be found in Moses Abramovitz' article on "Monopolistic Selling in a Changing Economy" (*Quarterly Journal of Economics,* Vol. 52, 1938): "The upswing of a cycle is a period in which the volume of profits is chiefly regarded; in the downswing it is security which businessmen chiefly seek" (p. 201).

Several authors have argued recently that the fear of loss or of smaller profits is stronger than the hope for more profits. This development is acknowledged and deplored by the Council of Economic Advisers, who write: "The profit motive has in somewhat alarming ways given way to the protective motive" (*Second Annual Report to the President,* December, 1947, p. 17).

During the last few years, the term "minimizing regrets" has been introduced into economic theory. The theoretical considerations connected with this concept and some other sophisticated theories of maximizing behavior may serve to stimulate research on the role of motivational forces. How to make the best out of the worst may be a widely prevailing aspiration under precarious conditions.

E. S. Mason, commenting briefly on special factors that enter into the motivation of large and powerful firms, writes that "the time horizon of such a firm is more distant" and that "the profit maximization deemed adequate to account for competitive behavior becomes attenuated and much less adequate in describing the behavior of the large firms concerned with long-run questions of market strategy" (*Review of Economics and Statistics,* Vol. 31, 1949, p. 105).

That psychological differences between individual businessmen, based perhaps on their past experience, account for differences in their policies has been maintained, among others, by J. R. Hicks. He says that some people's price expectations are fairly steady, while other people are more sensitive and change their expectations easily. "Sensitive traders make sensitive prices, insensitive traders sticky prices" (*Value and Capital,* Oxford, 1939, p. 271).

The volume, *Cost Behavior and Price Policy* (by the Committee on Price Determination, National Bureau of Economic Research, New York, 1943), may be cited as providing the best evidence for the statement that costs are the results of administrative decisions. The book not only contains clear formulations of the principles of cost determination but also reports on a few valuable empirical studies in this field.

The author's own experience is derived from (1) wartime surveys on business pricing methods which he directed (see George Katona, *Price Control and Business,* Cowles Commission for Research in Economics, Bloomington, Ind., 1945); (2) several small postwar business surveys in which he participated, sometimes as consultant; and (3) interviews with business owners and managers in five annual Surveys of Consumer Finances. None of these surveys was directed toward collecting quantitative data on business motivation or the frequency of different types of business decisions. Extensive qualitative information about businessmen's attitudes and opinions was, however, obtained. Similarly, information was obtained about considerations that enter into decision formation, and will be discussed in the next two chapters. In the wartime pricing surveys, habitual behavior and rigidity or flexibility of business conduct were subjected to special studies (see also the author's article in the *American Economic Review,* Vol. 36, 1946).

Surveys conducted among representative samples of businessmen for the purpose of clarifying their value systems are greatly needed. Since only fragmentary information is available, most conclusions must remain rather general. For instance, the reading of several hundred interviews with business executives may enable the author to formulate that "seeking adventure plays no great role for (or is not salient in the minds of) businessmen." But this does not necessarily mean that such motivations do not exist and do not find vicarious outlets. The generality and incompleteness of the conclusions may be illustrated further by a reference to the "desire for volume." A great number of interview findings make it clear that such a desire exists; but information about its frequency and role (its relation to the profit motive, for instance) is lacking.

The possible contribution of the survey method should not be overestimated. To be sure, well-conducted surveys could find out under what conditions and why businessmen at specific times in the past preferred higher volume at lower prices to lower volume at higher prices (see Griffin's statement quoted above and some observations on this point in the next chapter). But general principles clarifying the relation between desire for volume and for profit can hardly be proved by surveys, because answers to hypothetical questions are highly deceptive. A question such as, "Which would you prefer, a lower volume at higher prices or a higher volume at lower prices, if your profits were larger in the first than in the second case?" would be of very little value to indicate how a businessman, if he had the choice, actually would decide. Several unforeseen circumstances might enter into consideration if the choice were to arise and might not be thought of by the businessman answering the question.

Recent public-opinion surveys—for instance, those of Elmo Roper for *Fortune Magazine* and of Richard Centers—shed some light on the atmosphere in which American business operates at the present time. These surveys suffice to indicate that the "apologetic" attitude of some businessmen is not entirely without justification, because some people, at least, think of "business" as amoral and greedy and believe that businessmen in general are overpaid. But in this respect, again, far too little exact information is available.

During the last few years the Brookings Institution has been engaged in a study of concentration in American business, through intensive interviews with executives of about 30 giant corporations. This study promises to lead to a valuable clarification of the motivational forces prevailing in the leading American industrial corporations. The author of this book is indebted to A. D. H. Kaplan, the director of the Brookings study, for several observations, especially on the matter of branching out into new business areas through continuing with small sideline activities as well as through the search for high-margin lines. In a preliminary publication, Kaplan says: "The [giant] industrial corporation . . . tends to become a pool of technical and financial resources available to a group of related products and operations" ("The Influence of Size of Firms on the Functioning of the Economy," *American Economic Review,* Vol. 40, Supplement, 1950, pp. 81*f.*).

CHAPTER 10

OUTPUT AND PRICE DECISIONS

Business owners and executives face a variety of different situations which call for decision and action. We shall take up the analysis of two major types of decisions. First, we shall study decisions that concern the size of output, or volume, of business and the price of goods sold, and then, in the next chapter, investment decisions relating to capital expenditures on plants or machinery.

Pure theory raises a problem different from ours. It asks: How *should* businessmen proceed to maximize profits? The solution of this problem is considered useful both in the sense of establishing norms of behavior and of representing a first approximation to actual behavior. It is usually acknowledged that the answer to a second question, namely, "How *do* businessmen go ahead to make profits?" may be different from the solution established in theory. But it is frequently thought that the differences can be disregarded because they are due to the fact that not all businessmen are good businessmen, or to institutional and psychological conditions that forestall the adoption of the required or desired procedures.

Our problem is, in one respect, broader than the question raised in theory. We do not assume at the outset that business decisions aim directly and at all times toward maximizing or even making profits. Whether that is the case remains to be determined. In other respects, however, our objective is much narrower than that of economic theory. We shall study the factors contributing to specific decisions made under certain conditions, instead of attempting to arrive at generally valid answers regarding the how and why of all business procedures. But our analysis is in need of guiding lines and hypotheses. Some of the broad hypotheses that we shall use can be derived from psychological studies, primarily from the distinction between genuine decision making and habitual behavior and from the study of business motivation. Other hypotheses of great usefulness are found in economic theory, especially in marginalist theory.

MARGINALISM

What is marginalism? The aim of our discussion of marginalism, and of the following discussion of supply and demand schedules, is not to summarize statements made in introductory textbooks of economics, but to discern fundamental points of view that are often hidden in the elaborate systems, developed during the past fifty or one hundred years. We shall, therefore, disregard innumerable differences of emphasis or detail and try to present the frame of reference underlying the theories. To the question "What is marginalism?" we then find two kinds of answers. The first one, which will not be of great usefulness for our analysis of business behavior, is embodied in such statements as: Marginalism is the "logical process of finding a maximum"; [1] it shows how one should operate in order to achieve a maximum of ends with given means. Or: Marginalism is the same as rational behavior; it elaborates the procedures that are involved in weighing alternatives rationally. More specifically, the underlying principle of marginalism may be presented by citing the result of marginal analysis: Marginalism shows that profit maximization is achieved by equating marginal costs and marginal revenues.

According to these statements, profit maximization and marginalism are so closely connected that it is hardly possible to make any use of marginalism except for the purpose of determining the output and price that will yield maximum profits. There exists, however, another set of descriptions of the essence of marginalism. Marginalism is said to represent a certain point of view, namely, the focusing of attention on the effects of *changes* in conditions.[2]

Instead of considering a given situation in its entirety, the businessman may divide the situation, conceptually, into two parts. He may take the situation as it is today (or was yesterday) as one unit and regard the possible changes that confront him as a second unit. Then he may raise, in his mind, the question, "What difference would the change make?" For instance, if a manufacturer is asked whether he is willing to sell a large quantity of his product at less than his list price, he may ask himself, "What difference will it make to my business if I accept or if I reject the offer?" Marginalism represents the viewpoint that "every economic decision is taken for the sake of the difference it will make." [3] Both the effects of changes that depend on the businessman's decision, and of changes in conditions, for example, changes in the price of raw materials, may be considered. The changes are confronted with the existing or preceding conditions and the difference that the change involves is studied. Marginalism, then, represents a possible attitude in business life which leads to certain types of considerations or calculations.

---

[1] Fritz Machlup, "Marginal Analysis and Empirical Research," *American Economic Review,* Vol. 36, 1946, p. 519.

[2] "Marginal analysis really intends to explain the effects which certain *changes* in conditions may have upon the actions of the firm" (Machlup, *op. cit.,* p. 521).

[3] According to Jacob Viner, quoted by A. G. Hart, *Anticipations, Uncertainty and Dynamic Planning,* Chicago, 1940, p. 4.

It is not easy to find a simple example which would illustrate clearly the meaning of the question, "What difference does it make?" Because of the usual complexity of business decisions, we shall illustrate what we may call the "marginalist attitude" by an example taken from a somewhat different aspect of economic activity. Assume that John Smith is a successful writer in Hollywood who, in view of contracts already entered into, knows that his taxable income will amount to $50,000 during the current year. One day he is offered $1,000 for writing a short story. Then, in order to find out whether or not he should accept the offer, he looks up the income-tax schedules and finds that he would have to pay $750 in taxes on the additional $1,000 of income. (The marginal tax rate is 75 per cent at his income level.) The writer considers the possible new gain of $250; is it worth the trouble, should he spend several evenings in order to make that amount of additional money? Consideration of the differential effect of the added units may induce him to refuse the offer which, possibly, he might not have refused if he had viewed the situation in a different way, or even if he had figured out that on a $50,000 income he would have to pay (approximately) 53½ per cent in taxes and on a $51,000 income 54 per cent.

Our example shows that the marginalist attitude presupposes some rather specific and exact knowledge. In the case of Mr. Smith, the required knowledge was easily accessible; it could be obtained from the Bureau of Internal Revenue or from any of innumerable pamphlets on income taxes. But how can a businessman know what difference his acceptance or rejection of an offer, or his acting in one way or in another way, will make? The traditional answer to that question is embodied in the analysis of supply and demand schedules. If businessmen had the information concerning the relation of their output to the prices of their products which is represented in the supply and demand schedules of economic theory, they would be in a position to apply marginal considerations or marginal calculations.

SUPPLY AND DEMAND SCHEDULES

What are demand curves? We learn that they are diagrams "in which the total quantities that would be purchased are plotted opposite the corresponding prices." [4] This relation between quantities sold and prices is usually illustrated in the following way. Suppose 10 units of a certain product are sold at a price of $10; 12 units could then be sold at a price of $8, 14 units at $6, while 8 units could be sold at a higher price, say, $12. The larger the quantities sold, the lower the price, and the smaller the quantities, the higher the price. This relationship is expressed in the negative slope of the curve

[4] A. M. McIsaac and J. G. Smith, *Introduction to Economic Analysis*, Boston, 1937, p. 51.

(Fig. 8*a*). Conversely, supply curves show that at a lower price, smaller quantities of a particular commodity would be offered for sale than would be offered at a higher price.

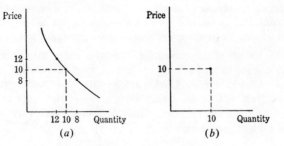

FIG. 8. Illustration of "Demand Curves."

How is the information embodied in demand and supply schedules obtained? Or, more generally, what do demand (and supply) curves mean? There are three possibilities. Demand curves may be theoretical, real, or subjective. Theoretical demand curves are constructions of theorists. Given certain assumptions, one may deduce demand curves, or the demand curves themselves may express certain hypotheses which the theorists set up in order to show what ought to take place in economic life. Most curves in the economic textbooks seem to be of that variety and represent illustrations.

It is also possible that demand curves depict the real situation as it is in a given moment or as it was during a specific past period. Such curves, if they exist at all, will be rare. Most standardized goods are sold at one price at a given time or at only a few prices—in case of price increases or decreases—during a short time interval. The quantities sold may vary substantially during a given period during which their price remains unchanged. Therefore, usually it will not be possible to compute curves containing several quantities and several prices that represent a real situation.

Third, demand curves may be subjective. They may exist in the imagination of businessmen, helping them in forming their decisions. These curves, which may be better called subjective sales curves, are relevant for our discussion. Before raising the question whether businessmen think in terms of such curves, we must study the scope and form of subjective sales curves.

Two rather obvious points must be mentioned first. Subjective sales curves cannot have the extension with which they are usually drawn; in other words, they cannot explain the relationship between all possible quantities and all possible prices. Second, subjective sales curves will, at best, be discrete, containing only certain points instead of taking the form of curves. Suppose in a given month an automobile manufacturer sells 20,000 cars at $1,500 each. It is possible that he has an idea about the price at which he could sell 10 or even 20 per cent more or fewer cars. But it is hardly possible that his imagination encompasses data about the prices he could charge if he were to produce only 1,000 cars or if he were to produce 100,000 cars. This point will not be elaborated further except for quoting the following clear renunciation of the usual wide range of demand curves:

". . . the length of the curves, i.e., the wide range they cover, was chiefly designed to enable those in the back rows of the class room to make out what goes on the blackboard; and to permit them to practice curve analysis without using magnifying glasses. The range of possibilities—prices, sales, outputs—which a business man may have in mind is probably quite narrow." [5]

Similarly, it might be sufficient to mention that it is possible for businessmen to think of increasing their sales or their prices by 5 or 10 per cent, but it is hardly possible for them to have in mind quantity-price relationships for every possible change between 5 and 10 per cent. In other words, businessmen may have an idea about the position of certain points of a demand schedule, but it will hardly ever be justified to speak of subjective sales *curves*. Figure 8*b* may express what is meant by subjective sales curves better than Fig. 8*a*.

Of much greater importance than these points is the discussion of one supposedly essential feature of demand curves, their negative slope. The statement that the larger the quantities sold, the lower their price, and the smaller the quantities, the higher their price, rests on considerations about basic principles of behavior. First of all, there is an assumption about individual scales of valuation. To quote again a clear statement from a textbook: Demand curves have a negative slope because there is "an inverse relation between the price and the quantity that would be purchased"—due to "differences in income, differences in taste, and the diminishing importance of the desires that remain unsatisfied as the quantity of a given commodity in one's possession is increased." [6] Of special importance is the third postulate, namely, that the more one has of a certain commodity, the smaller is the rate of satisfaction one derives from adding to one's stock of that commodity.

We may recall a classical example used to illustrate the principle. When a man is near starvation, a loaf of bread has enormous value for him, but after he has satisfied his hunger he places a much smaller value on a loaf of bread. Applied more generally to budgeting by consumers: the more one

[5] Machlup, *op cit.*, p. 522.
[6] McIsaac and Smith, *op. cit.*, p. 55.

has of anything, the less one values additional units thereof. The process of satiation is assumed to progress without interruption: human desires are thought to weaken steadily as the degree of satiation rises.

Fundamentally similar is a second underlying argument used to explain the inverse relation between quantities sold and prices. It generalizes not from the point of view of the buyers' situation but rather from what is assumed to be the universal experience of the sellers. That it is easier to sell goods at lower than at higher prices, or that in order to sell larger quantities prices have to be reduced, is assumed to be so obvious that it requires no proof and is taken as the basis for formulating a general law.

We shall not pursue the extensive theoretical discussions to which the elaboration of this principle has led in the past. It suffices to say that the principle assumes that a person is able to compare his satisfaction with, or the utility of, one commodity as against another (or of a commodity as against a quantity of money), but it is not necessarily assumed that satisfactions are measurable, or that the satisfactions of different persons are comparable. Elaboration of the principle has led to theories of substitution and of indifference curves. A person may compare bundles of commodities by making a preference ranking among sets of alternatives. Indifference curves show all combinations of quantities of goods which bring equal satisfaction so that it does not make any difference to a consumer which combination he chooses. The objectives we pursue in this book—the analysis of specific instances of decision formation—represent a much lower level of abstraction than these principles. We shall not concern ourselves with the principles of preference ranking, nor with axiomatic statements about the inverse relation between quantities of goods sold and their prices which are derived from assumptions about the optimal consumer choice (utility maximization).[7] We shall try to apply what we learn from economic theory to dynamic processes as they occur in our economy and ask: Does the amount demanded of a commodity increase (decrease) when its price decreases (increases)?

The most obvious instance of the inverse relation of quantity and price occurs under extreme conditions. If a certain desired product is extremely scarce it will have a high value, and if it is abundant it will have a low value. This consideration is of little use for the study of business decisions. We have learned already that businessmen's subjective sales curves do not have a wide range. They cannot be assumed to extend to extreme situations but

[7] Since reduction in price is considered as equivalent to increase in income, the "law of demand" has also been formulated in the form that the amount demanded of a good increases when income increases (and not only when price decreases). We shall disregard the frequently stated exception to that principle, namely, that it does not apply to "inferior goods." Higher income would not lead to increased consumption of margarine or potatoes, but rather of butter or meat.

only to situations closely resembling the prevailing quantities sold and the prevailing prices.

Other obvious instances can easily be listed by considering certain specific situations. For instance, if we consider perishable goods that must be sold quickly to buyers who are present at a given locality, the inverse relationship can easily be proved. Suppose I am the only dealer in Christmas trees in my town; the smaller the quantity I have, the higher I can set the price. If I have large, unsold quantities on Christmas Day, I must set the price very low to move my goods, which will be worthless the next day.

Finally, it is often thought obvious that an inverse relation between quantity and price prevails on the aggregate level. Suppose all consumers spent 10 billion dollars for all goods and services bought in a given month. They purchased 10 billion units of goods at an average price of $1 per unit. Suppose, further, that production increases by 10 per cent and next month sellers try to sell 11 billion units of goods while consumers continue to spend 10 billion dollars. Then next month the average price must be lower.

Can these considerations be of any help in the analysis of business decisions? In order to answer this question, we must study the assumption under which the inverse relation between aggregate quantities and prices was found to be valid. It was assumed that the amount of consumer expenditure was not affected by the larger production, in other words, that supply changed without regard to demand. Furthermore, we may express the argument in terms of consumer income rather than consumer expenditures. Suppose, in the first period, income after taxes amounted to 12 billion dollars, of which 2 billion were saved and the rest spent for 10 billion units at $1 per unit. Then, in the second period, in which 11 billion units are offered for sale, lower prices will result if consumers do not change their saving-spending ratio. The calculated inverse relation between quantity sold and price will prevail only if, in a period in which the quantity of goods offered for sale increases, (1) aggregate consumer income remains 12 billion dollars and (2) the amount saved out of income remains 2 billion dollars. It is, of course, possible that this will happen. But must it happen? Or will it happen as a rule? The same question may be put in terms of businessmen's decisions in the following form: In order to sell a larger quantity of goods, businessmen may reduce prices; is this the only means by which they can endeavor to increase their sales?

Three examples of the "obvious" nature of the demand curve's downward slope were presented to lead up to our main question: Under what conditions will businessmen's subjective sales curves have such a slope? As was said before, it is quite realistic for a businessman to ask himself the question, "Suppose I cut my price by 10 per cent, will I sell more goods?" The theory underlying the demand schedule presents a clear-cut answer to this question. But this answer, that lower prices will make sales increase, is correct only if other things are equal. What are these other things? Do they concern matters which, as a rule, businessmen disregard? Is the answer correct except, say, in case of outbreak of war, epidemics, or a sudden depression? We shall find that there are other possibilities which may make the answer incorrect and which are, usually or often, in the forefront of businessmen's thinking. The statement "If I reduce my price, my sales will increase" disregards the question of reactions to price reductions. It disregards the possibility that consumers and competitors may change their pattern of behavior in response to the changed conditions (to the reduction of prices). More specifically, it disregards expectations, expected developments as well as expected reactions. It is based on a mechanistic psychology according to which one item in the psychological field can be changed without affecting other items in the same field.

There is another basic problem involved in the attempt to answer the question, "Suppose I cut my price by 10 per cent, will I sell more or less goods?" This question, like the narrower one previously raised, is formulated as if I changed my price without any reason, or without reference to existing or expected conditions or changes in those conditions. This may happen but need not be the only or even the typical procedure.

Business decisions about output and price, like any other human decisions, are made if an opportunity or occasion is perceived and strong motivational forces press toward one or the other course of action. We shall therefore proceed by studying the conditions under which businessmen may have an incentive to change the quantity of their production or sales, or the price of their products, or both.

OUTPUT OR PRICE DECISIONS UNDER DIFFERENT CONDITIONS

It is relatively easy to list some of the conditions under which businessmen may consider a change in the quantity of their output or sales and in the prices they charge. The following schematic classification is not aimed to be complete. It is the result of preliminary observations about businessmen's behavior. We are in the position to describe various considerations businessmen have entertained under different conditions, but not to determine their frequency or even relative importance.

We may distinguish three basic situations of upswing, or business improvement, in which the need for decisions concerning changes in volume or prices may arise. The first situation (case 1a) is the expectation of larger demand. Without regard to anything a businessman has done or intends to do, a situation may arise in which he expects that the demand for his product will increase. It may be that he foresees an upward swing in the business cycle, due to which he expects an increase in the sale of all types of goods, including his own products. It may also be that because of changes in technology, population, or fashion, he expects that larger quantities of his product will be needed. Second (case 1*b*), it is possible that without regard to developments outside his own business, he develops a desire to obtain a larger share in the market, which is assumed to be constant. Third (case 1*c*), the underlying incentive for new decisions may be that costs have declined. Suppliers may have reduced their prices, or costs may have declined because of technological progress or other increases in productivity.

The parallel conditions of downswing, or unfavorable business developments, are, of course, the expectation of a downward trend of business (case 2*a*) and of an increase in costs due to higher prices charged by suppliers or increase in wages (case 2*c*). Consideration of case 2*b* may be omitted, because it may be assumed that businessmen as a rule will not voluntarily endeavor to reduce their sales.

Case 1a. Reactions to anticipated larger demand.   The empirical finding was cited earlier that people in general often hold opinions about the country's economic outlook with a fair degree of assurance. Some businessmen, at certain times possibly many businessmen, may be in a quandary and may have no clear notion about the prevailing business trend. But usually businessmen appear to have fairly definite notions about the economy's approximate position in the business cycle. They also have opinions about whether the next few months or the next year will bring an upswing, a downswing, or a fairly stable trend. Irrespective of whether these opinions later prove to be correct or false, they may influence business decisions. If a businessman believes that the general business situation will improve, and if he also thinks that this trend will affect his own product (as, of course, it may not necessarily do), we have an example of condition 1*a,* which may call for certain business decisions.

An optimistic general outlook is a rather common source of the expectation of larger demand for one's own product. But case 1*a* may also prevail in different circumstances. For instance, the owner of a bakery may anticipate larger sales because a new housing project has been completed in the neighborhood, or a manufacturer may anticipate larger sales because new uses for his product have been discovered, or because his regular customers have increased their business.

Let us consider three important responses that may be made in such conditions: (1) business volume may be kept unchanged and prices increased; (2) both volume and prices may be increased; and (3) volume may be increased at unchanged prices.

In studying businessmen's probable choice among the three possibilities cited, we may recall the observation reported in the preceding chapter that, in general, there exists a desire to increase business volume. In some cases, of course, when capacity production and sales have been reached, an immediate increase in volume may be impossible. In other cases, however, the striving toward larger volume has been found to be reinforced by certain special considerations.

First, there is evidence from answers by businessmen obtained in recent surveys that, under the conditions described, price increases are often considered to be risky. It has been found, in numerous case studies, that before embarking on price increases in anticipation of larger demand, businessmen consider the possible reactions of their customers and competitors. How will customers react to price increases? No answer can be given to this question which is valid in all circumstances. It is possible for customers to respond to price increases by buying larger quantities than before, provided they view the price increases as the beginning of a trend toward further price increases. It is also possible that customers' needs for a given product are such that price increases would not affect the quantity demanded. Finally, the quantity demanded may drop because of the price increases. In the light of information obtained in surveys, it appears that businessmen —or some businessmen at certain times—are aware of these different possibilities and are uncertain how their customers will react. That is why they consider price increases risky. This opinion of businessmen is reinforced when they think of the probable reactions of their competitors to price increases. They believe that if their competitors do not follow suit, the competitors may enlarge their share in the market at the expense of those who have raised prices. Again, uncertainty may prevail about how competitors would respond.

Interviews with businessmen have disclosed other reasons, too, for the tendency to prefer increased volume at unchanged prices to unchanged volume at higher prices. With the current institutional setup, prices are frequently a matter of public knowledge, whereas output, or volume of sales, is not. Also, increasing prices is often a technically involved process. It requires changing the prices of all of often numerous types of products and qualities, so as not to disturb the price relation between different products, whereas changes in output can be restricted to one or a few products. Retracting a decision after it has been put into effect is easier with respect to changes in output than with respect to changes in prices. Should, for instance, the anticipated increase in demand not materialize, output can easily be cut back to the level prevailing earlier. But reducing prices to the previous level may be considered as a public acknowledgment of a mistake and may, like any other price reduction, have adverse consequences on the business.

Some or all of these considerations may not be valid under certain conditions. Empirical data are not available about the frequency with which the different possible decisions have actually been made. All we can conclude is that businessmen will frequently react to the expectation of larger demand by increasing output and keeping prices unchanged. In terms of traditional demand-curve analysis, one may then say that the emergence of new expectations has a greater effect on the position of the subjective sales curve (in this case, a shift of the curve to the right) than on its shape (or on movements along the curve). Certain theoretical considerations about "elasticity of demand" appear to point toward a different conclusion. These considerations imply that businessmen, in general, can estimate the degree of responsiveness of their customers to changes in prices and can anticipate (even calculate in advance) the customers' reactions. Empirical studies are needed to determine whether and under what conditions that view is confirmed and the observation contradicted that businessmen often feel uncertain about how their customers and competitors would react to an increase in prices.

Case 2a. Reactions to anticipated smaller demand. A pessimistic general economic outlook appears to be the most important factor making for an expectation of lower sales. Businessmen may believe at a given time that a downward trend of business prevails or will develop in the near future. They may believe that the next few months will bring depression and unemployment, and they may expect or fear that their own businesses will be affected by the general trend. Major business decisions made in these circumstances can again be listed under three headings, similar to those discussed as responses to expected business upswing. Either business volume is kept unchanged and prices lowered, or volume is lowered while prices remain unchanged, or both volume and prices are reduced.

Following the traditional, simple formulation of the so-called "law of demand," the first decision is emphasized, namely, reducing prices in response to an expected downturn of business. There is one psychological consideration that may reinforce this response, the strong desire for volume and the reluctance to give up volume. But it has been found that businessmen often consider matters that speak against this decision and for responding in terms of output instead of in terms of prices.

It was argued before that businessmen have reason to consider increasing their prices a risky matter. Similar considerations apply with greater force to a reduction of prices. Many businessmen think, so it appears in the light of answers received in some recent surveys, that their customers' reaction to lowering prices cannot be foreseen. It is uncertain how customers will respond because they may respond in many ways, including the two extreme and opposite ways, namely, by increasing their purchases or by reducing them to the point of ceasing to buy. Observations about a variety of occasional reactions to price reductions are plentiful. To illustrate the two limiting cases, we may refer to a woman who considers buying a dress for $35 but cannot quite make up her mind; then she finds the price of the same dress reduced to $29.95; now she buys the dress without hesitation and feels that she made $5. As an example of an entirely different situation, the development of the lead market at the beginning of 1949 may be cited. After a lengthy and considerable upward movement during which lead prices reached unprecedentedly high levels, early in 1949 producers reduced the price by the small amount of 1½ cents. Newspapers reported that after that reduction the market dried up; no transactions were made at the reduced price at all.

In studying these and many other less extreme instances, it appears that the major difference between them may not be found in the type of product, in the type of customer (whether the product is purchased by consumers or by other businessmen), or in the size of the price reduction. The buyers' frame of reference and their expectations appear to account for the difference. A price reduction may be considered as leading to further price reductions; buyers may believe that the market has broken and a trend toward lower and lower prices has begun. Then price reductions may become a signal for abstaining from buying and for waiting for still lower prices. On the other hand, it is possible that a price reduction may be looked upon as temporary and therefore as providing a unique opportunity to purchase. Or buyers may assume that, with the reduction, prices have reached a new, attractive level at which they will stay. Again the buyers' reaction will be generally favorable.

Far too little is known about the underlying factors which determine the one or the other attitude. In some instances, the attitude may originate in the circumstances of the price reduction. Regular clearance sales or seasonal rebates may be cited as examples.[8] But in other instances, it is the general economic outlook which seems to determine the perception and the meaning of the price reduction. The perception of a part of the field—for instance, the reduction of the price of lead—is dependent on its whole, perhaps on the belief that a general deflationary trend prevails. We shall come back to the discussion of cumulative as against noncumulative expectations in later chapters. At this point it suffices to note that businessmen often have ample reason to consider the reactions of their customers to price reductions as uncertain.

[8] A specific example was the sale of of Waltham watches at 50 per cent of list prices by a large Boston department store in 1949. In this instance, consumers were made to realize that the price reduction represented a temporary move connected with the reorganization of the company, while watches not in stock would be priced in the future in accordance with the prevailing, much higher production costs. It was reported that on the day of sale, crowds jammed the store to buy the watches.

How will competitors react to price reductions? It has been found that businessmen frequently raise this question. Suppose competitors do not follow suit. Then the prices of the producer who decided to reduce his prices will be lower than those of competing producers. This may represent a competitive advantage but, in some cases, is thought to be unwelcome and disadvantageous. If two similar products are sold at different prices, the cheaper one may be thought by the buyers to be of lower quality and worth less. Again, businessmen may be faced with uncertainty concerning the effect of their action. If, on the other hand, competitors follow suit, the advantages expected from the price reduction would be shared by all producers and the share in the market of the firm initiating the price reduction would not increase.

A further consideration which, in the opinion of some businessmen, makes price reductions risky is that they are difficult to retract. Many businessmen feel that, if the price of an article is reduced in anticipation of a general economic decline, it will be difficult later to raise the price again—as may become necessary if, despite the lower prices, business volume falls below a critical point.

These considerations make it probable that many businessmen will respond to an expected business decline by reducing their output. It is not argued here that prices will not be reduced if lower sales are expected, but that businessmen have reason to prefer price rigidity. If a manufacturer, wholesaler, or retailer expects a business recession at a time when his own sales are still at high level, cutting production and purchases leads to a reduction of inventories. This is often considered the most effective preparation for a downward business trend.

Businessmen may, however, decide to act in various ways other than in terms of output or prices. If lower sales are anticipated, the decision may be to cut costs. Prices will then be reduced after cutting costs has proved to be feasible. This procedure has the advantage that the cost-price relation remains unchanged and therefore operating profits per unit are not lowered. Or, in anticipation of a depression, businessmen may make indirect price reductions by changing certain terms of sale or lowering quality, or they may change their products so as to stimulate sales in spite of adverse circumstances. Finally, the response to expected lower sales may consist in increasing sales efforts and the advertising budget. We turn now to a more appropriate situation for the discussion of these possible business measures.

Case 1b. Attempts to increase sales. The occasion for aspirations to increase business volume may arise in conjunction with a variety of developments. For instance, the expectation of an upward trend in business may give rise to a desire not only to participate in the upswing but also to increase one's share in the market. Similarly, an actual or expected reduction in costs, which we shall discuss shortly, may occasion attempts to enlarge sales volume. Adverse developments, such as an expected downturn in business or an increase in costs, may likewise serve to arouse interest in an increase in one's share in the market so as to counteract the expected general trend. It is, of course, possible that businessmen endeavor to obtain larger sales even if none of these developments has taken place or is expected. Changes in management or in capitalization, for instance, may present the occasion for business decisions of that type. In our present schematic discussion we shall study case 1b independently from the other cases, in spite of the fact that they are often or usually intertwined.

We take as a starting point the widespread desire to obtain a larger share in the market. What decisions and actions are frequently taken in response to such motivational forces? On the basis of some case studies, we may list the major types of business decisions without being in a position to discuss their relative frequency under varying conditions. Businessmen may embark on sales or advertising campaigns; they may introduce new products or brands, or change the quality of their products; they may attempt to cut their costs and thereafter prices; finally, they may start by reducing prices.

This is not the place to describe the wide variety of measures that may be undertaken in carrying out the first decision, the introduction of sales or advertising campaigns. The measures may range from such simple and inexpensive expedients as making a new window display in a retail store, or hiring a few salesmen, or sending salesmen to new territories, to advertising campaigns over the radio and in newspapers that involve expenditures of many millions of dollars. All these procedures have one thing in common which businessmen frequently consider a major advantage. Their cost is known in advance. The decision to embark on any of these policies involves a risk inasmuch as the money spent may not produce the desired effects. But the risk is limited, for it is known in advance how much money will be expended for the purpose of attempting to increase business volume.

The risks involved may also be limited with respect to the decision to introduce new products or to change the quality of one's product. In some cases the costs of such measures may be calculated in advance. Yet it is possible that the new product requires extensive capital expenditures which must be amortized over many years and may, therefore, involve substantial risks. And, in other instances, great uncertainty may prevail about the effects of the new policy because the introduction of new products may endanger the sales of the old ones.

The introduction of technological improvements may be a means to cut costs for the purpose of increasing business volume. Steps may be taken to alter the production process through the purchase of new machinery or to reorganize business procedures through a more efficient use of resources.

The degree of uncertainty involved in such decisions may be very small or considerable. After the success of such measures is assured, reducing prices so as to stimulate sales may appear a natural and easy step, involving much smaller risks than reducing prices without cutting costs.

That the final alternative, attempting to increase volume by reducing prices, is occasionally chosen is beyond doubt. But businessmen often explain that at those times when such policies are relatively easy, namely, when profits are substantial, the measure is frequently not needed. When, however, profits, or profit margins, are relatively small, a reduction of the cost-price ratio is fraught with great risks. Pursuing sales increases through price reductions does not appear to be a preferred method because businessmen are aware of possible drawbacks of such measures. We discussed before the possibility that in the minds of customers price reductions may arouse the expectation of still further price reductions and thus reduce demand and defeat their own purpose. We also said that lower prices may even carry the stigma of bad quality. In brief, then, attempting to increase volume through price reductions is considered risky business, the consequences of which can often not be foreseen.

Case 1c. Reactions to decline in costs. There are several typical situations in which business decisions in terms of output or price may be made in response to an actual or expected decline in costs. The first is when suppliers reduce their prices for current or future delivery. A manufacturer learns that in the future he will pay less for some of the raw materials he uses, or a wholesaler or retailer learns that he will obtain some of his goods at lower prices than before. Second, changes in technology or in rate of productivity may take place that are expected to lead to lower costs in the near or more distant future. Calculations may reveal that after certain new machines are put into operation, production costs will drop. Third, for the sake of completeness, a cut in wage rates must be listed. This is probably not a very frequent occurrence, even in periods of depression.

What are the probable reactions under such conditions? It is possible that nothing at all is done. Keeping output and prices unchanged when costs decline means higher profits. That this alternative is chosen may be more probable if the cost decline is restricted to the one firm in question, so that competitors are in a different situation and are not expected to change their output or prices.

Secondly, as said before, a decline in costs may provide the opportunity for attempting to increase business volume or the firm's share in the market. The money saved through a reduction in costs may be used for advertising or for the introduction of new products—or for cutting prices. When changes in technology or productivity enable a manufacturer to reduce the number of workers per unit poduced, he may endeavor to increase output rather than dismiss workers. On the other hand, that reaction appears to be less probable when the cost decline is due to suppliers' reducing their prices, from which all producers of the same product benefit. In that case, improvement of quality, that is, indirect price reductions, may be resorted to, or the response to lower costs may be exclusively in terms of lower prices.

The subjective considerations that speak against reducing prices need not be repeated here. It suffices to say that they carry less weight in the case of cost reductions than in any other instance. Still, it must be noted that price reductions are not the only possible response to an actual or an expected drop in costs.

Case 2c. Reactions to increase in costs. Increase in the prices quoted by suppliers and increase in wage rates are typical and important instances of situations requiring decisions about prices. Business decisions in terms of prices or output may also be called for because of an expectation of cost increases.

In this case, increasing prices is one of the possible reactions. Many businessmen seem to feel that price increases require some justification. Within that frame of reference, which in the last chapter was described as an apologetic attitude, some businessmen may have a guilt feeling or may fear adverse public opinion if they increase their prices without being able to explain publicly the inevitable necessity of this measure. Cost increases, and especially widely publicized wage increases, are considered the best justification for price increases. But raising prices is not necessarily the preferred reaction to higher costs because of the risks and uncertainties often associated with price increases. Case studies have shown many instances in which businessmen have tried to increase their sales in order to counteract higher costs.

Price increases may be the natural and quick decision made in inflationary periods. Then cost increases will be transmitted to customers without hesitation and to the full extent. We reserve the discussion of inflation for a later chapter.

HABITUAL BEHAVIOR AND GENUINE DECISION MAKING

In studying the diverse reactions of businessmen to "occasions" for price or output decisions, it was found that the consideration of uncertainty played a major role. Much of what has been said may be tentatively summarized by the statement that businessmen abhor uncertainty. They try to avoid decisions the consequences of which they cannot foresee, and try to make decisions the consequences of which are in their opinion least uncertain. A second preliminary conclusion which emerges from various observations is that many businessmen do not place great stock in their own power to influence conditions. They believe that their own businesses are affected by general trends but that their own actions have no influence, or only a very small influence, on those trends. The general trend is viewed, primarily, in terms of the current and expected demand of consumers. Fluctuations of consumer demand are watched carefully and business decisions adjusted to them. It seems that advertising is believed to be the main method by which businessmen have it in their own power to influence demand for their products.

These tentative conclusions appear to be in accord with what we know about the psychology of decision formation in general. The distinction between habitual behavior and genuine decision making has, in fact, been applied in the previous section when we searched for incentives that must be present to arouse the need for genuine decisions. And the observation that businessmen often seek the easiest and least uncertain solution may mean that behavior frequently remains habitual even when changes in conditions call for new decisions. It is, however, necessary to summarize what is known about habitual business behavior in a more systematic manner. After having done so, we shall again raise the question about the conditions under which genuine decisions occur.

There is ample evidence that routine behavior is very frequent in business life. Actions relating both to business volume and prices are often taken in the customary way without the process of weighing, choosing, and deciding. Habitual ways of thinking and acting, or rules of thumb, that even preclude the possibility of perceiving alternate courses of action may prevail. They may prevail within a firm, or within all firms of a given trade. They may even be formalized so that employees at a relatively low level may apply them and change volume or prices without consulting the centers of decision making.

There are good reasons for the widespread occurrence of habitual behavior. In our multiproduct firms, which purchase and sell a great number of different products and qualities at different prices, it is almost impossible to rely on the complex process of weighing all alternatives concerning every single action. It is necessary to set up principles or policies that can be carried over wherever and whenever they are thought to apply. Second, past experience which has proved to be satisfactory has great influence. Not only is it easier to act in the same way one has acted before under similar circumstances than to make a new decision, but it is also thought unnecessary and a waste of time to consider abandoning or changing the well-trodden paths of action. Were all circumstances and future developments known in every single instance, routine actions might perhaps have less compelling force. But in circumstances of uncertainty, doing the thing that was done before appears the safest way to proceed and the one involving the smallest amount of risk.

Empirical studies about the variety of routine behavior and rule-of-thumb decisions have not as yet progressed very far. What can be done at this point is to list some major habitual considerations that were found to prevail with respect to volume and prices.

1. Pricing Rules. Within a firm, or within an entire trade, certain pricing rules are often found to prevail. They are applied in a routine way; genuine decisions are needed in order to abandon or to change them, but not in order to apply them. A very important form of pricing is margin pricing. A retailer, for instance, buys at price X and sells at X plus some fixed percentage. The markup added to the purchase price may be fixed for all products sold and may remain unchanged over long periods. Or, there may be in a single firm several different markup rates, applied to different products or applied at different seasons. In other instances, instead of marking up by adding a percentage to the purchase price, the reverse system may prevail. The sales price may be considered as given, and the retailer purchases goods, if he can obtain them, at a certain traditional percentage of his sales price. In the case of a manufacturer operating on a markup principle, he adds a given percentage to his "costs" to determine his sales price. Not only is the percentage of markup traditionally set but the determination of costs is likewise ruled by certain habitual principles. Most frequently, the so-called variable costs alone are considered as costs, namely, raw materials and labor, while the margin is supposed to cover fixed costs (overhead, depreciation, interest, etc.), sales costs, and profits. Differences exist among firms and trades as to what the margin is supposed to cover. We discussed before (Chapter 4) certain pricing rules used by many restaurants, according to which food costs alone were considered as costs, and rent, lighting, heating, china, as well as wages, were thought to be covered through the markup rate. Whichever is the case, price changes may come about through the application of habitual margin rates rather than because of decisions to change prices. Fluctuating or flexible prices may be the result of rigid pricing methods.

Habitual pricing rules may be the basis of complex actions. An owner of a small store may have but one simple rule, such as: One-third is to be added to the purchase price. In large corporations, however, the pricing system may be formalized and incorporated in memos, records, or even printed books. The system of basing point prices, used for many decades by the steel industry, among others, was represented in very elaborate documents covering a variety of products sold in different localities. The system may have evolved, like most other habitual rules, as a result of complex considerations. Furthermore, changing the system, or abstaining from applying any small part of the system, would require new decisions on the policy level, but applying it does not necessitate consideration or action on the part of the board of directors, or president, or vice-president in charge of sales.

Habitual pricing rules are used in diverse circumstances. They are applied when sales are expanding and when they are contracting, and are generally thought to be applicable and useful without special study of the given situation. Furthermore, they are applied to new products as well as to products to which they have been applied before. A specific example may illustrate this statement in simple form. How does the owner of a small bakery determine the price of a cake which he has prepared for the first time? In one case study, it was found that the baker did not go around town to find out how other bakers price similar cakes. He did not think about the probable preferences of his customers and did not ask himself whether they would be willing to pay a few cents more for the new cake than for certain other products traditionally carried in his store. He first determined what he called costs, namely, the price of all ingredients—flour, sugar, chocolate, and so on—that go into the cake. Then he added a certain percentage to the costs, which percentage was traditional in his shop and was known to him to cover rent, labor, other costs, and profits. Finally, he divided cost plus markup by the number of cakes made and did some rounding. It was the same process that he applied to old products when the price of the ingredients changed. Should later experience show that the new product would not sell at the calculated price, genuine decisions may be called for; but often the action in that case will likewise be traditionally determined, namely, to give up baking the new cake.

It was said before that habitual pricing systems may extend to such measures as rebates, markdowns, promotions, and clearance sales. A wholesaler or a department store, for instance, may have a fixed system of reducing by a given percentage the prices of certain products if they are still unsold after a given time. Retailers may have a fixed system of seasonal sales, and the traditional principles may apply both to the range of products which are subject to markdowns and to the percentage of markdown.

It is not asserted here that habitual pricing necessarily conflicts with considerations dictated by the profit motive or even by profit maximization. What is implied is that the question of whether the new price will maximize profits frequently does not arise in the minds of businessmen. Short cuts are used that are not only simple but also have proved efficient and productive of profits in the past.

2. Inventory Considerations. A second form of habitual thinking has to do with the perception of changes in inventories and with reactions to such changes. In some firms, elaborate systems of inventory control prevail. Through such systems, care is taken to detect certain changes in inventories and to respond to them in a well-established way. The best known of such rules of thumb is the manufacturer's reduction of output in response to an increase in inventories of finished products beyond a certain point. Without being in a position to analyze inventory decisions in any detail, it must be emphasized on the basis of available observations that the flow of goods, the rate of turnover, or the flow of incoming orders may elicit reactions without genuine decisions. What, exactly, is considered a necessary occasion for change in output—for instance, how much inventories have to increase—may vary from firm to firm. The reaction itself may vary; it may, for instance, consist of markdowns instead of changes in output. The point is simply that some of such actions do not require a complex process of weighing and considering consequences. Again, genuine decisions in response to changes in the flow of sales and of inventories are not to be ruled out. But they must be understood against the background of habitual behavior.

3. Capacity Considerations. Business capacity is not an objectively given datum but a magnitude which businessmen determine on the basis of what they consider to be their normal production rate. It appears in the light of investigations, which are by no means conclusive, that many businessmen have notions about what the capacities of their businesses are, that they believe that near-capacity production is preferable to a lower rate of operation, and that operating at or close to capacity level represents the optimum size of output. If and when these opinions prevail, increasing the rate of output up to capacity may not require complex cost calculations. Genuine decisions are needed, on the other hand, in order to question the advisability of increasing the output and to make calculations on the increments in cost and revenues resulting from increased output. Similarly, there appears to be a habitual tendency to regard operations at a rate higher than capacity, which are possible through second shifts, overtime, speedup, etc., as unwelcome.

One possible basis for these attitudes toward production rates lies in accounting practices. The influence of the cost accountant on the thinking of business owners and business executives can hardly be overestimated, since most businessmen live with the concepts and the kind of figures supplied by the accountants. The division of costs into fixed and variable costs seems to have patricularly great influence. There appear to be some differences in different lines of business about what are considered fixed and what variable costs, but on the whole businessmen will identify variable costs with those costs which increase more or less proportionately to volume, and fixed costs with those which do not. Whether a given business operates with relatively large or relatively small fixed costs appears to be well known to the owners or executives and is often in the forefront of their thinking. The differences between businesses that operate with large or small fixed costs can be illustrated by the following simple scheme:

Sales	Fixed costs	Variable costs	Profits
		Firm *A*	
100	60	20	20
110	60	22	28
		Firm *B*	
100	20	60	20
110	20	66	24

In a firm having high fixed costs and low variable costs, profits will rise faster as sales increase, and fall faster as sales decrease, than in a firm having low fixed costs and high variable costs. The relative size of fixed costs is dependent not only on the type of business but also on the capitalization of the firm. To be sure, a hydroelectric power plant with large investments requiring high depreciation charges will have relatively higher fixed costs than a textile wholesaler, but within a given trade a firm financed primarily by mortgage or other liens will have greater fixed charges than a firm capitalized primarily by common stock. Striving toward operations that are close to capacity output will represent a much stronger incentive for enterprises with relatively high fixed costs than for those with relatively low fixed costs. This is, of course, in accordance with the principle of profit maximization. The point emphasized here is simply that the relation between capacity considerations and profits is not necessarily investigated in every step taken by businessmen; it may merely influence business actions in a routine way, inasmuch as businessmen may rely on the rule of thumb that represents part of their thinking carried over from past experience.

The term "capacity" must be understood in the broadest possible sense. In order to show how it may influence business behavior outside the field of manufacturing, to which it is usually applied, we may refer to surveys conducted among farmers. Theorists have frequently applied considerations of marginal calculus to hog production. The assumption is made that the most important factor determining fluctuations in hog production is the relation between corn price and hog price, inasmuch as that ratio determines the profitability of larger or smaller feeding and marketing programs. When, however, in recent surveys [9] hog farmers were asked about the considerations they actually·applied in determining the size of their herds and changes in the size, they referred first of all to matters that may be summarized under the term capacity. They spoke of the facilities available on their farms and of the number of hogs they and their families could tend. Small and middle-size farmers, especially, had a very clear notion about what size of herds they considered their capacity and identified that size with the optimum size. Increasing production beyond that size was considered difficult and was rarely attempted even under most favorable cost-price conditions, and reducing output below capacity size was likewise done reluctantly and only under most compelling adverse conditions.

4. **Liquidity Considerations.** There is some evidence that businessmen's habitual ways of thinking may encompass certain notions about what they deem to be the normal or required liquidity position. Prevailing accounting practices make the size of liquid resources and their fluctuations well known to business executives. In addition to bank deposits and government bonds, receivables and inventories may be considered as liquid assets or "working capital," from which short-term liabilities are deducted. There can be no doubt that businessmen in general aspire to a liquidity position which they consider comfortable. Certain amounts of net liquid assets, which of course vary from firm to firm and from trade to trade, are believed to represent the rock-bottom minimum. It is doubtful whether businessmen's rules of thumb contain any provisions about what to do if liquid assets substantially exceed that minimum. That means that a very liquid position may be maintained for long periods without necessarily inducing businessmen to plan for additional expenditures or investments. If, however, the liquidity position deteriorates and approaches what is considered to be the minimum requirement, the development is viewed as a danger signal. What has occasionally been called the "fetish of liquidity" may habitually induce businessmen to change their output or prices or to institute new sales-promotion measures.

5. **"Follow the Leader."** For the sake of completeness, we must mention the possibility that many firms habitually follow the price and output decisions of a leader. It is well known that in certain trades there exists a firm, usually the largest or the oldest, which traditionally assumes leadership in establishing new wages rates, production rates, or prices. To what extent such relationships are permanent and to what extent the leader's actions are followed more or less compulsively are not known. But in studying the habitual framework from which businessmen depart through genuine price or output decisions, it may be necessary to investigate the presence or absence of established leadership-follower relations. That relationship need not be compelling, but may mean simply that acting as the leader has acted

[9] Conducted by the Division of Program Surveys, Bureau of Agricultural Economics.

is relatively easy, and acting differently relatively difficult. Following the
leader's action may amount to more or less mechanical imitation. It may
mean compulsion in the sense that a firm's customers expect it to do the
same thing as the trade leader has done. But it may also represent trust in
the insight or intelligence of the leader and thus seem the best way to make
profits.

Habitual ways of business thinking have been enumerated in order to
gain acquaintance with some widespread rules of thumb and to understand
the background from which genuine business decisions arise. To repeat:
The making of a genuine decision often involves calling into question a
habitual pattern of action. It involves a realization that the situation calls
for a new decision and an attempt to understand the requirements of the
new situation. In this sense, genuine decisions mean a break with the past
and lead to flexible behavior.

Extensive investigations are needed to understand the various forms of
genuine decision making concerning output and price and to describe the
circumstances under which they may occur frequently. The schematic
presentation of business decisions given earlier may serve as a guide for
such studies. Anticipation of substantial changes in business trends or in
costs (cases 1a, 2a, 1c, and 2c) may represent some of the important
instances that elicit such decisions. There may be other instances, too, in
which confidently held expectations arise and lead to a restructuring of the
psychological field. Not enough is known at present about the formation
of business expectations, nor about the process of decision formation itself.

Decision formation may make use of the "marginalist attitude" and may
even take the form of marginal calculus. In other words, it is possible that
if and when a businessman feels himself to be in a crossroads situation, he
may make detailed calculations about the probable effects of various possible courses of action. The crucial question, "What difference does it make
whether I act this way or that?" may, however, be tackled in another way.
Some critics of marginal theory have argued that, in view of the number of
different factors involved, it is impossible for a businessman to make exact
calculations. Fritz Machlup [10] has replied that decisions may be made by
"sizing up the situation," which process requires only approximate estimates of some crucial factors or may even be made without any numerical
calculations or estimations. Machlup also points out that the terms used
by the businessmen, whether "marginal costs and marginal revenues," or
"changes in total costs and total revenues," or others, do not make any
difference. Weighing possible alternatives, considering anticipated developments and anticipated effects of a new decision, fit in with underlying prin-

[10] Machlup, *op. cit.*, pp. 525 and 534f.

ciples of marginalism and are, in our terminology, indications of genuine decisions.

"Sizing up" may denote the psychological process which we described in some detail in Chapter 4. Our thinking has a definite direction in problem solving—when we want to find out what the area of a trapezoid is, or whether we should change our output or prices. This direction may lead us to see the situation in a new way: certain parts of the trapezoid, or certain impending actions of government, competitors, or customers are seen as "disturbing," and certain kinds of decisions appear to be indicated. The problem-solving situation will hardly arise, and a solution through sizing up the situation will therefore not be arrived at, if the difference between the new and the old situation is small. But in those instances when the changes loom large, when therefore it really matters how we decide, the reorganization of the psychological field may present the solution without any need for calculations based on exact data.

The study of decision formation should also encompass the investigation of possible effects of business structure. We referred in the last chapter to the contradictory assertions that could be made regarding the frequency of routine actions by large and small firms. Similarly, it may be argued that only small firms need to resort to sizing up the situation. Firms which have large staffs, statistical and research divisions, and innumerable publications and predictions at their disposal can rely on detailed calculations of alternative courses of action. Again it is highly improbable that such a simple dichotomy correctly represents the actual situation. The mere quantity of available information and the size of the staff may be of little importance in themselves. But far too little is known about the relation of the process of decision formation to the size of the firm, the type of product, or the prevailing business trend (expansion or contraction).

Neither our description of genuine decision making nor the emphasis placed on habitual behavior is necessarily opposed to traditional economic analysis. As argued in Chapter 4, it is probable that rules of thumb and habitual standards are carried over from earlier genuine decisions, and those may have been intended to increase profits. But the present analysis differs from certain underlying assumptions of traditional theory. First of all, tenets of mechanistic psychology have no place in the analysis of business decisions. Only if it were true that there is necessarily a one-to-one correlation between a given stimulus and a given response can such "laws" as "the lower the price the larger the quantity demanded" be generally valid. Business firms are, however, not machines that react in a uniform manner to the same changes in their environment. Therefore, an analytical framework that considers a few factors only, and always the same few factors, can hardly be sufficient. Furthermore, in studying business decisions, it is necessary, and possible, to take uncertainty into account. Uncertainty means not only absence of knowledge about prevailing and expected conditions, or lack of experimentation with different possibilities, but also awareness of the possibility that the same action may have different results. For instance, some businessmen's decisions were found to be influenced by their opinion that their consumers and competitors might react in any of several ways to changes in prices. It is probable that when businessmen believe they know what the reactions to their actions will be, they will change their course of action more radically than when they are uncertain about those reactions. This conclusion again must be taken as a hypothesis that may be useful in future studies of business behavior as well as of economic policy.

NOTES TO CHAPTER 10

The survey sources of the empirical observations presented in this chapter were listed in the Notes to the preceding chapter. Problems of interviewing businessmen will be discussed further in Chapter 15.

For a detailed discussion of a variety of conventional and rule-of-thumb methods, see the volume *Cost Behavior and Price Policy* (by the Committee on Price Determination, National Bureau of Economic Research, New York, 1943). The evidence presented for the prevalence of such methods is most complete with respect to the calculation of various costs and the effect of accounting practices on busines behavior. The following statement supports the argument presented in the text: "It seems probable that anticipated shifts in the demand curve, to which the firm must adjust its decisions, have more relevance for price policy than does its shape" (*op. cit.,* p. 269). Demand curves "imagined by the firms" are referred to in that book and also in the studies of R. L. Hall and C. J. Hitch ("Price Theory and Business Behavior," *Oxford Economic Papers,* No. 2, 1939). Robert Triffin argues that the "only sales curve that is relevant is the subjective or imagined sales curve which expresses the expectations of the producer" (*Monopolistic Competition and General Equilibrium Theory,* Cambridge, 1940, p. 62).

That consideration of business expectations may affect the theory of supply and demand schedules has frequently been stated. For instance, Moses Abramovitz writes: "The curves of demand and supply are defined by the assumption that the anticipations of traders with respect to future prices do not change," and then argues that, "in fact, however, these anticipations change rapidly" (*An Approach to a Price Theory for a Changing Economy,* New York, 1939, p. 58).

J. R. Hicks refers to the "familiar textbook point that a fall in price may fail to increase demand, or may even diminish it, because it creates an expectation of the price falling farther" (*Value and Capital,* Oxford, 1939, p. 56). He does not attach great importance to this point, which he believes to be restricted to what he calls "speculative demand."

The literature on uncertainty is growing rapidly. F. H. Knight's book *Risk, Uncertainty and Profit* (New York, 1921) may be cited as an early important treatment of the problem. Albert G. Hart's book *Anticipations, Uncertainty and Dynamic Planning* (Chicago, 1940) contains valuable contributions to the subject. Jacob Marschak differentiates between various aspects of uncertainty, especially between the probability assigned to an expectation and the reliability of the estimate leading to the expectation ("Lack of Confidence," *Social Research*, Vol. 8, 1941, pp. 50*ff*.). Of interest are the papers presented by both Hart and Marschak, and the following discussion, at the December, 1948, meeting of the American Economic Association (see *American Economic Review*, Vol. 39, 1949, Supplement, pp. 171*ff*.). Hart in his paper rightly challenges the "strong tendency among theorists to push uncertainty under the rug by setting up 'certainty equivalents' to uncertain expectations" (*op. cit.*, p. 180). Similar arguments are to be found in R. A. Gordon's article cited before (*American Economic Review*, Vol. 38, 1948).

Fritz Machlup's paper "Marginal Analysis and Empirical Research" (*American Economic Review*, Vol. 36, 1946, pp. 519*ff*.) contains, in addition to a formulation of the essential features of marginalism—from which several passages were quoted in the text—a severe criticism of certain empirical studies (especially by R. A. Lester) which have attempted to show that the conduct of the firm differs from what marginal theory postulates. Our discussion of research methods in Chapter 15 is in substantial agreement with the methodological remarks of Machlup. In turn, Machlup's theory—not his methodological strictures—was criticized by several authors in subsequent issues of the *American Economic Review* (see especially Gordon's paper quoted above).

A broad attack on marginalism as contradicting a realistic description of business behavior was launched by W. J. Eiteman (*Price Determination—Business Practice versus Economic Theory*, Ann Arbor, 1949). Eiteman formulates a crucial question: "How do businessmen decide *when* it is advisable for them to raise or lower their prices?" (p. 14), and argues that changes in inventories (rate of turnover) have the greatest influence on managerial decisions about prices and output.

How businessmen regard their inventories, and changes in their inventories, will require much further research. Of great importance are the studies of Abramovitz. He divides the total stock of businessmen into several categories, "reflecting differences in motives behind inventory policy" ("Role of Inventories in Business Cycles," *Occasional Paper* 26, National Bureau of Economic Research, 1948).

Among recent case studies, mention should be made of E. P. Learned's valuable analysis of the price decisions and pricing policies of the Standard Oil Company of Ohio ("Pricing of Gasoline: A Case Study," *Harvard Business Review*, Vol. 26, 1948, pp. 723*ff*.). Learned shows that businessmen consider probable effects of, and probable reactions to, proposed prices. Many illustrations are given of the role of the company's share in the market and of leadership-follower relations. Especially interesting is the observation that the large company can "lead the market up" (take the initiative in raising the price of gasoline) but that "it is not wise to lead it down" (p. 731).

Chapter 11

INVESTMENT DECISIONS

By business investments are meant capital expenditures of business firms, such as erection of new plants or installation of new machinery. The purpose of such investments is to replace or improve existing facilities, or to create new facilities so that production and sales can be increased or the output and sale of new products initiated. Such capital expenditures must be differentiated from what may be called investment in business, that is, purchases of securities or loans to business firms made by private investors. These activities belong more properly in the category of decisions of households than in that of business decisions.

THE ROLE OF BUSINESS INVESTMENTS

In Chapter 7 we referred to the widely held thesis that business investment is the prime factor responsible for changes in economic trends. There we discussed the thesis that fluctuations in other economic activities, and especially in consumption expenditures, are not autonomous but dependent on fluctuations in income. In contradicting that position and in arguing that the rate of consumption may change independently of changes in rate of income and thus may be responsible for upswings or downswings in the economy, no attempt was made to detract from the importance of investments. A few words must be added here concerning what may be called the positive evidence for the role of business investment in generating economic trends. This evidence may be summarized thus: First, business investment is a major factor in the progress or growth of an economy. Second, it fluctuates greatly, and the direction and extent of its fluctuations cannot be explained by changes in other economic variables. Third, changes in investment have cumulative effects; they create changes in employment and income beyond their immediate scope.

There is ample statistical evidence that capital expenditures of business firms, in the aggregate, are large at certain times and small at other times. In searching for the causes of these fluctuations, a consideration may be mentioned first which, if viewed superficially, appears to be independent of psychological factors. Certain features are inherent in the functioning of our complex economy that cause capital expenditures to fluctuate much more widely than consumption or national income. These features of our economy have been described under the name "acceleration principle" [1] and are presented schematically in the accompanying table.

Year	Shoe production	Number of shoe machines used	Number of shoe machines produced		
			For replacement	For additions	Total
I	1,000,000	500	50	0	50
II	1,100,000	550	50	50	100
III	1,150,000	575	55	25	80

Suppose 1,000,000 pairs of shoes are produced in a given period (Year I) by 500 machines. Assume further that the machines can be used for 10 years and that one-tenth of the available machines are 10 years old. Then the replacement of old machines necessitates the production of 50 new machines without any change in the production of shoes. If, however, demand for shoes increases by 10 per cent in Year II, shoe producers will need 550 machines. Therefore, in addition to the machines needed for replacement, 50 more new shoe machines must be built. The second line in the table illustrates, then, that an increase of consumption by 10 per cent may lead to a 100 per cent increase in the capital expenditures of the shoe manufacturers and in the output of the factories producing shoe machinery. If we assume further that in Year III consumption and production of shoes increases by an additional 5 per cent, the required number of shoe machines will rise from 550 to 575. Only 25 new machines will be needed in that year (in addition to those needed for replacement), which means that the total production of shoe machines will drop from 100 to 80, in spite of an increase in shoe production.

Our schematic presentation may serve to illustrate the underlying principle, but it is not realistic. It was drawn as if there were no time lag between the production of shoe machinery and its use for the production of shoes. The output of new shoe machinery and the increased output of shoes were placed in the same period. In fact, capital expenditures must be planned well in advance. This does not mean, however, that increased output of consumption goods (of shoes, for instance) is impossible without a prior substantial increase in the output of capital goods (of shoe machinery,

---

[1] For a discussion of the acceleration principle, see Gottfried Haberler, *Prosperity and Depression*, League of Nations, Geneva, 1937, pp. 84*ff*. The example of fluctuations in the output of shoe machinery is adopted from that book.

for instance), because usually unused capacity exists or a higher rate of utilization of existing capacity is possible.

It was further assumed in our schema that a machine can be used for a predetermined number of years only and will be replaced at the end of that time, not earlier, not later. In fact, of course, when to replace an old machine depends on the manufacturers' decisions and represents the problem which we are about to study.

If such considerations are taken into account, it becomes doubtful that it was the 10 per cent increase in shoe consumption that brought forth the 100 per cent increase in the production of shoe machinery. If in a given year consumption rose slightly and capital expenditures sharply, other factors must have played a role, too. The producers of consumption goods must have anticipated an increase in consumption—lasting a longer period and not just for one year—and must have anticipated satisfactory price-profit ratios. Otherwise they would not have ordered the new machinery in addition to continuing with the replacement of their old machines. Or there must have been technological developments (improvements in the shoe machinery) that made the purchase of new machines necessary or advisable. Thus it is possible that business investment (the purchase of shoe machinery) is the result of increase in consumption, but it is also possible that it precedes the increase in consumption and is due to an expected increase or to technological changes. Whichever is the case, increased capital expenditures themselves will generate employment (of workers producing shoe machinery) and thereby create consumer income and perhaps added consumption.

The relation of investments to saving must next be discussed briefly in order to examine further the role of business investments in our economy. Investment requires caiptal. The funds invested may all be derived from saving done in the same period. It was, however, pointed out before that the quantity of funds that people plan to invest in a given period need not be the same as the quantity of funds people plan to save in that period. Previously accumulated and previously unused (hoarded) assets may be used for investment, or new funds may be created by banks through lending or by the government through deficits. Or some amounts saved may not be utilized in the same period but kept, for instance, in bank deposits for which the banks do not find productive use.

Those who make decisions to save and those who decide to invest are not necesarily the same people. Only in certain instances do the processes of saving and investing represent the same activity. If investment were to be defined as including investments by business firms, investments in business by private individuals, as well as other long-term and employment-producing uses of capital, a consumer's decision to use part of his income to build a house for his own use might mean at the same time saving as well as investment. Then, too, owners of unincorporated businesses sometimes use part of their profits to purchase capital equipment. And, most importantly, corporations resort to what is called internal financing. Instead of distributing their profits to their stockholders, they may use all or some of them for financing capital expenditures.

That is, however, not the whole story. Private households as well as business firms save money by adding to their bank deposits or by purchasing government bonds. And business firms often finance their investments by drawing on outside capital, borrowing money from banks, issuing stock, and so on. Not only may the savers and the investors be different people, but the two kinds of decisions may also be stimulated by different, even contradictory, considerations. As was shown before, there is a tendency to increase savings when bad times are expected. Without any detailed empirical studies, it appears probable, on the other hand, that decisions to invest will tend to be made primarily when good times are expected. Thus, there may be considerable differences between plans for saving and plans for investment.

It would seem, then, that certain simple explanations of investment decisions must be considered unsatisfactory. First, it is not possible to maintain that investment is a function of nothing but consumption and that fluctuations of investment follow those of consumption. Second, it is not correct to say that investment is a function of saving, because capital expenditures may exceed or may lag behind the rate of accumulation of new reserve funds. Finally, it is not possible to say that investment is a function of technological changes. It is hardly conceivable that the rate of technological progress is so extremely variable as to cause great scarcity of investment in some periods and very much larger investment opportunities in other periods. There may be some truth in every one of these arguments, but there may also be some truth in the reverse statements, namely, that consumption, or saving, or technological changes are to some extent functions of investment. Investment may add to consumption; it may also induce people to save, for instance, through offering attractive possibilities for the use of funds; and it may accelerate or generate research and the application of inventions.

HABITUAL BEHAVIOR

The most obvious feature of investment decisions by business firms is that they refer to the future. They may involve a period of several years, even of many years. When a public utility company, for instance, decides to build a new electric generating plant, it may take a few years to put that plant into operation. Furthermore, it may take even several decades to pay for the new plant. One may then assume that the decision to build such a plant involves considerations about the demand for electric current and about profits in the distant future. Sometimes, of course, the time lag between investment decision and utilization of the new capital equipment may be rather brief, but still it appears that future rather than current considerations must be involved. Can it therefore be asserted that investment decisions always require definite expectations and a restructuring of the frame of reference, that is, genuine decisions? Or is it possible that investments are made on the basis of habitual patterns or rules of thumb?

J. M. Keynes gave an answer to our question when he wrote that "[the entrepreneur] has no choice but to be guided by . . . expectations." [2] This statement is applied both to production and investment decisions, but with respect to the former, Keynes recognizes that the price at which an article to be produced is expected to be sold is usually judged in the light of its current price. On the other hand, investment, the purchase of a capital asset, is said to be based on long-term profit expectations, primarily on the expected yield of the asset in addition to its current cost. There is one passage in Keynes's book which constitutes a restriction of this argument. He says that in practice, as a rule, investors fall back on a *convention*: "The essence of this convention—though it does not, of course, work out quite so simply—lies in assuming that the existing state of affairs will continue indefinitely" (*op. cit.*, p. 152). Before discussing the role of expectations, we shall study the indications for conventional or habitual patterns of capital expenditures. We shall find that they occur under diverse conditions and play a great role in American economic life.

1. Replacement Based on Depreciation. The influence of accounting practices on businessmen's thinking has to be considered first. The practice of writing off machinery or plant over a specific number of years may mean more than an aid in determining profits through adding amounts of depreciation to costs. The practice may lead a businessman to think that a piece of machinery has a useful life of ten or twenty years and needs to be replaced after that time. Some observations indicate that in a certain sense it is true that a bell rings and calls for replacement. For some manufacturers, replacing a machine after the time set for its use has elapsed and it is fully written off, represents habitual behavior. Of course, it may happen that the signal is not heeded, and the machinery is kept in use and is not replaced even after it has been fully written off. This may require genuine decisions, as may changing depreciation rates, in order to arrive at shorter periods of use and quicker replacement. It appears that replacing

[2] J. M. Keynes, *General Theory of Employment, Interest, and Money*, New York, 1936, p. 46.

a machine that is not yet written off is an especially difficult decision, that is, one that requires compelling reasons.

These observations are confirmed by George Terborgh's study of replacement practices.[3] Terborgh argues (*op. cit.*, pp. 4*ff*.) that replacement .decisions should not be influenced by the book value, or unrecovered cost, of the asset considered for retirement. But "this prejudice exists in many places and must be reckoned with." "Not infrequently there is a marked unwillingness to 'take a loss' on the disposal of assets with substantial remaining book value, and their replacement is handicapped accordingly." He speaks of "a vague feeling that capital assets ought to be kept in commission over the service life assumed for depreciation purposes" and of ' capital expenditures being "influenced by the volume of depreciation accruals." No information is available, however, about the conditions under which such considerations are powerful and under which they are weak. Additional information would also be needed as to how depreciation rates are determined and how, and under what conditions, they are changed.

2. Replacement Based on Available Funds. If replacement of a capital asset is made dependent on the asset's having been written off, the question of raising capital for the next expenditure may not arise. The purchase of the new machine can be financed from the depreciation fund set up for the old machine, provided the depreciation reserves are kept in liquid funds. (Furthermore, the new machine must cost the same as the old one; this will not be the case if, as often happens, replacing means purchasing a better or larger machine.) There are indications that many businessmen are in the habit of making replacements only after funds have been accumulated for that purpose, through depreciation reserves or otherwise. The availability of such funds in itself may be a signal for replacement. And there may be a disposition, or a rule of thumb, to restrict replacement to the available internal funds.[4] To deviate from this rule and to borrow money for the replacement of existing and still usable facilities will be done only if compelling reasons exist. Such a procedure, then, requires genuine decisions.

3. Short Pay-off Requirement for Investment. Terborgh reports that the "use of conventional rule-of-thumb tests of replaceability [is] very common" (*op. cit.*, p. 12). These "shorthand aids to managerial judgment"

[3] George Terborgh, *Dynamic Equipment Policy*. Copyright, 1949. Courtesy of McGraw-Hill Book Company, Inc. The book contains, in addition to a discussion of how replacement and reequipment decisions are customarily made—a discussion that will be frequently quoted in the next few pages—a proposal for a new rational method for making reequipment decisions.

[4] Terborgh quotes a survey made by the Machinery and Allied Products Institute, according to which most member firms believe that their customers' current liquid position is a "determining or important" consideration in replacement decisions (*op. cit.*, p. 229).

apply not only to replacements but generally to purchases of new machinery. The most popular formula used is the short pay-off requirement, which in its simplest form may read, "No machine will be bought unless it pays for itself in two (three) years." Chapters XI and XII of Terborgh's book present ample evidence for the following findings about the currently prevailing practices among manufacturers: (a) The crucial consideration purchasers of machinery raise is the time period in which the new machine will "pay for itself." (b) Purchasers usually require that the new machine pay for itself in a very short period, namely, in two, three, or four years. The pay-off period required is much shorter than the service life of the machinery (which is taken into account when depreciation rates are set). It is not arrived at by complex calculations and has no rational justification. (c) The methods used to determine how much saving in costs a new machine will bring, and therefore when it will pay for itself, are likewise conventional short-cut procedures, in which "normal" rates of utilization are assumed. In summary, Terborgh characterizes the short pay-off requirement as "a part of our industrial folklore" (p. 187). He deplores the widespread use of the method and expresses the opinion that it induces business firms to operate machines that should long since have been replaced, thus bringing substantial reduction in costs.

The history of the short pay-off requirement and businessmen's attitudes toward it and their reasons for using it should be studied in much greater detail than has been done up to now. The prevailing uncertainty about the future, coupled with the irrevocability of the decision to purchase new capital equipment, may have much to do with the shortness of the pay-off requirements. We may refer to the finding, valid in various fields of economic behavior, that usually no action is taken if that action would make only a small difference. People decide to act in a certain way if thereby they are "obviously" better off, or very much better off, than by not doing so. Only then is uncertainty about future developments disregarded. If businessmen had definite expectations about their future sales and profits all the time, there would be no need for such cautious procedures and for shorthand rules of thumb in general. In the absence of definite expectations, however, they fall back on conventions that are not only simple but also involve little risk (or carry a large margin of safety).

4. Other Rules of Thumb for Investment. Terborgh describes various formulas other than the device of short pay-off requirement that sometimes guide decisions to replace machinery. Similarly, it is probable that regarding other forms of investment, or in fields other than manufacturing, a variety of rules of thumb prevail that represent standards habitually used. For purposes of illustration, two instances of such rules may be mentioned, which are said to be widely applied in the real-estate business. On what basis do private capitalists make their decisions about the advisability of building a new hotel, or hotel operators about expanding their facilities? It is said that the following rule of thumb prevails (or prevailed before the war): For every $1,000 of the original per-room investment, a room must average $1 income a day.[5] Or: Is there a rule which governs the price at which real estate (other than one-family homes and lots) changes hands? It is said that a multiple of gross income represents the "right" price and that there are conventional ways of calculating gross income and determining the multiple.

Occasional observations seem to indicate, furthermore, that business investments may, in some cases, represent little more than obeying the habitual pattern of "follow the leader." When technological developments make the installation of new machinery or the production of a new or changed article possible, it seems that genuine decisions are needed in order for the first firm to expend funds for the use of the new technique. But after one firm, and especially after the leading or dominating firm in the trade, has done so, a different situation may prevail. A firm may be compelled to spend large amounts of money on new equipment because its customers require the same features on its product—for instance, automatic gearshifts on automobiles—which they find on the competitor's product. Or a firm may habitually keep an eye on a trade leader and make capital expenditures if the leader does so.

We are not concerned here with the questions of fact: whether or not these or other rules of thumb have actually been widely applied. We cite the examples to call attention to the possibility that transactions which appear to an outsider as carefully deliberated decisions based on definite expectations may represent routine operations. Or that certain aspects of the considerations which are required for genuine investment decisions may be routinized.

GENUINE DECISIONS

We next take up the study of the role of expectations in capital expenditures. It is possible that expectations are dependent upon past experience instead of business investment following habitual patterns. That our expectations are based on past developments so that we expect that to happen which happened in the past is, as we showed before, one form of the origin of expectations. Thus an increase in the firm's sales or profits may make a business executive expect a further increase. Capital expenditures for the sake of business expansion, which require the expectation of larger future

[5] See the discussion of this rule, for instance, in *Business Week,* October 9, 1948, p. 94.

sales and profits, would then be undertaken in response to recent increases in sales and profits.

If that were the only way in which expectations originated, we could neglect expectations and consider past trends alone as sufficient indicators enabling us to predict future investment. In fact, in certain econometric calculations, a fairly good "fit" has been obtained between business investments actually made in a given period and those that were calculated on the basis of profits made in the preceding period. Further ex post variables —interest rates, stock of capital goods and of liquid funds, etc.—may be added to calculations to try to improve the fit between calculated investments and actual investments and to indicate that there is no need to take ex ante variables into account. Of course, such calculations, usually made for the entire economy or for branches of industry, do not prove that a causal connection exists between past profit or sales trends and investment decisions. In certain instances, or at certain times, it may happen that an individual firm's investment decision is influenced by past trends alone. In other instances, or at other times, it is probable that different factors enter into the picture. The mere fact of reversals in business trends lends weight to this probability. The assumption that an upward trend in sales and profits necessarily generates optimistic expectations and new investment (and a downward trend, pessimistic expectations and cessation of investments) is brought into question by the occurrence of turning points in the business cycle.

One of the crucial questions in the study of genuine decisions, therefore, concerns the origin of business expectations that lead to such decisions. From the preceding discussion of habitual patterns in capital expenditures, we must conclude that, although such patterns are not uncommon, investment decisions will sometimes be made without recourse to them or, even contrary to prevailing rules of thumb, on the basis of expected trends. We must also conclude that expected trends will sometimes differ substantially from past trends. Restructuring of the psychological field requires the presence of strong motivational forces. The emergence of something new, such as awareness of a technological change or of a change in business-cycle trends, may lead to the arousal of new expectations. But much relevant information is missing about the origin of expectations. Therefore, instead of a thorough analysis of decision formation, we can offer only a few suggestions and raise some pertinent questions.

It may be useful to differentiate between investment opportunities and investment decisions. Being aware of investment opportunities appears to be a necessary condition for genuine investment decisions but need not always lead to such decisions. Investment opportunity in this sense is a subjective notion. The question arises: When, under what conditions, do businessmen perceive that such opportunities exist, and still further, under what conditions do they search for such opportunities? Technology, for instance, may make progress and may nevertheless not be perceived as yielding investment opportunities. It is probable that the general economic outlook of businessmen has much to do with their perception of investment opportunities. When their business outlook is optimistic, or when they view the future with confidence, they may be more apt to perceive and to search for such opportunities. Uncertainty about the future or a pessimistic economic outlook may, then, impede investment, not only by causing businessmen to turn down opportunities after consideration, but also by making them unable to perceive opportunities.

The next problem to be studied is the mechanism through which perceived investment opportunities are transformed into actions. Detailed calculations made on the basis of definite expectations, or of a range or probability distribution of expectations, or marginal calculus, represent one possible way of arriving at a decision. Sizing up the situation and relying on a general notion about the advisability of an investment represents another possibility. In either case, several questions arise that refer partly to institutional facts. Who are the people who make the decisions in large or small business firms? What kind of information do they regularly require in order to be in a position to make their decisions? What kinds of decisions are made on the basis of fragmentary information, and what kinds of decisions require extensive, careful studies? How are "capital budgets" prepared and what is their function? It is known that some decisions require approval by a board of directors, while others, in the same firm, may be made without consulting the top executives. It is possible, but it is not known, that such differences are related to the presence or absence of habitual patterns of behavior.

The role of such factors as available liquid funds, the possibility of raising new funds, and interest rates will have to be studied. It is possible that when funds are available or can easily be raised investment opportunities are perceived, while lack of funds or tight capital markets make business executives, so to speak, blind to opportunities. But, of course, there must be exceptions, and instances in which firms have struggled against all odds to finance expansion projects deserve careful study. Even if liquid funds are available to finance capital expenditures, an investment decision is tantamount to a decision to lessen liquidity. Whether businessmen generally think in such terms, we do not know.

While in earlier economic literature investment was considered a function of interest rates, most recently scant attention has been given to the problem of the influence the size of interest may exert on investment decisions. This is partly due to the prevailing low interest rates and partly to the realization that availability of new funds (at any interest) and the question of the risks involved are of much greater importance than fluctuations in the interest rate by ½, 1, or even 2 per cent. Whether this neglect of the problem of interest is justified requires further study. Even during the first few postwar years of "cheap money," capital yields were very high and may have exerted a strong influence on investment decisions. We may present the problem (but not the answer) in a realistic way: In 1948, the XYZ Company, a manufacturer (dozens of well-known names could be inserted here), made a profit after taxes of $8 per common share and paid $5 dividends on each share; in 1949, its common stock is quoted at 50 on the New York Stock Exchange. Prospects for sales and profits are considered good and a plan for erecting a new plant comes up for consideration. Funds could be borrowed from banks at 2 or 3 per cent, but only against ample security (which is available in inventories, receivables, etc.) and for a relatively short period (after which, probably, the credit could be extended). New common stock could perhaps be sold, but at a yield of over 10 per cent. The company has substantial liquid funds, bringing practically no return, which could be increased by keeping dividends low during the next year or two and would then suffice for the new investment. In such circumstances, what is the interest rate which the company executives take into account when they consider the prospects of the planned capital expenditures? From all available information it appears that short-term credit is ruled out and the easy money rates of 2 or 3 per cent do not enter into consideration. Must the new project, in the opinion of the executives, promise to yield a profit of 10 per cent—the yield of the common stock at current market prices and current dividends—or a profit of considerably over 10 per cent, in view of the uncertainty to which prospective yields are subject? This question is raised to point out that interest rates, and attitudes toward interest rates, may play a substantial role in today's American economy.

No mention was made, in our example, of financing the expansion program through the flotation of a bond issue, although the current low bond yields are usually cited as *the* indicator of easy money conditions and of the lack of importance of interest rates for investment decisions. While manufacturers usually appear to be opposed to financing investment by bond issues—they are averse to increasing their fixed charges—railroads and public utilities customarily apply this procedure. They use capital goods over very long periods. Therefore, total interest charges (and compound interest) may represent a substantial burden even at the currently prevailing "low" bond yields (of, say, 3 to 4 per cent). It follows from these considerations that the importance of interest rates for investment requires further study.

Empirical studies of investment decisions are possible and promising because businessmen's attitudes and expectations can be determined and can be related to their behavior. Measuring the amount of orders outstanding and the amount of capital-expenditure plans of individual firms—as has been done during the past few years for the sake of estimating aggregate amounts of orders or investment plans for the entire economy—represents a first step in such investigations. A number of other financial facts—past sales, profits, current liquid assets, etc.—should be determined for the same individual firms and related to the investment plans. The same should be done with psychological variables: information should be gathered about sales and profit expectations, opinions about prospective business trends, attitudes toward the prevailing and the expected technological situation, and attitudes toward availability of capital and interest rates. The factors contributing to these attitudes and expectations and the degree of certainty with which they are held should be studied. Such studies would certainly be useful, because in all probability business expectations are not subject to sudden and violent changes which are unrelated to any other developments. The objective of such investigations would, therefore, be to determine what functional relations prevail in different circumstances among different variables, attitudinal as well as financial, in a large number of individual firms.

The procedure to be adopted in studying investment decisions may also be described in a somewhat different manner. It would be of little value to ask business executives directly what considerations they believe to be important for investments. But financial as well as attitudinal data could be—and should be—collected from business executives (1) who made important investments in the recent past, (2) who contemplated such plans but decided not to go forward with them, and (3) who had no such projects under consideration. Such studies would promise to clarify the factors that are responsible for the fluctuations in the timing and amplitude of investments in our economy. They might shed light on those crucial variables that are mentioned in the scientific as well as the popular literature under such names as "speculative spirit," "overoptimism," "pessimism," "lack of confidence." Under what conditions are businessmen aware of risks, what are their attitudes toward risks, and how do they react to risks?—all these questions are susceptible of empirical study.

NOTES TO CHAPTER 11

Surveys on capital expenditure plans will be described in Part Five. It will be pointed out there that, though those surveys represent substantial progress, their present scope and methods are not adequate to clarify the crucial problems of the how and why of investment decisions.

As mentioned in the text, economic literature contains opinions about business expectations which, if they were correct, would make studies of the relation between capital expenditures and attitudes unnecessary or unremunerative. One such view is that business expectations are always and necessarily a function of recent past experience. In view of what has been said in Chapters 4 and 7 (see especially the quotations from Angell and Klein on page 141, above), this argument will not be discussed further. A few quotations may, however, illustrate a second type of opinion. J. M. Keynes, for instance, writes about "expectations as to the future yield of capital-goods": "The basis for such expectations is very precarious. Being based on shifting and unreliable evidence, they are subject to sudden and violent changes" (*op. cit.*, p. 315). The marginal efficiency of capital—the crucial factor in investing—is "determined by the uncontrollable and disobedient psychology of the business world" (*op. cit.*, p. 317). Or, we read about business expectations in a recent textbook that they "change constantly and seem hopelessly unpredictable" (K. E. Boulding, *Economic Analysis*, New York, 1948, rev. ed., p. 835).

We know far too little about business expectations. But what we know seems to indicate that there is no justification for the statements quoted. Business expectations do not change constantly and do not change without cause. Their change requires a reorganization of the psychological field, which is undertaken only under stress due to strong motivational forces. Business expectations are held with confidence and influence action when, as does happen, they are based on the understanding of developments and not on hearsay or unconfirmed rumors. Finally, business psychology is not uncontrollable, as we shall try to show in the next part of this book.

Further investigations of expectations may be motivated by the following observation by Gerhard Colm: "Business expansion is largely guided by *existing* markets rather than by the confident anticipation that expansion will itself create *new* markets" (in *Economic Reconstruction*, edited by S. E. Harris, New York, 1945, p. 255). The conditions under which investment decisions are based on existing rather than expected conditions require study. Furthermore, Colm's statement seems to imply that business executives—at present or generally—are void of imagination; they do not foresee what could be brought about if they were to expand their facilities; their expectations are restricted to slight variations of existing conditions. This observation, if confirmed, would raise a fundamental psychological problem which could be fruitfully studied in diverse fields of human behavior.

After completion of the manuscript of this book, in the fall of 1950, the Survey Research Center conducted a study of Michigan manufacturers under the general direction of the author. Detailed personal interviews were made with owners or executives of approximately 200 manufacturing firms which were selected at random from records of the Michigan Unemployment Compensation Commission. Although the study was primarily concerned with factors influencing industrial mobility, questions were asked about past and expected investment decisions—expansion of plants and machinery—and about the considerations that were relevant in making those decisions. The findings, not yet published, indicate:

1. There are investments concerning which manufacturers feel that they had no choice and in which expectations concerning future developments play practically no role. The business executives say that they were compelled to expand their facilities, for instance, by an increase in the demand for their products.

2. There are investments which are made in order to improve the situation of the firm—to raise the level of sales or profits, to keep up with competitors, to reduce costs of production, or to increase the efficiency of operations. Definite expectations influence these decisions.

3. The more favorable a manufacturer judges the present as well as the expected trends in his own business, the more likely it is that he will entertain expansion plans. When business conditions are considered favorable, investments are frequently "automatic" or habitual. Sometimes, however, the expected improvement in one's business appears to be the result rather than the cause of the investment; these situations are usually characterized by genuine decision making.

PART FOUR

ECONOMIC FLUCTUATIONS

CHAPTER 12

ATTITUDES AND BEHAVIOR IN INFLATION

In studying fluctuations in economic activity, we shall be concerned primarily with the role of the decisions and actions of consumers and business firms in bringing about and arresting these fluctuations. Consumer and business behavior will no longer be viewed separately. Our analysis will be directed toward the interaction between the two kinds of decision makers and between what may be considered economic facts and people's attitudes.

Economic fluctuations of an extreme kind will be discussed first. It may be easier to recognize the characteristic features of decision formation and behavior during periods of full-fledged inflation or deflation than those that contribute to expansion or contraction during a business cycle. The study of inflation, of its origins as well as of the means to counteract it, is facilitated by the extensive set of observations made during and shortly after the Second World War.

HOW INFLATION COMES ABOUT

We shall speak of inflation as a general and sustained increase in the price level. This definition implies that an upward movement in prices for a short period only or in certain prices only—for instance, in grain or metal prices but not in others—does not represent inflation. When, however, as a result of a prolonged and general price movement the purchasing power of money undergoes a substantial decline, we acknowledge that inflation has occurred.

Inflation has been known for two thousand years or more. In ancient Egypt and Rome, in the Middle Ages as well as in modern times, inflation has been considered a major evil and events or persons responsible for it have been stigmatized. The traditional theories about the origin of inflation may be presented under the headings "too much money," "too few goods," and the combination of the two which, in its modern form, is the theory of the inflationary gap.

In earlier times, increase in money supply came about through the debasement of coins. The same quantity of silver, for instance, was used to coin more money. Printing paper money is a historically more recent form of creating additional supplies of money, and borrowing from banks the most recent form. In our present-day economy, currency and checks, paper money in vaults or pockets and demand deposits, are interchangeable; and, through lending, banks can increase the money supply. The well-known primary reason for any of these processes is government deficit. Because of war or extravagance of the ruler, for instance, the government spends more than it takes in and fills the gap by debasing coins, printing money, or borrowing from banks. The last process, in contrast to the first two, can also occur at the initiative of borrowers other than a government. Whatever the cause, the effect is the same: more money than before is said to compete for the same amount of goods and is therefore worth less. In other words, prices rise.

It follows logically and is well known historically that the process of inflation may also start through contraction of the supply of goods. In older times of relative economic isolation, when transportation was poor and slow and most of the money was spent on agricultural products, a series of crop failures resulted in the same quantity of money competing for a smaller quantity of goods. Or the quantity of goods available in a city or country under siege decreased rapidly; if the money supply remained the same, inflation resulted.

The modern formulation of the traditional theory considers both sides of the economy and their interaction. We learn that prices rise because the money supply increases more than the flow of goods. In a still more recent formulation, prices are said to rise if money incomes grow faster than the quantity of goods produced, or if incomes increase while the output of goods declines. In these circumstances, some money has no place to go and competes for the goods available. Thus, at the beginning of the Second World War, national income in the United States increased. Millions of people were newly employed or received higher wages than before to produce tanks, planes, and ships. But they could not spend their wages for the goods they produced. What people could spend their money for did not increase in quantity; in fact, it declined when production of automobiles and many other goods was prohibited and imports of consumption goods were reduced. Thus, in 1941 and 1942, experts calculated in advance the size of the inflationary gap which would result. The excess of incomes over the supply of goods available for purchase at unchanged prices could be expressed in percentages and represented a measure of the expected price increase— provided nothing were done to eliminate or reduce the gap.

It was, however, known centuries ago and has been repeatedly demonstrated in the twentieth century that these theories alone do not suffice. There have been periods of increasing money supply, and periods of decreasing supply of goods, in which prices did not rise. Moreover, the extent of price increases was usually not proportional to the size of the gap between the supply of money and goods. That there was no correspondence between the alleged cause and its effect has been amply demonstrated, for instance, in studies of the German hyperinflation of the twenties. Similar observations have been made during the last few years in Europe. Likewise in the United States, the large increase in money supply from 1942 to 1944 was accompanied by a moderate increase in prices, while prices rose substantially shortly after the end of the war when the money supply did not increase. The traditional way to cope with these problems has been to consider them as irregularities or deviations from the normal course of events, due to some additional rather nebulous and indeterminate factors. These factors have been identified under the terms "velocity of money turnover" and "willingness to spend." They play the role of a *deus ex machina*. Things are not as they ought to be, and so we name the culprits responsible: people sometimes, for some unexplained or unexplainable reason, do not use their greater supply of money and thus neutralize its effect. Or, prices do not advance even though incomes rise more than the flow of goods, because people are not willing to spend their money.

We have described one type of theory construction. The cause of a development, of inflationary price increases in this instance, is identified. If the cause is present but not its effect, then modifying, extraneous factors are postulated. In the theories just described, the causes were economic and the modifying factors psychological. It is, however, possible to reverse the procedure. Psychological factors may be called the primary causes of inflation, and inflation is then described as the result of mass hysteria.

This line of argument runs as follows: Certain opinions and beliefs may get hold of people, because of rumors, for instance, which may be wholly or partly unfounded. Correctness of the opinions is not essential; people's disposition to believe in them alone matters. If people in general are anxiety-ridden, they may embrace beliefs that are not well-founded and may act according to them. Runs on banks may originate in that way, as well as mistrust in the value of money and what was called in Europe "flight into real values" (exchange of bank notes for foreign currency, gold, or jewelry). Widespread fear that the value of money will decline is then identified as the real cause of inflation. If it is prevalent, even slight economic causes, such as a small increase in the money supply, may bring about vast price effects, or if the fear is absent, even a large increase in the money circulation may have no effect on prices.

We cannot accept either the purely economic or the purely psychological explanation of inflation, as we cannot consider economic and psychological factors separately. A purely economic theory of inflation presupposes an invariable connection between changes in the environment and people's reactions to them. It becomes questionable as soon as we recognize the possibility of different reactions to the same situation, depending on people's perceptions, attitudes, and expectations. A purely psychological theory, on the other hand, postulates, essentially, that expectations are almighty or, at least, that they are always self-justifying. Why do prices go up (or down)? Because the buyers expect them to go up (or down). Because of that belief, no matter whether it is well-founded or not, they purchase goods in advance and in excess of their needs and drive prices up (or abstain from buying and drive prices down). This may or may not happen. But the question is whether such price movements can result in inflation or deflation, in other words, whether the price movements can be sustained and enduring if the expectations themselves are not originally justified.

We must recall the psychological study of the origin of expectations. We found that expectations may originate in unjustified rumors. Things may sometimes be expected to happen because people are told that they will happen, or because they learn that others expect them to happen. But such expectations were found to be relatively weak and not to endure over long periods or to have great influence on behavior. On the other hand, expectations that are based on an understanding of why certain things must occur influence behavior to a much greater extent. If people learn that the money printing presses are operating at full speed, or that the supply of goods has been reduced sharply and cannot be increased, they have ample reason to expect price increases; they will be influenced by these reasons until they learn of other good reasons that will make them abandon or reverse their expectations. But expectations that spread only because of general anxiety and nervousness and are, in fact, not justified will hardly influence enough people over a long enough period of time to create inflation.

This means that we must make use of both economic and psychological factors to explain inflationary price increases. It is not by accident that historically most inflationary periods have coincided with or followed times of war. Enduring inflationary attitudes and expectations arise when there is a break with the past that compels us to reorganize our field. The outbreak of war, military defeat, perhaps a change in government, are typical instances of such a break and of what appears to many people to be the beginning of a new era. People then become aware that their customary ways of thinking are out of place; they grope for a new understanding of the situation and may find their previous habits of buying and saving to be inappropriate to it.

After the Second World War broke out, as we said before, money incomes in the United States rose and the supply of goods declined. These developments were widely known and understood. This does not mean that all or even many people had a sophisticated understanding of what was going on, but the news was viewed within a new frame of reference which greatly differed from the previous one. What spread from mouth to mouth and what people read in the papers and heard over the radio was not the simple assertion that prices would go up, but some notion of the economic processes that would result in a change from a buyers' market (ample choice for the sovereign customer) to a sellers' market (dominance of those who hold the scarce goods). Similarly, after the end of the war, when the abandonment of price controls was thought to be imminent, and later when it became a fact, people had some understanding of the underlying situation and derived strong expectations from that understanding.

Inflationary expectations differ somewhat from expectations studied previously. They may be characterized as "one-way expectations"; people realize that under the given conditions prices must go up and cannot possibly go down. As opposed to expectations based on weighing risks and concluding that, under certain given conditions, the chances are that, say, sales volume will probably go up rather than down, inflationary expectations are characterized by pointing exclusively in one direction. People not only expect prices to go up but are convinced that it would be out of the question for them to go down.

Furthermore, inflationary expectations are usually what may be called trend expectations. People believe that prices will advance a little at first, more and more later, and are convinced that the process is cumulative. Small price increases are not considered the fulfillment of their expectations but, on the contrary, as leading to, or being steps toward, further price increases. A deflationary spiral in its extreme form represents the reverse process. Price reductions give rise to expectations of further price reductions and induce businessmen and consumers alike to abstain from buying.

This is in sharp contrast to the common forms of business expectations discussed in the last two chapters. Expansion of manufacturing facilities, for instance, is usually based on noncumulative expectations. When the expectations are fulfilled and sales increase so that the new machinery installed is amply used, the manufacturer is confronted with a new situation. He may or may not expect a further expansion, depending on new insights and new considerations. The feeling of the prevalence of a trend, in which one step is thought to lead to the next, represents a different attitude that characterizes periods of inflation and, probably, of deflation and severe depression.

Without going into details, it may be mentioned that what has been called hyperinflation, which has occurred in our lifetime in many European and Asiatic countries but not in the United States, is characterized by a rather complete break with the past. The meaning of money and of money wages undergoes a change, and people measure their income and their wealth by standards other than the national currency. In the study of periods of hyperinflation, it is easy to recognize that people expect the trend of rising prices to be continuous.

Prolonged and extensive inflationary price movements occur because of certain economic processes *and* inflationary expectations. Excess of money over goods alone is not sufficient to give rise to inflationary developments. It may be called the inflationary potential. To transform an inflationary potential into actual inflation, people must be aware of the inflationary potential and must derive certain expectations from it. Inflationary expectations are not a necessary consequence of the presence of an inflationary potential, as we shall see in a moment when we study American wartime developments and especially the role and function of price control. Expectations and willingness to spend are intervening variables bringing about behavior that results in inflation. Both awareness of certain economic developments and the arousal of a new frame of reference are necessary to bring forth enduring expectations that influence the behavior of masses of people.

HOW TO FIGHT INFLATION

We have concluded that inflationary price increases are not automatic effects of certain economic conditions. Rather they are the result of people's behavior, which, in turn, is influenced by their understanding of those conditions. Similar conclusions emerge when we study the possible means of fighting inflation.

Measures intended to block inflationary price increases, like the causes of inflation, may be thought to be either economic or psychological. Legislative or administrative action is usually considered economic. For instance, steps can be taken to increase production or the supply of goods. Or regulations may be adopted to reduce the supply of money, or to slow down the rate of its increase, for example, by cutting government expenditures, reducing the quantity of money in circulation, or curtailing bank credit. Legislative action may also have the purpose of curtailing the purchasing power of consumers. Limitations imposed on incomes (wage ceilings, for instance), increases in taxes, and compulsion to purchase bonds fall in this category. A large group of government measures intended to arrest inflation comprises interference with the allocation and pricing of goods through control of the use of strategic materials, through rationing, and through price control. Among the psychological methods of fighting inflation, exhortation to cut down on spending and to increase saving is most frequently mentioned. Systematic, organized campaigns to induce people to purchase bonds belong in that category. But the scope of anti-inflationary psychological measures is much broader. This will become apparent when we cease to distinguish between the economic and the psychological and consider the effect of so-called economic measures on the behavior of businessmen and consumers.

We shall begin with a discussion of price control. From a certain point of view, price control may be thought to represent the most effective means of fighting inflation. When the government orders prices to remain at a given level, one might think that inflation—a general and sustained increase in prices—would thereby be made impossible. That this conclusion is not obvious may be readily understood if we consider the contrary view, according to which price control is ineffective as a weapon against inflation. At the time when price control was debated and introduced in the United States in 1942, the attack against it was frequently expressed in the catching phrase, "price control is tinkering with the thermometer." Price increases were merely symptoms of the inflation, the argument ran. The basic, underlying evil, the excess purchasing power, would not be affected by measures that dealt with the symptoms only. If we tried to control the "thermometer," the instrument that would measure the extent of the disease, the best we could hope for would be to postpone inflation. It was argued further that usually even that result would be unobtainable. All that a police state could achieve would be the maintenance of stable prices for certain quantities of staple products. But even under such conditions, black markets would develop which would faithfully mirror the course of inflation. Usually, however, there would also be diverse "gray markets": evasions of price control by deteriorating quality, by changing the composition of goods produced and sold, or by changing the terms of trade. In a complex economy not entirely devoid of goods beyond the barest necessities, excess purchasing power would soon leave price control an empty shell. The majority of business transactions and consumer purchases would reflect the inflationary trend despite price control.

Support for the argument that price control cannot stop inflation has also been found in other purely economic considerations. It has been pointed out that under price control, if it were effective, prices would be lower than they would be in the same circumstances without any control of prices. Therefore, in view of the postulate of economic theory that "the lower the prices the larger the quantity demanded," buyers would seek to purchase more goods under price control than in its absence. In brief, as it has often been formulated, "price control increases demand." This view represents the best starting point for an analysis of the effects of price control. We shall try to show that both extreme views cited are erroneous. Price control is not a weapon which alone can arrest inflation, but still it can, in certain circumstances, do a large part of the job.

We argued in Chapter 10 that quantities demanded do not depend on prevailing prices alone. The crucial factor which must be considered, in addition to the price level, is the expectation concerning the future trend of prices. Let us compare the behavior of purchasers—consumers as well as businessmen—in two situations. In the first, firm price controls are in force and people believe that they will be effective; they expect prices to remain stable. In the second, there are no price controls, the price level is higher than in the first situation, and people expect prices to increase. It is not necessarily true that in the first situation, in which prices are lower, the quantities demanded will be higher. It is possible that, despite the high price level prevailing in the second situation, the anticipation of further price increases will induce people to step up the rate of their purchases, to purchase in excess and .in advance of their needs—in other words, to demand a quantity of goods that far exceeds the quantity demanded in the first situation.

The two conditions just described are not just hypothetical constructions. High prices and the expectation of further price increases represent, as we have seen, the typical inflationary situation and the one which usually calls for the introduction of price control. The crucial question, then, is whether the first situation is realistic. Our argument was not that the quantity demanded would necessarily be relatively small under price control, but that this might occur *if* price control were trusted and generated expectations of price stability. If people have confidence in price control and believe that it will be effective, their demand may be so reduced that the expectation will come true. Should these conditions prevail, price control would not attack superficial symptoms of inflation but one of its basic causes, namely, inflationary expectations. It follows that the most important effect of price control may be found in the behavior of buyers and sellers, in their abstaining from hoarding and withholding goods, of stocking up and rushing to buy, and not merely in the stability of price quotations.

Whether price control has such results depends on people's attitudes toward it. Under what conditions will price control be approved by businessmen and consumers; when will it be trusted and believed to guarantee stable prices? Answers to this question can be derived from the study of the American experience with price control between 1942 and 1946. Detailed information is available not only concerning the legal measures themselves, the public announcements accompanying laws and executive orders, and the trend of retail sales, but also concerning reactions to price control which are less susceptible to statistical measurement. Evasions of price control, deterioration of quality, and "uptrading," as well as the attitudes of both businessmen and the general public toward price control, have been analyzed. Only a few of the crucial periods in the history of price control will be reviewed here briefly.

Prior to the issuance of the General Maximum Price Regulation (in April, 1942) there were advances not only in prices but also in retail sales of apparel and food; and the increase in sales was greater than the increase in disposable incomes. During the first few months after the general freezing order had been issued, accompanied by broadcasts of the President and announcements by the price administrator that "the ceilings will not be punctured," retail demand declined, prices remained stable, and evasions of control were rare. At the same time, the great majority of the American people approved of price control. At the beginning of 1943, however, the public was made aware of forthcoming shortages and the price administrator announced that "prices will advance about one-half of one per cent a month." In the first few months of that year, retail sales increased rapidly, and most businessmen expected prices to increase and price control to break down. Price regulations were frequently relaxed and evasions became very frequent. The "hold-the-line order" of April, 1943, coupled with firm measures of price control and clear-cut government announcements, succeeded in arresting that trend. The reversal was again noticeable in retail sales, evasions, and public attitudes. After the end of the war, however, when the general atmosphere changed completely, no efforts were made to make the business world and consumers believe that price control was really necessary; on the contrary, relaxation and ultimate abandonment of price control were generally predicted. Then direct as well as indirect price increases became frequent, and consumer demand became more pressing.

This brief account of certain phases of the history of price control must be supplemented by referring to anti-inflationary measures other than price control. It is not correct to attribute people's cooperative attitudes and behavior to firm price ceilings and the public explanation of their necessity alone. Wage control, rationing, allocation of scarce materials, tax measures, and war-bond drives contributed to the general atmosphere, as described in Chapter 5, which can be characterized briefly as one opposed to excessive spending. But price control itself played a big role, especially in times when it was well "sold" to the public—when businessmen understood that it would damage their reputations and be against their long-run interest to evade control, and when consumers understood that they would not lose by not stocking up. To repeat: We do not contend that price control alone can arrest inflation. Nor do we maintain that psychological weapons can win the fight against inflation. Exhortation of the public, appeals to patriotism, and public branding of black-marketeers alone would not have sufficed without firm legal measures that provided evidence that the government was intent on carrying out its policy not to let inflation interfere with the war effort.

The main lesson of the study of price control is, then, that it cannot be effective without the wholehearted cooperation of the public. Superficial obedience and passive compliance caused by fear of punishment are not enough. Businessmen as well as consumers must understand why the controls are needed, and must approve of them. The same conclusions may be derived from a study of other anti-inflationary controls, such as wage ceilings, quantity controls, and rationing. Whatever the regulation, the possibilities of evasion are numerous. No government can cope with widespread and widely approved noncompliance, nor can any system of regulations plug all loopholes and eliminate the introduction of new business practices that would defeat the purpose of the controls. Consumer rationing represents an especially complex form of control which greatly disturbs the customary relations between sellers and buyers. Moreover, it is extremely burdensome for businessmen as well as ultimate consumers, since it requires a great amount of time-consuming work. Price control is likewise burdensome, but at least it has some obvious advantages for all buyers—and businessmen are buyers as well as sellers.

Rationing has often been called the regulation that makes price control work: it makes it impossible for buyers to bid for all the goods they desire and can afford to buy. On the other hand, however, rationing calls general public attention to shortages and induces shoppers to forget about prices and to ask, "How much can I get for my coupons?" instead of the usual, "How much?" It follows that rationing requires most careful psychological preparation. Businessmen as well as consumers must understand why it is introduced and why it is inevitably necessary that it be introduced. Since such convincing explanations could not have been made for all kinds of goods during the war, the criticism leveled against the OPA that it erred in not rationing certain goods must be contradicted. Because of people's reactions and attitudes to rationing, there were good reasons to go slow with this type of interference with people's choice. The statement that price fixing inevitably must be supplemented by rationing does not appear to be justified.

There are no anti-inflationary economic measures that have automatic effects. People's reactions to the measures depend on how they perceive, understand, and interpret them. No proof for this statement is needed in the case of bond drives. Organized campaigns aimed at curtailment of spending and increase in saving are entirely dependent upon the creation of the right atmosphere. They cannot be successful unless the public is fully convinced that buying bonds is the right thing to do. People must feel that buying bonds is in their personal as well as in the general interest and that not participating is contrary to the behavior of their group. It is, however, much less recognized that the effect on inflation of even such compulsory measures as tax increases depends upon the reaction of the public and, therefore, upon the attitudes of the people. The following schematic example may serve to illustrate that point of view:

	Year I	Year II
Aggregate income before taxes, billions	$100	$120
Taxes, billions	−10	−18
Disposable income, billions	$ 90	$102
Amounts saved, billions	−9	−5
Consumer expenditures, billions	$ 81	$ 97
Consumer expenditures in per cent of income before taxes	81%	81%

We assume that in an inflationary period tax rates are advanced so sharply that they take away 50 per cent more of total incomes than previously. In Year II, for which the new tax rates apply, national income increases by 20 per cent and taxes consume 15 per cent of that income (as against 10 per cent of the income of the previous year). As the table shows, the tax increase achieves one result: disposable income rises to a lesser extent than income before taxes. But in the first year, one part of the disposable income, 10 per cent in our example, was saved and not spent. In the second year, then, by reducing their rate of saving, consumers are able to keep up their rate of exenditures in spite of the tax increase and thus stifle its effects. They are, as the table shows, in a position to increase their expenditures at the same rate as their incomes increase. That people may actually respond to larger incomes by saving less has been shown in Chapter 8.

It is possible, of course, for tax increases to have a considerable antiinflationary effect. If they are very large, they may reduce consumption expenditures. If additionally imposed taxes absorb the entire increase in consumer income and perhaps even the amounts consumers ordinarily save, people may have no choice but to spend less.[1] Usually such extensive tax increases are politically and socially not feasible or would have adverse effects on people's morale and production effort. Furthermore, these con-

---

[1] It must be kept in mind, however, that in addition to reducing the amount they save out of income, consumers can also supplement their expenditures by drawing on previously accumulated assets or by borrowing. It is possible for an economy as a whole to dissave, that is, for consumer expenditures to exceed aggregate disposable income.

siderations, like the example presented in the table above, reflect the aggregate situation only. Anti-inflationary tax increases must, however, be primarily directed toward restricting the expenditures of certain groups, namely, those that are in possession of the increased money supply. The difficulties involved in achieving such differential effects again cast doubt on the automatic effect of tax increases. Therefore, even tax increases require psychological preparation. People must understand that taxes are increased in order to curtail spending. If they approve of that objective, tax increases represent a powerful weapon in the fight against inflation.

One further anti-inflationary measure must be discussed, which is of much greater importance after a war than during a war when usually it cannot be applied. In 1946 and 1947 in the United States, it was fairly generally argued that inflation could be defeated by one means only, namely, by increased production. It is, of course, clear that the "inflationary potential," that is, the excess of available purchasing power over the supply of goods, can be reduced or even eliminated if supplies are increased sufficiently. But usually increasing the rate of production is a slow process, and substantial inflationary price increases can take place before production has been stepped up to the required level. Furthermore, "available purchasing power" is not a fixed quantity. Increased production may result in further increases in income, and incomes may be supplemented by drawing on assets or by borrowing. Therefore, the objectives of production increases will be achieved only if certain attitudes are present. If measures on the output side of the economy generate the expectation of ample future supplies and thus counteract previously prevalent inflationary expectations, the measures may play an important role in arresting inflation. In 1946 and 1947, this was not the case. This was a period of abandoning wartime restraints, of enjoying high levels of income, and of entertaining optimistic income expectations. Business associations and spokesmen proclaimed in vain that increased production would guarantee stable prices and that therefore price control and rationing would no longer be needed. Such pronouncements were mistrusted and were not sufficient to restructure people's frame of reference. Stabilization after an inflationary period requires a break with the past and a new start, just as does the onset of inflation.

Although substantial price increases did occur in the 1940's, especially following the premature abandonment of price controls after the war, the record on the whole is satisfactory. Never before has a country fought in a major war with such small inflationary effects as those felt in the United States during the Second World War. The credit for this achievement must go first of all to the greater economic knowledge of the people. That government as well as community and business leaders adopted more appropriate measures during the Second World War than, say, during the First, is only part of the story. They also explained the situation and its requirements more fully, and the people—on the whole, at most times—understood them and cooperated so as to make them effective. The knowledge that inflation was not an automatic effect of an excess supply of money, and therefore was not inevitable during a great war, helped to keep price increases down. But our general success should not blind us to the fact that there were times, both during and after the war, when "one-way expectations" prevailed, indicating that we have not yet fully learned the lesson. Cumulative, self-reinforcing processes, whether of an inflationary or deflationary character, still threaten to arise and to plague us again.

NOTES TO CHAPTER 12

The discussion of inflation has been kept relatively short because the author has previously published two books on the subject: *War without Inflation* (New York, 1942) and *Price Control and Business* (Bloomington, Ind., 1945). The objective of the first book was stated in its preface as follows:

". . . the efficacy of fiscal and economic measures of fighting inflation could be enhanced by the consideration of certain psychological facts and an adequate psychological preparation of the anti-inflationary measures. The attempt will therefore be made to set forth what the psychological facts are and of what the psychological preparation should consist" (pp. vii*f*.).

The conclusion drawn from the analysis was:

"Is war without inflation possible? A general and sustained upward movement in prices is not an automatic effect of economic factors . . . because prices are made to move in one or the other direction by the decisions and actions of men" (p. 197).

"Weapons capable of defeating inflation are in our possession; the question is only whether we understand how to use them and whether we have the will and the fortitude to do so" (p. 201).

The book supplements this chapter and contains numerous examples of such assertions as "price control is merely tinkering with the thermometer" or "price control increases demand."

The second book by the author contains data on businessmen's attitudes toward price control, on their behavior during price control (including evasions, quality deterioration, and "uptrading"), and on the influence of price control on demand. Evidence is presented there for the following statement:

"When price control was believed to be cracking and businessmen and consumers expected price increases, the former stocked up and the latter bought merchandise in excess and in advance of their requirements. When price control worked efficiently and was expected to insure price stability, purchases fell off" (p. 154).

The best treatises on the origin and course of large-scale inflations were written about the German inflation following the First World War. See F. D. Graham, *Exchange, Prices and Production in Hyper-inflation; Germany, 1920–23,* New York, 1930, and C. Bresciani-Turroni, *The Economics of Inflation,* London, 1937. For the traditional treatment of anti-inflationary measures, see A. C. Pigou, *The Political Economy of War,* New York, 1941 (1st ed., 1921).

Our discussion of trend expectations and the differentiation between expecting cumulative processes and expecting noncumulative processes is similar to Hicks's distinction between elastic and inelastic expectations. According to Hicks, the elasticity of an expectation is greater than unity when a change in the current price makes people "recognize a trend" so that the expected price changes in the same direction and at a greater rate than the current price; the elasticity is negative when a change in the current price is interpreted as the "culminating point" so that a reversal is expected (*Value and Capital,* Oxford, 1939, p. 205).

There are, however, several differences between Hicks's and our argument. Hicks makes a number of restrictive assumptions (for instance, he considers only the effect of a change in current prices on definite price expectations) and is mainly concerned with the cases in which the elasticity of expectations is zero or unity. The main conclusion of Hicks, that a system with highly elastic expectations is unstable while price rigidities exercise a stabilizing influence (see also Oscar Lange, *Price Flexibility and Employment,* Bloomington, Ind., 1944) will be discussed further in the next two chapters.

The term "self-justified expectations" is used by K. E. Boulding, who states that "What enough people expect will happen whether it was going to happen or not" (*The Economics of Peace,* New York, 1945, p. 138). Boulding rightly argues that flexibility is no cure for inflation: under inflationary conditions, letting prices go up will not equate production and consumption—"the law of supply and demand does not work" (p. 143). But "if people *knew* that deflation or inflation would both be prevented, they would not expect deflations or inflations, and as we have seen, it is the expectation of price and income movements which is the main factor in causing them" (pp. 164*f.*). Under what conditions expectations will justify themselves represents an important additional question not studied by Boulding.

Chapter 13

ATTITUDES AND BEHAVIOR IN BUSINESS CYCLES

We turn to the discussion of business and consumer behavior during the recurring alternations of expansion and contraction in economic activity that are described under the term "business cycles." Since inflation may be viewed as part of a business cycle, we shall be in the position to make use of much that has been said in the preceding chapter. But we shall have to take up new problems, because there need not be any general price increases during the upward phase of the cycle and because we have hardly touched thus far upon the discussion of contraction in business activity. We shall try to show in this chapter how psychological analysis may supplement the more traditional studies of business cycles.

THE PROBLEMS FOR ECONOMIC PSYCHOLOGY

It has been said occasionally that inflation in itself is not detrimental to an economy. Inflation, according to this view, must be fought and arrested in order to avoid the slump which it generates after it has run its course. The inevitability of a postinflationary collapse is assumed to be the main disadvantage of inflation. Contrary to this view, we must recognize that inflation disorganizes production and distribution because it upsets business cost calculations as well as family budgets. It brings about an arbitrary and inequitable redistribution of incomes and wealth—losses for those with bank deposits, bonds, insurance policies, and fixed incomes, and gains for those with debts. These effects lower morale and productivity. In an inflationary period, higher wages and speculative profits become people's main economic objective, instead of higher production and economic advancement. Thus there are ample and good reasons for trying to arrest inflationary movements.

These considerations do not apply to the usual upward phase of the business cycle, which is rightly termed the period of prosperity. Expanding production and sales, incomes and profits, even if accompanied by some moderate price increases, represent the most favorable economic climate known to us. Is it nevertheless necessary to stifle the upward phase of a business cycle to forestall inevitable collapse? "Stabilization" is usually

271

considered the aim of anticyclical policies. But that goal hardly seems an adequate one. Need for stabilization even at a high level of employment, output, and incomes seems to imply that expansion in itself is detrimental because of the subsequent collapse to which it must give rise. Yet continuous expansion is required for the sake of social and technological progress, to raise the living standards of a growing population and especially of underprivileged people.

A stationary economy is of necessity a declining economy. The desire for advancement and growth is, as we have seen, a powerful incentive of human behavior. The struggle for its attainment would quickly degenerate if it were to consist of nothing but striving for a larger share of the pie, the size of which remained unchanged. It follows that arresting the upward phase of a business cycle for the purpose of avoiding a later depression is a very unsatisfactory solution. From the discussion of certain aspects of behavior during economic fluctuations, we shall try to derive, at the end of this chapter, what the aim of anticyclical economic policy should perhaps be. Yet it is clear at the very outset that such a policy, in contrast to anti-inflationary measures with their clear-cut aims, must be very complex—and the knowledge available at present is woefully insufficient to give us any assurance of its being successful. We are still at the very beginning of our understanding of cyclical forces and cyclical behavior. Instead of answering the crucial questions of how cyclical fluctuations come about and how detrimental fluctuations can be avoided, we can attempt only to discern some of the major problems involved and to present a few hypotheses.

Business cycles are known to be characterized by periodic wavelike fluctuations, shown schematically in Fig. 9. Important differences in the

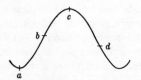

FIG. 9. Scheme of Business Cycle Fluctuations.

amplitude and duration of upswings and downswings are omitted from the scheme in order to point to the two major problems of all cycles in a simple way. One is the problem of the turning points; the other, that of the continuation of a trend that has begun. The first problem concerns points *a* and *c* in the figure. Why does a downward or an upward momentum end, and why is it replaced by a different trend? By asking why the turning points did not come earlier, we raise the second problem: Why is it that the curve did not turn downward at point *b* or upward at point *d*? This is the question about the reasons for the continuation of prevailing trends.

Previous discussions may help in the analysis of the second problem. Especially with reference to what may happen at point *b*, we may recall the discussion of sales and investment policies in Part Three. When one producer or distributor has succeeded in expanding his business volume, his competitors have a great incentive to do the same in order to keep their share in the market. When new technological procedures have been introduced by one or a few producers, the others may feel that they will lose their share in the market if they do not follow suit. Expansion is accompanied as well as stimulated by a favorable general economic outlook and, in turn, gives rise to it. Cumulative expectations that were described in analyzing inflation in the last chapter may arise with respect to business volume and incomes, as well as to prices. The achievement of higher volume may generate additional income and may create or reinforce optimistic expectations.

Similar considerations may be applied to the explanation of the continuation of a downward swing. Curtailment of business activity reduces the flow of incomes and is not only caused by but also generates pessimistic expectations. Thus, the main question concerns the turning points. Why is it that a trend, once established, is not self-perpetuating but, according to all past experience, terminates at a certain point, which may come relatively soon or relatively late? The theories of business cycles, which we shall now enumerate, are primarily explanations of the turning points.

Some students of business cycles have propounded what have been called "overinvestment theories." Overdevelopment of industries producing capital goods is thought to be primarily responsible for the upper turning point. Other students adhere to "underconsumption theories," blaming insufficiency of purchasing power due to "oversaving" or hoarding for the termination of the upswing and the collapse. According to monetary theories, on the other hand, fluctuations in the volume of money available to the economy represent the main cause of business cycles. Most commonly, the difference between the different schools is one of emphasis. Students of business cycles consider a great many different factors but assign to certain ones, for instance, to the volume of money or the rate of investment, the main responsibility for the turning points. In addition to the three types of theories mentioned, there are also "psychological theories" of the business cycle. According to these, "psychological phenomena," such as changes in people's attitudes, and not "economic phenomena," such as changes in money volume or investment, are the crucial factors responsible for the turning points. Gottfried Haberler devotes a chapter in his comprehensive review of business-cycle studies to theories of this kind.[1] In these theories, as he says,

> "Optimism and pessimism are regarded as causal factors which tend to induce or intensify the rise and fall of investment which are characteristic of the upswing and downswing respectively" (*op. cit.,* p. 136).

Contrary to this view, Haberler rightly argues that "there is really no fundamental difference between the economic theories already reviewed in these pages and the so-called psychological theories" (p. 133). In other words, all theories make assumptions about people's economic behavior. Therefore, it is not correct to speak of purely economic or purely psychological theories. It is true, however, that the analysis of the economic processes generating business cycles and characterizing their various phases has, on the whole, progressed without due regard to the role played by people's attitudes.

The task of economic psychology in analyzing business cycles may be formulated in the light of our previous discussions. Economic developments without regard to people's perceptions of them and reactions to them do not suffice for a full understanding of cyclical fluctuations. It is not enough to know, for instance, whether at a given moment investment is large or small, or is growing or declining, or whether funds for investment are ample or scarce. It is equally necessary to know how people, businessmen as well as consumers, view the different economic stimuli—the changes in their environment—with which they are confronted. There is no justification for assuming that the same stimuli will always bring forth the same reactions. People's reactions will depend on their frames of reference and their attitudes. In different phases of the cycle, attitudes, expectations, and the length of people's time perspective will differ and will affect their understanding of changes in the environment. We must therefore conclude that there exists multiple causation, and that economic developments and attitudes reinforce one another, so that they must be considered together.

PURELY ECONOMIC OR PURELY PSYCHOLOGICAL CAUSATION

These statements may be contradicted on two counts. First, it is possible that, at least under certain conditions, purely economic developments are so powerful that they will bring forth expansion or contraction, or a turning point, without regard to psychological factors. Second, it is possible that, at least under certain conditions, psychological factors are autonomous,

[1] *Prosperity and Depression,* League of Nations, Geneva, 1937, Chap. 6.

that is, they may generate changes in business trends irrespective of the underlying economic situation.

Overproduction in a certain field, brought about by the simultaneous great expansion of facilities on the part of several manufacturers, may serve to illustrate the first possibility. Each individual manufacturer may have been right in assuming that the output of his enlarged factory would easily be absorbed. But after several manufacturers have completed their expansion program, more goods may be produced than can be sold. Or building activity at a given locality and a certain time—for instance, the erection of skyscraper office buildings in downtown Manhattan in the late twenties—may have exceeded the need for space, and a period of feverish activity is followed by a slump. It may be assumed that in such circumstances attitudes and expectations play no role in bringing about the reversal of a trend in specific fields of business (although, in the examples just cited, the disillusionment of the manufacturers or builders may have resulted in a greater stoppage of new projects than demand conditions alone would have justified). The question to be raised is whether slumps or expansions in specific areas—arising, for instance, from technological changes or population movements—may form turning points of business cycles, that is, whether they may affect the entire economy. Can the transition from a period of upswing to one of downswing, or its reverse, result from several localized developments, or is there a need for psychological factors to account for the generality of the change?

It is also conceivable that in relatively undeveloped and poor economies cyclical fluctuations arise that are influenced but little, if at all, by psychological factors. The probability of business fluctuations being a function of changes in the volume of money may be greater if people on the whole have little discretionary purchasing power and small liquid reserves, and if only an insignificant part of the national output goes into postponable purchases. But in our current American economy with its relatively high reserves and incomes, expenditures on houses, on consumer durable goods, on plants and machinery represent a very substantial share of total output. Likewise, there is considerable production of goods for stock, rather than for current orders, and storage of goods for future use. Thus, a large part of business and consumer purchases is not inevitably necessary at a given moment but can be postponed for shorter or longer periods, or can be "bunched," that is, undertaken at the same time by many business firms and consumers. The same applies to luxury expenditures and to many uses of individual or business profits that depend on people's inclinations as well as on the availability of reserves or credit.

The assumption that in our economy psychological factors play a role in generating business fluctuations may best be explained by considering the other extreme view, according to which these factors are all-powerful so that underlying economic processes may be neglected. This point of view, occasionally expounded in economic writings, holds not only that changes in people's attitudes alone can bring about changes in business trends but also that changes in attitudes are not dependent on economic developments. The following statement, published in April, 1949, when signs of a weakening of economic activity began to appear, may serve as an illustration:

"The spending plans of businesses and consumers are always subject to change, and if a pervading conviction should develop that the end of inflation meant depression, it could swiftly lead to substantial curtailment, *regardless of the underlying economic prospects.*" [2]

The last phase concerns us most. It is here argued that changes in spending plans, capable of leading to substantial curtailment of business activity, may be brought forth by changes in people's attitudes that are independent of the underlying economic situation; more specifically, that people's convictions about the economic prospects, that is, what we have called their general economic outlook, may be pessimistic when underlying conditions do not justify pessimism and may, nevertheless, be effective in changing the trend in the economy.

In studying this argument, we may first refer to an individual instance that seems to justify it. A small retailer told an interviewer at the beginning of 1949 that he was buying as little as possible. When asked why, he replied that everybody was telling him that there would be a depression. To an inquiry about his own sales, he answered that they were about 12 per cent higher than in the same period the year before and were higher than ever before. Whether this example represents an exceptional or a fairly common instance is not important for our argument. We refer to it because it shows a flat contradiction between what may be called the underlying economic situation and a businessman's attitudes and expectations. The example also shows that actual behavior may be influenced by the expectations and not the underlying conditions. But, we may ask, for how long will the retailer continue to buy as little as possible and reduce his stocks if his sales remain at a record level? Without any reference to the individual situation, about which much important information is lacking, it appears probable that businessmen's attitudes will sooner or later change if they contradict their daily experiences and are based on nothing but hearsay. We have found in studying the development of inflationary expectations that they are probably not sustained for an extensive period if they have no

[2] *Annual Report* of the Federal Reserve Bank of New York for the year ended December 31, 1948, p. 9 (italics not in the original).

basis in fact, or if people do not understand how and why factual developments will make their expectations come true. Is it possible, we may ask, that pessimistic expectations are governed by a different set of rules?

Attitudes and behavior of one or a few businessmen, or attitudes and behavior in one specific field of trade, do not constitute a real test of the assumptions which we have set forth. It is possible that the theory of "self-fulfilling expectations" holds good in isolated instances. Assume, for instance, that regardless of the underlying situation, the opinion takes hold among influential members of the fur trade that fur prices are too high and are bound to fall. That this opinion alone will suffice to drive fur prices down cannot be called impossible. But general price movements encompassing all or most fields of business will hardly result from opinions that are not well-founded. It is true that we do not always expect that to happen which happened before. Therefore, we may expect price slumps or business contraction at a time when prices are rising and business activity is expanding. But such expectations require restructuring of people's psychological field, which is dependent on a new frame of reference. This frame of reference will not arise and will not take hold unless people understand that the underlying economic situation has changed. Slumps in prices or business activity must, therefore, be attributed to changes both in people's attitudes and in underlying economic processes. The typical case will be interaction and mutual reinforcement of economic and psychological factors. We turn now to the discussion of the forms of that interaction.

INTERACTION BETWEEN ATTITUDES AND ECONOMIC PROCESSES

One possible view about the origin of cyclical attitudes and expectations is that they are unequivocally determined by certain factual changes in the economy. It may be argued, for instance, that changes in government expenditures, money supply, or technology make a change in people's thinking inevitably necessary. It would then follow that attitudes would *lag behind* other changes in the economy and thus be of little value for the prediction of forthcoming business trends. Contrary to this view, it appears that, usually or often, there is some justification for the presence of different attitudes and expectations at the same time. What has been called "underlying economic prospects" is not something unequivocal and clear. During the same period there may prevail economic trends that point upward and others that point downward. In such circumstances, it may happen that one way of seeing the developments, which is not the only possible way, may become predominant.

We shall try to illustrate this point by a brief résumé of recent American developments. When the war ended in 1945, the following view of the underlying economic prospects was held by many experts and often appeared in print: For the past few years, economic activity has been sustained by government orders for war materials. They are about to cease, and millions of workers will be discharged. At the same time, the labor market will be clogged by millions of soldiers and sailors who will be demobilized. Between 1940 and 1945, prices were driven up because of the high incomes of the war workers and shortages in civilian consumption goods. Although increased production of peacetime goods will give employment to many people, this production cannot compensate for the adverse factors. Therefore, a downward trend in employment, production, and prices is imminent.

It was evident from surveys of attitudes and opinions that in 1945 and 1946 the majority of both consumers and businessmen did not think along those lines. People in general were optimistic; they expected their incomes to stay up or to rise, good times with plentiful employment to continue, and prices to advance. Did these opinions originate regardless of, or contrary to, the underlying economic situation? By no means. The view of certain experts as outlined above was just one of several possible ways of viewing the underlying prospects. It was also possible to believe at the time the war ended that all underlying trends pointed toward runaway inflation. One could argue that several years had passed during which members of the armed forces had not bought any clothing, consumers had not bought durable goods and had not repaired their houses, and businessmen had not kept up their plants and had emptied the trade channels of stocks. After the period of restrained buying that characterized the war years, consumers and business would hasten to purchase all kinds of goods. Producing these goods alone would guarantee high employment and large incomes. At the same time, there existed considerable pent-up purchasing power in the form of war bonds and bank deposits in the hands of consumers and business. When people began spending both their incomes and their accumulated liquid assets, runaway inflation would surely ensue.

In addition to these two extreme and contradictory views about the prevailing economic forces, various other intermediate opinions about underlying trends and prospects could emerge at the same time. This means that diverse attitudes and frames of reference of businessmen and consumers could have found justification in what may be termed economic facts. How most people actually viewed the situation could not be determined by studying the underlying economic processes themselves. On the other hand, by studying people's opinions, attitudes, and expectations it was possible to find out about two strong motivational forces that were widely held shortly after the end of the war. One of these was, as already mentioned in Chapter 5, the urge to keep one's liquid reserves intact, available for future emergencies, and not to spend them on consumer goods. The other was the great desire for goods, explained partly as a reaction to the previous restraint and partly by actual shortages in business as well as consumer inventories. The joint result of these attitudes and the economic factors is well known: large consumption of both durable and nondurable goods, increase in inventories, and extensive capital investments by business characterized the first few postwar years. These expenditures were made possible through a reduction in the rate of saving, but, on the whole, not by using up previously accumulated reserves. Therefore, the inflationary forces were strong and prices rose, but runaway inflation was not in the cards.

If, more properly, we study behavior on the microeconomic level, we find that many families dissaved during some of the postwar years. Willingness to spend grew at a time when incomes advanced and were expected to remain high. Many people who spent more than their incomes in one year to purchase durable goods and other good things of life did not feel that they had used up their reserve funds, since they had reason to think that they would replace them. And, in fact, a year of dissaving was preceded or followed in many cases by a year of high saving. The average rate of saving—which in 1947, 1948, and 1949 was low relative to the high incomes—was a resultant of high rates of saving by some families and dissaving by others. Less is known about business attitudes toward using liquid assets, but according to available indications they did not differ greatly from consumer attitudes. In the sense, then, that they induced some people and firms to spend more than their incomes during part of what they considered to be a prolonged period of good business, attitudes contributed substantially to the prosperity. But the attitudes alone cannot be credited with that accomplishment; without the favorable financial position of consumers and business firms—high incomes and liquid-asset holdings, relative freedom from debts—the attitudes would not have been influential and probably would not have arisen.

The threat of an impending depression was frequently discussed in 1947 and 1948, and in one respect the prevailing frame of reference of the people made them responsive to such rumors. Opinion surveys showed that very few people believed that the American economy was depression-proof. On the contrary, most people were of the opinion that alternate periods of upswing and downswing could not be avoided. During a period of full employment, then, most people thought that depression would come sometime; the question was only whether it would come sooner or later. This question, however, the majority of consumers as well as businessmen answered in 1947 and 1948 in the optimistic way: they did not believe there would be an early downturn of business trends. Their attitudes were dependent on how they viewed the underlying economic trends, and both attitudes and trends served as incentives to consumer and business spending.

What was the situation at the beginning of 1949? If we try to summarize its major aspects, at first without regard to people's attitudes and expectations, we again obtain a picture that has two sides. Some aspects of the economic situation appeared to justify great optimism: During three years of peacetime prosperity, speculative excesses had not developed. Business as well as consumers had borrowed relatively little and at very low interest rates, so that their incomes were subject to small prior charges. At the same time, the considerable expansion in plant capacities and business inventories kept pace with but did not exceed the increase in business volume. In all these respects, the comparison with, say, 1929 was very favorable. On the other hand, in contrast to the late twenties, prices had advanced during the first few postwar years and families whose incomes had not risen substantially were priced out of the market. Furthermore, in 1948 the rate of acceleration of business activity slowed down. When expansion of inventories and production facilities caught up with sales, shortages and sellers' markets disappeared.

How did the people themselves view the situation? Early in 1949 some people were pessimistic; they expected and feared a depression, which they considered inevitable. But the great majority of consumers as well as businessmen remained optimistic. In view of their high incomes and assets and their own substantial needs and desires for goods, they expected good times for themselves and for the entire economy. At the same time, the majority in all strata of the population expected inflation to end and prices to begin to decline slowly. While according to some theoretical considerations price declines are associated with a deterioration in business activity, the people themselves thought differently at the beginning of 1949. They had learned that inflation is an evil, and greeted what they thought to be the end of inflation as an assurance of continued good times.[3]

Further important indications of consumer attitudes are, as we saw in Part Two, people's buying intentions as regards houses and durable goods. At the beginning of 1949, there were as many prospective buyers in these markets as a year earlier (in the markets for automobiles and television sets, the number had grown). More of those who expected good times to prevail and prices to decline in 1949 expressed intentions to buy durable goods

---

[3] According to the Survey of Consumer Finances, 38 per cent of all spending units with definite opinions thought at the beginning of 1949 that prosperous times would continue *and* prices would decline. The proportion of spending units who thought that times would be bad and prices would decline was 18 per cent at the same time. Most of those who expected prices to decline did not expect their own incomes to go down. These findings were already mentioned on p. 166, above.

than any other group. Thus the consumer survey did not support the opinion that 1949 would be the year of the upper turning point in the business cycle.

These survey findings gave rise to two crucial questions: First, could a depression come about at a time when consumers' ability to buy was considerable and their attitudes optimistic? We may recall the behavior of the small retailer quoted earlier. Suppose a great many large firms were to decide, in spite of satisfactory sales, to cut their production and discharge some of their workers in order to reduce their inventories. Could businessmen alone create a depression in this way? Second, in conjunction with such a possible change in business behavior, how would consumers react if their optimistic expectations failed to materialize? Would consumer attitudes undergo a substantial and sudden change when employment decreased and some incomes declined? Should that be the case, then the conclusion derived from the 1949 Survey of Consumer Finances, that consumer purchases would remain as high in 1949 as they were in 1948, could prove to be erroneous.

No answer that is generally valid can, of course, be given to the two questions posed. But with respect to the developments in the year 1949, the answers are clear. Caution and desire to be on the safe side, even at the price of foregoing some profits, induced many business firms to curtail their operations in the spring. To doubts and uncertainty about the future, businessmen as a rule responded by cutting production rather than by reducing prices. For the first time since the beginning of the war, unemployment increased noticeably. Though rising unemployment filled the newspapers with gloomy predictions, consumer purchases did not shrink. Thus business firms that maintained their sales at 1948 levels at a time when they reduced their output or purchases curtailed their inventories substantially.

A nation-wide consumer survey conducted in July, 1949, revealed that, for the first time since the end of the war, the proportion of spending units earning less than they had a year earlier exceeded the proportion who were earning more. But the number of people who felt that their financial situation had deteriorated was not greater than at various times in earlier years, because in 1949 prices were not advancing (some had even gone down somewhat). There were people who felt they were seriously affected by the "depression"—mostly people with low incomes. Nevertheless, attitudes toward the future and buying intentions presented in July, 1949, the same optimistic picture as six months earlier. Again the majority of all important occupational groups throught that their incomes would go up or remain the same and that times, in general, were and would remain good. Intentions to purchase durable goods showed no lessening at all. As a survey conducted a few months later indicated, unexpected income declines did not affect greatly people's attitudes and expectations. Those who unexpectedly made less in 1949 than in 1948 commonly spoke of a slight "interruption" and did not feel frustrated and did not alter their optimistic outlook.[4]

Production indices showed a recovery in the third quarter of the year. This was attributed, in one thoughtful study, to the behavior of consumers—although, as usual, without reference to their attitudes.

"The force behind the recovery has been the immense buying power of the country, fortified by huge liquid savings and government supports. While pipelines were being emptied and commitments reduced through the Spring, demand for goods of everyday use was relatively sustained. The turn came naturally when stocks had to be replenished and commitments replaced" (*National City Bank of New York, Monthly Letter,* October, 1949, p. 112.)

Somewhat later, in summarizing the developments during the entire year, a government study concluded:

"The most important area of stability throughout 1949 was in the consumer sector of the economy" (*Survey of Current Business,* January, 1950, p. 2.)

The economic history of the year 1949, which will go down in business annals as a good year, provides evidence that both the business and the consumer sectors, as well as both financial position and attitudes, are influential in shaping economic trends. We may also conclude from the experience in that one year that the study of attitudes *may* provide reliable clues to economic behavior. Naturally, however, what happened in 1949 does not prove that depression can never originate and spread through business decisions alone. Nor does it indicate that attitudes and expectations cannot change unexpectedly and suddenly. Finally, the developments in 1949, of course, do not prove that attitudes are always reliable *advance* indicators of forthcoming trends and that surveys can always measure impending changes in attitudes.

TASKS FOR POLICY AND RESEARCH

Because of the interaction of a large number of variables, forecasting cyclical fluctuations will no doubt remain difficult and precarious for a long time to come. But as to the method which will prove most appropriate for that purpose, a prediction may be ventured. Forecasts of business trends will ultimately be based on a comprehensive theory consisting of verified

[4] These findings were referred to in the Notes to Chapter 6, on p. 121, above.

sets of functional relationships between all relevant economic as well as psychological variables. Both the what and the why must be studied, and answers must be supplied to the question of how the different sectors of the economy interact. In addition to information on past behavior and its underlying factors, data of a forward-looking character need to be assembled at frequent intervals. The orders business firms have on hand and the orders they have placed must be determined, together with the factors shaping business as well as consumer decisions, namely, people's economic attitudes, expectations, and intentions. Regression equations based on past behavior alone cannot provide a reliable clue to future behavior, because crucial changes in economic trends result from people's not doing what they had been doing before. Neither can historical analogies suffice, because human behavior is characterized by plasticity and learning.

Suppose information is available about impending cyclical trends and their underlying factors. What use can be made of this information? We began this chapter with the statement that the aims of economic policy are clear when full-fledged inflation threatens, and they are of course clear when severe depression threatens. Economic policy must then be directed toward forestalling what has been called the vicious circle. The process of price advances or declines that gives rise to an expectation of further price increases or decreases, and thus stimulates or restrains buying, must be arrested. "Cumulative expectations" represent a threat to the economy, and policies are required that forestall their arousal. This conclusion is perhaps applicable to every phase of the cycle. It is not the expansion of the economy—rising employment, incomes, production and investment— that should be fought, but rather people's expectation that expansion itself must lead to further expansion. The danger during the upswing consists in the bunching of capital expenditures by business and in durable-goods purchases by consumers. The main question, therefore, is whether optimistic attitudes and rising incomes, investments, and expenditures can be maintained without becoming excessive.

If the alternatives were absence of definite expectations, on the one hand, and of cumulative expectations of a self-justifying upward or downward movement, on the other hand, there would appear little hope for anticyclical policies. Rigid stabilization of some or all prices, or of rates of capital expenditure or durable-goods purchases, does not promise to be an adequate cure. At best, it would lead to inflexible behavior that would be detrimental to progress and would sooner or later cause difficulties when habitual behavior became inappropriate because of changed conditions. But flexible behavior appears to be possible on the basis of "noncumulative expectations." People may expect prices to fall to some extent and then remain stable, in which case price reductions would induce them to buy more and not less. People may also expect their incomes to increase and still not feel induced to bunch their expenditures. And businessmen may expect to undertake profitable capital expenditures that need not stimulate them to still further expansion. The question, then, is whether economic policy can be inaugurated that will hold off the emergence of expectations of a cumulative increase or decrease in prices, incomes, and sales, and yet will not counteract the development of all kinds of expectations. In addition, there is the question of whether economic policy can be flexible enough to cope with changing requirements—to stimulate expectations of expansion at certain times and of contraction at other times.

NOTES TO CHAPTER 13

The information presented about people's cyclical attitudes and expectations during the period 1945 to 1950 is taken from the Surveys of Consumer Finances. The distribution of income expectations and of the general economic outlook at various times was shown before in Table 9 (Chapter 6) and of price expectations in Table 34 (Chapter 8). For further data on several other relevant variables, including buying intentions, as they appeared at the beginning of 1949 and at earlier times, the reader is referred to two articles entitled "1949 Survey of Consumer Finances," Parts I and II, in the June, 1949, *Federal Reserve Bulletin*. That "many consumers who looked forward to lower prices during 1949 also were expecting good times for the country as a whole and for themselves as individuals" is discussed on page 642 of that Bulletin. A short summary of the survey findings was given in the paper "Sustained Consumer Purchases Indicated" by George Katona, *Michigan Business Review*, July, 1949, pp. 9*ff*.

Results of a smaller survey conducted by the Survey Research Center of the University of Michigan for the Federal Reserve Board in July, 1949, were presented in the article "Financial Position and Buying Plans of Consumers, July 1949" in the October, 1949, *Federal Reserve Bulletin*. As shown in that article, 36 per cent of the nation's spending units said in July, 1949, that their current incomes were lower than a year before, and 24 per cent that they were higher (the remaining 40 per cent said that they were about the same). Nevertheless, more units expected income increases than decreases, and more thought that good times were ahead than that bad times would come (see Table 11, Chapter 6).

No reference was made in the text to consumers' saving behavior as it may relate to the business cycle. But mention may be made here of some savings data for the period 1948–1949. It was not uncommonly argued, by way of explaining what some observers thought to represent a depression, that toward the end of 1948, consumers, having satisfied their pressing deferred demands, had decided to save a larger part of their incomes. This argument proved to be unjustified. In fact, consumers increased their expenditures, especially for postponable durable goods, in 1948 as well as in 1949, and—according to survey data—consumers *qua* consumers did not increase their rate of saving in either 1948 or in 1949 (see "1949 Survey of Consumer Finances," Part VIII, *Federal Reserve Bulletin,* January, 1950, and the paper by J. N. Morgan in the June, 1950, issue of the *American Economic Review*).

Samuel P. Hayes, Jr., in "The Business Cycle: Psychological Approaches" (*Political Science Quarterly,* Vol. 63, 1948, pp. 82*ff.*) pleads for business-cycle research through large-scale collection of data on economic behavior that should represent a coordinated attack of all social sciences. He stresses the need to know about the whys and wherefores, primarily through psychological surveys.

CHAPTER 14

ECONOMIC POLICY

Economic policy can make use of both economic and psychological weapons. To explain the term "economic weapon" it may suffice to list such measures as tax increases or decreases, changes in interest rates, social security legislation, antitrust suits. The most important psychological weapon at the disposal of the policy maker is publicity—the transmission of economic information and its interpretation. The major purpose of this chapter is to show that usually neither purely economic policy measures, nor purely psychological measures, will suffice alone; economic policy must make use of both kinds of measures to be effective.

PROBABLE REACTIONS TO POLICY

Economic change, and social change in general, may be desired, and deliberate action may therefore be taken, usually by the government, to bring it about. In other instances, economic or social conditions may undergo a change without any deliberate action. Frequently, of course, deliberate action is taken to promote or to counteract changes in underlying conditions that have occurred or threaten to occur. The fundamental question concerns, in all these instances, the response of people. How people will react either to new legislative action or to changed conditions represents a major problem for economic policy.

Examples of deliberate economic or social change are the introduction of old-age insurance, of inheritance taxes, or of guaranteed annual wages. Examples of economic change that is not intended are turns in the business cycle pointing toward depression or inflation. Examples of deliberate action taken to counteract economic changes are the introduction of price control, of credit restriction, or of facilitation of borrowing or investing.

It may seem that there is a problem of response to economic change that is specific to deliberate action. This is the question of compliance. In discussing price control, we mentioned that economic policy can be thwarted if people do not comply with the spirit as well as the letter of the law. In some other instances—tax reductions may serve as an example—the problem of compliance may not arise at all. This is, however, beside the point, because compliance with economic policy is a special case. The more general case is the reaction or response to change. Whatever form a new legislative action has, and whatever changes take place without deliberate action, the question arises whether businessmen's and consumers' reactions will be appropriate. People's attitudes and behavior may be such as to promote the purpose of a new law, or they may counteract it; and under changed conditions, people's attitudes and behavior may be such as to promote a business upswing, or they may hinder and defeat it.

An example of this argument has already been presented in Chapter 12, when it was shown that tax increases do not automatically have the intended or required effects. The same is true of tax reductions. Suppose individual and corporation income taxes are reduced in order to stimulate consumer spending and business investing. This purpose may not be achieved if consumers and businessmen decide to hoard the amounts they save in taxes. The tax reduction may then result in nothing but an increase in the unused funds of banks. Analogous is the case of such recovery programs as the New Deal program of pump priming and public works during the thirties. As a result of these measures, financed through government deficits, money volume was increased. But during certain periods of pump priming, other sectors of the economy reduced their expenditures and thereby counteracted the intended effects of government policy. Or, in response to a policy of raising interest rates, the volume of business and consumer borrowing may either decline, or increase, or remain unaffected. Credit expansion, that is, policies offering easy conditions to borrowers or enabling banks to offer such conditions, may be ineffective if the potential borrowers abstain from participating.

Technological changes represent a further important instance that serves to illustrate the argument. After new inventions have been made, it is not necessarily true that business firms hasten to make use of them. Attitudes and expectations, the general climate of opinion, play a role in the utilization of technological progress, and that role is often the decisive one. Adoption of technological change can be facilitated by economic policy, both by economic measures, such as tax regulations, and by publicity.

The development and use of economic measures that are called "automatic stabilizers" or "built-in flexibility" do not detract from our argument. Unemployment insurance, for instance, is called an automatic stabilizer because it automatically leads to larger government expenditures in bad times, when there are more unemployed and larger expenditures are needed, and to smaller government expenditures in good times. Policy measures with inherent flexible features are of great usefulness because they make rapid changes in policy possible without recourse to the usually slow machinery of legislative action. But the problem of the diversity of possible reactions arises with respect to automatic stabilizers just as with other policy measures. Even unemployment insurance, involving the disbursement of large sums of money to millions of unemployed, requires psychological preparation. Otherwise, it may cause widespread fear regarding the government's solvency, and contribute to the curtailment of expenditures on the part of business firms to an extent exceeding the additional government expenditures. With adequate preparation, however, business spending may remain unaffected and consumers' feeling of security may be increased.

We conclude from these considerations that (1) it is often possible to differentiate between appropriate and inappropriate response to economic policy and to economic change; (2) economic policy needs to consider the possible and probable responses to its measures and to changing conditions; (3) economic measures need to be supported by psychological preparation. Changes in economic conditions that arise or threaten without deliberate action also need to be supported or counteracted by psychological measures in addition to economic ones.

PUBLICITY

The aim of psychological policy measures, and of psychological preparation of economic measures, is to create the "right" climate by influencing people's attitudes and expectations. Publicity may be put into the service of this objective. The term "publicity" is used here in a sense that differentiates it from persuasion or propaganda. By publicity is meant, first, making economic information known to the public. Second, the term should imply a certain way of presentation or publication. Economic information should be made known in such a way as to be understood, that is, apprehended within the right or required frame of reference.

We have seen in earlier chapters that learning based on repetition is much less effective than learning based on understanding. It follows that admonitions and exhortations alone, even if reiterated over and over again through the radio, in newspapers or posters, are not the best means of influencing people's behavior substantially over an extensive period.[1] "Spend less," "invest more," "reduce prices," and many other similar pronouncements will be effective only if the people understand why it is in their own and the country's interest for them to do so. If and when the right kinds of attitudes prevail, stamping in through reiteration and even through moral pressure

---

[1] The success of repetitive methods in advertising does not refute our argument. A newly coined brand name—or a telephone number—cannot be learned in any way except by repetition. By bringing the name of certain brands of cigarettes or soap constantly before the ear or eye of the public, the advertiser appeals to people who are predisposed to purchase cigarettes or soap and channels their response to a special brand.

may be useful. The most effective exhortation of the last few years, the slogan "Buy War Bonds," was effective because it was accompanied by good reasons why buying bonds was in the interest of the individuals and the nation, and because people's attitudes and frames of reference were responsive to the arguments presented.

Instead of telling people what they ought to do, they may be told what will probably happen. In this respect, again, frequent reiteration alone is rarely effective enough. The announcement "recovery is around the corner" did not help to instill confidence toward the end of 1929 and the beginning of 1930 and did not induce people to spend and to invest. Similarly, industrial and trade associations reiterated in vain that "prices will remain stable" after price control was lifted in 1946. On the other hand, at certain times during the war the statement that "the ceilings will not be punctured" was effective, because (1) it was accompanied by action, the purpose of which was to make the statement come true, and (2) the statement was not merely made, but it was explained so that people understood why prices could and would remain stable.

Under the heading publicity, we must consider first the transmission of economic information. Acquainting as many people as possible with what is going on by publishing data or indices on incomes, production, or prices belongs in this category. Publication of such economic data is, from the point of view of those in charge of publicity, often separated from the interpretation of the data. But those who read or hear of such "facts" as, for instance, the previous month's change in the cost of living, will understand them within a certain frame of reference, even if the publicity makers carefully abstain from interpretation.[2] Instead of leaving people in the dark, or—as more usually happens—instead of leaving the task of interpreting the data to interested parties, the concept of publicity may encompass making known not only the data themselves but also what they mean. What economic developments mean, why they took place, and what consequences they may have is economic information that constitutes an important segment of publicity.

[2] Strictly speaking, the argument presented in the last two sentences, though sufficient for our present purposes, is not correct. The statement "The B.L.S. cost-of-living index is 166 this month as against 167 last month" is *not* an entirely factual report. By omitting to state that the index applies to lower-middle-income family expenditures, as determined several years ago, that changes in rents (under rent control) are not fully taken into account, as well as many other relevant factors concerning the construction of the index, the publicity maker did engage in interpretation. If he includes such references in his publication, he likewise cannot be purely factual, since he must decide what emphasis to place on the various factors. But it remains true that the hearer or reader of the statement interprets it further, for instance, by understanding it to mean that "inflation has ended at last" or "there is a downward trend in prices."

Separation between factual reporting and interpretation becomes, of course, more difficult, or even hardly possible, when we think of the publication of information relating to the prospects of a business cycle. Reporting on trends in the volume of credit used, investments made, orders received, as well as on business and consumer attitudes, expectations, and plans is part of economic publicity. The same is true of the transmission of economic knowledge, of chains of causation, and of theory.

Although publicity may influence people's attitudes and expectations, and thereby their behavior, it should not attempt to dictate their behavior. Businessmen and consumers should make up their own minds, but on the basis of the best and most complete information that can be provided to them. Placing data in the frame of reference in which they inherently belong is therefore a legitimate function of publicity and not to be derogated as propaganda. We may also use a much simpler word to call attention to that function: publicity needs to consist of *explanation* of data, in addition to presentation of data.

What does explaining mean? We defined in Chapter 4 the term which denotes the result of a successful process of explanation, namely, understanding. Understanding was said to consist of fitting diverse items into an integrated whole so that the gaps are closed. The main function of explaining is, then, to supply the appropriate greater whole, the frame of reference, that serves to integrate the individual items of information.

To be sure, not everything can be explained. The makers of policy and publicity themselves may not understand an economic development or may have divided and even contradictory opinions about it. In such circumstances, the best that can be done is to present the various sides of the argument. But in some instances, at least, the meaning of economic trends or of economic policy or legislative action is clear. The function and significance of publicity are then enhanced.

In certain circumstances, publicity may suffice without economic measures. Similarly, economic measures alone may do the job, especially under extreme conditions when excessively strong measures are taken, or when the climate is appropriate and people are responsive. Usually, however, the two kinds of measures must be applied jointly in order that they should be trusted and relied upon.

It may even happen that the main function of an economic measure consists of the publicity it creates. Publicity, or fear of adverse publicity, may then influence people to change their behavior. The major purpose of prosecuting black-market operators or tax evaders may be said to consist of its effect on honest people, who may then lean over backward in complying with the laws so as to avoid adverse publicity. It is possible—though no evidence for the argument can be presented at this time—that here may be found the main beneficial effect of antitrust policy. The instances in which trusts have been dissolved or business concerns compelled to change their practices are relatively few. But, possibly, in many more instances business firms have abstained from taking over their competitors or from destroying them, not so much because they feared legal action as because they feared that they would be publicly branded as monopolies.

Economic policy, and the differentiation between appropriate and inappropriate response to policy, are based on predictions. Any anti-inflationary measure, whether it is a tax increase, credit restriction, or price control, implies the expectation that inflationary trends and inflationary behavior of businessmen and consumers will continue if they are not counteracted. Similarly, tax reductions or easing of credit are undertaken because of certain definite assumptions about prospective business trends and about the reactions to those measures. Predictions are part and parcel of economic policy as well as of economic publicity. To be sure, it is bad practice to have people with authority make flat statements about future developments. Economic predictions need to be presented together with their basis. In order to achieve understanding of current and expected future developments on the part of businessmen and consumers, predictions are useful, provided they are made in such form that the people can judge for themselves whether they are well-founded. The purpose of publicizing predictions in that way is, to repeat, to influence attitudes and expectations.

COLLECTING INFORMATION ON PROBABLE REACTIONS

Policy makers need to be concerned not only with the transmission of economic information but also with its collection. From previous discussions we may draw an important practical conclusion as to a certain kind of information policy makers may need. It is mere common sense that they should have the best and most complete information at their disposal. But it is often not realized that such information must encompass information about probable future developments and, above all, information about probable reactions to policy. All too frequently, economic laws are enacted without careful advance study about how the people—those directly affected as well as others—will respond to the new law. Yet such information is essential for determining the appropriateness of the legislative action.

Our present methods of fact finding are not sufficiently developed to argue that it is always possible to obtain advance information on probable reactions to deliberate economic change. But such information may be obtainable more often than is commonly realized. Investigations about probable reactions have, until now, been carried out only in a few, relatively simple circumstances. During the early phases of the war, for instance, shortly after the introduction of payroll-deduction plans for the purchase of war bonds, a "victory tax" withheld from payrolls at source was contemplated. The Treasury was then confronted with the question as to whether its second measure would not defeat the first one. More generally, the problem was: What would be the effect of withholding income taxes on wage earners' spending and saving? In a survey directed toward answering this question, varied reactions were obtained on the part of people who did not understand the purpose, scope, or method of tax withholding. But those who were fully acquainted with it—and simple methods of explanation were developed for the purposes of the survey and were later adopted for general use—indicated favorable attitudes toward tax withholding and expressed the opinion that the new tax would not induce them to give up payroll deductions for war bonds. These survey indications were borne out by people's behavior after the new tax measure went into effect.

A second, somewhat different, example may be found in the control of installment credit after the war. The purpose of this measure was to curtail the use of installment credit and thereby to counteract prevailing inflationary trends. However, unfavorable consequences of such control were conceivable. First, evasion, practiced jointly by dealers and buyers, might have made the control ineffective. Second, just as maximum prices fixed by law tend to become minimum prices under which no sales are made, it was possible that the knowledge that one might not borrow more or for longer terms than fixed by the government would lead practically all buyers to avail themselves of the permissible rate of borrowing—even those buyers who would pay full cash if there was no regulation. Surveys showed that, at least in certain postwar periods, most businessmen as well as consumers were in favor of installment-credit control. Many dealers thought that they would not like to grant easier credit terms even if it were permissible; and many buyers, that they would not want to buy on easier terms. These attitudes did not indicate that control of installment credit was not necessary. The regulation gave emphasis to the government's anti-inflationary policy and made sure that dealers were not forced by a few of their competitors to grant easier credit terms against their wishes.

These few isolated examples of studying reactions to government measures are perhaps not typical. There is a difference between crystallized and uncrystallized public opinion, and there is little value in studying the probable reactions of those who do not understand clearly the what and the why of new economic measures. Deliberate economic action may be of such complexity that it cannot be explained fully before its enactment. Even in that case, it may be useful to find out about people's reactions shortly after the introduction of the measure. Furthermore, even if attitudes toward certain measures cannot be discovered in advance, the attitudes toward the conditions that the new measures are intended to remedy can usually be ascertained at an early stage. All such studies may belong among the tools of the policy makers.

The need for studying probable reactions to new developments can be illustrated further by referring briefly to pension plans agreed upon by labor unions and employers. In 1949 and 1950, in particular, labor unions fought for old-age security for their members and induced several large business concerns to contribute to it. To some avowedly insufficient extent, such security is provided by Federal and state social security legislation. Traditionally it has been provided, for all too few people, by their own effort, namely, by saving part of their incomes through life insurance (annuities) and other methods. How will private pension plans, those thus far established and more extensive ones that may come in the future, affect people's spending and saving behavior? Theoretically it is possible that the feeling of greater security will influence people to spend a larger share of their income than before. On the other hand, saving for old age or retirement is only one of many motives for saving. It is possible that pension plans will induce people to save more than before so that, together with what they will receive from the government and their employers, they will be assured of really adequate security after retirement. It is necessary, and possible, to study people's attitudes and reactions to pension plans. The task is not easy and cannot be accomplished by a few simple questions, but must encompass a detailed analysis of different groups of people's incentives and value systems and their relation to behavior.

POLICY BY WHOM?

We used the term policy makers to describe those in charge of economic policy. Inasmuch as economic policy has the form of legislative, administrative, or judicial action, the government in any of its three branches is the policy maker. But economic policy can also be made by other sectors of the economy. Decisions, for instance, of any of the billion-dollar corporations to make or not to make use of technological developments, or to increase or decrease their investments, may affect the entire economy and represent, in intent as well as in effect, economic policy. Participation of business in economic policy is not necessarily the result of the size of business corporations. Even if there were no giant business firms, there would be trade leaders, as there are leaders in most social groups. Action or inaction by leaders may influence the other members of the group and may inaugurate policy. Furthermore, labor organizations may fashion economic policy by setting up new aims for labor—wage increases, shorter hours, pension plans, for instance—or by abstaining from doing so.

In these considerations, we have disregarded that economic policy includes psychological action as well. Participation in policy, and even initiation of policy, by various sectors of the economy becomes obvious when economic publicity is considered. Publicity campaigns providing economic information, as well as propagandistic attempts to influence people's attitudes and expectations, may be undertaken by government, business, labor, as well as by community leaders, newspaper and radio commentators, and consumer organizations. Influencing the prevailing economic climate is not a monopoly of any group. This fact poses important problems to research. Which groups use the weapon of molding public opinion in economic matters most efficiently? In what circumstances does that power shift from one group to another? Are any methods of economic publicity at the disposal of certain groups only and not of other groups? These are some of the problems to which we do not know the answers.

The fact that there may be, and usually are, several policy makers raises the problem of conflict in economic policy. Insofar as one or the other group may succeed in initiating economic policy for selfish aims that are contrary to the public interest, the participation of certain groups in economic policy represents a drawback. But conflict between different aims and methods of policy is advantageous, because it contributes to the crystallization of policy by means of democratic processes and adds flexibility to the system. If it were true that the required economic policy were clearly and unquestionably known at every given period, a different opinion might perhaps be maintained and autocratic rule by those in possession of wisdom might be advocated. But such a situation does not prevail, and it is questionable whether it will ever be attained. Therefore, participation in shaping economic policy on the part of all sectors of the economy, and publicity of conflicting aims—not merely of different aims of conflicting interest groups—are welcome. The prevalence of conflict adds to the need for publicity and for explaining the reasons for different possible policies.

Rational resolution of conflicts in policy aims is more than the pious hope of an optimist. Business and labor leaders have become increasingly aware of their responsibility to the public as well as of the fact that their own interests can best be promoted by striving for what is in the general interest. To seek a larger share in a stable national output is much less promising than to strive for the same, if not larger, share in a growing national output. The redistribution of a stable national income and wealth for the sake of increasing the share of either business or labor would not only be more difficult but would also yield smaller results than an increase in national income or wealth. Depression and unemployment are calamities for the economy as a whole and at the same time the greatest threats to the self-interest of both business and labor. While most business and labor leaders are increasingly aware of their dependence on general trends, they may differ in the means they consider appropriate to achieve the common aims. But differences in means or methods are, as said before, justified, because no single method is known to be the right one, and conflicting attempts and suggestions may promote the crystallization of the best policy —although there is no assurance that they will do so.

The role of government in policy making is of necessity paramount. That government alone is in the position to enforce policies is obvious. Within the context of this book it is more important to clarify the role of government in economic publicity. The compilation and publication of economic information—of data on trends of income, production, prices, attitudes, and so forth—could possibly be accomplished without the participation of the government. At present, in addition to government agencies, business firms and business organizations, labor unions, research foundations, and universities contribute to this task. If, however, the government were to withdraw from this work and leave it entirely to private groups, the entire economy and the free-enterprise system would be endangered. Then a situation would be bound to develop in which relevant information would be available only, or available first, to those in a position to pay for it. The weaker members of the economy—consumers as well as small business—would be at a great disadvantage, and freezing of the prevailing economic status would be promoted.

Equal access to economic information can be made available to all people, and this is an important function of government in economic matters. Government should not have a monopoly in economic publicity—the present situation in which everyone who wishes may assemble and publicize economic information must be maintained—but it must be the leader in this field. If, as in these pages, publicity is differentiated from persuasion and propaganda, government leadership in publicity will promote individual liberties and the free-enterprise system as well.

IS TOO MUCH INFORMATION DETRIMENTAL TO THE ECONOMY?

Never before in history has more economic information been made generally available than at the present time in the United States. Not only has the quantity of economic data grown steadily and rapidly during the past century, but their quality and the means available for interpreting them have also improved greatly. At the same time, it might be argued, scant progress has been made in avoiding disastrous economic fluctuations. To be sure, inflation during the Second World War was kept within bounds, and economic knowledge of the leaders as well as the masses was shown to have contributed to that result. But the depression of the thirties was one of the severest and longest ever encountered, the frequency and threat of bankruptcies has not diminished, and there is no assurance that future disastrous depressions will be avoided.

The argument may be made more pointed by assigning to widespread economic information an important causal role in bringing about excessive trade fluctuations. When every incipient or localized difficulty—cutback of production, layoff of workers, decrease in prices—becomes generally known, depression may be thought to spread over all segments of the economy much faster than when such matters do not rapidly become public knowledge. Furthermore, being in the dark about various developments may enable some people and some businessmen to maintain one opinion, and other people or businessmen the opposite opinion. Diversity in attitudes and behavior may keep the economy on an even keel, whereas quick and complete publicity may promote uniform mass sentiments and mass action, and thus intensify fluctuations. The greater the economic publicity, the more probable may be the arousal of cumulative expectations, of expecting one step to lead to the next, in all fields of trade.

Numerous considerations can be mentioned in contradiction to this argument. Not only incipient and localized economic difficulties are publicized, but also incipient and localized signs of improvement. Further, as we have seen, what we have called the underlying economic situation usually has two sides. It provides the basis for different, and sometimes contradictory, opinions and attitudes. Risk and uncertainty are never absent, whatever the amount of information at our disposal, because future developments are not inevitable results of past trends but depend both on past trends and current action.

Still, unsolved problems remain. The argument that uniform mass behavior is promoted by widespread publicity cannot be shoved aside easily. We are at the very beginning of our understanding of the origin of attitudes and expectations and must admit the possibility that simultaneous similar action will be the consequence of many people's being in the possession of the same facts. This may be advantageous in certain circumstances and disadvantageous in other circumstances. Here we face one of the most important and most difficult tasks of economic psychology. In essence, it is the same problem which emerged from our analysis of business cycles and the prospects of economic stabilization.

The problem may be expressed in a set of value judgments reflecting aims of policy. We do not want people to stay in the dark; they should have at their disposal the best and most complete economic information possible. We do not want a rigidly stable economy; for the sake of economic and social progress, flexible behavior based on the emergence of new expectations should be encouraged. We do not want to restrict individual liberties, which in the economic field comprise opportunity and some degree of freedom of action for all; we want to maintain what is the essence of the free-enterprise system. Can these aims be accomplished without leaving the way open to excessive economic fluctuations? There is a need to influence people's attitudes and expectations, but they should not be constrained or manipulated.

In summary we may argue: Economic policy should consist of such measures as are not only desirable in themselves but are also likely to arouse those expectations that are called for at the given time. When inflation threatens, expectations of price stability need to be stimulated; when deflation is imminent, expectations of income increases need to be stimulated. Since expectations are not innate and are not the function of people's past experiences but are dependent on their understanding of events —including government measures and economic publicity—it is not impossible to achieve this objective. But whether it is probable that we shall achieve it in our lifetime is another question. The only road we know of toward that goal consists of more, and not less, publicity. Correct and complete public analysis of past economic trends and behavior, and their effects on the future, and of the probable effects of economic policies on the underlying situation as well as on people's expectations, represents a method that carries some promise of success.

NOTES TO CHAPTER 14

It follows from the argument presented in the text that the Council of Economic Advisers acts as policy maker not only if and when it proposes new legislative or administrative action but also when it publishes its semiannual economic reports. The comprehensive analysis of the position and prospects of the American economy, given in these reports, represents "publicity" and serves to influence attitudes and expectations. From some programmatic statements issued by the Council, it appears that it is aware of this function as well as of the need to study and analyze probable reactions to new developments and policies. It is also well aware of the current limitation of economic science in all these respects. The paper of E. G. Nourse, "Economics in the Public Service," *American Economic Review,* Vol. 37, Supplement, 1947, pp. 21*ff.*, and the *Third Annual Report* by the Council of Economic Advisers (December, 1948, especially pp. 28*f.*) indicate the early position of the Council most clearly.

That comprehensive economic planning would depend on full and accurate information about the nation's budget and the factors influencing expenditures and savings (which at present are not available), as well as on publication of that information, has been stated by W. H. Beveridge (*Full Employment in a Free Society,* New York, 1945).

The Council of Economic Advisers has not drawn the consequence from the limitations of our knowledge to initiate or suggest studies of probable re-actions to new policies. To what extent such studies can be made, and to what extent they have been made, through attitude surveys has been described in the May, 1946, number of *The Journal of Social Issues* entitled "Measuring Public Attitudes" (Angus Campbell, ed.). W. A. Nielsen points out in this publication that business firms spend millions of dollars to study probable reactions of consumers to their products, while the government does very little with respect to its much more important task. Angus Campbell shows that surveys were conducted, and many more could be usefully conducted, to answer the fol-lowing questions: "How well is the public informed? . . . How does the Government feel about actions the Government has taken? . . . How will the public feel about new Government action that is planned? . . . What is the public doing? . . . What is the public planning to do in the future? . . . Are there public needs on which the Government should take action?" (*op. cit.,* pp. 14*ff.*). Rensis Likert discusses similar functions of interview surveys and refers to the study of the relation between payroll taxes and payroll deduction for war bonds in "The Sample Interview Survey" (in *Current Trends in Psychology,* Pittsburgh, 1948, pp. 196*ff.*).

An analysis of the functions of government publicity and numerous examples of appropriate and inappropriate publicity are to be found in Chapter VII of *War without Inflation,* New York, 1942, by George Katona.

PART FIVE

RESEARCH METHODS

Chapter 15

ECONOMIC-PSYCHOLOGICAL SURVEYS

To a large extent economic research takes as its starting point data collected and published because of practical or legal requirements not related to research objectives. Profit-and-loss statements of corporations, quotations at security and commodity markets, or government publications on tax receipts or on exports and imports are by-products of administrative activity and at the same time basic data upon which economists have depended for the analysis and understanding of economic processes. During the past few decades, however, more and more fact finding has been initiated by considerations of the economists themselves. Price or production indices and data on consumer expenditures or business investment, for example, are at present assembled for the sake of research use as well as for practical needs.

Economic psychology, in contrast to other fields of economics, is not in a position to rely on basic material collected for practical or legal purposes. To be sure, it can and must make use of a multitude of available statistics and may search corporation reports and files for indications about the processes of decision formation. But psychological analysis of economic behavior, as a rule, must be based on empirical studies initiated and guided by the aims of that analysis. In this area, fact finding and analysis are interrelated and dependent on each other to a much greater extent than in any other field of economic research.

The most important research method of economic psychology is the sample-interview survey. By asking representative samples of consumers and businessmen about the what and the why of their decisions and actions, and by relating these findings to various characteristics of the respondents (income, assets, age, for instance), quantitative data are collected for the purpose of understanding economic behavior. This chapter will be devoted primarily to a description of the methods of economic-psychological surveys. In addition to this basic research tool, however, economic psychology may utilize two further methods. It can make use of psychological studies of noneconomic behavior, and it can derive valuable information from case studies. We shall turn first to a brief discussion of these research methods.

APPLICATION OF PSYCHOLOGICAL FINDINGS

Psychological principles and findings are often useful for the study of economic behavior. But the transition from psychological theory or from knowledge acquired through psychological experiments to economic behavior is not a simple task. The most common research method of psychology, the small-scale experiment with animals or human "subjects" in which the principle of controlled variation is applied, usually only provides hypotheses that may serve to guide research into economic behavior. In order for such experiments to produce results directly applicable to economic behavior, they must be planned with that aim in mind.

Use has been made in this book of a variety of psychological findings. As our first example, we may refer to the analysis of the learning process and of expectations. On the whole, the elaborate experimental work on learning has been carried out without regard to economic behavior. Similarly, discussions of the theory of learning, based on those experiments and stimulating many more experiments, have proceeded as if learning took place solely in noneconomic behavior. In the controversy between reinforcement theories of habit formation and learning with insight, for instance, it did not occur to most participants that evidence concerning many of the disputed points might be obtained in the field of economic behavior. Therefore, in analyzing habitual behavior of businessmen and consumers, or studying the origin of their expectations—to mention only two major issues—it was not possible simply to refer to psychological findings. It was necessary to reconsider the psychological theorems and also to make new experiments that differed from the traditional psychological experiments inasmuch as they were focused on the problems of economic behavior. The experiments on the formation of expectations, discussed in Chapter 4, may serve as an illustration of what the author believes to be true of decision formation in general: Psychological experiments may be useful for economic psychology but, in most cases, they must be conceived, or redone, with that purpose in mind.

The situation appears to be somewhat more favorable, and applicability of psychological experiments to economic behavior easier, in certain other fields. Levels of aspiration and their effects on behavior were originally studied in a rather restricted way (in intelligence tests, for instance), but in due time those studies were extended to group activities of more general significance. Thus, we were able to apply some aspects of motivational studies (for instance, those concerning satiation and frustration) to economic behavior without extensive new research. But the psychology of motivation is still in a rather preliminary and incomplete stage, and in building a theory of motivation psychologists have again failed to consider economic behavior as a field from which new evidence might have been drawn. Psychological research about motives is needed which is centered on problems that are apparent in economic motivation.

Similarly, psychological findings on group belonging, on relations between leaders and followers, and on the influence of reference groups, are useful for economic psychology. Yet their usefulness could be considerably enhanced through further research. Psychological experiments isolating crucial variables and comparing experimental and control groups could be made with the specific aim of clarifying issues of economic behavior. In addition to laboratory experiments in which groups with different economic motives are formed and their behavior observed, field experiments could be carried out under more realistic but less controlled conditions. Attempts in this direction have been made in studying communication between economic groups, in manipulating social behavior in housing projects, and, above all, in investigating management-employee relations and the factors conducive to increased coherence, morale, and productivity of small work groups.

These few words may suffice to substantiate the assertion that psychological experiments belong among the research methods of economic psychology. What is needed to make better use of that method is, first of all, greater interest in economic behavior on the part of psychologists. Up to now, social psychology has made progress primarily through studying family and social groups, or social and political beliefs and attitudes, through investigating morale, leadership, prestige, prejudice, propaganda, cooperation and aggression among children, or in situations of religious, racial, labor, and political conflict. There is no reason why social-psychological experiments and field investigations should not be devoted to the study of the development of spending or saving habits or to the analysis of cooperation and conflict between business executives. The process of investing would provide a particularly interesting field for social-psychological studies.

CASE STUDIES

The second research method available to economic psychology is the case study. Searching for detailed, intimate knowledge about individual cases is somewhat in disrepute among psychologists, although it has been usefully applied to the study of exceptional cases, especially in clinical psychology. Yet the investigation of the frequency or generality of traits requires hypotheses that often cannot be obtained except from the careful observation of individual cases. The problem of decision formation may serve to illustrate this point. Reports by scientifically trained business executives about their own behavior and decisions, and reports by students of economic psychology who serve as interns in business firms and are in a position to observe decision formation at close range, are greatly needed. To obtain the history of exceptional instances, such as what went on before a firm arrived at a crucial decision that either made or broke it, would be only one of the aims of such case studies. We also need detailed recording of the course of events preceding such decisions as increasing or decreasing prices, output, or inventories. What has been going on should be studied, including the memoranda, inquiries, informal and formal conferences, as well as the attitudes, motives, incentives, and expectations of the persons concerned. The major purpose of such case studies would be the formulation of hypotheses to be tested in further quantitative studies.

Economic case studies are quite numerous but, for the most part, they do not extend to psychological considerations. Yet even when the investigator has not considered the study of motives or expectations as his major goal, the findings have often been useful for such studies. As one example for many, the study of setting gasoline prices by the Standard Oil Company of Ohio may be mentioned. This study, referred to in the Notes to Chapter 10, contributes to answering questions about the conditions under which a large company assumes price leadership and under which it follows the market. Case studies about a few businessmen's attitudes toward price control and the influence of these attitudes on their behavior were directed by the author for the purpose of supplementing a sample survey during the war.

Related to case studies are surveys that are not based on a sample. Certain firms or families may be selected for study, for instance, simply on the basis of their availability to the investigator. Clarification of sequences of behavior or insights into the dynamics of decision making may result from such studies. The investigator should, however, always keep in mind that generalizations about the frequency of forms of behavior cannot be derived from case studies. Such quantitative information, which is the basis of scientific understanding and prediction, is beyond the case-study stage.

HISTORY AND FUNCTION OF SAMPLE SURVEYS

The practice of seeking economic information from individual persons and firms is being continued on an ever-increasing scale. The traditional method of gathering such information has been to take a complete census of all the individuals or firms the information is intended to cover, enumerating the characteristics under study. Thus, for data on retail dry-goods sales, for example, each of the thousands of retail firms selling dry goods would be asked to supply figures on its sales. Recent progress in sampling has made this extensive and expensive procedure unnecessary in many instances. In addition, as we shall show later in this chapter, especially with respect to psychological information, sample surveys may be more accurate than complete enumerations. At present, an important purpose of the decennial census is to provide basic data that enable experts to draw representative samples.

The Bureau of the Census itself conducts numerous economic sample surveys. It collects information by this method, for instance, on the number of employed and unemployed workers in the nation. Fact gathering through consulting with a sample of individual firms is the basis of the cost-of-living index compiled by the Bureau of Labor Statistics. In both instances, concepts are defined, questions are prepared, a sample is drawn, the households or firms falling in the sample are personally visited, facts are ascertained by asking questions or by looking at price tags, and the sample findings are expressed in terms of the "universe" (all people or firms from which the sample was drawn).

In discussing the methods of economic psychology, we are not concerned with purely economic surveys. Nevertheless, we must mention two such surveys that represent important milestones of research and are the forerunners of the psychological-economic surveys to be studied here. In 1935–1936, the Study of Consumer Purchases was conducted as part of the WPA program: a very large number of households was visited and, for each family or individual, data were obtained on income and on expenditures. In 1941–1942, the Bureau of Labor Statistics (together with a division of the Department of Agriculture) made a similar nation-wide study on a much smaller scale.

During the same period, in the decade before Pearl Harbor, scientific progress was considerable in several related noneconomic fields as well. Psychologists turned to the problem of attitude measurement. They devised methods for the quantification of attitudes and opinions and tested them in many small surveys, conducted most commonly among college students. Second, sampling as part of mathematical statistics made rapid progress and opened the way for determining, within established margins of error, values representative of a population consisting of millions of units by collecting information from a few thousand or even a few hundred cases. Third, polling organizations were established and made sample surveys well known, popular, and widely trusted. Their success in the late thirties and early forties in predicting election results on the basis of small-sample interviews demonstrated to the public at large that people in all walks of life could be approached with what might seem rather personal questions and that answers obtained from a small sample could have significance far beyond the importance of the relatively few people who were actually interrogated.

Commercial market research made successful use of the same methods at the same time by determining people's brand preferences or listening and reading habits. Advertising agencies, periodicals, and the radio industry became big users of the sample interview survey.

During the war, several government agencies took up the task of measuring people's attitudes toward public issues connected with the war, among them many economic issues. Their purpose was to advise policy makers about the need for and the methods of disseminating information and, in some cases, also about the need for new regulations. The Army and Navy Departments had special staffs conducting surveys among soldiers and sailors concerning their motivation, attitudes, fears, and expectations. Methods of measuring the intensity of opinions, especially, were greatly improved by the work in the Army. The Division of Program Surveys, an agency established in the Department of Agriculture under the direction of Rensis Likert, conducted a number of surveys on wartime issues and pioneered in devising psychological methods of interviewing. In 1942, that Division began its program of psychological-economic surveys with a series of surveys conducted for the War Finance Division of the Treasury Department. Their major purpose was the measurement and improvement of the effectiveness of war bond drives. Then, in 1944, the Division of Program Surveys began its operations for the Board of Governors of the Federal Reserve System. The major original purpose of these surveys was to measure the distribution of liquid-asset holdings among the nation's consumer units, and the attitudes of consumer units toward those holdings. The surveys soon developed, however, into projects encompassing practically all aspects of economic psychology in the consumer sector of the economy. Since 1946, these Surveys of Consumer Finances have been conducted by the Survey Research Center of the University of Michigan, which was established in that year by the principal personnel of the Division of Program Surveys.

Before discussing the methods of these surveys, two brief remarks need to be made. Consumer surveys, though they do not deal with business firms as such, determine the financial position and financial attitudes of all kinds of people, including businessmen. Their methods, moreover, as we shall see later, are applicable to surveys conducted among business firms.

Second, the major aims of economic-psychological surveys among consumers may here be restated. For methods are the functions of the purposes for which they have been developed. Two purposes of these surveys may be distinguished. The first is to analyze what has happened and to assess recent and current developments. The second is the study of functional relationships between different variables, the testing of hypotheses about economic behavior.

To achieve these purposes, it is necessary to collect microeconomic financial data as well as data on financial attitudes. The two kinds of data must be collected in the same survey in order to enable the investigator to study their interrelationship. A single survey yields what may be called spatial variation of cross-section data; several consecutive surveys yield time trends of such data. The survey data are not to be used in isolation but in conjunction with data collected by other methods, especially with aggregative financial data concerning, for instance, the size of, and change in, national income, total savings, and total expenditures. Survey data supplement aggregative information not only by showing the distribution of aggregates—for instance, the distribution of income, of income changes, or of liquid-asset holdings—but also by shedding light on the dynamics of economic behavior, inasmuch as they attempt to answer why a certain kind of behavior occurred.

SAMPLING DESIGN

The aim of sampling is to make the sample as representative as possible, so that measurements based on a sample can be taken as equivalent to similar measurements based on the universe from which the sample was drawn. This ideal can be approximated but not fully achieved. The sampling error expresses the probable range of differences between measurements derived from a sample and measurements of the universe, or between measurements from one sample and measurements from many other samples drawn from the same universe.

Two kinds of sampling methods are in use, judgment sampling and probability sampling. In some cases, the selection of individuals to form a sample is a matter of judgment; in other cases, the selection is by chance, and judgment is confined to definitions and restrictions imposed on the design of the sample.

An example of judgment sampling is the quota sampling used by the major polling organizations (Gallup, Roper, etc.), for instance, in the presidential election polls. In 1948, the pollsters failed to designate the winner, whereas on many previous occasions their predictions had proved to be correct. We are not concerned here with the success or failure of the polls—which is due to several factors in addition to sampling—but with weaknesses of judgment sampling which are inherent in that method even if in a particular instance it happens to yield what later is found to be the correct result. In quota sampling, the interviewers are instructed to fill their quotas by contacting people of specified sex, age, race, and "economic level." It depends on the interviewer's judgment whether or not a prospective respondent qualifies. This procedure leaves much of the selection of the sample to human decisions, which cannot be controlled and variations in which cannot be determined. People who are difficult to reach or who do not like to be interviewed have a smaller chance of falling into the sample than other people. In judgment sampling, the probability of selecting a respondent is not known. Therefore, the probable limits of sampling variability (the sampling error) cannot be determined.

In probability samples, every member of the universe—that is, of the population studied—has an equal or known chance of being selected. Interviewers' bias in selecting respondents is excluded, and sampling errors can be calculated. There are two major forms of probability sampling, list sampling and area sampling. Suppose the universe in which we are interested and from which we want to draw a representative sample consists of all families who are permanent residents in a given town at a given time, or of all employees of an industrial corporation at a given time. Suppose, further, that lists containing the names of all members of the universe are available. (With respect to residents of towns, this is the case in many European countries but not the United States; with respect to industrial employees, this is more generally true.) Then a sample can be drawn by counting out every tenth or twentieth or hundredth name on the list. This method of selection permits no exercise of choice on the part of the investigator.

When no lists are available as, for instance, for the total population of the United States, more complex procedures must be used. Area sampling permits the determination of the location of each respondent so that no latitude is left to the interviewer in selecting the respondents. In order to draw a representative sample of all families in the United States, the process of random selection must be repeated several times. First, as in many samples used by the Census Bureau as well as in the samples of the Surveys of Consumer Finances, a random sample of counties is chosen. (A list of all counties in the United States is, of course, available.) Then a sample of towns and open country areas within the selected counties is drawn. Then, within a city, for instance, a sample of blocks is selected (by numbering all blocks in the city from maps). Then all dwelling units in the selected blocks are listed—enumerated through field trips—and a random sample of dwelling units is drawn. Finally, all respondents living in the selected dwelling units are listed, and either one of them is chosen at random or all of them constitute the sample. This procedure determines precisely which individuals the interviewer must call on.[1]

One drawback of area sampling is that complete coverage of all units

---

[1] The given description of the principles of sampling remains correct even though in actual practice the procedure is somewhat more complicated. In most surveys, for instance, stratified samples are used. (Stratification represents a method of systematic

selected in a sample can usually not be attained. The inhabitants of some of the dwelling units chosen may not be found at home or may refuse to be interviewed. Through repeated calls made at different times and through letters addressed to those who have refused to be interviewed, the deficiency may be reduced, but not eliminated. A second drawback of area sampling consists in its being rather expensive, appreciably more expensive than quota sampling. Quota sampling, on the other hand, can be improved by checking sample data with such census data as race, sex, age, etc., and then classifying and weighting the original sample data by census categories.[2] Such treatment of the data does not guarantee, however, that appreciable bias will not occur. For reliable, scientific investigations, aimed at a predetermined substantial degree of precision, there is no substitute for probability sampling.

Sampling of business firms can usually be made from available lists and follows, in principle, the same pattern as sampling of households, with this exception: For most purposes, in a household sample every family, irrespective of its size, income, or wealth, may rightfully have the same weight. In sampling business concerns, however, for most purposes firms of different sizes—for instance, the U.S. Steel Corporation and a small grocery store—cannot be given the same weight. True, for some purposes special weighting measures may be necessary in a household sample, but in a business sample such weighting is almost inevitable. Weighting by capital, number of employees, or other criteria, makes the sample design more complicated. The within-household sampling is likewise simpler than the within-firm sampling. Often special investigations are needed to determine whom to interview in a given business firm. There may even be several decision makers in one firm, or decision making may shift to different persons at different times.

The size of a sample, that is, the number of cases designated for interviewing, depends upon the following major considerations: (1) The degree of accuracy of results desired—the sampling error being a function of, among other things, the number of cases. (2) The variability of the characteristic to be measured—a larger sample being required, for example, to measure the distribution of the population by income, which has a wide range, than by home ownership. (3) The desired breakdowns of the find-

---

and, nevertheless, unbiased selection.) The details of sampling design and sampling statistics are outside the scope of this book.

The procedures described above have the additional advantage of making it easy to check upon the performance of the interviewers.

[2] This procedure may also be applied when the original interview material is based on nothing but the availability of respondents. This was done, for instance, by Kinsey in his *Sexual Behavior in the Human Male*.

ings—fewer cases being needed if national estimates alone are required than if, in addition, regional or occupational distributions are desired.

Since the variability of incomes may be as great in the State of New York as it is in the nation as a whole, the size of the sample for a national consumer-income survey need not exceed (or need not exceed greatly) the size for a New York State income survey (assuming the same degree of precision and the same kinds of breakdowns). The better the sampling design, the smaller the sample needed to achieve the objectives. In carefully designed area samples, to the surprise of the layman, interviewing one out of 40,000 cases has proved to yield results with a satisfactory (and known) degree of precision.

Since much of the material used in this book has been obtained from the Surveys of Consumer Finances, a few words need to be added about the sampling design of these particular surveys. The universe from which the sample is drawn consists of all consumer units in the continental United States living in private households. Members of the armed forces living in military reservations, residents in hospitals and other institutions, and the floating population (residents in hotels and large boarding houses) are excluded. Area sampling is used to select a representative cross section of dwelling units. Areas in which people of high income are assumed to live are oversampled. The reason is that such people constitute a small percentage of the total population, and therefore the number of them who would fall into a small sample if they were chosen at the standard sampling rate would be too small for purposes of study. Weights are used to compensate for the oversampling. The sample of each survey consists of approximately 3,500 spending units located in the 12 largest metropolitan areas and in 54 other sampling points (mostly counties). The exact location of each dwelling unit is given to the interviewers, and every effort is made to obtain personal interviews with the heads of each spending unit residing in the designated dwelling. In case of failure, no substitution is permitted.

PERSONAL INTERVIEWS VS. MAIL QUESTIONNAIRES

Two possible ways of approaching the selected respondents are by visiting them personally or by writing to them. Mail-questionnaire surveys are known to have great disadvantages. Many of those who receive such questionnaires do not respond. A 30 or 40 per cent response to a mail questionnaire is ordinarily considered a highly satisfactory result; occasionally the response rate is higher, but usually it is much lower. Some people just do not want to be bothered, others are not interested in the questionnaire sent to them, and still others do not want to commit themselves in writing. Those who do not respond may have special reasons for not responding and may differ in income, assets, or opinions from those who do respond. Therefore, there is no assurance that information obtained by mail is derived from an unbiased selection of respondents.

There may be instances in which the relatively low response rate of mail questionnaires does not constitute a great drawback. In certain surveys, one may not be concerned with the opinions of those who are not interested enough to reply. For instance, if a scientific society wants to poll its members as to whether its next convention should be near the East Coast, in the Middle West, or on the West Coast, it may be assumed that those who do not respond do not care where the convention will be held. Or if an automobile company asks people about their preferences concerning certain new features to be added to their car, the results obtained from those who care to respond may be of some interest. But for scientific surveys that require a proportional representation of all situations and opinions, the low reponse rate practically excludes the use of mail questionnaires. People in unusual or extreme circumstances may fail to respond; such failure would bias the results. Furthermore, "don't know" answers are relatively infrequent in mail questionnaires—those who do not know the answers usually do not care to reply—and such answers may be of great importance.[3]

A second disadvantage of mail questionnaires is likewise well known: mail questionnaires must be short and simple. Otherwise the chance of getting a substantial proportion of replies becomes extremely small. Lengthy and complex inquiries, therefore, cannot ordinarily be made through the mail (except in those instances in which members of a group are highly motivated to reply to a questionnaire sent by their organization).

Less attention has been given to a third basic fault of mail inquiries. There is no assurance that the respondents understand the written questions, and no assurance that the analysts understand the replies. Even carefully formulated and relatively simple questions may be misunderstood by the respondents, and simple answers misunderstood by the analysts—and there are no ways of finding out the real meaning of the answers. Mail questionnaires share this disadvantage with certain forms of personal interviews; therefore, this point will be discussed in the next two sections.

THE INTERVIEW

There are various forms of personal interviews. At the one extreme, the interviewer makes use of no questionnaire whatsoever, and at the other he

[3] The only way to assure that nonresponse will not bias the results of mail questionnaires is to interview in person a representative sample of those who do not answer the request for response by mail. This process, however, greatly diminishes the main advantage of mail questionnaires, their comparative inexpensiveness.

may use a detailed reporting form with spaces to be filled in, usually with check marks or figures, under abbreviated headings. Especially in sociological or business surveys and case studies, in which a small number of respondents is interviewed by those in charge of the survey, the first method has been used to advantage. In these cases, the interviewer may believe that he need not have a standardized questionnaire. Like many personnel officers when they interview applicants for jobs, he knows what he wants to find out and formulates on the spur of the moment the right questions to obtain the information he needs. This procedure is not without danger, because the interviewers, being fully aware of the purposes of the survey and the implications of their questions, are often led to ask questions which by their phrasing bias the results. Furthermore, the questions asked by different interviewers may differ. Therefore, interviewing without a questionnaire does not yield comparable data from different respondents. Because of the possible influence of the wording of a question on the replies received, survey measurements derived from a large number of respondents must be based on identical, and therefore predetermined, questions.

Having interviewers fill out reporting forms which contain not questions but column headings, such as occupation, age, number of workers, size of farm, etc., is the traditional method of censuses and enumerative surveys. Except where applied to very simple, factual matters, the procedure is not adequate. Careful studies have revealed that different interviewers formulate different questions for the same purpose and that these questions often yield differences in the answers. When the inquiry is directed toward such complex matters as income, assets, or attitudes, reporting forms cannot be depended on.

Between these two extreme forms of interviewing are those which make use of a questionnaire prepared in advance. There are different kinds of questionnaires. Some resemble the reporting forms, and others the conversational interview that makes use of no preformulated questions at all. A questionnaire in which the questions are so formulated that they allow only for yes, no, or "don't know" answers, to be indicated by the interviewer by means of check marks in the three boxes that appear after each question, is very similar to a reporting form. The task of the interviewer is simple— he only reads the questions and makes check marks—and the quantification and tabulation of results become almost automatic. Closely resembling this method are multiple-choice questions: the respondent is given a set of alternatives and chooses the one which most closely agrees with his situation or opinion. These questions have been dubbed "cafeteria" questions, since they restrict the respondent's choice of opinion much as a customer's choice of dishes is restricted in a cafeteria.

The fixed-question—free-answer method of interviewing differs from the methods just described. It makes use of open-ended questions, which call for full answers in the respondent's own words.[4] Although the questions are formulated in advance and are used in every instance without any change in sequence or wording, the interview becomes a conversation between interviewer and respondent instead of a cut-and-dried interrogation. The respondent is encouraged to express his opinion in his own words or to describe his situation in detail. The questions are usually supplemented by what are called nondirective probes. In case of a brief or unclear answer, the interviewer follows up with a remark such as "That is interesting, would you tell me more about it?" (or: "What do you have in mind?" or: "Why do you say so?") This approach, together with carefully prepared introductory statements about the purposes and the importance of the survey, is conducive to creating rapport between interviewers and respondents. Motivating the respondent to give complete and truthful answers, and to spend a comparatively long time with the interviewer, are primary conditions for the success of psychological-economic surveys and can best be achieved by making the interview an interesting experience to the respondent.

Using the methods just described, which have been worked out by the organization conducting the Surveys of Consumer Finances and have been applied in those surveys, places a great responsibilty on the interviewers. Interviewers must be able to gain the confidence of respondents and talk to them—whether laborers or business executives—as equals. They must understand the meaning of each question and the context of the entire interview. They must be able to take notes that reproduce faithfully the respondent's meaning—preferably verbatim notes. It follows that interviewers must be selected on the basis of careful personal screening and must be trained by an experienced supervisor. Knowledge of the subject matter of a survey alone is far from sufficient to qualify a person for interviewing; good economists may not be good interviewers.

Much preliminary work must be done to develop a "good" questionnaire. Each question must be carefully pretested from the point of view of its carrying the intended meaning in simple, understandable words and also from the point of view of avoiding suggestive leads. The sequence of the questions must be carefully planned with these same aims in mind as well as the aim of building rapport.

Interviews for the Surveys of Consumer Finances may consist of twenty or more pages, they contain over 150 questions, and, on the average, last one hour. When the completed interviews are returned to the central office, they are edited for completeness and consistency. Sometimes they are sent back to the interviewers for a second interview. Then follows the process

[4] Examples of open-ended questions will be presented in the next section of this chapter.

of quantification of data, which represents a difficult problem specific to interviews using open-ended questions and verbatim recording of answers. "Coding," the technical term for that process, is relatively simple with respect to such data as amounts of income or ownership of automobiles. Regarding attitudes and expectations, however, summarizing information that is often varied and lengthy becomes rather difficult. Experience indicates that reliable quantification of such data into a few major categories is possible. The reliability of this operation can be checked by having it performed twice by two persons.[5]

The complexity of interviewing carries with it certain severe limitations on surveys. First of all, each survey is limited with respect to the number of questions that may be asked. In economic research, interest prevails usually for many more problems than can be included in one survey. In addition, clarifying a simple economic issue often requires a great many questions. Yet the length of an interview is limited by the time respondents are willing to devote to it and by the span of their interest. Second, the size of the sample is severely limited. For various important economic purposes, as we shall see in a moment, it would be of great advantage to have samples of many thousands of respondents. But it would be very difficult to obtain carefully trained interviewers in sufficient numbers to conduct such a large-scale survey in a reasonably short period of time, and it would be still more difficult to ensure uniformity of procedures and uniformity of analysis.

ON QUESTIONS AND INTERVIEW CONTENT

What are the areas of study to which economic surveys may most fruitfully be applied? What are the areas to which the survey approach cannot be applied or should be applied with caution only? The discussion of these problems presents an opportunity to give illustrations of different kinds of interview questions, their value, and their pitfalls.

There is no need to consider the problem of question wording itself in any detail. That all questions must be simple and aimed at one point only is generally acknowledged, just as is the well-documented finding of numerous investigations that relatively small changes in question wording may influence the answers. That simple, brief answers may convey different meanings is, however, a more complicated matter. We shall therefore begin our discussion of interview content by one of the simplest inquiries included in economic surveys and proceed then to questions of greater complexity.

[5] Much of the color and feeling tone of the interviews cannot, of course, be conveyed in coding and quantifying. The analyst may therefore append to his report what are, in effect, case studies consisting of direct quotations from the interviews, often with thumbnail sketches of the respondents quoted.

The question, "Do you own a car?" appears to be so simple that the form of the question may be thought to be unimportant, and reporting forms and check marks for the answer may be thought to be adequate. What are the actual answers interviewers receive when this question is asked in the course of a conversational interview? Brief answers of yes or no are rare; people more commonly reply with fuller statements—such as, "Sure, we have a 1941 Ford" or "No, we would like to have one but cannot afford it." If that were all, one could say that noting down the detailed answers does not contribute anything to the objective of determining the number of automobile owners. (It gives additional information which may or may not be needed.) But a person may reply that he has a station wagon, or a truck, or a tractor, or a taxi. A salesmen, or the owner of a business firm, may reply that he has a car at his disposal but that it is registered in the name of his company. In such cases, the question arises how, for the purposes of the given survey, "car ownership" is defined. Theoretically, it is possible to give the set of definitions to the interviewers and ask them to make the check marks by keeping the definitions in mind. But interviewers in the course of an interview are overburdened with innumerable tasks; hence greater reliability is obtained if the definitions are uniformly applied in the central office, that is, if the interviewer has only to write out the answers.

The same point may be illustrated by discussing not car ownership but car purchases (for instance, during the calendar year preceding the interview) and the prices paid for the cars bought. Studying the results of such inquiries, it can be shown that single, direct questions do not yield exact values. Even if the question specifies that one would like to know the total price paid, including trade-in values, people in some cases include and in some cases exclude charges for "extras" and installment charges. In interviews conducted in a conversational manner, it is possible to make sure that the respondents understand what the question implies; and by having the interviewers write down the answers as nearly verbatim as possible, it can be made sure that the analysts understand what the answers really mean.

Proceeding to somewhat more complex questions, we may refer to an inquiry about expectations which, in the Survey of Consumer Finances conducted early in 1949, read as follows: "What do you think will happen to the prices of the things you buy during 1949—do you think they will go up, or down, or stay about where they are now?" This question, as far as it goes, is a multiple-choice question. (Yet it is formulated so as to make it relatively simple for the respondent to answer, "I don't know" or "How should I know?") As such it does not suffice to give clear and reliable information about the price expectations held by the respondents. In the surveys, it is followed by several open-ended questions as, for instance,

"Why will they [the prices] do that?" or "Why do you think so?" and also by questions about the prices of different types of commodities and the degree of expected price changes. By scrutinizing detailed answers to all these questions, one finds that the respondent may have replied to the first question, "They will go up," because he expected rents to go up, while his real answer to the question, as revealed by later answers, was "Prices of things I buy will remain the same." By probing about reasons for opinions, one may make sure that the respondents understand the question (or how they understand it), and one may make sure that the analysts understand the answers.

The why question is the most important and most useful open-ended question in surveys. A questionnaire may properly include, for instance, a question such as, "Are you making as much money now as a year ago, or more, or less?" if this question is followed by one asking, "Why is that?" or "How come you made more (less)?" The second question may be useful in obtaining tabulations of factors contributing to income changes—such as higher or lower wage rates, more or less overtime, change in job, more or fewer people in the family working, etc. But even if these factors are of no interest for the study, the why question adds to the reliability of information on income increases or decreases and often serves to clarify the answers to the first question. For instance, an answer "same" may be revealed to refer to the same hourly wage rate received, and yet "a year ago" the respondent may have worked full time and "at present" half time.

In order to present a further example of open-ended questions, we may cite a section of the questionnaire used in the 1949 Survey of Consumer Finances:

> "Have you heard of a regulation on the amount you pay down and the time you can take to pay for an automobile, furniture, or household appliance you buy on installment? . . . What do you think of that regulation? . . . Why do you think so?"

The first question, seeking the respondent's level of information, was not expected to yield reliable data about the proportion of people who had heard of the regulation of installment credit. It was probable that some people would answer such a question in the affirmative because they would be reluctant to reveal their ignorance. The purpose of that question was to weed out those people of whom the next question could not be asked, and to introduce that open-ended question: "What do you think of the regulation?"

What has been called the "funnel arrangement" of questions represents a useful solution to some interviewing problems. First, a rather general question is asked, but it is followed by one in the same area that is somewhat narrower, and finally by a specific question. Suppose we wish to find out why a person with substantial means has no investments in common stock. Instead of asking him directly—which may make it difficult for him to reveal his ignorance about the stock market and may induce him to invent an answer—we may better start out with general and impersonal questions. We may try to find out in what forms, in his opinion, people should keep their savings and what the advantages and disadvantages of different kinds of investments are. We may want to know whether the respondent spontaneously mentions common stock, or considerations of "yield" or "speculation," before we ask direct and possibly suggestive questions.

These principles of interviewing are of particular importance if we turn to inquiries into what many people consider personal matters, such as, for instance, the size of their bank deposits. First, again, problems of definition arise. The questionnaire must be drawn up so as to encompass all kinds of bank deposits (checking accounts, savings accounts, shares in savings and loan associations, etc.) and all the accounts a person or a family has. Then there is the question of rapport. Obviously, an interviewer cannot just ring a doorbell and ask about the size of the person's bank deposits. In this respect, the study of people's opinions and of their financial position in one and the same survey, and therefore in the same interview, helps to a great extent. Attitudinal questions letting people express their opinions and voice their grievances help to build rapport. Embedded into attitudinal questions, questions regarding personal matters can be asked with much greater chance of success. After a person has expressed his opinions about bank deposits or common stock, he may be much more willing to tell the truth about his having or not having such investments.

These considerations should not imply that answers can be obtained to all kinds of questions from all respondents. If respondents refuse to answer certain questions, second inquiries or letters may help, but some errors due to nonresponse will aways remain, as will some reporting errors. With respect to certain questions, people's reluctance to answer has proved to be so large that the questions have had to be excluded from the survey. The most conspicuous examples of such failures have been inquiries about currency holdings. In repeated attempts it has been impossible to find out how much cash people have locked away in safe-deposit boxes or elsewhere.

There are other questions, too, which, though they may be easily asked and usually bring prompt replies, must be used with caution or even excluded from surveys. Questions referring to distant past events need to be mentioned first in this connection. Studies about memory errors, conducted by asking the same people the same question at different intervals, have confirmed the well-known psychological findings that memory is selective and later developments falsify our recollection of earlier events. Asking people now about their income before the war may therefore be useless for the purpose of determining prewar income distributions (of people still alive).[6] The question may, however, be useful in grouping people into those who think that they now make more and those who think that they now make less than before the war, which current attitudes may be relevant in certain respects. Questions about remote past motives and attitudes seem, however, to be rather useless. People will willingly tell why they bought their houses several years ago, or whether they expected inflation or unemployment at the end of the war—but there seems to be no way to find out whether their answers reflect what they actually thought at the time.

Asking people how they would behave if certain developments should occur—President Roosevelt called such questions "iffy"—is a kind of question that must be used with great caution. If the contingency mentioned is one of which most people had never thought before, or one which appears unrealistic at a given moment, the answers may be misleading. When, for instance, in a consumer survey conducted shortly after the end of the war, people were asked whether they would buy certain goods if their prices fell by 10 per cent, most people replied in the affirmative. Further inquiries revealed, however, that at the same time most people expected prices to go up or at least to stay stable. The supposition of the 10 per cent drop in the prices of automobiles, for instance, was apparently understood by many people as if a gift of 10 per cent were offered to them. Their answers hardly disclosed how they actually would act if prices fell. On the other hand, of course, it may be useful to ask those people who say that their incomes will probably or possibly decline how they will behave—what they will purchase, how much they will save, etc.—if their expectation comes true.

A further type of question which by itself may be misleading and should be used only as an introduction to a detailed inquiry is one which asks for general opinions about broad issues. When, for instance, during the war, businessmen were asked, "What do you think of price control?" the replies often reflected political arguments or statements publicized by trade associations at the given moment. Detailed inquiry about how different provisions of price control had worked out in the respondent's own business, and how he felt about these provisions, frequently contradicted the answers received to the general question. If we ask a business executive, "How do you set your prices?" or "What are the major considerations you take into account before investing money?" most commonly we receive replies reproducing textbook statements or rationalizations about what would be an intelligent

---

[6] In recent, still unpublished studies it has been found that even the passage of one year makes a great difference. Data on people's income in 1947 obtained at the beginning of 1949 differed in many instances from the same data obtained at the beginning of 1948. The differences reflected, among other things, income developments in 1948.

or a desired procedure. There is no assurance that the replies reflect actual behavior. Generalizations about price setting and investing ought to emerge from analysis of specific information. Detailed inquiries about the how and the why of specific instances of recent price and investment decisions, and correlation of such information with other characteristics of the businessmen concerned, appear to be the most promising method of such studies.[7]

In summary, then, the most important issues to which psychological-economic surveys may be properly addressed can be listed as follows: First, such surveys may serve to determine what respondents (households as well as firms) have done in the recent past and why they have done so. As an example: surveys can find out how many spending units in the nation bought cars during the year preceding the interview, what kind of spending units bought cars, and for what reasons they bought cars at that time. Second, surveys may serve to determine the financial position of the respondents at the time of the interview and the attitudes of the respondents toward their situation. As an example: surveys can ascertain the amounts of government bonds owned, the characteristics of people holding such bonds, and people's attitudes toward keeping or cashing those bonds. Third, surveys may serve to determine the plans and expectations of respondents and the factors responsible for them. As an example: it is possible to measure income expectations as well as people's intentions to buy certain durable goods during the year following the interview. The frequency of the intentions to buy will not provide a measure of prospective demand, but will reflect attitudes prevailing at the time of the interview from which, in certain circumstances, prospective changes in demand may be deduced.

RELIABILITY OF SURVEY DATA

Sample interview surveys, if properly conducted, yield information on the true order of magnitude of data but do not necessarily produce exact values. Information derived from such surveys is subject to sampling errors, to reporting errors, and to errors due to nonreporting.[8]

Sampling errors arise from the very fact that a sample is used instead of a complete enumeration. In probability sampling, such errors can be determined for each value as well as for differences in values. A sampling error does not measure the actual error of a particular sample finding but indicates the range on either side of the sample estimate within which the "true value" is expected to lie with a stated degree of probability (assuming there are no errors other than the sampling error). The size of the sampling

[7] This point has been elaborated in Chapter 5.

[8] We disregard here that errors may occur also in the recording of information by the interviewer and coder and in the tabulation and analysis process.

error depends on several factors, among which the size and the spread of the sample are important. The larger the sample, the smaller the sampling error, other things being equal.

As an illustration, the size of the sampling error in the Survey of Consumer Finances with its 3,500 "cases"—spending units in this instance—may be mentioned. In one of these surveys it was found, for instance, that 20 per cent of all spending units had incomes between $3,000 and $4,000 in 1948. The sampling error of this estimate is slightly less than 2 percentage points. This means that, except for nonsampling errors, the chances are 95 out of 100 that the true value lies within the range of 18 and 22 per cent. Furthermore, the chances are about 68 out of 100 that the true value lies within the range of 19 and 21 per cent. When, from data obtained in the same survey, data about the income size distribution of skilled workers are computed, the sampling error is larger because the estimate is based on a smaller cell (only some of the 3,500 heads of spending units interviewed are skilled workers).

Reporting errors and nonresponse errors are not precisely measurable. They may be as large as or larger than sampling errors. Reporting errors differ greatly according to the type of information under consideration. From data obtained through interviewing the same respondents twice, and from comparing survey findings with nonsurvey data, it appears probable that reporting errors are larger with respect to such quantitative financial data as the size of bank deposits held than with respect to automobile ownership or attitudinal information. Reporting errors are due primarily to errors of memory and sometimes to intentional falsification of the information given.

Nonresponse errors arise fom the fact that some respondents designated in a sample refuse to be interviewed, or refuse to give certain information, or cannot be found at home on repeated calls. Complex technical methods can be and have been used to reduce the effect of nonresponse errors, but in population samples they cannot be wholly excluded. Refusal to be interviewed is usually more frequent among high-income than among low-income families. The most important method of reducing reporting errors, as well as errors due to refusal to be interviewed, is the proper motivation of the respondent. Survey designs must be adapted to that purpose.

Some information about the joint effect of all survey errors can be derived from a comparison of aggregate data derived from surveys with outside estimates. Determining such aggregates as the total income of all families, or the number of automobiles owned, or the amounts paid for new automobiles purchased in a given year is, however, not the major purpose of the surveys discussed in these pages. Not only do microeconomic data represent distributions of income, automobile ownership, or purchase prices of automobiles (and of attitudes)—the information that the surveys are seeking—but the errors involved in such distribution data are also usually smaller than those in aggregate survey data. Moreover, comparisons between survey aggregates and outside estimates are often very complicated because of differences in definition and coverage. In those instances in which relatively reliable comparisons could be made—for instance, with respect to the number of automobile owners, the amount of United States government E bonds held, and also the amount of aggregate personal money income before taxes in different years—comparisons between Survey of Consumer Finances data and other estimates have shown differences of approximately 10 per cent.

In many instances, aggregates calculated from surveys were found to be consistently lower than estimates derived by other methods. Sampling errors are random errors that may cause either over- or underestimates and cannot explain the consistency of underestimations. There are, however, good reasons why reporting and nonresponse errors should cause survey findings to be lower than estimates derived from records of wages, salaries, or dividends paid out or bonds outstanding. Evidence indicates that the direction of the reporting and nonresponse errors is constant in successive surveys conducted by the same methods, and also that their extent does not vary greatly from survey to survey. It follows, then, that comparison of data obtained in successive surveys, or time trends of data, may be more reliable than survey information about conditions that prevail at one time. The reliability of year-to-year comparisons is subject primarily to random variations in the samples, which are measured by the sampling error.[9]

The fact that sampling errors increase when the size of the sample decreases imposes severe limitations on the analysis of survey data. In addition to information about all households in the nation, consumer surveys need to determine the characteristics of certain groups of households. When the population is divided into a small number of groups—for instance, into five or ten income groups—relatively satisfactory data can be obtained from a sample of 3,500 units. But it may be important to measure the characteristics or the behavior of groups that are homogeneous with respect to several variables. The testing of economic hypotheses, in particular, often requires the simultaneous study of several factors. For instance, as we have seen in an earlier chapter, it would be desirable, in studying saving, to be able to make separate groupings of people who are similar, not only in regard to present income, but also in regard to past income, income expec-

[9] The most important statistical information to supplement survey tabulations consists, therefore, of the presentation of sampling errors of differences. For the size of sampling errors in the Surveys of Consumer Finances, see "Methods of the Survey of Consumer Finances," *Federal Reserve Bulletin,* July, 1950.

tations, age, and size of liquid-asset holdings. But if we divided a sample of 3,500 units into such highly refined categories, the resulting groups would be so small that any inferences we might draw from comparing them with one another would have no firm statistical base.

The simplest method of overcoming this difficulty would appear to be to increase the size of the sample. In many instances, however, this is not a practicable solution. Even disregarding considerations of cost, it is almost inevitable that various nonrandom errors would increase if the size of the sample were increased considerably. Interviewers would then be likely to be less carefully selected and less well trained; uniformity of interviewing procedures could not be assured, nor could the best methods of reducing reporting errors and checking the findings be applied. The relative importance of nonsampling errors presents a strong argument for using small samples. Furthermore, it follows from these considerations that complete enumeration (census) is not necessarily more reliable than a sample survey. With respect to information that is subject to large reporting errors, census data would be relatively unreliable. To collect such information, a census would be a waste of money. The Bureau of the Census is well aware of this fact and therefore conducts many of its enumerations on a sample basis.

To overcome the limitations imposed by the size of the sample, several complex methods may be used. One of them, applied in the Surveys of Consumer Finances and mentioned before, is to oversample those parts of the universe that are of special interest but would appear only in relatively few instances if a straight cross-section sample were used. Another method is to test hypotheses by considering the samples of two or more successive surveys jointly. Finally, statistical methods of holding certain variables constant or studying covariation within a large cell may be used.

SURVEYS OF BUSINESSMEN AND BUSINESS FIRMS

The importance of fixed-question—free-answer interviewing and of motivating the respondents may loom even larger in interviewing business owners or executives concerning their business affairs than in consumer interviewing. Businessmen must be interested in a survey and appreciate its aims in order to reveal what some of them may consider business secrets. Since business records are frequently kept in forms different from the terms of the survey, and definitions of investments, costs, or inventories differ in different firms, clarification of the meaning of replies and comparability of the information received poses difficult problems that can be solved only through detailed interviewing. Perhaps the most effective method of getting businessmen to cooperate in surveys is to give them an opportunity to express their own opinions, to discuss their own grievances, and to give their own views about how things should be done. Such methods were used in the wartime survey of pricing practices conducted by the Cowles Commission for Research in Economics, information from which was used especially in Part Three of this book.

In several recent business surveys, which yielded valuable results, somewhat different methods were used. A brief discussion of their methods is, therefore, in order. We shall refer only to surveys that deal primarily or partly with psychological variables, thereby disregarding the enumeration of economic data (prices charged, orders received, etc.).

Two Federal agencies, the Securities and Exchange Commission and the Office of Business Economics in the Department of Commerce, are conducting quarterly surveys concerning past and expected nonfarm plant and equipment outlays. Close to 1,000 corporations registered with the SEC and more than 1,000 unregistered manufacturing concerns are canvassed. The method used is the mail questionnaire. Form letters are sent to the business firms asking for three kinds of information: expenditures for new plant, expenditures for new machinery and equipment, and expenditures for used plant and equipment. The firms are asked to write down the amounts of each of these expenditures (1) for the last quarter, before the receipt of the inquiry, (2) for the current quarter, and (3) for the next quarter. In addition, once a year, annual past and annual anticipated expenditures are also requested.

Not much information is available about the sampling aspects of this survey nor about the frequency and significance of nonresponse. The form of the questions used raises several problems already discussed. As has been pointed out, the meaning of a concept may differ from respondent to respondent, and when only a single direct question is asked there is no assurance that every respondent will understand the terms in the same way. The blank of the SEC survey calls for exclusion of "costs incurred for maintenance and repairs," which may or may not be a simple procedure for a firm and may or may not be uniformly applied. The problem of meaning looms especially large with respect to the study of anticipated expenditures. They may include such categories as projects under way, orders placed or money appropriated for projects definitely decided upon, reproduction of budget estimates approved by the board of directors or chief executives, as well as more or less vague ideas about plans, intentions, or anticipated needs. To what extent each firm includes each category is not known. To the extent that reported anticipated expenditures represent projects under way or orders placed, a relatively close correspondence between anticipated expenditures and actual expenditures as determined several months later is to be expected.[10]

What is missing in these surveys are, of course, the why questions, intended to clarify the factors responsible for anticipated behavior. The form of the SEC inquiry compels the business firm to state one definite amount of expenditure for a given future quarter. Some expenditures may, however, be of what is called in surveys the "depend on" type. If sales increase, or if certain technological developments take place, or if prices fall, a firm would act in a certain way; otherwise, it would act in a different way. Since the SEC surveys do not include information about contingencies or study the factors responsible for various expectations, these surveys may be considered a useful preliminary step but not the final answer to the analysis of prospective investment expenditures.

The SEC–Commerce Department surveys are, of course, not planned for the purpose of enriching our knowledge of the dynamics of business decisions. With respect to their primary purpose, to present advance information as to an increase or decrease in future capital expenditures, errors in any single survey may be of small importance provided successive surveys are comparable (that is, if reporting and nonresponse errors of successive surveys are similar in direction and extent). The following crucial question emerges therefore: Do businessmen include tentative expenditure plans in their reports to the same extent when conditions seem to be improving as when they seem to be deteriorating? We do not as yet know the answer to this question.

The problems and questions raised about the SEC–Commerce Department inquiry are understandable in view of the present relatively undeveloped stage of surveying business firms. Not so easily justified, however, is the form in which the results are published, which consists of nothing but extrapolated aggregate expenditure data (by five groups of industries). Certainly the size distribution of the anticipated expenditures, and the proportion and distribution of increases and decreases, should be made available.

A second organization which has recently started surveying business expectations for the purpose of determining prospective business trends is Dun & Bradstreet, Inc. This organization uses the method of personal interviews with the executives of a sample of large business concerns. The sample is drawn from carefully collected lists but the firms are not weighted by size. Questions are asked about the amount of sales, new orders received,

---

[10] This is especially true in a time of shortages such as prevailed shortly after the war, when the time elapsed between placing orders and receiving machinery or equipment was considerable and therefore no last-minute orders could be placed and cancellations of orders were rare.

inventories, net profits, number of employees, and level of selling prices. In addition to questions about past changes, the respondents are asked for each of these items to compare the next future quarter with the corresponding period of the previous year. According to the technique used in earlier mail inquiries, which apparently has been maintained, the interviewer inquires concerning each item whether there will be "any change (plus, minus, or zero)" and then about what the "approximate extent of change in per cent" will be. This form of questioning no doubt reduces the "don't know" and "depends-on" answers: the questions suggest to the respondent that he ought to know how many per cent the dollar volume of his sales or profits will increase or decrease. The underlying theoretical assumption appears to be that every businessman has definite expectations concerning every aspect of his business.

The frequent and prompt publication of the change in the proportion of business firms expecting higher, lower, or unchanged sales, orders, and profits, represents a valuable index of business sentiment. Of great interest would be a comparison of expressed expectations with subsequent reports about actual developments on the part of the same firms.

The annual McGraw-Hill Survey, conducted during the last few years by the Department of Economics of the McGraw-Hill Publishing Company, consists of several carefully formulated questions concerning expected capital expenditures. The sample, drawn from business listings, covers "larger" firms of each industry only. A mail questionnaire is used. No information is available about the response rate. One of the merits of the survey is that it provides information about types of planned expenditure (expansion, modernization, also methods of financing) in addition to dollar amounts of plans, and also about some contingencies and long-range needs of business firms. The data are presented by type of industry.

What is most needed in the field of business surveys is more basic research rather than additional collection of data thought to be useful for practical purposes. Figures on construction contracts and permits, for instance, are collected and published regularly and present useful information on relevant ex ante variables. But information on the considerations that enter into builders' or contractors' decisions to construct apartment houses and one-family houses for sale may ultimately be of much greater usefulness for predicting forthcoming business trends and assisting economic policies. Such information could be collected through repeated surveys in which executives of firms engaged in "speculative building" are interviewed about what they had done in the recent past and why, what projects they considered but did not carry out, what plans they are considering at the given moment, and what developments the carrying out of these plans depends on.

RESEARCH PROSPECTS

Experiments constitute the most important research method of natural science. There is a widespread belief that in social science, and especially in economics, experiments are impossible. This opinion appears to be correct only if the term "experiment" is defined in a rather restricted way.

Experimentation has been characterized as cross-examining nature. More specifically, its essence is the controlled variation of isolated variables. By keeping all variables constant except the one which he wants to manipulate, the experimenter observes the effects of experimentally produced changes on that variable. The manipulation by the experimenter may, however, not be essential for experiments, although it facilitates and hastens the observations. One variable may happen to undergo certain measurable changes due to forces not produced by the experimenter. That all variables except one remain constant is likewise not inevitably necessary, and in many scientific experiments this goal is not accomplished. In biological and psychological experiments, especially, the experimenter must often accept small variations in conditions. The assumption is made that if an experiment is repeated often enough, the changes in variables other than the experimental variable will cancel out. Thus, in an experiment in which rats run a maze once under conditions of hunger and once under conditions of thirst, it is assumed that all other differences can be disregarded, provided a sufficiently large number of rats is used and the experiment is repeated a sufficient number of times.

Similar conditions prevail in social sciences, including economic psychology. The fact that experimental manipulation may not be possible does not preclude the use of a common form of experiment, namely, the before-after experiment. A situation may be observed before an event takes place—such as the enactment of a new law or the outbreak of war—and again after it has taken place. Of course, if the event is not anticipated, the situation may not be observed systematically before the event, and in some instances the observer may have to wait several years until the changes that are needed to test hypotheses actually occur (for instance, effects of depression cannot be observed in prosperous times).

Breaking down survey data obtained through detailed interviewing appears to approach the criterion of cross-examining nature. When, for instance, the social scientist intends to study the effects of changes in income, he does not need to manipulate incomes; he can make controlled observations without controlling conditions. From data obtained in carefully conducted surveys, he can keep the other relevant variables constant by observing the behavior of groups whose members are identical with respect to these other variables—current income level, wealth, age, and expectations. The technical difficulties involved in this procedure have been mentioned before. In addition to the problems raised by the number of variables that need to be considered, there is no doubt that "control of conditions" is achieved to a much greater extent in experimentation than in the process of analytical breakdown of data. To some extent it helps in this respect if the fact gathering and the analysis are done by the same person or the same organization—which is usually the case in experiments as well as in economic sample surveys. In spite of all the difficulties involved in attempting to create the equivalent of experimental variation through analysis, some progress has already been achieved with this method and there are reasonable hopes for greater success in the future.

In social psychology, progress has recently been made in carrying out experiments by manipulating variables. A new type of experiment, "action research," initiated primarily by Kurt Lewin and his associates, consists of first observing social behavior, then injecting certain experimentally induced changes in that behavior—for instance, by spreading a rumor or by changing the leaders of a group—and then observing social behavior again. Such methods may be applied to economic psychology in the future. Even if experimental variation were to be achieved only with a very small group of selected families, responses to certain changes in needs or prices could be usefully investigated. That one of the large social-science research groups will one day be in a position to create experimental changes in supply or demand and observe the effects of these changes does not appear impossible.

Panel studies with groups of consumers offer other interesting possibilities. A group of people may be interviewed, say, every month over a period of a year, or once a year over a period of ten years. By using this method, changes in conditions and resulting changes in behavior may be studied. The theory of consumer demand may profit from monthly panel studies, and the theory of saving may profit from linking consumption and saving patterns with life cycles.

The psychological analysis of economic behavior is, as has been repeatedly stated in these pages, in its very beginning. Similarly, its research methods have not yet been fully developed. Research methods currently in use must be improved and new avenues of research opened up. Although the direction of progress cannot be predicted, it appears that detailed interviewing surveys, yielding quantitative data based on a random sample of consumers or business managers, will for a long time remain the most important research tool of economic psychology. Such surveys represent a basic method of social science and should be applied to an increasing extent to the study of economic behavior.

Psychological-economic surveys are at the same time a method of basic research and of research intended to satisfy practical needs. Attempting to arrive at valid generalizations—the aim of basic research—can be combined with endeavoring to find solutions to specific problems of the day and even represents what will ultimately prove the best means of achieving practical aims. If this function of scientific research is more widely understood, larger funds than heretofore may be channeled to studies that are basic and therefore practical.

NOTES TO CHAPTER 15

SAMPLING

The following publications may be referred to regarding sampling theory, statistics, and techniques: M. H. Hansen and W. N. Hurwitz, "On the Theory of Sampling from Finite Populations," *Annals of Mathematical Statistics,* Vol. 14, 1943, pp. 333*ff.*; Frank Yates, *Sampling Methods for Censuses and Surveys,* London, New York, 1949; E. E. Houseman, "Designs of Samples for Surveys," *Agricultural Economics Research,* Vol. 1, 1949; W. Edwards Deming, *Some Theory of Sampling,* New York, 1950.

The sample of the Surveys of Consumer Finances is discussed in "Methods of the Survey of Consumer Finances," *Federal Reserve Bulletin,* July, 1950, and Appendix to articles on Survey of Consumer Finances, *Federal Reserve Bulletin,* June, 1947, June, 1948, and June, 1949; Roe Goodman, "Sampling for the 1947 Survey of Consumer Finances," *Journal of the American Statistical Association,* Vol. 42, 1947, pp. 439*ff.*; Roe Goodman and E. E. Maccoby, "Sampling Methods and Sampling Errors in Surveys of Consumer Finances," *International Journal of Opinion and Attitude Research,* Vol. 2, 1948, pp. 349*ff.*

For sampling within households, see Leslie Kish, "A Procedure for Objective Respondent Selection within the Household," *Journal of the American Statistical Association,* Vol. 44, 1949, pp. 380*ff.*

For principles of sampling business firms, see George Katona, *Price Control and Business,* Bloomington, Ind., 1945.

The sample of each annual Survey of Consumer Finances consisted of people not previously interviewed, with the exception of the 1949 Survey. The sample of that survey contained, in addition to "new" respondents, a sample of urban respondents who had been interviewed in the 1948 Survey (and who had not moved during 1948). A subsample of the 1949 Survey respondents was also reinterviewed in a special survey conducted in November, 1949. Frequent use has been made in this book of the results of these two consecutive interviews with identical respondents. (The analysis of the reinterviews has been made possible by grants of the Rockefeller Foundation to the University of Michigan.)

The failure of the 1948 election polls led to the publication of several studies on quota and area sampling (as well as on other problems of polling and interviewing). The book published by the Social Science Research Council, *The Pre-*

election Polls of 1948, New York, 1949, contains valuable data. Articles by Rensis Likert, "The Public Opinion Polls," *Scientific American,* Vol. 179, 1948, pp. 7*ff.*, and Daniel Katz, "Polling Methods and the 1948 Polling Failure," *International Journal of Opinion and Attitude Research,* Vol. 2, 1948–1949, pp. 469*ff.*, emphasize differences between polling and scientific survey methods.

MAIL QUESTIONNAIRES

For specific problems involving mail questionnaires, see the articles by M. H. Hansen and W. N. Hurwitz, "The Problem of Non-response in Sample Surveys," *Journal of the American Statistical Association,* Vol. 41, 1946, pp. 517*ff.*, and "Controlling Bias in Mail Questionnaires," J. A. Clausen and R. N. Ford, *Journal of the American Statistical Association,* Vol. 42, 1947, pp. 497*ff.*

Mail questionnaires with a very low rate of response are still being used to assemble important economic information that is then published in a form which suggests that the surveys have yielded exact and reliable data. As one example for many, the article "Income of Dentists, 1942–1948" in the *Survey of Current Business,* January, 1950, pp. 8*ff.*, may be mentioned. The mail questionnaire requested data about the gross income, cost of practice, net income from independent practice, etc., for each of the years 1944 to 1948. The proportion of usable returns was 11.3 per cent. Because the response rate of members of the American Dental Association was higher than that of nonmembers, the information received from members and nonmembers was weighted differently. Yet it is impossible to tell whether high-income Dental Association members replied more or less frequently than low-income members, and high-income nonmembers more or less frequently than low-income nonmembers. Nevertheless, the results of the questionnaire have been used to publish numerous tables on the mean and median income of all dentists, and of groups of dentists, in different years. (In previous studies of similar kind, the response rate to mail questionnaires varied between 9½ and 30 per cent; see Milton Friedman and Simon Kuznets, *Income from Independent Professional Practice,* National Bureau of Economic Research, New York, 1945.)

A mail questionnaire sent to 430 Southern manufacturing firms, of which 58 firms sent usable replies, is the basis of an analysis of important business decisions by R. A. Lester ("Shortcomings of Marginal Analysis and Wage-Employment Problems," *American Economic Review,* Vol. 36, 1946, pp. 63*ff.*). The questionnaire used by Lester and his method of analysis have been severely criticized by Fritz Machlup ("Marginal Analysis and Empirical Research," *American Economic Review,* Vol. 36, 1946, pp. 519*ff.*). Although Machlup's demonstration of the pitfalls of Lester's methods has, as far as the author knows, not been contradicted, Lester's "findings" are still widely quoted.

In the well-known election poll conducted by the *Literary Digest* in 1936, the response rate was approximately 20 per cent out of a mailing of ten million. The erroneous prediction made—that Roosevelt would be defeated—was due, in that case, to a biased sample as well as to the nonresponse.

Interviewing

For a discussion of the interviewing methods developed by the Division of Program Surveys, see E. E. Maccoby and R. R. Holt, "How Surveys Are Made," *Journal of Social Issues*, Vol. 2, 1946, pp. 45*ff.*, and also L. S. Cottrell, Jr., and Sylvia Eberhart, *American Opinion on World Affairs in the Atomic Age*, Princeton, N. J., 1948. (The last-named book contains also a verbatim reproduction of interviews on international affairs.) The interviewing method as applied to the Surveys of Consumer Finances has been discussed in the articles of the *Federal Reserve Bulletin*, cited above, as well as in the following papers: Angus Campbell and George Katona, "A National Survey of Wartime Savings," *Public Opinion Quarterly*, Vol. 10, 1946, pp. 373*ff.*; E. E. Maccoby, "Interviewing Problems in Financial Surveys," *International Journal of Opinion and Attitude Research*, Vol. 1, 1947; Rensis Likert, "The Sample Interview Survey," in *Current Trends in Psychology*, Pittsburgh, 1948.

Methodological aspects of the Surveys of Consumer Finances are discussed in the articles by Selma F. Goldsmith, and by R. Wasson, A. Hurwitz, and I. Schweiger in the forthcoming Volume 13 of *Studies in Income and Wealth* (National Bureau of Economic Research).

On question wording, see Hadley Cantril, *Gauging Public Opinion*, Princeton, N. J., 1944, and on various interviewing methods, P. F. Lazarsfeld, "The Controversy over Detailed Interviews," *Public Opinion Quarterly*, Vol. 8, 1944, pp. 38*ff.*

Problems of analysis of interview data are discussed by Quinn McNemar, "Opinion-Attitude Methodology," *Psychological Bulletin*, Vol. 43, 1946, pp. 289*ff.*, and by Hans Zeisel, *Say It with Figures*, New York, London, 1947.

The large-scale 1935–1936 Study of Consumer Purchases resulted in two important publications (*Consumer Incomes in the United States: Their Distribution in 1935–36*, and *Consumer Expenditures in the United States: Estimates for 1935–36*, by the National Resources Committee, 1938 and 1939), while the most important report of the 1941–1942 study is "Family Spending and Saving in Wartime," *Bulletin* 822 of the U.S. Department of Labor, Bureau of Labor Statistics, 1945. In addition to the Surveys of Consumer Finances, postwar consumer-income surveys have also been made by the Bureau of the Census, and consumer-opinion surveys by the National Opinion Research Center and *Fortune Magazine*. The Dominion Bureau of Statistics in Canada uses in its Surveys of Family Expenditures the interesting method of distributing questionnaires and calling for them some time later. During the personal visit, it is possible for the interviewer to go through the blanks with the respondents.

Sampling and interviewing methods of the Division of Program Surveys have also been used in the studies of morale conducted by the U.S. Strategic Bombing Surveys under the direction of Rensis Likert.

As an illustration of interviewing techniques, detailed accounts of some aspects of the Survey of Consumer Finances interviews will be presented here. Following are some of the phrases which have been used by interviewers as part of their introductory remarks:

"My name is ————, and I am working for the Survey Research Center. We are doing a survey for the government [or for the Federal Reserve Board] here in ———— ———— and other cities over the country. We are interested in how people are getting along financially and what their outlook is for the future. This survey is concerned with saving and spending, and so we like to talk to the head of the household [wage earner] whenever we can."

"Probably you'd like to know how I happened to stop here. In a city of this size they just select houses around the block by chance and this just happened to be the one."

"During the years since the war, there have been a lot of economic changes in the country—in people's incomes, in the amount of money they can save, and in their plans for spending the money they saved during the war. The information in this survey is needed by businessmen, the government, labor unions, and many other groups concerned with the economic welfare of the country."

The introduction is varied according to the socioeconomic status of the person to whom it is addressed. Sometimes the respondents are told:

"We made a survey like this a year ago and another the year before. We have interviewed over 9,000 people all around the country. Here I can show you how they used the answers that people made in that survey. You can see that no names are mentioned or anything like that—it's just a question of how many people answer the questions in the different ways."

Three important points are illustrated by an experience of one interviewer, which will be retold here. First, questions relating to such financial data as income, assets, and debts must be addressed to the head of the household, who usually can be reached only in the evening. (Most census blanks are filled out by the housewife and many surveys are satisfied with interviewing whoever happens to be at home.) Second, personal information is often revealed to a stranger though it would not be told to an acquaintance or relative. Finally, interviewing is both a difficult job and an art that requires ability to talk to people, understanding of human relations, and perseverance. The following account is, of course, not typical:

"My respondent—a small businessman about 50 years of age—was pleasant and cooperative as long as I asked him about his opinions and about housing and automobiles. When I came to the income questions, he replied, 'I'm not giving that information to anybody.' I tried in vain to explain the importance of the information for the survey. He refused even to indicate the approximate range of his income or his assets. Finally I gave up. His wife, who during the interview had sat in the corner of the room, knitting, accompanied me to the door and said: 'Don't take it so hard; I'm married to him for twenty-five years and I don't know how much money he makes.'

"This gave me an idea. I talked to the wife and found out that Wednesday evenings she attended a club meeting downtown. So I returned the following Wednesday, found the man alone at home, told him that I had forgotten to ask a few questions during my previous visit, and in the course of the conversation obtained income data without much difficulty."

Parts of an interview obtained in the 1948 Survey of Consumer Finances will be reproduced here to illustrate the fixed-question—free-answer interviewing method. The respondent was a junior high school teacher, veteran, between 35 and 44 years of age, married, having a 5-year-old daughter.

Q.: Would you say *you* people are better off or worse off financially now than you were a year ago?

A.: That question is a little hard to answer in a way, but I would say worse off, for the simple reason that we had the expense of moving to the Coast from Virginia last August and we think the price of our home here is inflated.

Q.: Any other reason?

A.: No, only that we have the debt now for the home and furniture we bought here.

Q.: Are you making as much money now as you were a year ago, more or less?

A.: Yes, we are making about an equal salary.

Q.: How about a year from now—do you think that you will be making more money or less money than you are now, or will you be making about the same?

A.: Well, my salary will be more next year.

Q.: Why will that be?

A.: Last year the teachers' salaries were increased and might be raised again some. And the salaries are also based on the type of diploma you hold. I am taking courses summers and expect an increase based upon additional credits I will have earned.

Q.: Now considering the country as a whole, do you think we will have good times or bad times or what during the next twelve months or so?

A.: Well, I think that would be based on whether the high cost of living is decreased or increased. I definitely don't think we can go on just as we are. We think prices are definitely going to have to come down. So I suppose I could say I think things will be fair and some better. I don't look for a *great* drop in prices but some decrease, and that should make for some improvement, it would seem to me.

Q.: Do you consider that we are having good times or bad times now?

A.: I would say they are just fair now; I wouldn't say these are really good times because prices are just out of line for set incomes.

Following these questions, information was obtained about the house and the furniture bought by the respondent and about his income. The following attitudinal questions, asked later in the interview, serve not only the purpose of obtaining relevant information but also facilitate inquiries about respondent's assets.

Q.: Suppose a man has some money over and above what he needs for his regular expenses. What do you think he should do nowadays—spend it to raise his standard of living, save it, or what?

A.: I'd say to save it for future needs when he might have illness or have to buy a home or some real need might arise.

Q.: Why do you think that is best?

A.: Well, he wouldn't have to go into debt and could continue right along with his usual standard of living and still have money to meet unexpected expenses or emergencies as illness.

Q.: Suppose he decides not to spend that money. He can either put it in a bank or in bonds or he can invest it. What do you think would be the wisest thing for him to do with the money nowadays—put it in the bank, buy savings bonds with it, invest it in real estate, or buy common stock with it?

A.: Bonds, I think. Real estate is too greatly inflated to invest in, as we found out having to buy our home. Or putting his money in the bank is equally good compared with bonds. It can be cashed out either from bonds or bank very readily when needed and draws interest both places if left. Real estate has upkeep expense and depreciates.

Q.: You didn't discuss stock. What do you think about that?

A.: No, I wouldn't recommend stock. Only a few people know enough about that to keep from making a poor investment.

BUSINESS SURVEYS

The report on the wartime surveys on business pricing is contained in George Katona's *Price Control and Business,* Bloomington, Ind., 1945.

The Securities and Exchange Commission–Commerce Department data on plant and equipment expenditures are regularly published in the *Survey of Current Business* (for example, in the issue of December, 1949). After the manuscript for this book was completed, a detailed analysis was published of the relation between anticipated and actual capital expenditures as determined in these surveys (Irwin Friend and Jean Bronfenbrenner, "Business Investment Programs and Their Realization," *Survey of Current Business,* December, 1950, pp. 11ff.). It discloses a fairly wide dispersion between the actual annual outlays and the expectations of identical firms. The largest firms were, however, much more accurate in their anticipations than the smallest firms. In a special mail questionnaire a check list of reasons for differences between actual and anticipated expenditures in 1949 was presented to those firms which showed large percentage differences in the extent of realizing their plans. Although much interesting information has been obtained, the check-list method is not sufficient to provide reliable information about the factors influencing decision formation.

Dun & Bradstreet, Inc., began its studies on business expectations with a "Survey on Business Expectations and Governmental Policies" for the Joint Committee on the Economic Report in 1947 (mimeographed report).

The McGraw-Hill surveys are published in *Business Week* (see the issues of Jan. 22, 1949, and Jan. 21, 1950).

An evaluation of the surveys of actual and intended business investments has been presented by the Council of Economic Advisers in the *Midyear Economic Report of the President*, July, 1949, pp. 75*ff.*, Washington, D.C., 1949.

In addition to the surveys mentioned in the text, the *Fortune* Forum of Executive Opinion collects a variety of interesting data on the opinions and expectations of executives regarding both their own businesses and business in general. The method used is the mail questionnaire containing multiple-choice questions. A research project on "Expectations and Business Fluctuations," conducted at the University of Illinois, may also be referred to because it is expected to contribute in the future to the clarification of several problems discussed in this book. The study published by Friend and Bronfenbrenner, referred to above, is an outgrowth of that research project.

RESEARCH PROSPECTS

On experimentation in social science, see Ernest Greenwood, *Experimental Sociology*, New York, 1945, and F. Stuart Chapin, *Experimental Designs in Sociological Research*, New York, 1947. On action research, see Dorwin Cartwright, "Basic and Applied Social Psychology," *Philosophy of Science*, Vol. 6, 1949, pp. 198*ff.*

Panel studies have been used and studied primarily by Paul F. Lazarsfeld, who points to their particular importance for the purpose of clarifying turnover in opinions. See, for instance, P. F. Lazarsfeld, Bernard Berelson, and Hazel Gaudet, *The People's Choice*, New York, 1948, 2d ed.

Simon Kuznets, in his presidential address delivered at the December, 1949, annual meeting of the American Statistical Association ("Conditions of Statistical Research," *Journal of the American Statistical Association*, Vol. 45, 1950, pp. 1*ff.*), analyzes the supply of statistics and the errors involved in statistics not based on experimentation. He points out that the supply of data is "capricious" because of its origin in social needs and its dependence on administrative decisions and costs. For planning the supply of statistics in the future, he emphasizes the necessity of relating basic research to the collection of primary data. Specifically, he calls attention to one shortcoming in many of our statistical data collected for purposes other than scientific study: "As a rule, collectors and publishers of primary data do not deem it their obligation to accompany a series by a detailed description of how it was obtained; and users, also, for the most part, tend to accept a series, particularly one issued by a governmental agency, at its face value without inquiring into its reliability" (*op. cit.*, p. 12). Kuznets' demand for "explicit description of how the data were obtained" is particularly applicable to psychological-economic data.

SELECTED BIBLIOGRAPHY

ABRAMOVITZ, MOSES: *An Approach to a Price Theory for a Changing Economy,* Columbia University Press, New York, 1939.

ABRAMOVITZ, MOSES: "Role of Inventories in Business Cycles," *Occasional Paper* 26, National Bureau of Economic Research, 1948.

ANGELL, J. W.: *Investment and Business Cycles,* McGraw-Hill, New York, 1941.

ASCH, S. E.: "The Doctrine of Suggestion, Prestige and Imitation in Social Psychology," *Psychological Review,* Vol. 55, 1948.

BEAN, L. H.: "Relation of Disposable Income and the Business Cycle to Expenditures," *Review of Economic Statistics,* Vol. 28, 1946.

BOULDING, K. E.: "The Incidence of a Profits Tax," *American Economic Review,* Vol. 34, 1944.

BOULDING, K. E.: *The Economics of Peace,* Prentice-Hall, New York, 1945.

BOULDING, K. E.: *Economic Analysis,* Harper, New York, 1948 (rev. ed.).

BRADY, D. S.: "Expenditures, Savings, and Income," *Review of Economic Statistics,* Vol. 28, 1946.

BRADY, D. S., and R. D. FRIEDMAN: "Savings and the Income Distribution," *Studies in Income and Wealth,* Vol. 10, National Bureau of Economic Research, New York, 1947.

BRIDGMAN, P. W.: *The Logic of Modern Physics,* Macmillan, New York, 1938.

Bureau of Labor Statistics, U.S. Department of Labor, "Family Spending and Saving in Wartime," *Bulletin* 822, 1944.

BURNS, A. R.: *Economic Research and the Keynesian Thinking of Our Times,* National Bureau of Economic Research, New York, 1946.

BURNS, A. R.: "Keynesian Economics Once Again," *Review of Economic Statistics,* Vol. 29, 1947.

CAMPBELL, ANGUS: "The Uses of Interview Surveys in Federal Administration," *Journal of Social Issues,* Vol. 2, 1946.

CAMPBELL, ANGUS, and GEORGE KATONA: "A National Survey of Wartime Savings," *Public Opinion Quarterly,* Vol. 10, 1946.

CANTRIL, HADLEY: *The Psychology of Social Movements,* Wiley, New York, 1941.

CANTRIL, HADLEY: *Gauging Public Opinion,* Princeton University Press, Princeton, N. J., 1944.

CARTWRIGHT, DORWIN: "Some Principles of Mass Persuasion," *Human Relations,* Vol. 2, 1949.

CARTWRIGHT, DORWIN: "Basic and Applied Social Psychology," *Philosophy of Science,* Vol. 6, 1949.

CENTERS, RICHARD: "Motivational Aspects of Occupational Stratification," *Journal of Social Psychology,* Vol. 28, 1948.

CENTERS, RICHARD, and HADLEY CANTRIL: "Income Satisfaction and Income Aspiration," *Journal of Abnormal and Social Psychology,* Vol. 41, 1946.

CHAPIN, F. S.: *Experimental Designs in Sociological Research,* Harper, New York, 1947.

CLARK, J. M.: "Economics and Modern Psychology," *Journal of Political Economy,* Vol. 26, 1918.

Committee on Price Determination, *Cost Behavior and Price Policy,* National Bureau of Economic Research, New York, 1943.

COTTRELL, L. S., JR., and SYLVIA EBERHART: *American Opinion on World Affairs in the Atomic Age,* Princeton University Press, Princeton, N. J., 1948.

Council of Economic Advisers, *Annual Report to the President,* issued every year since December, 1946, U.S. Government Printing Office, Washington, D.C.

DEMING, W. E.: *Some Theory of Sampling,* Wiley, New York, 1950.

DEWHURST, J. F., and ASSOCIATES: *America's Needs and Resources,* Twentieth Century Fund, New York, 1947.

DICKINSON, Z. CLARK: *Economic Motives,* Harvard University Press, Cambridge, Mass., 1922.

DUESENBERRY, J. S.: "Income-Consumption Relations and Their Implications" in *Income, Employment and Public Policy: Essays in Honor of Alvin H. Hansen,* Norton, New York, 1948.

The Economic Report of the President, transmitted to Congress in January of every year since January, 1947, and *Midyear Economic Report of the President,* transmitted to Congress in July of every year since July, 1948, U.S. Government Printing Office, Washington, D.C.

EITEMAN, W. J.: *Price Determination—Business Practice versus Economic Theory,* Bureau of Business Research, University of Michigan Press, Ann Arbor, 1949.

EZEKIEL, MORDECAI: "Statistical Investigations of Saving, Consumption, and Investment," *American Economic Review,* Vol. 32, 1942.

FRIEND, IRWIN, and JEAN BRONFENBRENNER: "Business Investment Programs and Their Realization," *Survey of Current Business,* December, 1950.

FRIEDMAN, MILTON: "A Monetary and Fiscal Framework for Economic Stability," *American Economic Review,* Vol. 38, 1948.

FRIEDMAN, MILTON, and SIMON KUZNETS: *Income from Independent Professional Practice,* National Bureau of Economic Research, New York, 1945.

GARVY, GEORGE: "The Role of Dissaving in Economic Analysis," *Journal of Political Economy,* Vol. 56, 1948.

GOODMAN, ROE: "Sampling for the 1947 Survey of Consumer Finances," *Journal of the American Statistical Association,* Vol. 42, 1947.

GOODMAN, ROE, and E. MACCOBY: "Sampling Methods and Sampling Errors in Surveys of Consumer Finances," *International Journal of Opinion and Attitude Research,* Vol. 2, 1948.

GORDON, R. A.: *Business Leadership in the Large Corporation,* Brookings Institution, Washington, D. C., 1945.

GORDON, R. A.: "Short-period Price-Determination in Theory and Practice," *American Economic Review,* Vol. 38, 1948.

GREENWOOD, ERNEST: *Experimental Sociology,* King's Crown Press, New York, 1945.

GRIFFIN, C. E.: *Enterprise in a Free Society,* Irwin, Chicago, 1949.

HABERLER, GOTTFRIED: *Prosperity and Depression,* League of Nations, Geneva, 1937.

HABERLER, GOTTFRIED: "The Place of the General Theory of Employment, Interest and Money in the History of Economic Thought," *Review of Economic Statistics,* Vol. 28, 1946.

HALL, R. L., and C. J. HITCH: "Price Theory and Business Behavior," *Oxford Economic Papers,* No. 2, 1939.

HANSEN, ALVIN: "Keynes and the General Theory," *Review of Economic Statistics,* Vol. 28, 1946.

HANSEN, M. H., and W. N. HURWITZ: "On the Theory of Sampling from Finite Populations," *Annals of Mathematical Statistics,* Vol. 14, 1943.

HANSEN, M. H., and W. N. HURWITZ: "The Problem of Non-response in Sample Surveys," *Journal of the American Statistical Association,* Vol. 41, 1946.

HARRIS, S. E. (ed.): *Economic Reconstruction,* McGraw-Hill, New York, 1945.

HART, A. G.: *Anticipations, Uncertainty and Dynamic Planning,* University of Chicago Press, Chicago, 1940.

HART, A. G.: "Liquidity and Uncertainty," *American Economic Review,* Vol. 39, Supplement, 1949.

HAYES, S. P., JR.: "The Business Cycle: Psychological Approaches," *Political Science Quarterly,* Vol. 63, 1948.

HAYES, S. P., JR.: "Some Psychological Problems of Economics," *Psychological Bulletin,* Vol. 47, 1950.

HICKS, J. R.: *Value and Capital,* Clarendon Press, New York, 1939.

HILGARD, E. R. *Theories of Learning,* Appleton-Century-Crofts, New York, 1948.

HILGARD, E. R., "Human Motives and the Concept of the Self," *American Psychologist,* Vol. 4, 1949.

HOUSEMAN, E. E.: "Designs of Samples for Surveys," *Agricultural Economics Research,* Vol. 1, 1949.

HULL, C. L.: *Principles of Behavior,* Appleton-Century-Crofts, New York, 1943.

HUNT, J. McV. (ed.): *Personality and the Behavior Disorders,* Ronald Press, New York, 1944.

HUTCHISON, T. W.: *The Significance and Basic Postulates of Economic Theory,* Macmillan, London, 1938.

JOHNSON, A. H.: "Market Potentials, 1948," *Harvard Business Review,* Vol. 26, 1948.

JOHNSON, A. H.: *Consumer Purchasing Power—1949,* J. Walter Thompson Company, New York, 1949.

KAPLAN, A. D. H.: "The Influence of Size of Firms on the Functioning of the Economy," *American Economic Review,* Vol. 40, Supplement, 1950.

KATONA, GEORGE: *Organizing and Memorizing: Studies in the Psychology of Learning and Teaching,* Columbia University Press, New York, 1940.

KATONA, GEORGE: *War without Inflation: The Psychological Approach to Problems of War Economy,* Columbia University Press, New York, 1942.

KATONA, GEORGE: "The Role of the Frame of Reference in War and Post-war Economy," *American Journal of Sociology,* Vol. 44, 1944.

KATONA, GEORGE: *Price Control and Business,* Cowles Commission for Research in Economics, Principia Press, Bloomington, Ind., 1945.

KATONA, GEORGE: "Psychological Analysis of Business Decisions and Expectations," *American Economic Review,* Vol. 36, 1946.

KATONA, GEORGE: "Contribution of Psychological Data to Economic Analysis," *Journal of the American Statistical Association,* Vol. 42, 1947.

KATONA, GEORGE: "Financial Surveys among Consumers," *Human Relations,* Vol. 2, 1949.

KATONA, GEORGE: "Effect of Income Changes on the Rate of Saving," *Review of Economics and Statistics,* Vol. 31, 1949.

KATONA, GEORGE: "Analysis of Dissaving," *American Economic Review,* Vol. 39, 1949.

KATONA, GEORGE, and J. A. FISHER: "Post-war Income Changes of Identical Consumer Units," *Studies in Income and Wealth,* Vol. 13, National Bureau of Economic Research, New York, 1951.

KATONA, GEORGE, and RENSIS LIKERT: "Relationship between Consumer Expenditures and Savings: The Contribution of Survey Research," *Review of Economic Statistics*, Vol. 28, 1946.

KATZ, DANIEL: "Polling Methods and the 1948 Polling Failure," *International Journal of Opinion and Attitude Research*, Vol. 2, 1948–1949.

KEYNES, J. M.: *The General Theory of Employment, Interest, and Money*, Harcourt, Brace, New York, 1936.

KEYNES, J. M.: "The General Theory of Employment," *Quarterly Journal of Economics*, Vol. 51, 1937.

KLEIN, L. R.: "A Post-mortem on Transition Predictions of National Product," *Journal of Political Economy*, Vol. 54, 1946.

KLEIN, L. R.: *The Keynesian Revolution*, Macmillan, New York, 1947.

KNIGHT, F. H.: *Risk, Uncertainty, and Profit*, Houghton Mifflin, New York, 1921.

KNIGHT, F. H.: *The Ethics of Competition*, Harper, New York, 1935.

KOEHLER, WOLFGANG: *Gestalt Psychology*, Liveright, New York, 1929.

KOEHLER, WOLFGANG: *Dynamics in Psychology*, Liveright, New York, 1940.

KOFFKA, KURT: *Principles of Gestalt Psychology*, Harcourt, Brace, New York, 1935.

KRECH, DAVID, and R. S. CRUTCHFIELD: *Theory and Problems of Social Psychology*, McGraw-Hill, New York, 1948.

KUZNETS, SIMON: "Conditions of Statistical Research," *Journal of the American Statistical Association*, Vol. 45, 1950.

LAZARSFELD, P. F.: "The Controversy over Detailed Interviews," *Public Opinion Quarterly*, Vol. 8, 1944.

LAZARSFELD, P. F., BERNARD BERELSON, and HAZEL GAUDET: *The People's Choice*, Columbia University Press, New York, 1948, 2d ed.

LEARNED, E. P.: "Pricing of Gasoline: A Case Study," *Harvard Business Review*, Vol. 26, 1948.

LEAVENS, D. H.: "Diversification of Investments," *Trusts and Estates*, May, 1945.

LESTER, R. A.: "Shortcomings of Marginal Analysis and Wage-Employment Problems," *American Economic Review*, Vol. 36, 1946.

LEWIN, KURT: *A Dynamic Theory of Personality*, McGraw-Hill, New York, 1935.

LEWIN, KURT: *The Conceptual Representation and the Measurement of Psychological Forces*, University of North Carolina, Durham, N.C., 1938.

LEWIN, KURT: "Frontiers in Group Dynamics," *Human Relations*, Vol. 1, 1947 (reprinted in *Field Theory in Social Science*, Harper, New York, 1951).

LEWIN, KURT, TAMARA DAMBO, LEON FESTINGER, and P. S. SEARS: "Level of Aspiration," in *Personality and the Behavior Disorders*, edited by J. McV. Hunt, Ronald Press, New York, 1944.

LIKERT, RENSIS: "The Sample Interview Survey," in *Current Trends in Psychology*, University of Pittsburgh Press, Pittsburgh, 1948.

LIKERT, RENSIS: "The Public Opinion Polls," *Scientific American*, Vol. 179, 1948.

LIVINGSTON, S. M.: *Markets after the War*, Bureau of Foreign and Domestic Commerce of the Department of Commerce, U.S. Government Printing Office, Washington, D.C., 1943.

LIVINGSTON, S. M.: "Forecasting Postwar Demand," *Econometrica*, Vol. 13, 1945.

MACCOBY, E. E.: "Interviewing Problems in Financial Surveys," *International Journal of Opinion and Attitude Research*, Vol. 1, 1947.

MACCOBY, E. E., and R. R. HOLT: "How Surveys Are Made," *Journal of Social Issues*, Vol. 2, 1946.

MACHLUP, FRITZ: "Why Bother with Methodology?" *Economica*, New Series, Vol. 3, 1936.

MACHLUP, FRITZ: "Marginal Analysis and Empirical Research," *American Economic Review,* Vol. 36, 1946.

MACK, R. P.: "The Direction of Change in Income and the Consumption Function," *Review of Economic Statistics,* Vol. 30, 1948.

MAIER, N. R. F.: *Psychology in Industry,* Houghton Mifflin, Boston, 1946.

MARSCHAK, JACOB: "Lack of Confidence," *Social Research,* Vol. 8, 1941.

MARSCHAK, JACOB: "Role of Liquidity under Complete and Incomplete Information," *American Economic Review,* Vol. 39, Supplement, 1949.

MASON, E. S.: "Various Views on the Monopoly Problem," *Review of Economic Statistics,* Vol. 31, 1949.

MASSERMAN, J. H.: *Behavior and Neurosis,* University of Chicago Press, Chicago, 1943.

MAYER, KURT: "Toward Understanding Economic Behavior," *American Journal of Economics and Sociology,* Vol. 8, 1949.

MAYO, ELTON: *The Social Problems of an Industrial Civilization,* Harvard University Press, Cambridge, Mass., 1945.

McNEMAR, QUINN: "Opinion-Attitude Methodology," *Psychological Bulletin,* Vol. 43, 1946.

MENDERSHAUSEN, HORST: *Changes in Income Distributions during the Great Depression,* National Bureau of Economic Research, New York, 1946; Foreword by Jacob Marschak.

METZLER, L. A.: "Three Lags in the Circular Flow of Income," in *Income, Employment and Public Policy: Essays in Honor of Alvin H. Hansen,* Norton, New York, 1948.

MITCHELL, W. C.: "Human Behavior and Economics," *Quarterly Journal of Economics,* Vol. 29, 1914.

MODIGLIANI, FRANCO: "Fluctuations in the Saving-Income Ratio," *Studies in Income and Wealth,* Vol. 11, National Bureau of Economic Research, New York, 1948.

MORGAN, J. N.: "Individual Savings in 1947 and 1948," *American Economic Review,* Vol. 40, 1950.

MOSAK, J. L.: "Forecasting Postwar Demand," *Econometrica,* Vol. 13, 1945.

MOULTON, H. G.: *Controlling Factors in Economic Development,* Brookings Institution, Washington, D.C., 1949.

MUENZINGER, K. F.: *Psychology, the Science of Behavior,* Harper, New York, 1942.

National Resources Committee, *Consumer Incomes in the United States: Their Distribution in 1935–36,* and *Consumer Expenditures in the United States: Estimates for 1935–36,* Washington, D.C., 1938 and 1939.

National Survey of Liquid Asset Holdings, Bureau of Agricultural Economics, June, July, and August, 1946, and *Federal Reserve Bulletin,* June, July, and August, 1946.

NEWCOMB, T. M.: *Social Psychology,* Dryden, New York, 1950.

NIELSEN, W. A.: "Attitude Research and Government," *Journal of Social Issues,* Vol. 2, 1946.

NOURSE, E. G.: *Price Making in a Democracy,* Brookings Institution, Washington, D.C., 1944.

NOURSE, E. G.: "Economics in the Public Service," *American Economic Review,* Vol. 37, Supplement, 1947.

OHLIN, BERTIL: "Some Notes on the Stockholm Theory of Savings and Investment," *Economic Journal,* Vol. 47, 1937.

REYNOLDS, L. G.: "Toward a Short-run Theory of Wages," *American Economic Review,* Vol. 38, 1948.

ROBBINS, LIONEL: *An Essay on the Nature and Significance of Economic Science,* Macmillan, London, 1932.

SCHUMPETER, J. A.: *Business Cycles,* McGraw-Hill, New York, 1939.

SCHUMPETER, J. A.: "Keynes and Statistics," *Review of Economic Statistics,* Vol. 28, 1946.

SHACKLE, G. L. S.: "The Expectational Dynamics of the Individual," *Economica,* Vol. 10, 1943.

SHACKLE, G. L. S.: *Expectation in Economics,* Cambridge University Press, New York, 1949.

SHERIF, M., and H. CANTRIL: *The Psychology of Ego Involvements,* Wiley, New York, 1947.

SLICHTER, S. H.: "The State of Economics," *Items,* Social Science Research Council, Vol. 3, September, 1949.

SMITHIES, ARTHUR: "Forecasting Postwar Demand," *Econometrica,* Vol. 13, 1945.

Social Science Research Council, *The Pre-election Polls of 1948,* New York, 1949.

Survey of Consumer Finances, conducted by the Survey Research Center of the University of Michigan for the Board of Governors of the Federal Reserve System:

    1947 Survey, *Federal Reserve Bulletin,* June, July, and August, 1947.

    1948 Survey, *Federal Reserve Bulletin,* June, July, August, and September, 1948.

    1949 Survey, *Federal Reserve Bulletin,* June, July, August, September, October, November, 1949, and January, 1950.

    1950 Survey, *Federal Reserve Bulletin,* June, July, August, November, and December, 1950.

Survey of Consumer Finances, Methods of, Appendix to *Federal Reserve Bulletin* of June, 1947, June, 1948, and June, 1949, and article in *Federal Reserve Bulletin* of July, 1950.

Surveys of Liquid Asset Holdings, *Federal Reserve Bulletin,* September, 1945.

TERBORGH, GEORGE: *Dynamic Equipment Policy,* McGraw-Hill, New York, 1949.

TOLMAN, E. C.: *Purposive Behavior in Animals and Men,* Appleton-Century-Crofts, New York, 1932.

TRIFFIN, ROBERT: *Monopolistic Competition and General Equilibrium Theory,* Harvard University Press, Cambridge, Mass., 1940.

Twentieth Century Fund, *Financing American Prosperity,* New York, 1945. Articles by J. M. Clark, Fritz Machlup, S. H. Slichter, and J. H. Williams.

WERTHEIMER, MAX: *Productive Thinking,* Harper, New York, 1945.

WOLFLE, DAEL, RENSIS LIKERT, D. G. MARQUIS, and R. R. SEARS: "Standards for Appraising Psychological Research," *American Psychologist,* Vol. 4, 1949.

WOODWORTH, R. S.: *Contemporary Schools of Psychology,* Ronald Press, New York, 1948, rev. ed.

WOYTINSKY, W. S.: "Relationship between Consumers' Expenditures, Savings, and Disposable Income," *Review of Economic Statistics,* Vol. 28, 1946.

WOYTINSKY, W. S.: "What Was Wrong in Forecasts of Postwar Depression?" *Journal of Political Economy,* Vol. 55, 1947.

YATES, FRANK: *Sampling Methods for Censuses and Surveys,* Hafner, London, New York, 1949.

YOUNG, R. A., and DUNCAN McC. HOLTHAUSEN: "Values and Limitations of Consumer Financial Surveys for Economic Research," *Federal Reserve Bulletin,* March, 1947.

ZEISEL, HANS: *Say It with Figures,* Harper, New York, 1947.

INDEX

Expectations, inflationary, 260–262, 268
and investment, 244, 247
origin of, 53*f*., 95, 104–142, 166*f*.,
199*f*., 248, 252, 260
and prediction, 174*f*., 190
self-justifying, 260, 270, 277
treatment of, by economists, 140*f*.,
147*f*.
trend (cumulative), 261, 270, 273,
283*f*.
(*See also* Economic outlook; Expected
income; Price expectations)
Expected income, definiteness of, 96
fulfillment of, 96, 119
measurement of, 117*f*., 179, 181
origin of, 141*f*.
reasons for, 117
relation of, to level of aspiration, 93
to past changes, 93–95, 120*f*., 140*f*.
and savings, 157*f*., 179*f*.
and spending, 182*f*.
stability of, 118
Experiments, 302, 326*f*.
Explanation, 57, 290
Ezekiel, Mordecai, 186, 336

F

Federal Reserve Bank of New York,
276
Federal Reserve Board, 81*f*., 85, 113,
306, 340
Festinger, Leon, 121, 338
Field, and field theory, 32, 35–40, 89
Fisher, J. A., 177, 337
Ford, R. N., 329
Fortune Magazine, 213, 334
Frame of reference, 35*f*., 41, 47
Friedman, Milton, 187, 329, 336
Friedman, R. D., 114, 335
Friend, Irwin, 187, 189, 333, 334, 336
Frustration, 93

G

Gallup, George, 307
Garvy, George, 186, 336
Gaudet, Hazel, 334, 338
Genuine decisions, of business firms, 50–
52, 236*f*.

Genuine decisions, of consumers, 67*f*.
in investments, 247*f*.
psychology of, 49*f*.
Gestalt psychology, 31, 40*f*.
Goldsmith, S. F., 330
Goodman, Roe, 328, 336
Gordon, R. A., 210, 211, 239, 336
Government as policy maker, 293, 295,
297
Graham, F. D., 270
Greenwood, Ernest, 334, 336
Griffin, C. E., 210, 212, 336
Groups, belonging to, 37–39, 96, 109*f*.
by executives, 196–198
and individuals, 37–41, 71
reference, 39, 96

H

Haavelmo, T., 24
Haberler, Gottfried, 14, 167, 186, 241,
274, 336
Habitual behavior, of businessmen, 50–
52, 230–236
of consumers, 67*f*.
and expectations, 56*f*.
and income changes, 142–144, 148
in investments, 243–247, 253
psychology of, 48–50
Hall, R. L., 238, 336
Hansen, A. H., 146, 187, 336
Hansen, M. H., 328, 329, 337
Harris, S. E., 337
Hart, A. G., 14, 85, 126, 186, 215, 239,
337
Hayes, S. P., Jr., 285, 337
Hicks, J. R., 24, 148, 211, 238, 270,
337
Hilgard, E. R., 58, 59, 337
Hitch, C. J., 238, 336
Holt, R. R., 330, 338
Holthausen, Duncan McC., 82, 340
Home ownership, 65, 102, 105
Houseman, E. E., 328, 337
Hull, C. L., 57, 337
Hurwitz, A., 330
Hurwitz, W. N., 328, 329, 337
Hutchison, T. W., 13, 337
Hypotheses, 15, 29, 138*f*., 144, 146,
238